KIRSH: A GUIDE TO CONSTRUCTION LIENS IN ONTARIO

KIRSH: A GUIDE TO CONSTRUCTION LIENS IN ONTARIO

HARVEY J. KIRSH
B.A., LL.B., LL.M.

BUTTERWORTHS
Toronto

Kirsh: A Guide to Construction Liens in Ontario

© 1984 Butterworth & Co. (Canada) Ltd.

Printed and bound in Canada

The Butterworth Group of Companies

Canada
Butterworth & Co. (Canada) Ltd., Toronto and Vancouver
United Kingdom:
Butterworth & Co. (Publishers) Ltd., London
Australia:
Butterworths Pty Ltd., Sydney, Melbourne, Brisbane, Adelaide and Perth
New Zealand:
Butterworths of New Zealand Ltd., Wellington and Auckland
Singapore:
Butterworth & Co. (Asia) Pte. Ltd., Singapore
South Africa:
Butterworth Publishers (Pty) Ltd., Durban and Pretoria
United States:
Butterworth Legal Publishers, Boston, Seattle and Austin
Mason Publishing Company, St. Paul
D & S Publishers, Clearwater

Canadian Cataloguing in Publication Data

Kirsh, Harvey J.
  Kirsh: a guide to construction liens in Ontario

Includes index.
ISBN 0-409-84286-9

1. Ontario. Construction Lien Act.   2. Liens — Ontario.
I. Title.

KEO325.K57 1983   346.713′074   C83-099176-X

Sponsoring Editor — M. Paul
Editor — D. Florkow
Production — J. Shepherd

To my father, Alex,
My late mother, Freda,
And my sons, Lowell and Evan

To my father, Alex,
My grandmother, Leeds,
And my sons, Lowell and Evan

Author's Foreword

This book is meant to be a practical guidebook or manual on the new *Construction Lien Act, 1983* for lawyers and for persons involved in the construction industry, such as architects, engineers, trade contractors and subcontractors, material suppliers, developers and builders.

It was my intention to use straightforward, non-technical language, to the extent possible, and to attempt to explain complicated legal concepts by using simple examples and illustrations.

Generally, the book canvasses the relevant considerations which pertain to the financing and the flow of funds on a construction project, from the point of view of the various persons involved in the construction pyramid. Additionally, it sets out a step-by-step description of the practice and procedures involved in a typical lien action, along with a discussion of tactical considerations.

The Appendices contain not only the prescribed forms and current regulations under the Act, but also a large number of sample precedents created specifically for this text. Furthermore, both the *Construction Lien Act* and its predecessor, the *Mechanics' Lien Act,* are reproduced in full, along with two Tables of Concordance. This will assist persons who may be involved in researching all of the cases which have been decided under a particular statutory provision, or who are seeking to illuminate a problem by putting it in its historical context.

Although every provision in the legislation is referred to in the footnotes where it was appropriate to do so, I have tended to avoid extensive footnoting of case authorities, except to exemplify a statement in the text by referring to a specific case in point.

Throughout, references have been made to the proposed new amendments to the Act which, as of the date of this writing, have not as yet been presented to the Legislature. Although those proposed amendments may ultimately be changed by the time they receive Third Reading, their inclusion by reference in the book serves to highlight certain problems and considerations which were not anticipated when the Act was originally proclaimed in force in April of 1983.

I should like to take this opportunity to thank those persons who have assisted me greatly in this project: Harry Radomski, who read and commented upon portions of the manuscript and who assisted in the preparation of the precedents; David Florkow, of Butterworth & Co. (Canada) Ltd., who edited the manuscript and the various proofs; The Mortgage Insurance Company of Canada, which provided me with permission to reproduce its lien holdback deficiency bonds (see Precedent

Nos. 67 and 68); Joanne Saliba, who did an excellent job on word processing the manuscript; my secretary, Mirella Iaboni, who provided invaluable assistance in typing the manuscript and in meeting the unreasonable deadlines which I often set; and my partners at Blaney, Pasternak, Smela & Watson, who provided encouragement and support.

Finally, I wish to thank my sons, Lowell and Evan, for letting me feel their unfailing and continous love over the last few years during which this book was being written. Some day when they are older they will read this and understand.

Harvey J. Kirsh
Toronto, Canada
October, 1983.

Preface: I

Harvey Kirsh's guide to the *Construction Lien Act, 1983* provides an excellent critical analysis of the new legislation.

The new Act, which was given Royal Assent on January 27, 1983 and applies to all construction contracts entered into on or after April 2, 1983, effects substantial changes in mechanics' lien legislation in Ontario.

Mr. Kirsh's work is an informative and clearly written analysis of the new Act and should be an extremely useful resource not only for the legal profession but also for lay persons in the construction industry and lending institutions. For the practitioner who is familiar with the prior legislation, the book provides a context in which to analyze the new legislation, by highlighting those areas which are new or substantially revised, and by indicating those provisions which effect a codification of, or a departure from, prior case law, or which codify or establish procedural matters.

The author has also supplied a number of useful precedents which will assist the inexperienced practitioner in preparing his or her case. Additionally, his inclusion of commentary from Discussion Papers and Advisory Committee Reports which were prepared in analysis of the draft legislation affords useful insights into the aetiology of the new law.

I have known Harvey Kirsh since 1973 when he entered practice after obtaining his LL.M. from Harvard Law School and being called to the bar of Ontario. In September of 1974 he left Toronto to teach for a year at Queen's Law School. Since his return to Toronto, he has been associated with the firm of Blaney, Pasternak, Smela & Watson, where he practices commercial litigation with an emphasis on property and construction cases. He also served on the Attorney General's Advisory Committee to examine the draft *Construction Lien Act*.

Mr. Kirsh is a most able practitioner who has now added this most valuable publication to his list of accomplishments.

Master Benzion Sischy, Q.C.
Supreme Court of Ontario

Preface: II

Perhaps some day lien legislation will be so clearly expressed that a guide to it would be redundant. That day has not arrived.

Construction-related transactions are often complex. Owners, lenders and contractors may need guidance in determining the requirements of the Act. The extensive codification of lien law in the Ontario statute has not eliminated the need to know many of the cases decided under earlier legislation.

Harvey Kirsh has created a very readable, helpful guide to the Act. It is well-organized, the text is supplemented by useful notes and the precedents given are valuable. While cross-references are provided to related provisions of the Act and citations are given for all the leading cases, the guide does not overwhelm the reader with irrelevant detail. While providing the reader with as much of the history and background of a provision as is needed to understand the context in which it operates, the guide is not an economic or philosophical polemic.

The guide is a practical book for practical people. It should be very useful to both lawyers and those in the construction industry.

Stephen V. Fram, Esq.
Chairman,
Attorney General's Advisory
Committee on the Draft
Construction Lien Act

Writing a book is an adventure; to begin with it is a toy, then an amusement, then it becomes a mistress, and then it becomes a master, and then it becomes a tyrant, and the last phase is that just as you are about to be reconciled to your servitude you kill the monster and strew him about to the public.

— Winston S. Churchill

Table of Contents

CHAPTER 1

INTRODUCTION

CHAPTER 2

THE LIEN

CHAPTER 3

THE STATUTORY HOLDBACKS

CHAPTER 4

EXPIRY, PRESERVATION AND PERFECTION OF LIENS

CHAPTER 5

THE TRUST FUND

CHAPTER 6

RIGHT TO INFORMATION

CHAPTER 7

DISCHARGE OF PRESERVED OR PERFECTED LIENS

CHAPTER 8

EXTRAORDINARY REMEDIES

CHAPTER 9

JURISDICTION, PRACTICE AND PROCEDURE

CHAPTER 10

PRIORITIES

CHAPTER 11

CROWN LANDS, MUNICIPALLY-OWNED PUBLIC STREETS AND HIGHWAYS, AND RAILWAY RIGHTS-OF-WAY

Table of Cases

A

D

E

F

G

H

I

J

K

L

M

N

O

P

R

Chapter 1

Introduction

A. ORIGIN OF LIEN LEGISLATION

The first mechanics' lien legislation was enacted in Maryland in 1791.[1] It was apparently inspired by the desire of Thomas Jefferson and James Madison to stimulate and encourage the rapid building of the City of Washington as the permanent seat of the government of the United States.[2] That Act granted a lien in favour of "master builders," bricklayers, carpenters, joiners, "undertakers" or workmen "on the house and the ground on which the same is erected"[3] so as to encourage builders "to undertake the building and finishing houses within the said city, by securing to them a just and effectual remedy for their advances and earnings."[4]

Lien legislation was subsequently enacted by other state legislatures, perhaps as an acknowledgment that, in a young and growing country, not only was it important to foster mechanical, commercial and industrial pursuits, but it was also manifestly equitable to provide security for the payment for labour and materials which enhanced the value of the lands into which they were incorporated.[5]

There is also speculation that the origin of the lien is traceable to the fact that many of the new settlers in that country, many of whom came from continental Europe, were influenced by the European civil law traditions which protected and regulated workmen's rights.[6]

The first mechanics' lien Act in Ontario, *An Act to establish Liens in favour of Mechanics, Machinists and Others,* was enacted in 1873.[7] It restricted the right to lien to those persons who contracted directly with

---

[1] An Act concerning the territory of Columbia and the city of Washington, Laws of Maryland, c. 45, passed December 19, 1791.

[2] See Phillips, *A Treatise on the Law of Mechanics' Liens on Real and Personal Property,* 3rd ed. (1893), at 11-13; and Mitchell S. Cutler and Leonard Shapiro, "The Maryland Mechanics' Lien Law — Its Scope and Effect" (1968), 28 Md. L. Rev. 225 at 225.

[3] Note 1, *supra,* Section X.

[4] *Ibid.*

[5] For a discussion of the early development of lien legislation, see Wallace, *Mechanics' Lien Laws in Canada,* 3rd ed. (1920), at 2ff.

[6] *Ibid.*

[7] 36 Vict. c. 27.

the owner of the land,[8] but provided subcontractors with the right to establish a "charge" against any monies owing by the owner to the contractor.[9] A subsequent amendment, enacted in 1874,[10] gave subcontractors lien rights in the land.

There were obviously many amendments and consolidations throughout the next 110 years,[11] each attempting to clarify the law and to adapt it to changing social and economic conditions.

B. THE LIEN AS A REMEDY

Mechanics' lien rights did not exist at common law or in equity. The lien was and is strictly a creation of statute law, deriving its existence and scope exclusively from the enabling legislation. It exists as a remedy in the nature of a charge against an interest in property, whether freehold or leasehold, to secure a preference of payment for the supply of labour or materials used in improving that property.

As Samuel L. Phillips wrote in his landmark American treatise on the law of mechanics' liens,[12]

A mechanic's lien is not property, or a right in or to property; it is neither a *jus in re* nor a *jus ad rem*. It is simply a right to charge the property it affects, with the payment of a particular debt, in preference and priority to other debts, so far as the statute confers such preference, if all the requisitions of the statute are observed.... It does not create even after being judicially established by judgment or decree, any privity of estate, or right of entry thereunder, but is in the nature of a legal charge, running with the land, encumbering it in every change of ownership, and preventing subsequent alienations or encumbrances only by making them subordinate to the rights of the lien-holder.[13]

The most significant aspect of the lien remedy is that it is available to all those persons who supply services or materials to a particular construction project, despite the fact that there may be no privity of contract with the owner. The mechanical subcontractor who supplies and installs a heating, air-conditioning and ventilating system in a new home, for example, would have lien rights against the owner's interest in the property, notwithstanding that the mechanical subcontractor's contract is with the general contractor and not the owner. The ultimate realization of those rights would potentially give the subcontractor a personal judgment

[8] *Ibid.*, s. 1.
[9] *Ibid.*, s. 11.
[10] 38 Vict. c. 20.
[11] For an interesting discussion of the initial difficulties and resistance which the lien legislation met in its early years, see Wallace, *supra*, note 5, at 4-9.
[12] Phillips, *supra*, note 2.
[13] *Ibid.*, at 16-17.

against the general contractor, and the right to a judicial sale of the owner's interest in the property.

The typical construction project may be viewed as a pyramid. At the apex is the owner. Below him is the general contractor whom he retains to carry out the construction and to hire, supervise and co-ordinate the sub-trades. Below the general contractor is the first tier of subcontractors. These might include, for example, the electrical, excavating, painting and mechanical subcontractors. The pyramid begins to expand at this level. Each subcontractor may in turn engage the services of other sub-contractors for specialized aspects of the work. For example, the mechanical subcontractor would engage sheet metal, plumbing and heating subcontractors, and the painting subcontractor would employ painters and would purchase materials from a paint supplier. It can therefore be seen that the proliferation of subcontractors further broadens the base of the notional pyramid.

As one commentator observed,

> This pyramid results in a complex web of relationships. Each person arranges for the supply of specific services or materials to the improvement, knowing that those services and materials may well be supplied by persons other than the person with whom he deals. Conversely, each supplier looks to those who have employed him for payment, knowing that the money for that payment must come from someone further up the pyramid. Because defective performance of any part of the contract work may result in a stoppage of payment, and the consequent flow of monies down the pyramid, a supplier of services or materials in a construction project may be greatly affected by the behaviour of people with whom he has no contractual relationship. While in theory, proper performance by a supplier entitles him to demand payment from the person to whom the supply was made, in practice the chances of such payment are largely contingent upon the continuous flow of contract monies from the owner down the pyramid.[14]

This practical reality lends support to the view that ordinary contractual remedies may be inadequate for construction-related claims:

> Those who invest their services and materials in the improvement of real property need assurance in the form of security over the property before they are willing to provide those services and materials at a reasonable cost. The need for the type of remedies provided by the *Mechanics' Lien Act*, and the proposed *Construction Lien Act*, emanate from the complicated nature of contractual relationships within the construction industry, and the credit-granting practices which are an integral part of that industry.[15]

Given this framework, it is not surprising to observe that the ostensible purpose of lien legislation is to provide an informal, inexpen-

---

[14] Stephen Fram, "Is the Construction Lien Act Really Necessary?", at 3-4 in *The New Construction Lien Act — Bill 139* (materials distributed at a conference sponsored by Oyez Limited, October 7 and 8, 1982, Toronto).

[15] *Ibid.*, at 2.

sive, expeditious, yet formidable, remedy for enforcing construction claims. The *Construction Lien Act, 1983*, for example, decrees that "[t]he procedure in [a lien] action shall be as far as possible of a summary character . . .",[16] and penalizes litigants in costs "[w]here the least expensive course is not taken . . .".[17] Further, interlocutory proceedings, other than those provided for in the Act, shall not be taken without the consent of the court;[18] and no appeal lies from an interlocutory order.[19]

Despite the fact that lien legislation is a derogation from the common law, the courts have traditionally refused to construe it strictly, but have rather taken the view that it is remedial legislation deserving of a liberal interpretation, particularly with respect to the enforcement of the rights it confers upon those to whom it applies.[20] However, the provisions determining whether a particular claimant is entitled to a lien,[21] and those essentially creating the lien, such as the sections prescribing the time periods for preserving and perfecting lien rights, are to be strictly construed.[22]

The *Construction Lien Act, 1983* also carries forward the spirit of the curative provision found in earlier mechanics' lien legislation to the effect that failure to comply strictly with those sections which prescribe the content and form of certificates, declarations and claims for lien does not render those documents invalid, unless some person has been prejudiced, and then only to the extent of the prejudice suffered.[23]

C. EVOLUTION OF THE CONSTRUCTION LIEN ACT, 1983

(i) The Need for New Legislation

The call for reform of lien legislation in Ontario arose out of the fact that trade contractors were dissatisfied with the efficacy of the *Mechanics' Lien Act*. As Stephen Fram wrote,

> While the construction industry is of the view that lien legislation is necessary, it is widely believed that the present operation of the *Mechanics' Lien Act* is unsatis-

---

[16] Section 69(1).
[17] Section 88(2).
[18] Section 69(2).
[19] Section 73(3)(b).
[20] See *Clarkson Co. Ltd., Trustee in Bankruptcy of L. Di Cecco Co. Ltd. et al. and Ace Lbr. Ltd. et al.,* [1963] S.C.R. 110, 36 D.L.R. (2d) 554, 4 C.B.R. (N.S.) 116; revg. [1962] O.R. 748, 33 D.L.R. (2d) 701.
[21] *Ibid.*
[22] See, generally, Wallace, *supra*, note 5, Chapter III: "Construction of Mechanics' Lien Acts."
[23] Section 6. But see "Affidavit of Verification" (heading B(ii) of Chapter 4).

factory. It is believed that the Act does not now provide the protection it was intended to afford and that the rights provided by the Act are vague and ill-defined and subject to much confusion. Lawyers litigating lien claims, and the courts adjudicating in cases of dispute, are of the view that procedures for enforcing lien claims are confused.[24]

The "process" involved in the recent revamping of lien legislation was rather unique. In November of 1980, the Ministry of the Attorney General responded to the sweeping recommendations for change contained in a brief submitted to it in 1978 by The Council of Ontario Contractors Associations by preparing and distributing a Discussion Paper, containing extensive proposals for the reform of the existing lien law as well as draft legislation.[25]

As a result of the Attorney General's invitation to participate in the process of formulating new law, numerous briefs and submissions were received from individuals, companies and associations involved in the construction industry, thereby providing valuable feedback and critical commentary.

In May of 1981, the Attorney General established an Advisory Committee on the Draft *Construction Lien Act*, composed of lawyers expert in mechanics' lien law and knowledgeable about the working of the legislation from the perspective of labour, material suppliers, sub-contractors, contractors, owners, commercial sureties, mortgage lenders, municipalities, the Crown and the courts.[26]

The Advisory Committee was given the following terms of reference:

1. To review the draft Act and to consider the responses to the Discussion Paper from all perspectives of the construction industry;
2. To prepare a Report of the Committee's findings and recommendations; and
3. To examine and approve draft legislation modifying the provisions of the draft Act to implement the Committee's recommendations.

The Committee was also encouraged to develop its own proposals for reform, based upon the expertise and experience of its members.

Despite the differing points of view which were held by the Committee members, informed and pragmatic compromises gave rise to

---

[24] Stephen Fram, note 14, *supra,* at 7.
[25] Ministry of the Attorney General, *Discussion Paper on the Draft Construction Lien Act* (November 1980).
[26] See April 20, 1982 *Statement by The Honourable R. Roy McMurtry, Attorney General for Ontario, on the Tabling of the Report of the Advisory Committee on the Draft Construction Lien Act,* at 1.

a unanimous Report.[27] As the Committee's letter of transmittal to the Attorney General provides, in part:

> Many diverse groups comprise the construction industry. . . . The interests of these sectors rarely coincide. Consequently, from the beginning of our deliberations, it was clear to us that any attempt to reform the mechanics' lien law of the Province would require a spirit of compromise and cooperation between diverse groups. Acting in this spirit, we have attempted to devise a scheme that strikes a balance between the often competing interests of the various sectors of the industry. Though as individuals we were not always in agreement with each of the proposed changes, nevertheless, as a group we can and do support this Report as a package.[28]

On April 20, 1982, the Attorney General tabled the Committee's Report in the Ontario Legislature, summarizing the major recommendations as follows:

> Mr. Speaker, the Report confirms that there is a continuing need for lien legislation to protect those who have supplied services and materials to the construction or improvement of buildings.
>
> The Report, while containing very significant recommendations for change, continues the approach to lien legislation developed in Ontario over the past century. For example, the concepts of the lien and trust remedies and the requirements of holdback are retained.
>
> The Report recommends the reduction of the rate of holdback from the existing 15% of the price of services and material supplied, to 10%. While the Report states that the reduction is justified on the basis of the low margins of profit in the construction industry and the high cost of financing the holdback, the Report makes it clear that the reduction should not be effected without certain other measures to ensure that hardship does not result.
>
> The Report recommends the extension of the special priority afforded to workers' lien claims for wages from the existing 30 days to 40 working days. Since as much as 30% of these wages are now paid into workers' trust funds to cover vacation pay and health & welfare benefits, it is recommended that the trustees for the workers' trust funds be able to enforce payment directly on behalf of workers. To make this realistic, it is also recommended that trustees for these funds have the right to obtain access to payroll records of the employer to determine whether there are arrears in the payment to the funds.
>
> The Report recommends that the time for preserving a lien be extended from the existing 37 days to 45 days. The Committee found that 37 days is too short for a potential claimant to adequately determine whether to preserve a lien, while the 60 day period proposed in the Discussion Paper would delay payment of the holdback too long.
>
> The Report deals extensively with the expiry of lien rights to ensure that no

---

[27] *Report of the Attorney General's Advisory Committee on the Draft Construction Lien Act* (April 1982).

[28] Letter of transmittal from Stephen V. Fram, Lloyd D. Cadsby, Q.C., Howard Devry, Q.C., James F. Heal, Harvey Kirsh, Raymond Koskie, Q.C., Master D.D. MacRae, Norman Ross, James Shapland, Leonard W. Stewart, Q.C., Robert Stupart, Q.C., and Paul Thomson to The Honourable R. Roy McMurtry, Q.C., Attorney General for Ontario, dated April 8, 1982, in the *Report of the Attorney General's Advisory Committee on the Draft Construction Lien Act* (April 1982).

legal impediment would exist to delay payment of the holdback. In this connection, the Committee recommends that the concept of substantial performance, introduced into lien legislation in 1969, be limited in application to the main contract, and that certification of substantial performance of the main contract be made known to the suppliers of services and materials by publication. The effect of these and other recommended changes should be to greatly speed payment of the holdback related to the substantially performed contract while providing protection for the finishing trades and their suppliers.

The Report recommends that there be security for the holdbacks. Too frequently today, high interest rates on mortgages eliminate the owner's interest in a project, leaving lien claimants without any protection despite their contribution to the project and the fact that payment has been withheld from them by law. To correct this injustice, the Committee recommends limited adjustments to the priorities of liens over mortgages. In the Committee's view, this adjustment of priorities will accomplish, without administrative overhead and in a manner that is commercially reasonable, most of the major benefits that would have resulted from the joint trust account proposals to secure the holdback set out in the Discussion Paper.

The Report's recommendations with respect to lien claims are designed to make the lien process more effective. At present, the Act sometimes requires a prudent claimant to claim far more than the price of services or materials he has supplied. These exaggerated claims impede the proper flow of construction funds. The recommendations, if implemented, would permit a person to claim only the amount owed to him, without jeopardizing his right to claim a lien for additional services and materials he may supply.

The extensive recommendations with respect to court procedures for dealing with lien claims are designed to speed the resolution of lien actions. One of the key recommendations in this respect is that defendants be required to file a defence to a claim quickly or lose their right to defend. The present procedure is grossly defective in this respect and results in lengthy delays in what is intended to be a summary process.

The Report contains a complete draft of legislation to implement the Committee's recommendations. After a century of major and minor amendments to the lien legislation, there is little doubt of the necessity for a new beginning. While the complexity of the subject matter and the need for certainty of obligations do not make the draft legislation light reading, I believe that major improvements have been made.

Mr. Speaker, I hope that in the near future I will be introducing legislation based on the Report of my Advisory Committee.[29]

The tabling of the Advisory Committee's Report in the Legislature culminated in the Government's introduction of Bill 139 ("An Act to revise the Mechanics' Lien Act"), which received First Reading on June 8, 1982. In introducing the Bill, the Attorney General commented that "substantative changes [to the Bill], because they may affect the delicate compromises which have made this legislation possible, will not be made without compelling reasons for doing so."[30]

---

[29] April 20, 1982 *Statement by The Honourable R. Roy McMurtry, Attorney General for Ontario*, note 26, *supra*, at 3-6.

[30] June 8, 1982 *Statement by The Honourable R. Roy McMurtry, Attorney General for Ontario, on the Introduction for First Reading of the Construction Lien Act*, at 2.

Subsequently, however, the Canadian Bankers' Association, The Canadian Institute of Public Real Estate Companies and The Urban Development Institute made representations to the Cabinet in an attempt to have the Government reconsider passage of the new Act. The developers' and bankers' resistence stemmed from the suggestion that the priority provisions in the Act would substantially increase the risk to lenders, which would in turn cause them to charge more for financing or to demand more security. The Canadian Institute of Public Real Estate Companies wrote to the Attorney General, alleging that "[p]rojects and the associated financing applications in process at the time of implementation of the Act will be delayed until lenders adopt formal policies and procedures in reaction to the proposed changes. . . . Given the current economic environment, and specifically the unhealthy state of the construction industry in Ontario, it seems to us that any legislative changes that would immediately result in increased costs to the building industry and would delay or possibly eliminate projects being contemplated should be considered most carefully at this time."[31]

As a result of this aggressive opposition, representatives of the Attorney General entered into discussions with developers and lenders with a view to finding some form of compromise. In the meantime, Second Reading of the Bill was indefinitely postponed.

After the 1982 Christmas recess, Bill 139 was withdrawn by the Government, and Bill 216 was introduced in its place. Bill 216, which was substantially the same as Bill 139 but with certain minor modifications, received First Reading on January 24, 1983, Second and Third Readings on January 25, 1983 and Royal Assent on January 27, 1983.

(ii) The Transition to New Legislation

The *Construction Lien Act, 1983* came into force on April 2,1983, and applies to all contracts, and to all subcontracts arising under those contracts, entered into on or after that date.[32]

The *Mechanics' Lien Act* continues to apply, however, to all contracts entered into before April 2, 1983, and to all subcontracts arising under those contracts.[33]

It is to be noted that the definition of the word "contract" under the *Construction Lien Act, 1983* means "the contract between the owner and the contractor, *and includes any amendment to that contract.*"[34] Pursuant to s. 92(3), if a contract, which was entered into before April 2, 1983, is

---

[31] "Contractors, bankers battling over new lien act," *Globe and Mail*, Tuesday, December 14, 1982, at B6.
[32] Section 92(1).
[33] Section 92(2).
[34] Section 1(1) 3 (emphasis added).

amended in good faith after that date, the *Mechanics' Lien Act* would apply to that amendment and to all subcontracts arising under it.

The operation of the transitional provisions contained in the Act can be best illustrated by the use of an example. Where a subcontract is entered into on, say, May 1, 1983, the provisions of the *Mechanics' Lien Act* would apply to it if it arises under a contract which was entered into on, say, April 1, 1983; whereas the provisions of the *Construction Lien Act, 1983* would apply if the subcontract arises under a contract which was entered into on, say, April 2, 1983.

As can be seen, the date the contract was entered into, which is always a question of fact, is pivotal. In seeking to preserve his lien, a subcontractor would therefore be well advised to make an inquiry of the owner or the contractor, under s. 32(1) of the *Mechanics' Lien Act* or s. 39(1) of the *Construction Lien Act, 1983,* as to the contract date.[35]

It is difficult to speculate how the courts will apply cases decided under the authority of the *Mechanics' Lien Act* to new situations arising under the *Construction Lien Act, 1983.* One might argue that the earlier judicial decisions have no application since the wording in the new Act is in most cases different than that found in the *Mechanics' Lien Act.* Even if the wording of some of the new provisions were exactly the same, one might argue that the context is different, and that the same words must be considered anew. Furthermore, the common law presumption that a judicial interpretation is to be carried forward from one statute to the next has been abolished by virtue of s. 19 of the *Interpretation Act.*[36]

Having said that, however, it is probable that the earlier judicial decisions will at least have a strong persuasive influence in circumstances where the spirit and intent of both the former and the new provisions are the same.

D. AMENDMENTS TO THE CONSTRUCTION LIEN ACT, 1983

After the *Construction Lien Act, 1983* was proclaimed in force, institutional lenders continued their lobbying efforts to have the priority provisions of the legislation reconsidered or at least clarified by amendment.[37]

---

[35] Neither s. 32(1) of the *Mechanics' Lien Act* nor s. 39(1) of the *Construction Lien Act, 1983* specifically oblige the contractor or owner to provide information as to the date the contract was entered into, although the *Mechanics' Lien Act* provision does oblige the owner or his agent to produce for inspection "the contract or agreement with the contractor for or in respect of which the work was or is to be done or the materials were or are to placed or furnished, if the contract or agreement is in writing. . . ."

[36] R.S.O. 1980, c. 219.

[37] "Insurers leery about new lien act," *Globe and Mail,* Friday, June 24, 1983, at B2.

Additionally, insurance companies were reluctant to create new types of bonding, such as a lien holdback deficiency bond, in response to the new Act,[38] partly out of the lack of certainty as to how the courts would interpret the new legislation. The headline of an article on p. 2 of the Business Section of the June 24, 1983 *Globe and Mail* confirmed that, "Insurers leery about new lien act."

Another problem area in the new legislation related to the position, both practical and legal, of purchasers of new homes, particularly where the possibility existed that they might be construed to be statutory owners under the Act. As Stephen Fram wrote to the members of the Attorney General's Advisory Committee on the Draft *Construction Lien Act* on June 1, 1983,

> [P]urchasers [of new homes] have considerable latitude in selecting components of the home. Nevertheless, the transfer of title and payment does not occur until closing. It seems to me, that as a practical matter, a purchaser waiting in the moving van with his three children and the dog are often not in a position to withhold the holdback from the builder. I tend to think that the best course would be to provide such purchasers are not owners within the meaning of the Act. Subsection 9 constitutes the payment to the builder a trust. In addition, it may be desirable to give all those persons who contribute services and materials the right to demand from the builder information regarding the proposed date of closing for any sale of a house.

In order to allay some of these fears and anxieties, and to clarify certain aspects of the legislation, the Attorney General made the following statement to the Ontario Legislature on May 20, 1983:

> Mr. Speaker, on January 25th, 1983, the House gave 2nd and 3rd Reading to Bill 216, the Construction Lien Act, 1983. The Act came into force on April 2nd. Some Members of the Legislature and others have raised a problem that is causing hardship to new home purchasers. I have been asked to intervene to redress the problem. It is my intention to do so.
>
> Many lenders were surprised by the speed with which the House, on a non-partisan basis, enacted the lien legislation and they appear to have been unprepared for it coming into force so quickly. As a result, some of the provisions of the Act have been interpreted in a manner not in accord with our intentions.
>
> The problem raised by the Member for Oshawa relates particularly to subsection 80(5), dealing with the priority of liens over mortgages registered subsequent to the commencement of an improvement.
>
> When a purchaser of a new home, who has not had the house built for him or her and, therefore, is not an "owner" under the Act, closes the transaction, advances the purchase price and receives a conveyance from the builder, it is clear that if no liens are registered at the time and the purchaser has no written notice of a lien, the interest of the purchaser has priority over any lien. That is the effect of subsection 80(6).
>
> It has long been, and in my opinion, is now the law, that a mortgage arranged by the purchaser, who is not an owner, advanced and registered at closing also has priority over liens which have not been registered.

---

[38] *Ibid.*

It was not our intention to confiscate part of the interest of mortgagees lending to purchasers. The lien is a right over the interest in the property of the person who had the improvement made.

While several highly regarded lawyers have given the same opinion as I have just expressed, doubt remains in the mind of some lenders. They have not been advancing 10 or more percent of the price on closing. Some purchasers of new homes have been forced to arrange interim financing for a period of up to sixty days from closing. Not only could this be harmful to the individual purchaser, but it also could put a cloud over purchasing a home and might thereby harm the construction industry which is important to the economic health of the province.

I could refer the interpretation of the subsection to the courts and wait for clarification. However, that would not be the desire of the Government or of Members opposite.

While I had hoped to wait for at least a year before making amendments to the Act, I believe that there should be amendments in the near future to clarify the intention of the legislation.

The effect of the amendments that I will bring forward will be to make it clear that a mortgage of a purchaser's interest in a new home is not subject to the priorities of subsections 80(2) or of 80(5). These amendments will be retroactive to April 2nd when the Act came into force.

In addition, the conveyancing Bar has requested that there be legislative clarification of when a purchaser of a new home becomes an owner, and thereby becomes responsible for holdback. The amendments will clarify this issue.

Mr. Speaker, I trust that the lenders in the province will act on this statement of intention to bring forward legislation. It is not necessary, and it is undesirable, for a lender to a purchaser to be concerned about the priority of liens under subsections 80(2) or 80(5). Because of my wish to consult those involved, a Ministry official will be meeting with lawyers representing lenders to work out the details of these amendments. Representatives of contractors and of labour will also be consulted.

To avoid misunderstandings, I want to emphasis that the principles of the Act and holdback security will not be reconsidered in connection with these proposed amendments. Holdback security in the present form will remain until all segments of the construction industry can agree on a better method for protecting the vital interests of those who supply services and material to improve real property.

Thank you, Mr. Speaker.

At the date of this writing, it is anticipated that First Reading of the proposed amending legislation will take place early in the Fall sitting of the Legislature, in October of 1983. The amendments, though, will be retroactive to April 2, 1983.

On July 8, 1983, the Ministry of the Attorney General circulated the following discussion draft of, and comments on, the proposed amendments to the Act:

(PROPOSED) CONSTRUCTION LIEN AMENDMENT ACT, 1983

1.-(1) Subsection 1(1) of the *Construction Lien Act, 1983*, being chapter 6, is amended by adding thereto the following paragraphs:

7a. "home" means,

    i. a self-contained one-family dwelling, detached or attached to one or more others by common wall,

    ii. a building composed of more than one and not more than two self-contained, one-family dwellings under one ownership, or

    iii. a condominium dwelling unit, including the common elements,

and includes any structure or works used in conjunction therewith;

7b. "home buyer" means a person who buys the interest of an owner in a premises that is a home, whether built or not at the time the agreement of purchase and sale in respect thereof is entered into, where not more than 20 per cent of the purchase price is paid prior to the conveyance and where the home is not conveyed until it is ready for occupancy, evidenced in the case of a new home by the issuance under the *Building Code Act* of a permit authorizing occupancy or the issuance under the *Ontario New Home Warranties Plan Act* of a certificate of completion and possession.

1.-(2) Paragraph 15 of subsection 1(1) of the said Act is amended by adding at the end thereof "but does not include a home buyer."

COMMENTS

Case law under the prior Act (the *Mechanics' Lien Act*) would have classified as owners persons purchasing housing not yet built, from sample, that is, from a builder's model or plans. Since the definition of owner is basically the same under the *Construction Lien Act, 1983,* the same result is probable.

It has been decided that the costs of having most house purchasers classified as owners would inflate the price of new housing without an equivalent benefit to those who supply services and materials to new housing.

Therefore, section 1 of the proposed bill excludes a "home buyer" from the definition of owner. The result would be that no liens could be claimed against the interest of a home buyer, unless lien claims were registered on title or written notice of a lien was given to the home buyer, before the conveyance of the premises. Other changes protect the interest of a mortgagee where a mortgage is given or assumed by a home buyer (Section

8 of the proposed bill). Therefore, on closing, a home buyer would receive the full advance of the mortgage and a builder selling to a home buyer would receive the full balance of the purchase price.

The definition of "home" is similar to that contained in the *Ontario New Home Warranties Plan Act*. However, seasonal housing is not excluded. The definition would include all residential housing bought as a home.

The definition of "home buyer" is intended to encompass purchasers whose intention is to buy a home and not to have one built. The total deposits a "home buyer" may make is limited to 20 per cent. This is a somewhat arbitrary figure, but reflects the fact that, where deposits are greater than this amount, the purchaser is financing construction. It also is designed to protect suppliers of services and materials by ensuring that there is a significant amount at stake at closing to deal with liens that are registered. The definition requires the conveyance of both the land and home only after the home is ready for occupancy. This will prevent avoidance of the Act and permit those working on the home site to know when they may lose their lien rights. Those who have left the site will be able to demand relevant information (see section 6 of the proposed bill). One of two different forms of documentation are required to evidence the readiness for occupancy of new homes. This will provide certainty to all parties to the conveyance.

2. Subsection 3(3) of the said Act is repealed and the following substituted therefor:

(3) Despite subsection 14(1), an architect or the holder of a certificate of practice under the *Architects Act* and the employees thereof do not have a lien.

COMMENTS

Under subsection 3(3) of the Act, architects do not have lien rights. It was intended that this would include employees of architects. The governing body for architects, the Ontario Association of Architects, considers it unprofessional conduct for an architect to not pay his or her employees. The amendment set out in section 2 of the proposed bill removes lien rights from the employees of an architect.

3. Section 5 of the said Act is amended by adding thereto the following subsection:

(2) Without restricting the generality of subsection (1), an agreement of purchase and sale that provides for the making or completion of an improvement shall, where the purchaser is an owner, be deemed to provide for the retention of a holdback by the purchaser, and tender by the purchaser on closing is not defective by reason only that the purchaser does not tender the amount of the holdback.

COMMENTS

A purchaser of housing built from the builder's model or plans or a person having a home built who is not a "home buyer" would be an owner and have the statutory obligations of an owner. So too would a purchaser of commercial or industrial property who had improvements made to the premises prior to taking the conveyance.

Some doubt has existed whether a purchaser who is an owner could force the vendor to give possession while retaining statutory holdback. Section 3 of the proposed bill provides that a purchaser who is an owner may force the vendor to give possession while retaining holdback.

The effect of this amendment on a purchaser of housing is that the purchaser who is not a "home buyer" and is an owner can comply with the statutory obligation. The mortgagee may not advance the holdback on closing but the purchaser will not be prejudiced by having to obtain interim financing.

The effect of sections 1 and 3 on a builder is to provide a choice. A builder who obtains a significant part of the financing from a home purchaser before closing must realize that the person is an owner under the Act and holdback must be retained by that purchaser on closing. A builder who is financing construction on his own credit, and obtains a deposit of 20 per cent or less, will obtain the full balance of the purchase price on closing with the home buyer.

4. Section 36 of the said Act is amended by adding thereto the following subsection:

(6) A person who has preserved a lien, but who has extended a period of credit for the payment of the amount to which the lien relates,

may commence an action for the purpose of perfecting his lien even though the period of credit has not at the time expired, but where the action is so commenced, the action is stayed until the expiration of the period of credit, unless the court is satisfied that the stay is unfair in the circumstances and orders that the action proceed.

COMMENTS

Section 4 of the proposed bill corrects a defect in the Act. Under the Act, the time for bringing an action is not extended where a period of credit for payment has been granted. However, it is ordinarily improper to bring an action to enforce a debt that is not yet payable. The amendment which adds a new subsection 36(6) will allow a person to perfect his lien rights before they expire by bringing an action. However, the action is stayed until the debt is payable unless the stay is lifted by a judge.

5. Subsection 37(2) of the said Act is amended by striking out "an application" in the first and second lines and inserting in lieu thereof "a motion".

COMMENTS

Sections 5 and 7 of the proposed bill are amendments to replace the word "application" by the word "motion". This is not a change of substance.

6. Subsection 39(1) of the said Act is amended by adding thereto the following paragraph:

3. By an owner who is selling his interest in a premises that is a home, with,

    i. a copy of the agreement of purchase and sale, and
   ii. the date on which a permit authorizing occupancy or a certificate of completion and possession has been issued.

COMMENTS

In new home construction, activity on the site increases to ready the home for occupancy just prior to closing. Those on or near the site will be aware of when a home sale is about to close. However, some suppliers of services and materials would find it useful to determine whether a purchaser is a home buyer, when the sale is likely to be closed, and when the home is ready for occupancy. The provision will allow them to obtain this information.

7. Subsection 44(4) of the said Act is amended by striking out "application" in the fourth line and inserting in lieu thereof "motion".

COMMENTS

See Comments under Section 5, above.

8.-(1) Subsection 80(5) of the said Act is repealed and the following substituted therefor:

(5) Where a mortgage affecting the owner's interest in the premises is registered after the time when the first lien arose in respect of an improvement, the liens arising from the improvement have priority over the mortgage to the extent of any deficiency in the holdbacks required to be retained by the owner under Part IV.

8.-(2) Subsection 80(10) of the said Act is repealed and the following substituted therefor:

(10) A purchaser who takes title from a mortgagee takes title to the premises free of the priority of the liens created by subsections (2) and (5) where,

   (a) a financial guarantee bond; or
   (b) a letter of credit or letter of guarantee from a Canadian chartered bank,

in a form prescribed is registered on the title to the premises, and the security of the bond, letter of credit or letter of guarantee thereupon takes the place of the priority created by those subsections, and persons who have proved liens have a right of action against the surety on the bond or the issuer of the letter of credit or letter of guarantee.

(11) Subsections (2) and (5) do not apply to a mortgage given or assumed by a home buyer.

COMMENTS

A revision to subsection 80(5) will make it clear that a mortgage of the interest in premises of a person who is not an owner under the Act is not affected by the priority of liens. This conclusion follows from the concept of a lien as set out in section 14(1) of the Act: a lien attaches to an owner's interest in premises.

A consequence of excluding a home buyer from the definition of owner is that a mortgage given by a home buyer would not be subject to the priority of liens. This, by itself, would leave mortgages taken out by the builder but assumed by a home buyer subject to the priority of liens. This would be an anomalous position quite disadvantageous to home buyers. Mortgages are assumed because the interest rates and terms are better than a mortgage that could be arranged by the home buyer. Having decided that a home buyer should not be an owner under the Act, it is sensible to put mortgages assumed by a home buyer in the same position as mortgages given by a home buyer. A new subsection 80(11) provides that subsections 80(2) and (5) do not apply to a mortgage given or assumed by a home buyer.

Section 80(10) has been revised to provide that where a mortgagee sells the interest of an owner the purchaser can take the premises free of the priority created by subsections 80(2) and (5) where either a financial guarantee bond or a letter of credit, in a form prescribed, is registered on title. This will permit the Canadian chartered banks to provide equivalent protection to lien claimants to that provided by the bonding industry.

9. This Act shall be deemed to have come into force on the 2nd day of April, 1983.

COMMENTS

The proposed amendment deals primarily with matters that needed clarification. Even the most substantive change, that is, excluding home buyers from the definition of owner, reflects what most persons thought that the law already provided. Therefore, in keeping with the Attorney General's statement of May 20, the proposed bill provides that it is retroactive to April 2nd, 1983.

10. The short title of this Act is the *Construction Lien Amendment Act, 1983.*

Chapter 2

The Lien

A. CREATION OF THE LIEN

(i) Generally

As indicated in the preceeding chapter, the lien is purely a creature of statute, and did not exist either at common law or in equity.

Section 14(1) of the *Construction Lien Act, 1983,* which creates the lien, provides as follows:

> 14(1) A person who supplies services or materials to an improvement for an owner, contractor or subcontractor, has a lien upon the interest of the owner in the premises improved for the price of those services or materials.

Inasmuch as most of the words in that section are defined terms, any discussion of it would essentially be an exercise in statutory interpretation, requiring dissection of those words and their underlying concepts.

(a) "A person"

In a general sense, "person" is meant to include "contractors,"[1] "subcontractors"[2] and "workers."[3] Material suppliers and lessors of equipment (either with[4] or without[5] an operator) would come under the definition of either "contractor" or "subcontractor," depending upon whom they contracted with. Furthermore, as will be seen below, certain design professionals, other than architects,[6] are also "persons" who would in some circumstances be entitled to a lien.[7]

In its literal meaning, the word "person" is relatively self-explanatory. This sense, though, is extended by the *Interpretation Act*,[8] which

---

[1] See s. 1(1) 4.
[2] See s. 1(1) 23.
[3] See s. 1(1) 27.
[4] See s. 1(1) 25, i.
[5] See s. 1(1) 12, ii.
[6] See s. 3(3).
[7] See s. 1(1) 25, ii.
[8] R.S.O. 1980, c. 219.

defines "person" to include "a corporation and the heirs, executors, administrators or other legal representatives of a person to whom the context can apply according to law."[9] The latter part of this definition is consistent with the notions of assignment and devolution of lien rights found in the *Construction Lien Act, 1983*.[10]

Reported cases have made it clear that the "person" referred to in s. 14(1) will be interpreted to be the one who actually contracted to supply services or materials to the improvement.[11] The fact that these cases have come before the courts have made the articulation of this obvious principle necessary.

(b) "who supplies services or materials"

Section 1(1)21 of the Act declares that "services *or* materials" includes both services *and* materials.[12]

"Supply of services" means any work done or service performed "upon or in respect of[13] an improvement,"[14] and is deemed to include:

(a) the rental of equipment *with* an operator;[15] and

---

9 *Ibid.*, s. 30(28).

10 See s. 75.

11 See, for example, *Inter Property Invts. Ltd. v. Trpchich et al.* (1975), 11 O.R. (2d) 568 (S.C.), where the headnote provides, in part:

> Where a lien is filed by a limited company for work which was performed by the president of the company in his personal capacity it is not a valid lien. Moreover, the president cannot be added as a party plaintiff *nunc pro tunc*. Because of the failure of the president to file a claim for lien and certificate of action there are no lien rights which he could enforce in his personal capacity. Thus to add him as a party plaintiff *nunc pro tunc* would be to convert the character of the action from a mechanics' lien action to a personal action on a contract.

By way of further examples, see *Re Mechanics' Lien Act; Rodewalt v. Plasky* (1959), 30 W.W.R. 457 (Alta. S.C.); *Waisman and Ross c.o.b. Waisman, Ross & Assoc. v. Crown Trust Co.*, [1970] S.C.R. 553, 72 W.W.R. 531, 9 D.L.R. (3d) 733; *Chick Lbr. & Fuel Co. v. Moorehouse*, 41 Man. R. 574, [1933] 3 W.W.R. 465, [1934] 1 D.L.R. 364 (C.A.); and *Simac v. Waltman; Roskar v. Heidner's Trustee et al.*, [1947] O.W.N. 264 (H.C.).

12 "In ordinary usage, 'and' is conjunctive and 'or' disjunctive. But to carry out the intention of the legislature it may be necessary to read 'and' in place of the conjunction 'or', and vice versa.": *Maxwell on the Interpretation of Statutes*, 12th ed. (1969) at 232–233. Section 1(1) 21 obviates the necessity of speculating as to legislative intent where the phrase "services or materials" is used.

13 For a discussion of the interpretation of the words "in respect of . . . any land", in a mechanics' lien context, see *George Wimpey Can. Ltd. v. Peelton Hills Ltd. et al.* (1981), 31 O.R. (2d) 563, 119 D.L.R. (3d) 408, 14 M.P.L.R. 1, 16 R.P.R. 222, affd. 35 O.R. (2d) 787, 132 D.L.R. (3d) 732, 42 C.B.R. (N.S.) 1, 18 M.P.L.R. 65, 23 R.P.R. 123; leave to appeal to S.C.C. refused (1982), 43 N.R. 618n. In that case, a contractor entered into an agreement with P. Ltd. to install services and to construct roads and sidewalks on road allowances, which were conveyed to the municipality prior to the work being performed. P. Ltd. also conveyed the subdivision lots adjoining the road allowances to A. Ltd., taking back a mortgage. The contractor claimed that the work done on the road created a lien which could be asserted against P. Ltd.'s interest in the

(b) where construction does not in fact begin, the supply of a "design, plan, drawing or specification" that *in itself* enhances the value of the owner's interest in the land.[16]

The latter provision was inserted in the Act so as to accommodate the claim of, for example, an engineer who might have undertaken extensive work and incurred considerable expenses in preparing the drawings and specifications with respect to a building which is never in fact constructed.

An architect's right to assert a lien under the authority of Ontario's mechanics' lien legislation was never entirely clear. Earlier cases appear to have held that, while an architect may have been entitled to a lien for supervisory services, and might have claimed a lien for preparing plans when he also supervised construction in accordance with those plans,[17] he was not entitled to a lien for the preparation of the plans alone, particularly where the building did not proceed.[18] Under the *Construction Lien Act, 1983,* however, an architect or the holder of a certificate of practice under the *Architects Act,*[19] is clearly not entitled to a lien,[20] despite ss. 14(1) and 1(1) 25 ii.

---

subdivision lots, since the work was performed "in respect of" those lots. The Divisional Court, whose decision was upheld by the Court of Appeal, held that the lien could only be claimed against lands on which work was done or materials were placed, and not against adjoining lands.

14 Section 1(1) 25. The generality of this provision might serve to open the door to a variety of lien claims which hitherto may not have been recognized as being legitimate. For example, *quaere* whether a solicitor, who has been intimately involved in all steps leading up to the registration of a plan of subdivision, would have a lien for services performed "in respect of an improvement." *Quaere* whether the same solicitor would argue that he or she is entitled to a lien, where it would mean that the owner would then be obliged to comply with the holdback provisions in the Act.

15 Section 1(1) 25, i. Contrast this with the rental of equipment *without* an operator, which is defined as being "materials" under s. 1(1) 12, ii.

16 Section 1(1) 25, ii.

17 *Read v. Whitney* (1919), 45 O.L.R. 377, 48 D.L.R. 305 (C.A.); *Burgess v. Khoury (Albrechtsen's Claim),* [1948] O.W.N. 789 (H.C.). But see *Beling Cement Const. Ltd. v. J.C. Contractors Ltd. et al.; Bourdeau & Marquis Drywall & Insulation Inc. v. J.C. Contractors Ltd.; Pederson c.o.b. J.P. Const. v. J.C. Contractors Ltd.; N. Pollard & Son Ltd. v. J.C. Contractors Ltd.* (1980), 13 R.P.R. 306 (Ont. S.C.).

18 *Burgess v. Khoury (Albrechtsen's Claim), supra,* note 17. But see *William McNally Const. Ltd. v. Demlakian* (1979), 31 C.B.R. (N.S.) 287, 9 R.P.R. 70 (leave to appeal refused (1979), 27 O.R. (2d) 118 (H.C.)), and *Armbro Materials & Const. Ltd. v. 230056 Invts. Ltd. et al.* (1975), 9 O.R. (2d) 226, 60 D.L.R. (3d) 68 (S.C.) (this decision, though, is distinguishable since it deals with the claim of an engineer, and specifically differentiates it from the claim of an architect).

19 R.S.O. 1980, c. 26.

20 Section 3(3). It may be noted that the proposed *Construction Lien Amendment Act, 1983,* which is expected to receive First Reading in October of 1983 and which will be deemed to have come into force on April 2, 1983, purports to repeal s. 3(3) and to substitute the following therefor:

    Despite subsection 14(1), an architect or the holder of a certificate of practice under the *Architects Act* and the employees thereof do not have a lien.

"Materials" are defined to mean:

> . . . every kind of movable property,
>   i. that becomes, or is intended to become, part of the improvement, or that is used directly in the making of the improvement, or that is used to facilitate directly the making of the improvement,
>   ii. that is equipment rented without an operator for use in the making of the improvement.[21]

By virtue of s. 1(2), "materials" are "supplied to an improvement" when at least one of the following conditions are met:

(a) when they are placed on the land[22] on which the improvement is being made;[23]

(b) when they are placed upon land designated by the owner[24] or his agent[25] that is in the immediate vicinity[26] of the premises.[27] However, the placing of materials on the designated land does not, of itself, make that land subject to a lien;[28]

(c) when they are incorporated into, or used in making, or facilitating the making of,[29] the improvement.[30]

A person's lien arises and takes effect when he first supplies his

---

[21] Section 1(1) 12. Contrast the latter portion of this definition with the rental of equipment *with* an operator, which is defined as being the "supply of services" under s. 1(1) 24, i.

[22] "Land" is defined to include "any building, structure or works affixed to the land, or an appurtenance to any of them, but does not include the improvement": s. 1(1) 10.

[23] Section 1(2)(a).

[24] That is, the "statutory" owner: see s. 1(1) 15.

[25] It is a question of fact as to whether a particular person is an agent of the statutory owner. In most cases, the person who is superintending the construction, such as the architect or the general contractor, would be perceived by all to be acting in that role. Section 1(3) of the Act, though, assists in the determination of the factual agency issue by deeming the contractor or a subcontractor, to whom materials are supplied and who makes the actual land designation, to be the owner's agent for that purpose, unless the material supplier has actual notice to the contrary. In order to avoid potential problems, perhaps the material supplier would be well advised to have the person, who designates the land where the materials are to be placed, sign the delivery receipt in the expressed capacity of "agent for owner."

[26] It is a question of fact whether the land upon which materials are placed is in the "immediate vicinity" of the premises. The main thrust of this provision, though, is to clarify the fact that the delivery of materials to, say, the owner's warehouse, for subsequent delivery to the construction site when required, does *not* constitute the supply of materials to the improvement, in which case no lien would arise unless and until the materials are actually placed on the land and/or incorporated into the improvement.

[27] See s. 1(1) 19.

[28] Section 1(2)(b).

[29] For example, the rental of equipment without an operator would be used in "facilitating the making" of the improvement: see s. 1(1) 12, ii.

[30] Section 1(2)(c).

services or materials to the improvement.[31] Materials, in particular, may be supplied pursuant to either a series of separate contracts or a "prevenient arrangement." The latter is in effect a single contract whereby the person requiring the materials undertakes to order them, as they are required, from a particular supplier. Although the prices and quantities may not be defined until orders are placed, the entire transaction, which might extend over the entire life of a construction project, is based upon the original understanding between the parties. As will be seen later, the fact that materials may have been supplied under a prevenient arrangement, rather than under a series of separate contracts, may significantly affect the calculation of the material supplier's 45-day lien period.

(c) "to an improvement"

The distinction made between the defined terms for "land," "premises" and "improvement" in the Act require careful consideration.

"Improvement" is defined to mean:

> i. any alteration, addition or repair to, or
> ii. any construction, erection or installation on,
> any land, and includes the demolition or removal of any building, structure or works or part thereof. . . .[32]

This defined term is meant to be construed as the physical results of the supply of services or materials, whether those results take the form of a new building structure; an addition to, or an alteration or repair of, an existing structure; or the demolition or removal of all or part of an existing structure.

"Land" is defined to include not only the actual real property, but also "any building, structure or works affixed to the land, or an appurtenance to any of them," but expressly does not include the "improvement."[33]

"Premises" is defined to include the "improvement," "all materials supplied to the improvement," and "the land occupied by the improvement, or enjoyed therewith,[34] or the land upon or in respect of which the improvement was done or made."[35]

At the risk of oversimplification, the foregoing concepts might be more easily understood by the use of a representational illustration:

---

[31] Section 15.
[32] Section 1(1)8.
[33] Section 1(1)10.
[34] See, for example, *Wray & Sons Ltd. v. Stewart,* [1958] O.W.N. 65 (C.A.) and *Crown Lbr. Co. v. McTaggart Motors Ltd.* (1961), 34 W.W.R. 370 (Alta. S.C.). But see *Sparks & McKay v. Lord; Dom. Lbr. & Coal Co. v. Lord* (1929), 63 O.L.R. 393, [1929] 2 D.L.R. 32 (C.A.); affd. as to *Sparks & McKay (sub nom. Steedman v. Sparks & McKay)*; revd. as to *Dom. Lbr. & Coal Co. (sub nom. Steedman v. Dom. Lbr. & Coal Co.),* [1930] S.C.R. 351, [1930] 3 D.L.R. 185.
[35] Section 1(1) 19.

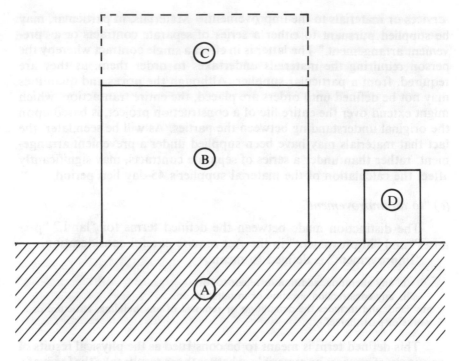

"A" represents the real property to which "B", a building, is affixed. A contractor is retained to build an addition, "C", on top of "B" for the purpose of adding more interior space to the existing structure. A subcontractor delivers a quantity of bricks and lumber ("D") to the site, and these materials are intended to be used in the construction of the addition.

The "improvement", as defined, would refer only to "C". It does not include either the pre-existing building ("B"), the real property ("A"), or the materials ("D") supplied by the subcontractor.

The "land" includes both the real property ("A") and the pre-existing building ("B"), but does not include either the addition ("C") or the materials ("D").

The "premises" collectively includes the real property ("A"), the pre-existing building ("B"), the addition ("C"), and all materials ("D"). In fact, the above diagram could be entitled "The Premises".

If the contractor had initially been engaged to construct a building ("B") on *vacant* land ("A"), the "improvement" would be represented by "B", the "land" would include only "A", and the premises would include "A", "B" and "D".

(d) "for an owner, contractor or subcontractor"

"Owner" is a defined term under the Act, and does not necessarily refer to the registered owner of the land. For this reason, the "owner" described and defined in s. 1(1) 15 of the Act is generally referred to as the "statutory owner" so as to avoid confusion with the "registered owner."

Section 1(1) 15 provides that "owner" means:

15. . . . any person,[36] including the Crown,[37] having an interest in a premises[38] at whose request and,

    i. upon whose credit, or

    ii. on whose behalf, or

    iii. with whose privity or consent, or

    iv. for whose direct benefit,

an improvement is made to the premises;[39]

For a thorough discussion of the extension of the concept of statutory ownership to persons other than the registered owner of the land, see heading B in this chapter, entitled "Who is an Owner?".

The definitions of "contractor" and "subcontractor" in the Act are substantially the same as those found in the *Mechanics' Lien Act.* "Contractor" is defined to mean "a person contracting with or employed

---

[36] The introductory words of the definition of "owner" under the *Mechanics' Lien Act,* R.S.O. 1980, c. 261, s. 1(1)(f) were as follows:

    (f) "owner" includes any person and corporation, including the Crown, a municipal corporation and a railway company . . ."

The omission of the references to a "corporation", a "municipal corporation" and a "railway company" in the *Construction Lien Act, 1983* derives from the fact that the word "person" is sufficiently broad so as comprehend those entities.

[37] The reference here is to the provincial, not the federal, Crown: see s. 1(1)6.

[38] "Interest in the premises" is defined to mean "an estate or interest of any nature, and includes a statutory right given or reserved to the Crown to enter any lands or premises belonging to any person or public authority for the purpose of doing any work, construction, repair or maintenance in, upon, through, over or under any lands or premises": s. 1(1)9.

[39] The proposed *Construction Lien Amendment Act, 1983,* which is expected to receive First Reading in October of 1983 and which will be deemed to have come into force on April 2, 1983, purports to amend s. 1(1)15 by adding at the end thereof the words "but does not include a home buyer." The amending legislation defines "home buyer" to mean "a person who buys the interest of an owner in a premises that is a home, whether built or not at the time the agreement of purchase and sale in respect thereof is entered into, where not more than 20 per cent of the purchase price is paid prior to the conveyance and where the home is not conveyed until it is ready for occupancy, evidenced in the case of a new home by the issuance under the *Building Code Act* of a permit authorizing occupancy or the issuance under the *Ontario New Home Warranties Plan Act* of a certificate of completion and possession." Furthermore, "home" is defined to mean,

    i. a self-contained one-family dwelling, detached or attached to one or more others by common wall,

    ii. a building composed of more than one and not more than two self-contained, one-family dwellings under one ownership, or

    iii. a condominium dwelling unit, including the common elements,

and includes any structure or works used in conjunction therewith.

directly by the owner or his agent to supply services or materials to an improvement;"[40] and "subcontractor" is defined to mean "a person not contracting with or employed directly by the owner or his agent but who supplies services or materials to the improvement under an agreement with the contractor or under him with another subcontractor."[41]

As the Attorney General's Advisory Committee on the Draft *Construction Lien Act* observed:

> It is customary for construction projects to be organized upon what is known as a pyramid pattern. An owner will hire a contractor to make an improvement to his property. The contractor, in turn, will hire a number of specialist subcontractors, each of whom will work on a particular aspect of the project. Only the contractor has direct contractual relations with the owner.[42]

(e) "has a lien upon the interest of the owner in the premises improved"[43]

As will be discussed in detail below, the "interest of the [statutory] owner in the premises" could be an interest in the freehold, the leasehold, a mortgage or charge, an agreement of purchase and sale, and perhaps other aspects of or rights in real property.

(f) "for the price of those services or materials"

"Price" is defined by the Act to mean,

> ... the contract or subcontract price,
>   i. agreed upon between the parties, or
>   ii. where no specific price has been agreed upon between them, the actual value of the services or materials that have been supplied to the improvement under the contract or subcontract.[44]

Reference to the notion of "actual value," as contained in the foregoing definition, would seem to imply that, in the absence of an agreed price, the equitable doctrine of *quantum meruit*[45] would apply.

Inasmuch as the lien is limited to the "price" of services or materials, the Act provides that every claim for lien shall set out, among other things,

---

[40] Section 1(1)4.
[41] Section 1(1)23.
[42] *Report of the Attorney General's Advisory Committee on the Draft Construction Lien Act* (April 1982), at 4–5.
[43] "Improved" is defined to have a corresponding meaning to "improvement," according to the definition section of the Act (see concluding words of s. 1(1)8).
[44] Section 1(1)20.
[45] "An action on a *quantum meruit* is an action of *assumpsit* grounded on a promise, express or implied, to pay the plaintiff for work and labour so much as his trouble is really worth.": *Mozley and Whiteley's Law Dictionary*, 9th ed. (1977), at 265.

only "the amount claimed in respect of services or materials *that have been supplied.*"[46] Furthermore, the Act creates a civil cause of action in favour of any person who suffers damage as a result of the preservation or the giving of formal notice of a lien which the claimant "knows or ought to know is grossly in excess of the amount which he is owed."[47]

By way of comparison, the *Mechanics' Lien Act* permitted the registration of a claim for lien setting out, among other things, "the sum claimed as due *or to become due.*"[48] Additionally, the *Mechanics' Lien Act* contained no sanctions against the registration of an inflated claim for lien, perhaps on the assumption that any person who suffers damage as a result might have had a cause of action for slander of title.

(ii) The Lien as a Charge

As seen above, s. 14(1) of the Act creates the lien and constitutes it as an interest in the premises. The lien claimant's position is reinforced and further secured by s. 21 which provides that a lien is a charge upon the holdbacks which are required to be retained under the Act, and upon "any additional amount owed in relation to the improvement by a payer to the contractor or to any subcontractor whose contract or subcontract was in whole or in part performed by the supply of services or materials giving rise to the lien."

If, for example, the owner's architect has issued an interim progress certificate confirming that the value of the services or materials that have been supplied to the improvement totals $100,000, the sum of $10,000 represents holdback and is required to be retained by the owner[49] "until all liens that may be claimed against . . . [it] have expired as provided in Part V, or have been satisfied, discharged or provided for under section 44."[50] If the owner holds back more than $10,000, (perhaps to secure a warranty with respect to the performance of future remedial work), the excess amount held back is also subject to the charge.[51] The charge against any excess amount held back, though, is subject to the owner's right to set off "all outstanding debts, claims or damages, whether or not related to the improvement."[52]

---

[46] Section 34(5)(d); emphasis added.
[47] Section 35(a).
[48] *Mechanics' Lien Act,* R.S.O. 1980, c. 261, s. 17(1)(c); emphasis added. Note, however, that a notice of claim to holdback, which was to have been served in circumstances where the lien did not attach to the land, was to set out, among other things, only "the sum claimed as due," and not the sum which was to become due: see *Mechanics' Lien Act,* s. 23(7)(c).
[49] Section 22.
[50] *Ibid.*
[51] Section 21.
[52] Section 17(3).

According to the Attorney General's Advisory Committee:

> The major effect of this provision is that where an owner complies with the Act, the holdback fund and, subject to subsection 17(2), any additional amount owed to the contractor related to the improvement, will take the place of the premises, and the lien then becomes converted to a charge against those amounts. In other words, an owner may protect his interest in the premises from seizure and sale merely by complying with the payment and holdback provisions of the Act.[53]

(iii) Claim for Interest

It was not uncommon for a claim for lien, registered pursuant to the *Mechanics' Lien Act,* to include a claim for the principal amount alleged to be owing, plus interest, plus costs. Although experience has shown that courts were not averse to awarding interest to the lien claimant,[54] nonetheless the theoretical right of entitlement to a lien for interest was never clear.

The Attorney General's Advisory Committee on the Draft *Construction Lien Act* was of the view, though, that "there should be no lien right for interest because interest does not represent an improvement to the value of the premises."[55]

Accordingly, s. 14(2) of the Act provides that "[n]o person is entitled to a lien for any interest on the amount owed to him in respect of the services and materials that have been supplied by him. . . ." The section preserves the right, though, to recover interest as part of a personal judgment which may be obtained in the lien action. By way of example, the court might determine that a particular subcontractor is entitled to a lien against the owner's interest in the premises for the sum of $10,000, as well as a personal judgment[56] against the contractor, with whom there was privity of contract, for $10,000 *plus interest.*

In determining the amount of and entitlement to interest, the court may have regard to the pre-judgment interest provision in the *Judicature Act.*[57]

(iv) Limitations on the Value of a Lien

As confirmed by s. 17 of the Act, the lien of a person is limited to the amount owing to him in relation to the improvement. The obvious

---

[53] *Report of the Attorney General's Advisory Committee on the Draft Construction Lien Act* (April 1982), at 59.

[54] See, for example, *Nor-Min Supplies Ltd. et al. v. C.N.R. et al.* (1979), 27 O.R. (2d) 390, 106 D.L.R. (3d) 325, 10 R.P.R. 62 (C.A.); *Bird Const. Co. Ltd. v. Ownix Devs. Ltd. et al.* (1981), 33 O.R. (2d) 807, 125 D.L.R. (3d) 680, 20 R.P.R. 196 (C.A.).

[55] *Report of the Attorney General's Advisory Committee on the Draft Construction Lien Act* (April 1982), at 48.

[56] See s. 65.

[57] *Judicature Act,* R.S.O. 1980, c. 223, s. 36. The authority for invoking this provision of the *Judicature Act* is contained in s. 69(3) of the *Construction Lien Act, 1983.*

corollary to this is that a person is not entitled to a lien for an amount owing to him which does *not* relate to the improvement.[58] Furthermore, a lien may not exceed "the amount owing to him (the lien claimant)," specifically the "price," as defined[59] by the Act, of the services or materials supplied.[60] As indicated above, s. 34(5)(d) provides that "[e]very claim for lien shall set out . . . the amount claimed in respect of services or materials that *have been supplied"* (emphasis added).

Subject to the holdback obligations of the statutory owner, the value of a lien is further limited "to the least amount owed in relation to the improvement by a payer to the contractor or to any subcontractor whose contract or subcontract was in whole or in part performed by the supply of services or materials giving rise to the lien."[61] The thrust of this clause is to make the "payer" liable for an amount no greater than that amount which he owes directly to the person immediately below him on the construction pyramid. For example, an owner might owe a contractor the sum of $10,000 for a completed contract. In turn, the contractor might owe all of his subcontractors collectively the total sum of $7,500 for their completed subcontracts. If the contractor and all of the subcontractors asserted their lien rights, the total amount claimed would be $17,500. Obviously, the claims of the subcontractors, in this example, would be subsumed under the claim of the contractor. Section 17(1) makes it clear that, subject to his holdback obligations, and assuming that there has been no breach of trust, the owner's maximum liability is limited to the amount which he owes to the contractor, namely $10,000.

In *Rockett Lbr. and Bldg. Supplies Ltd. v. Papageorgiou et al.,*[62] His Honour Judge Blair, sitting as a Local Judge of the Supreme Court of Ontario, was called upon to make a decision with regard to the lien of a particular roofing subcontractor. The contractor, Tom Papageorgiou, had entered into a roofing subcontract with one John Marlatt whereby Marlatt agreed to do the total roofing, which was to include a flat roof, for a price of $2,600. Marlatt, in turn, subcontracted all of the work that he had contracted to do, with the exception of the flat roof, to Bob Mac-Dougall c.o.b. Bob MacDougall Roofing for the same price of $2,600. MacDougall completed his work and, when he did not receive any payment, registered a $2,600 claim for lien.

---

[58] It is interesting to contrast this principle with the right available to an owner to counterclaim in a lien action "in respect of *any* claim that he may be entitled to make against that person (the plaintiff/lien claimant), *whether or not that claim is related to the making of the improvement"* (emphasis added): s. 57(2)(a). Also see s. 17(3) regarding the entitlement, albeit qualified, of a payer to set off, as against the person he is liable to pay, "all outstanding debts, claims or damages, whether or not related to the improvement."

[59] See s. 1(1)20.

[60] See s. 14(1).

[61] Section 17(1).

[62] [1979] 2 A.C.W.S. 291.

Counsel for Papageorgiou argued that MacDougall's lien ought not to exceed $2,115, being the difference between the Papageorgiou-Marlatt subcontract price ($2,600) and the cost to complete the flat roof ($485). MacDougall's position was simply that his subcontract price was $2,600, that he completed his work, and that his lien should therefore be for the full amount. Marlatt did not appear and was not represented at trial.

On the basis of the evidence before him, Judge Blair saw fit to limit the amount of MacDougall's lien to $2,115, although he awarded personal judgment against Marlatt for the full amount:

> Counsel for the general contractor submits that the claimant is entitled to a lien in the amount of $2,600.00 less $485.00. No evidence was given as to any payment from the general contractor to Marlatt, but counsel for Mr. Papageorgiou admits that nothing was paid by him to Marlatt. . . . I find that the amount owing by the general contractor to Marlatt is $2,115.00, and the lien claimant is limited thereby pursuant to section 10 of the Act.[63] The claimant is, therefore, entitled to a lien in the amount of $2,115.00, and personal judgment against Marlatt in the amount of $2,600.00.[64]

A further limitation on the value of a lien derives from s. 17(2) of the Act. According to the Attorney General's Advisory Committee:

> The subsection makes it clear that the value of all the liens claimed by persons who supply services and materials to the same contractor or subcontractor[65] cannot exceed the amount owed to that contractor or subcontractor.[66]

Finally, the last limitation on the value of a lien relates to set-off. In determining the amount of a lien, the payer, subject to any holdback obligations which he may have,[67] is entitled to take into account, and to set off from the monies owing to the person he is liable to pay, "all outstanding debts, claims or damages, whether or not related to the improvement."[68]

---

[63] Blair L.J.S.C. was commenting on s. 10 of the *Mechanics' Lien Act*, R.S.O. 1970, c. 267, which provided as follows:

Save as herein otherwise provided, where the lien is claimed by any person other than the contractor, the amount that may be claimed in respect thereof is limited to the amount owing to the contractor or subcontractor or other person for whom the work has been done or the materials were placed or furnished.

[64] Quoted from p. 2 of transcript of unreported text of decision of Blair L.J.S.C. (on file with the author).

[65] Section 17(2) is expressed in terms of "the total value of the liens of all members of a class, as defined in section 81. . . ." Section 81 provides:

81. All persons having a lien who have supplied services or materials to the same payer comprise a class, and a person who has supplied services or materials to more than one payer is a member of every class to the extent to which his lien relates to that class.

[66] *Report of the Attorney General's Advisory Committee on the Draft Construction Lien Act* (April 1982), at 53.

[67] See s. 30.

[68] Section 17(3).

(v) Waiver of Lien

Section 6 of the *Mechanics' Lien Act,* which created the general right to a lien under that statute, was introduced with the phrase, "[u]nless he signs an express agreement to the contrary. . . ." This meant that a contractor or a subcontractor could contract out of his lien rights. Although lien waivers were rarely obtained (except in circumstances where an owner or a contractor felt that more security than merely a statutory declaration was required upon the release of the holdback), particularly because any attempt to extract them from the trades smacked of overreaching, the option to negotiate for them was available. One could expect that, in situations of unequal bargaining power, especially in a depressed economy where the number of construction starts have diminished, the eagerness for work might have caused a subcontractor to waive his lien rights prospectively.

In recognition of the potential of this situation for abuse, the Legislature saw fit to prohibit lien waivers. Section 4 of the *Construction Lien Act, 1983* now provides:

> 4. An agreement by any person who supplies services or materials to an improvement that this Act does not apply to him or that the remedies provided by it are not available for his benefit is void.

It has been suggested, though, that in practical terms the provision of a "declaration of last supply" by a contractor or a subcontractor, under s. 31(5) of the Act, is tantamount to a waiver if the lien is not preserved within the 45-day period next following the date of "last supply" contained in the declaration.[69]

Since s. 4 renders *any* purported waiver of the provisions of the Act void, it is necessary to consider whether a void clause in a contract is severable from the other provisions, and, if not, whether the entire contract would therefore be void. Section 5 of the Act speaks to this issue, by deeming that every contract or subcontract is to be amended in so far as is necessary so as to be in conformity with the Act in all respects.

(vi) Curative Provision

Historically, mechanics' lien legislation has been contrued so as to give effect to its spirit rather than its letter. Furthermore, s. 19 of the *Mechanics' Lien Act* provided that "substantial compliance" with certain sections of that Act (dealing with the contents, registration and verifica-

---

[69] See Douglas Macklem, "The Construction Lien Claim", at 44–45 in *The New Construction Lien Act — Bill 139* (materials distributed at seminar sponsored by Oyez Limited, October 7 and 8, 1982, Toronto).

tion of a claim for lien;[70] the contents, service and verification of a notice of claim to holdback,[71] where the lien did not attach to the land; and the commencement of an action, including the filing and service of pleadings)[72] was sufficient, and no lien was to have been invalidated by reason of a lack of strict compliance, unless some person was caused to suffer prejudice, and then only to the extent of that prejudice. Nothing in that Act, though, dispensed with the requirement for timely registration of a claim for lien[73] and a certificate of action,[74] or timely service of a notice of claim to holdback.[75]

Over time, even the concept of "substantial compliance" was considerably eroded, to the point where, for example, claims for lien registered against the wrong land,[76] or supported by defective affidavits of verification,[77] were nevertheless validated on the ground that no prejudice had been suffered.

In considering the earlier legislation and the consequent jurisprudence, the Attorney General's Advisory Committee concluded "that section 19 [the curative section] of the existing Act [i.e., the *Mechanics' Lien Act*], as it has been interpreted by the courts, has too wide an application:"[78]

> In our view, the concept of substantial compliance jeopardizes the operational success of a statute such as the *Construction Lien Act*. We see it as opening the door to endless litigation. Over and above this concern, it is possible that many payers may feel insecure in making payments, if the curative provisions of the Act are given too extensive an application.[79]

Furthermore:

> The Committee appreciates the concerns that form should not be allowed to triumph over substance, and that a party should not be unduly penalized because of some trifling error in procedure.... [However,] the owner and payers have a right to expect that all claims will be made on time and in accordance with the procedure set down in the Act. . . . Indeed, if it is not necessary to comply with a prescribed procedure, one questions the need for prescribing that procedure in the first place.[80]

---

70 See *Mechanics' Lien Act*, ss. 17 and 18.
71 *Ibid.*, s. 23.
72 *Ibid.*, s. 33.
73 *Ibid.*, s. 24(1).
74 *Ibid.*, ss. 24(2), 26 and 27.
75 *Ibid.*, ss. 23(2), 23(5) and 25.
76 See, for example, *Nor-Min Supplies Ltd. et al. v. C.N.R. et al., supra*, note 54.
77 See, for example, *North York Steel Fabricators Ltd. v. City of Hamilton et al.* (1980), 27 O.R. (2d) 456, 107 D.L.R. (3d) 647, 33 C.B.R. (N.S.) 266, 16 C.P.C. 261, 13 R.P.R. 231 (C.A.); and *Alumex Industs. Ltd. v. Djelwah* (1978), 20 O.R. (2d) 92, 7 C.P.C. 25 (M.C.).
78 *Report of the Attorney General's Advisory Committee on the Draft Construction Lien Act* (April 1982), at 32.
79 *Ibid.*
80 *Ibid.*, at 31-32.

Consequently, the curative section of the Act, s. 6, purports to protect against the invalidation of any certificate, declaration or claim for lien only as a result of failure to comply strictly with the following sections: s. 32(2) (dealing with the form and content of a certificate or declaration of substantial performance of the contract); s. 32(5) (dealing with the form and manner of publication of a certificate or a declaration of substantial performance of the contract in a construction trade newspaper); s. 33(1) (dealing with the form of certification of completion of a subcontract); or s. 34(5) (dealing with the form and content of a claim for lien); ". . . unless in the opinion of the court a person has been prejudiced thereby, and then only to the extent of the prejudice suffered." However, it is now evident that, for example, a claim for lien registered against the wrong land, or supported by a defective affidavit of verification, will be invalidated, despite the fact that no person may have suffered any prejudice as a result of the defect.

B. WHO IS AN OWNER?

(i) Generally

As discussed earlier, the registered owner of land is not to be confused with the "statutory owner" contemplated by the Act, although in many cases they may be one and the same person.

Section 1(1) 15 defines "owner" to mean:

> any person,[81] including the Crown,[82] having an interest in a premises[83] at whose request and,
> - i. upon whose credit, or
> - ii. on whose behalf, or
> - iii. with whose privity or consent, or
> - iv. for whose direct benefit,
>
> an improvement is made to the premises;[84]

It is especially worth noting that, although sub-paras. i through iv in the above definition are, as amongst themselves, disjunctive, one or more of the elements contained therein must be combined, in a conjunctive sense, with the notion of "request" in order for the definition to apply. That is to say, there must be a request for an improvement to be made to the premises, and the request must be combined notionally with at least one of the elements contained in the four sub-paragraphs, in order for the definition of "owner" to be met.

---

[81] See note 36, *supra*.
[82] See s. 1(1)6 and note 37, *supra*.
[83] See s. 1(1)9.
[84] See note 39, *supra*.

The "request" contemplated by the definition need not necessarily be expressed, but rather may be implied from the course of conduct of the "person . . . having an interest in [the] premises."[85] "Direct dealing" is not necessarily required before a request can be found.[86]

(ii) The Tenant as Owner

Where a person supplies labour or materials to a tenant in respect of leased premises, the interest of the tenant in those premises is subject to a lien. An example of this would be where a tenant, who has leased a store in a shopping centre, retains a contractor to construct the interior of the store and to supply shelving, lighting fixtures, partitions, display cases, and so on. In the typical situation, there would be privity of contract only between the tenant and the contractor. The landlord, whose interest is in the freehold, would not be a party to the contract, and might have either limited or no involvement. In this simple example, the tenant has an "interest in the premises," being a leasehold interest, and has expressly requested the contractor to carry out the work. Furthermore, the "improvement" is being made to the premises "upon [his] credit,"[87] "on [his] behalf,"[88] "with [his] privity [and] consent,"[89] and "for [his] direct benefit."[90] Consequently, it is clear that the tenant would be a statutory owner and would therefore have imposed upon him all the statutory requirements contemplated by the Act, including trust and holdback obligations.

The tenant might conceivably also be a statutory owner where the landlord acts as contractor and retains sub-trades to effect improvements to the leased premises. The statutory obligations which this would impose upon the tenant would be quite complex since the construction expenses payable by the tenant would usually be amortized over the term of the lease and would likely be paid to the landlord as "additional rent." The tenant's ability to comply with his holdback obligation would therefore be affected. Is he to hold back that part of the rent relating to the amortized construction expenses until such time as all the sub-trades' lien rights have expired? Might this cause him to be in breach of the lease? Furthermore, if he borrowed money to pay the rent, would part of that money be

---

[85] See, for example, *City of Hamilton v. Cipriani et al.*, [1977] 1 S.C.R. 169, 67 D.L.R. (3d) 1, 9 N.R. 83; *Nor. Elec. Co. Ltd. v. Mfrs. Life Ins. Co.*, [1977] 2 S.C.R. 762, 18 N.S.R. (2d) 32, 79 D.L.R. (3d) 336, 12 N.R. 216. (Subsequent references are to 79 D.L.R.)

[86] *City of Hamilton v. Cipriani et al., supra,* note 85.

[87] See s. 1(1) 15, i.

[88] See s. 1(1) 15, ii.

[89] See s. 1(1) 15, iii.

[90] See s. 1(1) 15, iv.

impressed with a trust under s. 7 of the Act? Would part of the rent received by the landlord be impressed with a trust under s. 8 of the Act? The facts of each situation would have to be analyzed in their individual contexts.

Upon establishing a lien against the tenant's leasehold interest in the premises, the lien claimant's ultimate potential remedy would be to sell that interest. In order to protect a lien claimant's rights in this regard, s. 19(2) of the Act provides that "[n]o forfeiture of a lease to, or termination of a lease by, a landlord, except for non-payment of rent, deprives any person having a lien against the leasehold of the benefit of his lien."

In practical terms, however, the lien claimant's remedy is often illusory. Firstly, it is not always easy to find a prospective purchaser of simply a leasehold interest. Often a purchaser wants to buy all the assets of the business to continue it as a going concern. Secondly, a leasehold interest is often difficult to value, and the sale of it usually requires the full co-operation of the landlord. And thirdly, in most cases the tenant may not have paid his suppliers because of financial difficulties. This would ordinarily mean that he probably could not manage to pay the rent as well, in which case the landlord would ordinarily be entitled to terminate the lease. To do so for non-payment of rent, though, the landlord would be obliged to give[91] notice in writing[92] of his intention, and of the amount of the unpaid rent, to each person who has registered a claim for lien against the premises.[93] Any lien claimant who receives such a notice would have ten days from the date of receipt[94] to pay to the landlord the amount of the unpaid rent, and the amount so paid may be added by that lien claimant to his claim.[95] However, if it is unlikely that a purchaser of the leasehold will quickly be found, or if the lien claimant's interest in the premises is subordinate to that of a leasehold mortgagee, it might be imprudent for the lien claimant to preserve the lease by bringing the rent into good standing. As a result, the lien claimant could be relinquishing his ultimate remedy, and would have to be satisfied with a personal judgment.[96]

---

[91] See s. 89(1).

[92] See Form 4 prescribed by O. Reg. 159/83 filed March 18, 1983, under the *Construction Lien Act, 1983*.

[93] Section 19(3).

[94] Section 89(2) provides that, "[i]n the absence of evidence to the contrary, a document or notice sent to a person by certified or registered mail shall be deemed to have been received by him on the fifth day following the date on which it was mailed, exclusive of Saturdays and holidays"; and s. 89(4) provides that, "[w]here a document or notice is sent by registered mail, the date appearing on the postal registration receipt shall be deemed conclusively to be the date of mailing."

[95] Section 19(4).

[96] See s. 65.

(iii) The Landlord as Owner

There are two situations where a landlord's interest in premises may be subject to a lien for the supply of services or materials to the tenant.

(1) Under certain circumstances, the landlord may be held to be a statutory owner with respect to work done on the tenant's premises. The most obvious example would be where the landlord retains a contractor to carry out improvements on the leased premises. The element of "request" would thereby be combined with one or more of the other requisite components of s. 1(1) 15 of the Act to give rise to the conclusion that the landlord would be a statutory owner. Aside from any personal judgment, the lien claimant's ultimate potential remedy would be to obtain an order for the sale of the landlord's interest in the premises, namely the freehold, despite the anticipated argument that it was only the leasehold which was improved as a result of the lien claimant's work. The rationale would be that the landlord would not have requisitioned the work unless he expected to receive some direct or indirect benefit from it.

The landlord may also be held to be a statutory owner in circumstances where there has been no privity of contract with a contractor regarding improvements to the leased premises, but where the conduct of the landlord was such as to give rise to the implication of statutory ownership. Until 1977, many of the decisions in this area were rationalized on the basis that, where the landlord could be said to have had "direct dealings" with the tenant's contractor, those dealings brought the landlord within the four corners of the statutory definition of "owner" by implication.[97] The apparent requirement of "direct dealing," though, was brought into question in the 1977 decision of the Supreme Court of Canada in the case of *City of Hamilton v. Cipriani et al.,*[98] where Laskin C.J.C. commented:

> The City was and remained the "owner" within s. 1(d) so as to make its land lienable under s. 5, and it is idle formalism to contend that the work was not done at its request. I do not regard *Marshall Brick Co. v. York Farmers Colonization Co.* as standing in the way of this conclusion. That case turned largely on the words "privity and consent" which were then conjunctive under the statute and they are now disjunctive. If the submission is that direct dealing is required before a request can be found, I am unable to accept such a limitation under the present *Mechanics' Lien Act.*[99]

---

[97] See, for example, *Orr v. Robertson* (1915), 34 O.L.R. 147, 23 D.L.R. 17 (C.A.); *John A. Marshall Brick Co. v. York Farmers Colonization Co.* (1916), 54 S.C.R. 569, 36 D.L.R. 420; affg. 35 O.L.R. 542, 28 D.L.R. 464 *(sub nom. Marshall Brick Co. v. Irving); Dalgleish v. Prescott Arena Co. Ltd.,* [1951] O.R. 121 (C.A.); *Swalm v. Fairway Finance Ltd.* (1965), 52 W.W.R. 626 (Alta. Dist. Ct.). But see *MacDonald-Rowe Woodworking Co. Ltd. v. MacDonald* (1963), 39 D.L.R. (2d) 63, 49 M.P.R. 91 (P.E.I.C.A.).

[98] Note 85, *supra.*

[99] *Ibid.,* at 173 S.C.R.

As a result, it appears that the absence of "direct dealings" on the part of the landlord may not be fatal to the lien claimant's contention that the landlord comes within the definition of statutory owner by implication.[100]

(2) Another situation where a lien claimant may subject a landlord's interest in premises to a lien, for the supply of services or materials to the tenant, is contemplated by s. 19(1) of the Act:

> 19(1) Where the interest of the owner to which the lien attaches is leasehold, the interest of the landlord[101] shall also be subject to the lien to the same extent as the interest of the owner if the contractor[102] gives[103] the landlord written notice[104] of the improvement to be made,[105] unless the landlord, within fifteen days[106] of receiving the notice[107] from the contractor, gives[108] the contractor written notice[109] that the landlord assumes no responsibility for the improvement to be made.

---

[100] For an analysis of the development and current import of the notion of "direct dealings", see C. E. Woollcombe, "Owners and Encumbrancers", at 1–28 in *The Mysteries of Mechanics' Liens* (materials distributed at conference sponsored by The Canadian Bar Association (Ontario), May 5, 1978, Toronto).

[101] The term "landlord" is not defined in the Act. Where it is a sub-tenant who retains a contractor and requisitions the work, *quaere* whether the term "landlord" could be extended to apply to both the landlord, under the head lease, and the tenant, under the sublease. It may be interesting to observe that s. 8(1) of the *Mechanics' Lien Act,* which is similar to s. 19(1) of the *Construction Lien Act, 1983* provides that notice is to be given to the "owner in fee simple or his agent".

[102] Section 8(1) of the *Mechanics' Lien Act* permitted "the person doing the work or placing or furnishing the materials" to give notice to the owner. *Quaere* why, under the *Construction Lien Act, 1983,* a subcontractor is precluded from utilizing this provision (*i.e.,* s. 19(1)). *Quaere* also whether a subcontractor can take the benefit of the section where the contractor has in fact implemented this section.

[103] See s. 89(1).

[104] See Form 2 prescribed by O. Reg. 159/83 filed March 18, 1983, under the *Construction Lien Act, 1983.*

[105] The words "to be made" clearly imply that the notice must be given to the landlord *prior to* the commencement of work. Furthermore, given that the written notice, if sent by certified or registered mail, is deemed to have been received by the landlord "on the fifth day following the date on which it was mailed, exclusive of Saturdays and holidays" (s. 89(2)); that the landlord then has 15 days to respond by written notice, which, if sent, would involve the passage of five more days; and that the landlord's notice would serve to disclaim responsibility "for the improvement *to be made*" (emphasis added); it is therefore suggested that it would be prudent for the contractor to send his notice to the landlord *at least* 25 days before commencing work, if he wishes to satisfy himself first that the landlord will not disclaim responsibility.

[106] *Quaere* whether a response on the 16th day would mean that the landlord has assumed responsibility for the improvement. It is to be noted that the curative provision, s. 6, makes no reference to s. 19.

[107] See s. 89(2).

[108] See s. 89(1).

[109] See Form 3 prescribed by O. Reg. 159/83 filed March 18, 1983, under the *Construction Lien Act, 1983.*

As indicated, the contractor's notice must be in writing,[110] and must be given before the services or materials are supplied.[111]

(iv) The Mortgagee as Owner

Under certain circumstances, a mortgagee may be held to be a statutory owner, and his interest in a premises may therefore be subject to a lien for the supply of services or materials to the improvement.[112]

A rather important decision in this area, *Nor. Elec. Co. Ltd. v. Mfrs. Life Ins. Co.,*[113] concerned a construction financing arrangement involving a sale, leaseback and mortgage. In that case, Manufacturers Insurance Co. ("Manufacturers") entered into an agreement with Metropolitan Projects Limited ("Metropolitan") to provide $1,236,000 in financing for the proposed construction of an apartment building on land owned by Metropolitan in the City of Halifax. Pursuant to the agreement, Metropolitan conveyed the land to Manufacturers for $164,000, and Manufacturers then leased the land back to Metropolitan for a term of 80 years. The rental payments under the lease, in part, were expressed as a percentage of Metropolitan's gross receipts, after a floor figure had been reached. Metropolitan then mortgaged its leasehold interest in the land to Manufacturers, purportedly as security for loan advances which were to be made as the work progressed. Shortly after $1,150,600 in loan advances were completed (the balance of $85,400 being earmarked as a "holdback" fund to finish construction), 17 lien claims were registered against the title to the land. Within one month of the date the first lien claim was registered, Metropolitan filed a proposal under the *Bankruptcy Act,* which was approved by the court shortly thereafter. The proposal was not successful and Metropolitan became bankrupt six months later.

In the circumstances, given the precarious financial state of Metropolitan, the lien claimants attempted to implicate Manufacturers by pleading, among other things, that Manufacturers and Metropolitan were joint venturers in constructing the apartment building and furthermore that Manufacturers was a statutory owner.

In a mechanics' lien action, the trial judge held that the lien claimant was entitled to a lien upon Manufacturers' reversion under the lease, and that Manufacturers and Metropolitan were joint venturers in the project, but rejected the argument that the lien attached to Manufacturers' leasehold mortgage.

---

[110] See *Nuspel v. Lem Foo,* [1949] O.W.N. 476 (H.C.).

[111] See *Patsis et al. v. 75–89 Gosford Ltd. et al.; Papas et al. v. Patsis et al.,* [1973] 1 O.R. 629, 32 D.L.R. (3d) 31 (H.C.).

[112] See, for example, *Bird Const. Co. Ltd. v. Ownix Devs. Ltd. et al., supra,* note 54; *Muzzo Bros. Ltd. v. Cadillac Fairview Corp. Ltd. et al.* (1981), 34 O.R. (2d) 461, 21 R.P.R. 23 (S.C.).

[113] Note 85, *supra.*

The Nova Scotia Court of Appeal set aside the trial judgment, holding that Manufacturers was not a statutory owner but merely supplied financing by means of a sale-leaseback-mortgage device.[114]

In a 5-2 decision, the Supreme Court of Canada allowed the appeal from the Nova Scotia Court of Appeal, holding that Manufacturers was indeed a statutory owner, and that the lien claimant was therefore entitled to realize its lien claim out of the $85,400 holdback fund which had been retained by Manufacturers. In the majority decision, Laskin C.J.C. wrote:

> In my opinion, although there is a lender-borrower aspect to the transaction between the developer and the respondent, the substance of it gives it a far different complexion.[115]
>
> . . .
>
> It is my brother Martand's conclusion that on the facts herein the respondent is an owner as that term is defined in s. 1(d) of the Act. . . . That conclusion is based on the view that under the arrangement with Metropolitan, by which the respondent obtained an estate or interest in the land upon which the apartment building was constructed, the work of construction was done at its request and with its privity and consent. I agree with this assessment so far as it goes.[116]
>
> . . .
>
> I would go further than the Nova Scotia Court of Appeal and further than my brother Martand in assessing whether the respondent is an "owner" under s. 1(d). In my opinion, the work herein can properly be said to have been done also on the respondent's behalf, if not also for its direct benefit. . . . The outright purchase by the respondent of the land on which the apartment building was to be built, the fact that title to the building would belong to the respondent no less than the title to the land, without any revestment right in Metropolitan, and the fact that, to the knowledge of the respondent, Metropolitan was to act as contractor on the project which was to proceed according to plans and specifications approved by the respondent and under the latter's financial control, are significant indications to me that the work was being done and the materials furnished more on behalf of the respondent than on behalf of Metropolitan, and more for its direct benefit than for the direct benefit of Metropolitan.[117]

(v) The Purchaser as Owner[118]

The question as to whether or not a purchaser of property is a statutory owner lends itself to the same analysis as that which would be

---

[114] See (1975), 53 D.L.R. (3d) 303.
[115] Note 85, *supra,* at 337.
[116] Note 85, *supra,* at 340.
[117] Note 85, *supra,* at 341.
[118] So as to clarify the position of purchasers of new housing in particular, the Ministry of the Attorney General has proposed that the *Construction Lien Act, 1983* be amended by adding the words "but does not include a home buyer" to the end of the definition of

applied to any person having an interest in a premises. The nub of the issue is whether a particular set of facts gives rise to the conclusion, by inference or otherwise, that the purchaser comes within the definition of "owner."

Assuming that there is a concluded agreement of purchase and sale which has not as yet closed, the purchaser would have an equitable interest in the premises.

The fact that, for example, a home is being purchased from a builder based upon a selection of one of a number of model-home styles would ordinarily not be sufficient to give rise to an implication that the work is being "requested" by the purchaser.[119] However, if the purchaser is involved in choosing the quality and type of materials, or in directing or implementing changes in the work, an argument could be made that, in so doing, he has made a "request" for the "improvement," and that the improvement is being effected on his behalf, with his consent, and for his direct benefit. This would be the case irrespective of whether there were any direct dealings or privity of contract between the purchaser and the contractor.[120]

If a purchaser is a statutory owner, it makes no difference whether his deed is registered before or after a claim for lien. On the other hand, if a purchaser is not a statutory owner, and he registers his deed after the

---

"owner." "Home buyer" is defined in the amending legislation to mean "a person who buys the interest of an owner in a premises that is a home, whether built or not at the time the agreement of purchase and sale in respect thereof is entered into, where not more than 20 per cent of the purchase price is paid prior to the conveyance and where the home is not conveyed until it is ready for occupancy, evidenced in the case of a new home by the issuance under the *Building Code Act* of a permit authorizing occupancy or the issuance under the *Ontario New Home Warranties Plan Act* of a certificate of completion and possession." Furthermore, "home" is defined to mean,
  i. a self-contained one-family dwelling, detached or attached to one or more others by common wall,
  ii. a building composed of more than one and not more than two self-contained, one-family dwellings under one ownership, or
  iii. a condominium dwelling unit, including the common elements,
  and includes any structure or works used in conjunction therewith.
Section 5 of the *Construction Lien Act, 1983* would also be amended by the addition of the following subsection:
    Without restricting the generality of subsection (1), an agreement of purchase and sale that provides for the making or completion of an improvement shall, where the purchaser is an owner, be deemed to provide for the retention of a holdback by the purchaser, and tender by the purchaser on closing is not defective by reason only that the purchaser does not tender the amount of the holdback.

[119] See, for example, *Sterling Lbr. Co. v. Jones* (1916), 36 O.L.R. 153, 29 D.L.R. 688 (C.A.).
[120] *City of Hamilton v. Cipriani et al., supra*, note 85; *Nor. Elec. Co. Ltd. v. Mfrs. Life Ins. Co., supra*, note 85.

contractor's work has been completed but before any lien has been preserved or before he receives written notice of lien, the deed would have full priority over the claim for lien.[121] If the claim for lien were registered before closing, no doubt its discharge would be a valid requisition on title, since it would have priority over a deed registered subsequently.[122]

(vi) Joint or Common Interests

Section 7 of the *Mechanics' Lien Act* provided that, where a married woman owned or had an interest in lands, and where improvements were made to those lands with the privity or consent of her husband, he was presumed conclusively to have been acting as her agent as well as for himself, unless the contractor received actual notice to the contrary before the services or materials were supplied.

Section 18 of the *Construction Lien Act, 1983* has expanded this concept to deal with any interest held by the owner jointly or in common with another person, such as a spouse,[123] a partner, a joint venturer, and so on. So long as that other person "knew or ought reasonably to have known" of the making of the improvement, the joint or common interest of that person in the premises is also subject to the lien, unless the contractor receives actual notice,[124] before services or materials are supplied, that that person assumes no responsibility for the improvement that is to be made.

As the Attorney General's Advisory Committee commented:

> Since the improvement will be mutually beneficial to both owners, they should both be responsible for the costs of the improvement if the one who arranged to have work done defaults in payment.[125]

---

121 Section 80(6).

122 *Harrell et al. v. Mosier et al.,* [1956] O.R. 152, 1 D.L.R. (2d) 671 (C.A.). Also see ss. 78 and 80(1).

123 In his paper, "The Construction Lien Claim," *supra*, note 69, at 23, Douglas Macklem asked:
> Query, whether the provisions of the *Family Law Reform Act* will be interpreted by the Courts as creating the kind of common interest in the property which is contemplated by Section 18 in those circumstances where the wife is the sole owner of the subject premises, so as to make the premises subject to the lien when the improvement is contracted for by the husband?

124 Assuming that the premises are registered in the names of a husband and wife as joint tenants, and the husband contracts for the supply of services or materials, presumably his wife may exculpate herself from any liability by merely advising the contractor that she assumes no responsibility.

125 *Report of the Attorney General's Advisory Committee on the Draft Construction Lien Act* (April 1982), at 55.

C. THE GENERAL LIEN

The concept of a "general lien" exists mainly to facilitate the realization of claims by persons who supply services or materials to housing subdivisions.[126]

Section 20 of the Act provides:

> 20. Where an owner enters into a single contract for improvements on more than one premises owned by him, any person supplying services or materials under that contract, or under a subcontract under that contract, may choose to have his lien follow the form of the contract and be a general lien against each of those premises for the price of all services and materials he supplied to all the premises.

Suppose, for example, that an owner of 15 subdivision lots enters into an agreement[127] with a contractor whereby the contractor agrees to erect a house on each lot for $75,000 per house, making the total contract price $1,125,000. So long as the requirements contained in s. 20 are met, the contractor would be entitled to a general lien against *each* lot for the price of *all* services and materials which he supplied to *all* of the lots. Accordingly, if the contractor were obliged to abandon the work at a time when he had received payment of only $675,000 of the $800,000 then owing, he would be entitled to preserve[128] and perfect[129] a $125,000 lien against *each* lot, despite the fact that each house may be at a different stage of construction and that the amount owing on account of certain houses may exceed that owing on others. The problem of allocating the amount owing for each individual house out of the total supply of services or materials is therefore avoided.

It is important to note that a general lien is available with respect to the supply of services or materials,[130] and may be applied to both a contract or any subcontract under that contract.[131] This would mean that, in addition to the contractor, any subcontractor who, in the above example, supplied services or materials to more than one of the 15 houses under construction would be entitled to a general lien in respect of those houses covered by his subcontract.

---

[126] *Ibid.*, at 58.

[127] Section 20 provides that the agreement must constitute a *"single contract* for improvements on more than one premises" (emphasis added), which in each case is a question of fact.

[128] Section 34(7).

[129] Section 36(5).

[130] Compare s. 37 of the *Mechanics' Lien Act,* which provided for a general lien only for the supply of materials. However, s. 18(1) provided that a "claim for lien may include claims against any number of properties," although s. 18(2) authorized the judicial officer trying the action "equitably to apportion against the respective properties the amounts included in any claim or claims under subsection (1)."

[131] Compare s. 37 of the *Mechanics' Lien Act* which provided for a general lien only in favour of the person supplying the materials to the owner, namely, the contractor.

If the owner should sell several of the houses that are subject to an *un*preserved general lien, the general lien nevertheless continues to apply, to its full extent, against those premises which where subject to the lien but were not sold.[132] This situation would obtain where several of the houses were sold, and deeds were registered, prior to the preservation of the general lien. The intent purportedly is to diminish the prejudice suffered by the lien claimant as a result of losing a portion of his security.

If the owner wishes to sell several of the houses that are encumbered by a preserved or a perfected general lien, he will have to clear the title to the particular premises being sold in order to close the sale transactions. In this regard, the owner might attempt to negotiate with the lien claimant for a partial discharge of the general lien[133] in consideration for a part payment on account, which ordinarily would be derived from the proceeds realized on closing. From the general lien claimant's perspective, his agreement to discharge his lien, by the registration of a release[134] in the prescribed form,[135] would have no effect upon, and would be without prejudice to, his general lien as it relates to the other premises to which it applies.[136]

Alternatively, the owner may clear the title to the premises being sold by making a payment into court or posting appropriate security, and obtaining an order vacating the registration of the preserved or perfected general lien and any certificate of action in respect of that lien.[137] In these circumstances, "the court may apportion the general lien between the premises in respect of which the application is made and all other premises that are subject to the lien."[138]

Section 84 of the Act deals with the issue of priority as between a general lien claim and other lien claims registered against a particular premises. If, for example, a subcontractor supplies $3,000 worth of drywall and insulation materials to each of 15 premises, he would be entitled to register a $45,000 general lien claim against the title to each of

---

[132] Section 76(1).

[133] See s. 42.

[134] Under s. 29(1) of the *Mechanics' Lien Act,* a claim for lien could be discharged "by the registration of a receipt acknowledging payment". However, once an action had been commenced, a court order was required: s. 29(2)(b).

[135] See Form 14 prescribed by O. Reg. 159/83 filed March 18, 1983, under the *Construction Lien Act, 1983.*

[136] Section 42. Also see s. 76(2).

[137] Section 44(1). See Precedent Nos. 20, 21 and 22.

[138] Section 44(4). *Quaere* what evidence the court would require in order to make an informed decision as to apportionment. Presumably the evidence of the lien claimant as to the price of the services or materials supplied to the particular premises being sold would be very relevant; however, s. 44(1) contemplates an application to the court, probably by the owner, "without notice to any other person". It would therefore appear that the only evidence before the court would be the uncontroverted affidavit evidence of the owner or his architect.

the premises. A plumbing subcontractor of the same class,[139] though, may only have liened premises no. 4 for $5,000. The abstract of title for premises no. 4 would reveal the registration of two lien claims in the respective sums of $45,000 and $5,000.

In the circumstances, since the drywall subcontractor supplied only $3,000 worth of services and materials to premises no. 4, it would be inequitable to permit him to recover nine times the amount which would ordinarily be recovered by the plumbing subcontractor on a *pro rata* distribution.

Accordingly, s. 84 sets forth a formula which deals with the relative priorities of the two lien claims. Under the formula,

> (a) the general lien shall rank with the other liens according to the rules of priority set out in section 82 only to the extent of,
> > (i) the total value of the general lien,
> > divided by,
> > (ii) the total number of premises to which the person having the general lien supplied services or materials under his contract or subcontract.

Section 84(b) goes on to provide that, "in respect of the balance of the general lien, it shall rank next in priority to all other liens against the premises, whether or not of the same class." Therefore, if $4,000 in equity were realized upon the judicial sale of premises no. 4, it would be distributed rateably[140] as between the two subcontractors, in which case the drywall subcontractor would recover $1,500, *i.e.*, $\dfrac{\$3,000}{(\$3,000 + \$5,000)} \times$ $4,000, and the plumbing subcontractor would recover $2,500, *i.e.*, $\dfrac{\$5,000}{(\$3,000 + \$5,000)} \times \$4,000$. If, on the other hand, $8,500 of sale proceeds were realized, the drywall subcontractor would receive $3,000, the plumbing subcontractor $5,000 and, assuming there were no other lien claimants, the balance of $500 would go to the drywall subcontractor on account of his general lien.

---

[139] See s. 81.
[140] Section 82.

Chapter 3

The Statutory Holdbacks

A. WHAT IS HOLDBACK?

Any person who is obligated to make a payment pursuant to a contract or a subcontract under which a lien may arise is obliged, by Part IV of the *Construction Lien Act, 1983,* to withhold ten percent of the "price"[1] of the services or materials, as they are actually supplied, for a specified period of time.[2]

By way of example, if an owner makes progress payments to a contractor from time to time on the basis of the architect's certification of the value of the services or materials supplied under the contract, the owner is obliged to retain ten percent of the certified amount as "holdback".[3] Similarly, the contractor must withhold ten percent of the amount owing by him to each of his subcontractors; each subcontractor must withhold ten percent of the amount owing to each of his subcontractors; and so on down the construction pyramid.

All persons who supply services or materials to an improvement have a lien for the value or "price" thereof "upon the interest of the owner in the premises improved."[4] This lien constitutes a charge against the monies which are required to be held back under Part IV of the Act.[5]

The concept of a "holdback" was established in order to provide some financial protection for those persons who have worked on or have supplied materials to a project, thereby enhancing its value, but who would not otherwise be entitled to assert any direct claim against the owner since they had no privity of contract with him. Notionally, accord-

---

[1] "Price" is defined by s. 1(1) 20 of the Act as the contract or subcontract price,
   i. agreed upon between the parties, or
   ii. where no specific price has been agreed upon between them, the actual value of the services or materials that have been supplied to the improvement under the contract or subcontract;

[2] *I.e.,* "until all liens that may be claimed against the holdback have expired as provided in Part V, or have been satisfied, discharged or provided for under section 44 (payment into court)": s. 22.

[3] See s. 1(1) 7.

[4] Section 14(1).

[5] Section 21.

ing to the Act, the trades would always be able to look to the holdback funds as providing them with a modicum of security in the event that, for whatever reason, there is an interruption in the downward flow of payments.

So long as an owner properly retains the ten percent holdback (and any "additional amount" owing to the contractor as contemplated by s. 21), the money so retained will take the place of the "premises improved," and the lien claimant will be unable ultimately to obtain a court order for the sale of the owner's interest in the property. The owner's position is further protected by the fact that the lien is limited in amount to the sum which he owes to the contractor.[6]

B. BASIC HOLDBACK AND HOLDBACK FOR FINISHING WORK

Under the *Mechanics' Lien Act*, it was not uncommon to find that a construction project had been "substantially performed"[7] before the finishing trades, such as the landscape contractors and carpet-layers, commenced their work. This meant that it was possible for the holdback to have been released before the finishing trades had an opportunity to register their claims for lien. Accordingly, even though all parties may have complied with the Act, the finishing trades could have been prejudiced to the extent that they may have been deprived of the right to look to the holdback to satisfy all or part of their claims.

To rectify this problem, the *Construction Lien Act, 1983* has provided for two distinct holdbacks:

(a) the "basic holdback", which represents ten percent of the price of services or materials as they are actually supplied under the contract or subcontract.[8] This holdback is for the benefit of those trades who supply services or materials to the improvement before the date of certification or declaration of substantial performance of the contract, and is required to be retained "until all liens that may be claimed against the holdback have expired as provided in Part V,[9] or have been satisfied, discharged or provided for under section 44 (payment into court)";[10] and

(b) the "holdback for finishing work," which is contemplated where a contract has been certified or declared to have been substan-

---

[6] Section 17(1).
[7] See the *Mechanics' Lien Act*, R.S.O. 1980, c. 226, s. 1(3).
[8] Section 22(1).
[9] See, in particular, ss. 31(2) and (3).
[10] Section 22(1).

tially performed but services or materials remain to be supplied in order to complete the contract.[11] In the circumstances, a separate holdback, equal to ten percent of the price of the remaining services or materials, as they are supplied under the contract or a subcontract, must be retained, in the case of the owner, for a period of 45 days from the earlier of the dates of completion or abandonment of the contract;[12] and in the case of the contractor or a subcontractor, for a period of 45 days from the earlier of the date of the last supply of services or materials to the improvement, or the date of certification of completion of the particular subcontract.[13] Alternatively, the holdback for finishing work may be released when all liens that may be claimed against it "have been satisfied, discharged or provided for under section 44."[14]

The obligation to retain basic holdback and holdback for finishing work applies irrespective of whether the contract or subcontract provides for partial payments or payment on completion.[15] Notwithstanding s. 17 of the Act, which essentially provides that an owner is liable for no more than what he owes to his contractor, if an owner neglects to fulfill his holdback obligation, he is exposed to personal liability to those lien claimants who have valid liens against his interest in the premises for the full amount that he ought to have held back,[16] even though he may have no contractual liability to make any further payments to the contractor.[17]

Accordingly, lien claimants under the *Construction Lien Act, 1983* are entitled to obtain judgment against an owner upon his failure to retain a holdback. This provision takes on an added dimension when consideration is given to the prospect that, in certain instances, a mortgagee (for example) may be held to be a statutory owner,[18] and would therefore be exposed to direct personal liability to the lien claimants pursuant to s. 23(1).

---

[11] Section 22(2).

[12] Section 31(2)(b).

[13] Section 31(3)(b).

[14] Section 22(2).

[15] Section 22(3).

[16] Section 23(1).

[17] Section 22(3). The *Report of the Attorney General's Advisory Committee on the Draft Construction Lien Act* (April 1982) contains the following comment (at p. 62), with respect to s. 22(3):

> This subsection modifies the rule set out in section 17 that the owner is not liable for more than he owes to the contractor. Where there is a default by the contractor on a contract which calls for payment on completion, the owner is still liable for the holdback to the other suppliers to the improvement, even though he may not be liable for payment on the contract to the contractor.

[18] See "The Mortgagee as Owner" (heading B(iv) of Chapter 2).

Section 23(2) provides that "[t]he personal liability of an owner under subsection (1) may only be determined in an action under this Act". Therefore, only a person having a perfected lien would be entitled to this relief,[19] since a "trust claim shall not be joined with a lien claim but may be brought in any court of competent jurisdiction."[20] This stands to reason inasmuch as an owner has no holdback obligation to those whose lien rights have expired.

C. PAYMENTS IN REDUCTION OF HOLDBACK

(i) Progress Payments

So long as a person has received no written notice of a lien,[21] he may make payment of up to 90 percent of the contract or subcontract price without exposing himself to any liability under the Act.[22] This provision allows for the regularized flow of funds, other than holdback, to the trades during the course of construction.

However, if the payer receives the notice referred to above, he is obliged to hold back an amount sufficient to satisfy the lien[23] in addition to the holdback,[24] but may pay out the balance of the monies owing.[25] For example, if an owner owes a contractor the sum of $100,000, he would ordinarily be obliged to withhold $10,000, and would be entitled to make payment of $90,000 without jeopardy. However, if a subcontractor served the owner with written notice of $25,000 lien, the owner would be obliged to withhold the $25,000 lien claim as well as the $10,000 holdback, but would be entitled to make payment of the $65,000 balance to the contractor. Since this can radically affect the cash flow and hence the financial stability of the contractor, it is in the contractor's best interests to attempt to resolve all lien claims as expeditiously as possible.

It should be noted that a contractor has a remedy under the Act, in the form of a civil cause of action for damages, against any subcontractor who serves the owner with a written notice of lien for an amount which the

---

[19] See s. 1(1) 1, which defines "action" to mean an action under Part VIII.

[20] Section 50(2).

[21] See Precedent No. 18. "Written notice of a lien" is defined by s. 1(1)29 of the Act to include "a claim for lien and any written notice given by a lien claimant that,
　　i. identifies his payer and identifies the premises, and
　　ii. states the amount that he has not been paid and is owed to him by his payer.

[22] Section 24(1).

[23] It is to be noted that "an amount sufficient to satisfy the lien," as referred to in s. 24(2), is not to include any provision for interest: see s. 14(2).

[24] Section 21.

[25] Section 24(2).

subcontractor knows or ought to know is grossly inflated,[26] or where the subcontractor knows or ought to know that he does not have a lien,[27] which causes the contractor to suffer damages for, among other things, the loss of use of monies that would otherwise have been payable.

(ii) Reduction of Holdback Upon Completion of a Particular Subcontract

When a particular subcontract has been certified completed,[28] the amount of holdback retained with respect to that subcontract may be released and paid out, so long as all liens relating to the completed subcontract have expired,[29] or have been satisfied, discharged, or provided for under s. 44.[30]

This will mean that, assuming that no liens were preserved in the interim, the holdback relating to the certified subcontract may be paid out 45 days after either the date of certification[31] or the date of the last supply of services or materials to the improvement,[32] whichever occurs first.[33] This applies irrespective of whether the subcontract was certified before[34] or after[35] the date of certification or declaration of substantial performance of the contract, and irrespective of whether there is in fact no certification or declaration of substantial performance of the contract.[36]

If this portion of the holdback is paid out in accordance with the foregoing, all liens against it will be discharged to the extent of the amount paid.[37]

(iii) Payout of Basic Holdback

Each payer who has a statutory obligation to retain the basic holdback may nevertheless release it and pay it out, without incurring liability, so long as all liens which may be claimed against it have expired,[38] or have been satisfied, discharged, or provided for under s. 44.[39]

---

[26] Section 35(a).
[27] Section 35(b).
[28] Section 33.
[29] See s. 31(3).
[30] Section 25.
[31] Sections 31(3)(a)(iii) and 31(3)(b)(ii).
[32] Sections 31(3)(a)(ii) and 31(3)(b)(i).
[33] Sections 31(3)(a) and 31(3)(b).
[34] Section 31(3)(a).
[35] Section 31(3)(b).
[36] *Ibid.*
[37] Section 29.
[38] See ss. 31(2)(a) and 31(3)(a).
[39] Section 26.

This will mean that, in the case of the owner, the basic holdback may be paid out 45 days after (a) the date of publication of a copy of the certificate or declaration of substantial performance of the contract,[40] or (b) the date the contract is completed,[41] or (c) the date the contract is abandoned,[42] whichever occurs first.[43]

In the case of a contractor or a subcontractor, the basic holdback may be paid out 45 days after (a) the date of publication of a copy of the certificate or declaration of substantial performance of the contract,[44] or (b) the date of the last supply of services or materials to the improvement,[45] or (c) the date a particular subcontract is certified complete,[46] whichever occurs first.[47]

The foregoing assumes, of course, that no liens are preserved in the interim.

Once the basic holdback has been paid out in accordance with s. 26, all liens against it are discharged.[48]

(iv) Payout of Holdback for Finishing Work

Each payer who has a statutory obligation to retain holdback for finishing work may nevertheless release and pay it out, without incurring liability, so long as all liens which may be claimed against it have expired,[49] or have been satisfied, discharged, or provided for under s. 44.[50]

This means that, in the case of the owner, the holdback for finishing work may be paid out 45 days after the date the contract is completed[51] or abandoned,[52] whichever occurs first,[53] assuming that no liens are preserved in the interim.

In the case of a contractor or a subcontractor, the holdback for finishing work may be paid out 45 days after the date of last supply of services or materials to the improvement,[54] or the date a particular

---

[40] Section 31(2)(a)(i).
[41] Sections 31(2)(a)(ii) and 31(2)(b)(i).
[42] Sections 31(2)(a)(ii) and 31(2)(b)(ii).
[43] Section 31(2).
[44] Section 31(3)(a)(i).
[45] Sections 31(3)(a)(ii) and 31(3)(b)(i).
[46] Sections 31(3)(a)(iii) and 31(3)(b)(ii).
[47] Section 31(3).
[48] Section 29.
[49] See ss. 31(2)(b) and 31(3)(b).
[50] Section 27.
[51] Section 31(2)(b)(i).
[52] Section 31(2)(b)(ii).
[53] Section 31(2)(b).
[54] Section 31(3)(b)(i).

subcontract is certified complete,[55] whichever occurs first,[56] again assuming that no liens are preserved in the interim.

Once the holdback for finishing work has been paid out in accordance with s. 27, all liens against it are discharged.[57]

D. DIRECT PAYMENT TO PERSON HAVING LIEN

Section 28 of the Act provides that, where an owner, contractor or subcontractor makes a direct payment to "any person having a lien"[58] with whom he does not have privity of contract, that payment is deemed to be a payment to the person who was contractually obliged (*i.e.*, "the proper payer") to pay the person having the lien. In these circumstances, the amount so paid may be deducted from the debt owing to the proper payer of the person having the lien, but only so long as written notice[59] of the actual payment or the intention to pay[60] is given[61] to the proper payer.

There is a risk, though, in an owner (for example) making the permitted payment. It may be that, unbeknownst to the owner, the contractor has taken the position with his subcontractor that the latter's work is inadequate and defective. The owner, by paying the subcontractor directly, would thereby be preventing the contractor from carrying out the general contract properly, and from effectively asserting a set-off claim against the subcontractor to attempt to force the latter to complete or to rectify deficiencies in the work. Therefore, in practical terms, unless the contractor expressly directs and authorizes it, the owner would probably be best advised in most circumstances not to make payment to the subcontractor.

This procedure ought to be considered, however, where a contractor has abandoned his work, or has become incapable of completing it for whatever reason. A direct payment to the subcontractor in these circumstances might avoid the difficulties which the owner would face in having

---

55 Section 31(3)(b)(ii).

56 Section 31(3)(b).

57 Section 29.

58 It is to be noted that a "person having a lien" includes both a lien claimant, who would have a preserved or perfected lien (see s. 1(1) 11) and a person with an unpreserved lien: s. 1(1) 18.

59 See Precedent No. 2.

60 The written notice may be given either before or after the payment is made. In most cases, it would probably be prudent to give the notice beforehand, so as to give the "proper payer" an opportunity to voice his objection to it. If no such objection is raised, it would not thereafter lie in the mouth of the proper payer to complain that the payment was improper and ought not to have been made because of a set-off claim which the proper payer had, as against the recipient of the payment, for defective or incomplete work.

61 See s. 89.

his dealings with his land affected by the registration of lien claims, not to mention the time and expense involved in unnecessary litigation.

The direct payment contemplated by s. 28 does not reduce the amount of holdback which is required to be retained under Part IV of the Act. Furthermore, it also does not reduce any additional amount which is required to be retained by virtue of having received a written notice of lien from any person other than the recipient of the payment.[62]

E. NO SET-OFF AGAINST HOLDBACK

If a contractor abandons his work or otherwise fails to complete his contract, his subcontractors are nevertheless entitled to enforce their lien rights.[63] In these circumstances, though, the owner would likely be inclined to resist the claims of the subcontractors on the basis that the expected increased costs of completion of the contract would give the owner a claim, in the form of a set-off, against the defaulting contractor.

According to the Act, however, although there may be a right of set-off against trust funds,[64] no such right exists with regard to holdback.[65]

This principle is consistent with the general theory that the Act serves to protect the trades at the lower levels of the construction pyramid who do not have privity of contract with the owner, but who have nonetheless conferred a benefit upon his interest in the land in the form of the supply of labour and materials. If the owner were to have an unrestricted right to set off those claims which he might have against his contractor for defective or incomplete work, the sub-trades, who might have had no involvement whatever in performing that work, would be put at a serious disadvantage. Accordingly, the holdback has been set up as an almost sacrosanct fund which may not be diminished by the owner's claim of set-off against the contractor. Where, however, the subcontractors have failed to preserve their liens within the time periods set forth in the Act,[66] the holdback loses its character *qua* holdback, and a claim against the contractor for defective or incomplete work may then be set off against it.[67] In the same vein, if all liens that may be claimed against the holdback have been satisfied, discharged, or provided for under s. 44 (payment into court), then a set-off claim may be asserted against those monies which would otherwise have been characterized as holdback.[68]

---

[62] See s. 24.
[63] Sections 74 and 30.
[64] Section 12. Also see "Set-off Against Trust Funds" (heading E of Chapter 5).
[65] Section 30.
[66] See Part V, and in particular s. 31(3).
[67] Section 12.
[68] Section 30.

Chapter 4

Expiry, Preservation and Perfection of Liens

A. ARCHITECT'S/ENGINEER'S CERTIFICATION

(i) Generally

In a large percentage of construction projects, the agreement between the owner and the contractor contemplates that the owner will engage a "payment certifier,"[1] such as an architect or an engineer, who will supervise and review the status of the work, and who will issue progress certificates from time to time.

The issuance of these certificates serves the following purposes:

    (a) to permit the mortgagee to follow the progress of construction so that timely mortgage advances may be made, and so that the mortgagee may be regularly satisfied as to the security of its position;

    (b) to assist the owner in calculating the amount of the holdback inasmuch as "holdback" is defined[2] in terms of a percentage of the value of services or materials supplied;

    (c) to provide the owner with particulars of any deficiencies in the work which must be rectified; and

    (d) to create a trust fund (the "certificate trust") for the benefit of all persons who supplied services or materials to the improvement.[3]

In recognition of the cash flow requirements of the building trades, virtually all construction contracts, including the standardized forms authorized by the Canadian Construction Association, provide for interim progress payments to be made as the work proceeds. In this regard, the owner is entitled to rely on a progress certificate in making a payment on account of the contract, and may, without jeopardy, release

---

[1] Section 1(1) 17 defines "payment certifier" to mean "an architect, engineer or any other person upon whose certificate payments are made under a contract or subcontract".

[2] See s. 1(1) 7.

[3] See s. 7(2), and "The Certificate Trust" (heading B(ii) of Chapter 5).

[4] Section 24(1).

up to 90 percent of the certified amount,[4] so long as he has not received written notice of a lien.[5] The foregoing figure of 90 percent recognizes the owner's obligation to retain holdback irrespective of any contractual liability which he may have to make partial payments to the contractor from time to time.[6]

When the *Mechanics' Lien Act* was in force, most owners required, as a condition of making an interim progress payment, that their contractors provide them with further assurance, in the form of a statutory declaration,[7] that all subcontractors had been paid up to date, except for holdback, and that all assessments and levies[8] had been paid in full. Owners will no doubt continue to rely upon statutory declarations (in a revised form)[9] with respect to progress payments, notwithstanding that no specific provision is made for them under the *Construction Lien Act, 1983.* The Act, however, does provide for a "declaration"[10] to be made by a person who has completed his supply of services or materials to the improvement. Section 31(5) contemplates a person, who has supplied services or materials to an improvement, making a declaration[11] in the prescribed form[12] declaring (a) the date of last supply of services or materials, and (b) that he will not supply any further services or materials. Such a declaration is deemed to be true against the person making the declaration.[13] In particular, the date of last supply of services or materials referred to in the declaration could be relied upon by the owner as being

---

[5] Sections 24(1) and (2). Also see s. 1(1) 29 and Precedent No. 18.

[6] Section 22(3).

[7] The *Mechanics' Lien Act,* R.S.O. 1980, c. 261 did not require the provision of statutory declarations in connection with interim progress payments, although their informal use in the industry has been common and widespread. These declarations are "statutory" in that they are written statements sworn under oath pursuant to the provisions of the *Evidence Act,* R.S.O. 1980, c. 145 (see s. 43). Since a false deposition would give rise to possible criminal consequences (see the *Criminal Code,* R.S.C. 1970, c. C-34, s. 122.1), owners traditionally appear to have been content to rely upon them as being truthful and accurate.

[8] *E.g.,* worker's compensation assessments.

[9] See Precedent No. 1.

[10] See s. 31(5), and Form 5 prescribed by O. Reg. 159/83 filed March 18, 1983, under the *Construction Lien Act, 1983.*

[11] Such a declaration would probably be made pursuant to a contractual obligation, or perhaps voluntarily, by a subcontractor who wanted the contractor to apply for certification of completion of his subcontract (see s. 33(1)).

[12] See Form 5 prescribed by O. Reg. 159/83 filed March 18, 1983, under the *Construction Lien Act, 1983.*

[13] Section 31(5). *Quaere* whether s. 31(5) could form the basis of a civil cause of action in favour of, say, an owner who relied upon a declaration, as if it were a representation, in releasing holdback monies, only to find out that the declaration was inaccurate or untruthful and that, to the owner's detriment, the holdback monies had been released prematurely.

the date when the declarant's lien period commenced to run,[14] assuming that that period had not commenced to run earlier.[15]

Although the Act does provide a remedy to anyone who suffers damages[16] where the payment certifier refuses or neglects to certify substantial performance of the contract within a reasonable time after receiving an application therefor,[17] there is no statutory remedy to force the issuance of an interim progress certificate.[18] This shortcoming is especially significant where, as sometimes happens, a contract provides that the issuance of a certificate is a condition precedent to payment. In the circumstances, in the absence of a provision similar to s. 12(4) of the *Mechanics' Lien Act,* an injured person's only claim would be for damages for negligence (*i.e.,* nonfeasance) for the wrongful withholding of a certificate.

(ii) What is "Substantial Performance of the Contract"?

Under the *Mechanics' Lien Act,* a contractor was entitled to register a claim for lien "before or during the performance of the contract . . . or within thirty-seven days after the completion or abandonment of the contract. . . ."[19] Prior to the 1969 amendments to the *Mechanics' Lien Act,* though, ascertaining the precise date of "completion of the contract" was a difficult question of fact. In order to avoid "completing" a contract, contractors were known to do all of their work, with the exception of some minor finishing work. Their obvious objective was to attempt to prevent the 37-day lien period from commencing to run, thereby preserving or "freezing" their lien rights until such time as they were able to satisfy themselves that payment was forthcoming.

This abuse was addressed in 1966 by the Ontario Law Reform Commission:

> The term "completion of the contract" appears several times in the legislation. These words have caused some confusion in the cases. A trivial piece of work of little value may be held to be the "completion of the contract". It is recommended that this phrase be defined as follows: "completion of the contract means substantial performance, not necessarily total performance, of the contract."[20]

---

[14] See ss. 31(2)(a)(ii), 31(2)(b), 31(3)(a)(ii) and 31(3)(b)(i).

[15] See ss. 31(2)(a)(i), 31(2)(b), 31(3)(a)(i), 31(3)(a)(iii) and 31(3)(b)(ii).

[16] Damages must be reasonably foreseeable: see s. 1(1) 24.

[17] Section 32(3). Liability under this section is premised upon there being "no reasonable doubt that the contract has, in fact, been substantially performed."

[18] Contrast this with s. 12(4) of the *Mechanics' Lien Act.*

[19] The *Mechanics' Lien Act,* s. 22(1).

[20] *Report of the Ontario Law Reform Commission, The Mechanics' Lien Act* (February 22, 1966), at 12.

By virtue of the foregoing, the *Mechanics' Lien Act* was amended in 1969[21] so as to adopt the Ontario Law Reform Commission's recommendation. No doubt the Legislature was of the view, though, that the notion of "substantial performance of the contract" would give rise to at least as much interpretation-seeking litigation as the term "completion of the contract" did previously. Consequently, the *Mechanics' Lien Act, 1968-69* contained the following additional provisions which attempted to create a formula for defining substantial performance with some degree of accuracy:

> 1(3) For the purposes of this Act, a contract shall be deemed to be substantially performed,
> - (a) when the work or a substantial part thereof is ready for use or is being used for the purpose intended; and
> - (b) when the work to be done under the contract is capable of completion or correction at a cost of not more than,
>   - (i) 3 per cent of the first $250,000 of the contract price,
>   - (ii) 2 per cent of the next $250,000 of the contract price, and
>   - (iii) 1 per cent of the balance of the contract price.

> 1(4) For the purposes of this Act, where the work or a substantial part thereof is ready for use or is being used for the purpose intended and where the work cannot be completed expeditiously for reasons beyond the control of the contractor, the value of the work to be completed shall be deducted from the contract price in determining substantial performance.

Needless to say, litigation on this issue flourished. In any event, it could be argued that these amendments resolved more problems than they created, and certainly eliminated abuses of the type referred to above.

The formula for determining when a contract has been substantially performed has been carried through into the *Construction Lien Act, 1983*,[22] although the definition of "completion of the contract" was eliminated as being no longer relevant. Section 2(1) of the Act, which is substantially the same as s. 1(3) of the *Mechanics' Lien Act, 1968-69* quoted above, provides as follows:

> 2(1) For the purposes of this Act, a contract is substantially performed,
> - (a) when the improvement to be made under that contract or a substantial part thereof is ready for use or is being used for the purposes intended; and
> - (b) when the improvement to be made under that contract is capable of completion[23] or, where there is a known defect, correction, at a cost of not more than,
>   - (i) 3 per cent of the first $500,000 of the contract price,
>   - (ii) 2 per cent of the next $500,000 of the contract price, and
>   - (iii) 1 per cent of the balance of the contract price.

---

21 See S.O. 1968-69, c. 65.

22 Section 2.

23 See s. 2(3), which provides that, "[f]or the purposes of this Act, a contract shall be deemed to be completed and services or materials shall be deemed to be last supplied to the improvement when the price of completion, correction of a known defect or last supply is not more than the lesser of,
   (a) 1 per cent of the contract price; and
   (b) $1,000."

As indicated, a contract is not substantially performed until two criteria are met: the improvement must be used, or ready for use, for the purposes intended; and the improvement must be capable of completion or, where there is a known (*i.e.,* not hidden) defect, correction, at a cost which would not exceed an amount established by formula.

The formula deserves exemplification. Assuming that the contract "price"[24] is $400,000, the contract would be substantially performed when the improvement is capable of completion or correction at a cost of no more than $12,000 (*i.e.,* "3 per cent of the first $500,000 of the contract price").[25] If, for example, the contract price is $2,000,000, then the contract would be substantially performed when the improvement is capable of completion or correction at a cost of no more than $35,000 (*i.e.,* "3 per cent of the first $500,000 of the contract price, 2 per cent of the next $500,000 of the contract price, and 1 per cent of the balance of the contract price,"[26] being $15,000 plus $10,000 plus $10,000).

The definition of "price" in the Act does not appear to resolve the issue as to whether "extras" to the contract are part of or separate from it, and hence whether or not "extras" ought to be included in applying the substantial performance formula.[27] This issue was commented upon by Locke J. in *Bd. of Trustees of Rocky Mountain School Div. No. 15 v. Atlas Lbr. Co. Ltd.,*[28] a 1954 decision of the Supreme Court of Canada, where His Lordship adopted[29] the following quotation from the *Cyclopedia of Law and Procedure:*

> Where labor or materials are furnished under separate contracts, even though such contracts are between the same persons and relate to the same building or improvement, the contracts cannot be tacked together so as to enlarge the time for filing a lien for what was done or furnished under either, but a lien must be filed for what was done or furnished under each contract within the statutory period after its compliance. Where, however, all the work is done or all the materials are furnished under one entire continuing contract, although at different times, a lien claim or statement filed within the statutory period after the last item was done or furnished is sufficient as to all the items; and in order that the contract may be a continuing one within this rule it is not necessary that all the work or materials should be ordered at one time, that the amount of work or materials should be determined at the time of the first order, or that the prices should be then agreed upon, or the time of payment fixed; but a mere general arrangement to furnish labor or materials for a particular building or improvement is sufficient, if complied with, even though the original arrangement was not legally binding. Whether there was one general contract or several separate contracts is a question of fact. . . ."[30]

---

[24] See s. 1(1) 20.

[25] Section 2(1)(b)(i).

[26] Section 2(1)(b).

[27] This issue also arises in connection with the calculation of the holdbacks, in that any increases in the contract price would thereby increase the amount which would have to be retained. See *Baines v. Harman,* 60 O.L.R. 223, [1927] 2 D.L.R. 743 (C.A.) and *Smith v. Bernhart* (1909), 2 Sask. L.R. 315, 11 W.L.R. 623 (S.C.T.D.).

[28] [1954] S.C.R. 589, [1955] 1 D.L.R. 161.

[29] *Ibid.,* at 604-605 S.C.R., 175-176 D.L.R.

[30] 27 Cyc. 114.

In this regard, the 1976 Ontario decision of *Crestile Ltd. v. New Generation Properties Inc.*[31] is also worthy of note. There, on a reference of a Supreme Court mechanics' lien action, Master MacRae had to determine the date of substantial performance using the formula then extant under the Ontario Act:

> I know of no case in which the meaning to be ascribed to the words "contract price" has been discussed nor was I referred to any. In the circumstances of this case I interpret it to mean the price of the work done by the plaintiff pursuant to its original contract as altered and augmented by the addition of extras pursuant to the agreements between the parties.[32]

In point of fact, this approach has been carried through into the *Construction Lien Act, 1983* by virtue of the fact that "contract" is defined not only to mean "the contract between the owner and the contractor,"[33] but also to include, for the sake of clarity, "any amendment to that contract."[34]

The substantial performance formula under the *Construction Lien Act, 1983* uses a $500,000 figure as its basis, rather than the $250,000 figure which was used under the *Mechanics' Lien Act.*[35] The effect of this is that, in construction projects where the contract price exceeds $250,000, substantial performance of the contract will occur earlier than it did under the *Mechanics' Lien Act.* For example, a $300,000 contract under the *Mechanics' Lien Act* would be deemed to be substantially performed when the cost of completion or correction of the work was $8,500 (*i.e.,* "3 per cent of the first $250,000 of the contract price [plus] 2 per cent of the next $250,000 of the contract price,"[36] being $7,500 plus $1,000), whereas the same contract would be substantially performed under the *Construction Lien Act, 1983* when the cost of completion or correction of the improvement is $9,000 (*i.e.,* "3 per cent of the first $500,000 of the contract price").[37] The higher the contract price, the greater the discrepancy. Although this will mean that contractors will have to be more diligent in ensuring that their lien rights do not expire (since their lien period will in most cases commence to run from an earlier date), this is offset somewhat by the extension of the lien period from 37[38] to 45 days.[39]

Furthermore, the substantial performance formula under the *Construction Lien Act, 1983* contemplates the taking into account of the

---

[31] (1976), 13 O.R. (2d) 670, 24 C.B.R. (N.S.) 95 (M.C.).

[32] *Ibid.,* at 672 O.R., 96 C.B.R. (N.S.).

[33] Section 1(1) 3.

[34] *Ibid.*

[35] "This change has been made to account for the depreciation in the value of the dollar, since the doctrine of substantial performance was first incorporated into the Act": *Report of the Attorney General's Advisory Committee on the Draft Construction Lien Act* (April 1982), at 26.

[36] The *Mechanics' Lien Act,* s. 1(3)(b).

[37] Section 2(1)(b).

[38] The *Mechanics' Lien Act,* s. 22.

[39] Section 31.

cost of correction of known defects only, which promotes a certain fairness to both owners[40] and contractors.[41]

Finally, the discussion regarding substantial performance would be incomplete without considering s. 2(2) of the Act, the thrust of which is the same as s. 1(4) of the *Mechanics' Lien Act* (quoted above). According to s. 2(2), if for any reason beyond the control of the contractor the improvement can not be completed[42] expeditiously, or where the owner and the contractor agree[43] not to complete the improvement expeditiously, the "price" of the services or materials remaining to be supplied is to be deducted from the contract price in determining substantial performance. For example, if inclement weather causes delay in completion of the work at a time when the value of the remainder of the work to be done under a $600,000 contract is $50,000, the contract price is deemed to be $550,000 for the purposes of the substantial performance formula. Therefore, while substantial performance would otherwise have occurred when the cost of completion or correction is $17,000, the delay caused by the weather conditions advanced substantial performance to the date when the cost of completion or correction is $16,000. The contractor ought to be alerted to this provision inasmuch as it could advance the date on which his lien rights expire.

(iii) Certification or Declaration of Substantial Performance of Contract

Under s. 32(1) 1 of the Act, it is incumbent upon the payment certifier, upon the application of the contractor, to determine and to certify[44] the substantial performance of the contract.[45] If there is no

---

[40] If the cost of correction of latent defects were to be included, this could delay the time of substantial performance, thereby extending the potential expiry date of the contractor's lien rights.

[41] "Under the new definition [of substantial performance], it is now clear that only 'patent defects' are to be taken into consideration in determining whether or not there has been substantial performance of the contract. A patent defect is one which is self-evident. Under the existing definition [under the *Mechanics' Lien Act*], many owners have refused to release the holdback for many months after the apparent substantial performance of the contract, for fear that there may be latent, or hidden, defects in the work which has been done. It is clear that it was never intended for the holdback provisions of the Act to be used for this purpose.": *Report of the Attorney General's Advisory Committee on the Draft Construction Lien Act* (April 1982), at 26-27.

[42] See s. 2(3).

[43] *Quaere* whether the "agreement" between the owner and the contractor can be implied (by their actions or inaction). *Quaere* also whether it can be oral, given s. 4 of the *Statute of Frauds,* R.S.O. 1980, c. 481.

[44] See Form 6 prescribed by O. Reg. 159/83 filed March 18, 1983, under the *Construction Lien Act, 1983.* Also see ss. 32(1) 2 and 32(2).

[45] It is to be noted that only a contract, and not a subcontract, may be certified as having been substantially performed. (Compare with ss. 22, 1(1)(a) and 1(3) of the *Mechanics' Lien Act,* and see *Union Elec. Supply Co. Ltd. v. Joice-Sweanor Elec. Ltd.* (1975), 7 O.R. (2d) 227, 54 D.L.R. (3d) 683 (C.A.)).

payment certifier, however, the owner and the contractor are obliged jointly to provide the requisite certification.[46] In either case, in order to avoid any problems of proof, the actual date set in the certificate is conclusive for all purposes to be the date the contract was substantially performed.[47]

Where the payment certifier certifies the substantial performance of the contract, he must, within seven days, give[48] a copy of the certificate to the owner and to the contractor.[49] Failure to do so exposes the payment certifier to liability to any person who suffers damages as a result.[50]

Within seven days of receiving a copy of the certificate,[51] whether it be signed by the payment certifier or the owner,[52] the contractor is obliged to publish it once,[53] in a construction trade newspaper[54] so that all of the trades will have sufficient notice in order to take whatever steps may be required, if necessary, to protect against the expiry of their lien rights. If the contractor fails to do so within the prescribed time, then any person may publish it.[55]

The construction trade newspaper is required to publish a copy of the certificate, upon commercially reasonable terms, in the prescribed form and manner;[56] but no certificate is invalidated by reason only of failure to comply strictly with the prescribed form and manner of publication authorized by the Act, unless, in the opinion of a court, a person has been prejudiced thereby, and then only to the extent of the prejudice suffered.[57]

Most significantly, a certificate of substantial performance has no effect until a copy of it has been published.[58] Since the 45-day lien period contemplated by ss. 31(2)(a) and 31(3)(a) might not commence to run until the date of publication, any delay in publishing it could postpone the

---

[46] Section 32(1) 1.
[47] Section 32(1) 3.
[48] See s. 89(1).
[49] Section 32(1) 4.
[50] Section 32(4). Also see s. 1(1) 24.
[51] Section 32(1) 6.
[52] Ibid.
[53] Section 32(1) 5. Also see s. 90(c), and s. 3(1) of O. Reg. 159/83 filed March 18, 1983, under the Construction Lien Act, 1983.
[54] "Construction trade newspaper" is defined to mean "a newspaper having circulation generally throughout Ontario, that is published no less frequently than on all days except Saturdays and holidays, and in which calls for tender on construction contracts are customarily published, and that is primarily devoted to the publication of matters of concern to the construction industry": s. 1(1) 2. At the date of this writing, the only newspaper in Ontario which would appear to come within this definition is the Daily Commercial News.
[55] Section 32(1) 6.
[56] Section 32(5). Also see s. 32(2), and s. 3(1) of O. Reg. 159/83 filed March 18, 1983, under the Construction Lien Act, 1983.
[57] Section 6.
[58] Section 32(1) 10.

release of the basic holdback,[59] to the detriment of the contractor and all persons who have supplied services or materials to the improvement.

Once a copy of the certificate of substantial performance has been published, any person may request the contractor to provide advice as to the date of publication and the name of the construction trade newspaper.[60] Failure to provide this information, or knowingly or negligently misstating the information, exposes the contractor to liability for any damages which may be suffered by the person who made the request.[61] In any event, though, the person requesting the information is entitled to bring a motion[62] to the court[63] for an order enforcing compliance.[64]

If certification of substantial performance of the contract does not appear to be forthcoming, either through neglect or refusal, "any person" may apply[65] to the court[66] for a declaration of substantial performance, which declaration, if granted, would have the same force and effect as a certificate.[67]

The date of the declaration is deemed to be the date the contract was substantially performed,[68] [u]nless the court otherwise orders."[69]

By virtue of s. 32(1) 9, the person who applied to the court for the declaration is obliged to publish a copy of it once in a construction trade newspaper, although there is no penalty or liability for failure to do so. Presumably, though, the person applying would have been of the view that it was preferable to apply quickly for the declaration rather than to wait for the issuance of the certificate, and, given the fact that the declaration has no effect until a copy of it is published,[70] the person who applied for it would probably waste no time in arranging for publication.

---

[59] See s. 26.

[60] Section 39(4).

[61] Section 39(5).

[62] See Precedent Nos. 6, 7 and 8.

[63] Section 52(1) dictates whether the motion is to be made to a master, an appointed local master or a local judge.

[64] Section 39(6).

[65] See Precedent Nos. 3, 4 and 5.

[66] The application would be made to a local judge or a Justice of the Supreme Court: see s. 52(2)(c). Given the delays inherent in Weekly Court applications, as compared with applications to the master, and considering the fact that most such applications would probably not be opposed, it is suggested that the procedure set down in the Act may not facilitate the expeditious release of holdback monies.

[67] Section 32(1) 7.

[68] Section 32(1) 8.

[69] *Ibid.* The date of substantial performance of the contract has a significant effect upon the expiry of lien rights (see ss. 31(2) and (3)) and the creation of a trust fund (the "substantial performance trust": see s. 7(3)). Accordingly, these factors ought to be borne in mind by an applicant seeking a court declaration of substantial performance, since the applicant may obtain a benefit, or may avoid an injustice, by petitioning the court to declare the date of substantial performance to be a date other than the day the declaration is made.

The construction trade newspaper is required to publish a copy of the declaration, upon commercially reasonable terms, in the prescribed form and manner;[71] but, as with certificates, no declaration is invalidated by reason only of a failure to comply strictly with the prescribed form and manner of publication authorized by the Act, unless, in the opinion of a court, a person has been prejudiced thereby, and then only to the extent of the prejudice suffered.[72]

(iv) Certification of Completion of a Subcontract[73]

The payment certifier also has a role to play in determining and certifying completion[74] of a subcontract, upon the request of the contractor.[75] Alternatively, the owner and the contractor may[76] provide the requisite certification.[77] In either case, the actual day when the certification of completion of a subcontract is made is deemed to be the day on which the subcontract was completed.[78]

---

[70] Section 32(1) 10.

[71] Section 32(5). Also see s. 90(c), and s. 3(2) of O. Reg. 159/83 filed March 18, 1983, under the *Construction Lien Act, 1983*.

[72] Section 6.

[73] Section 1(1) 22 defines "subcontract" to mean "any agreement between the contractor and a subcontractor, or between two or more subcontractors, relating to the supply of services or materials to the improvement and includes any amendment to that agreement".

[74] See Form 7 prescribed by O. Reg. 159/83 filed March 18, 1983, under the *Construction Lien Act, 1983*. "Completion," with regard to a subcontract, is not a defined term, and therefore literally means total completion. Unlike the situation under the *Mechanics' Lien Act*, a subcontract is not capable of being "substantially performed": see note 45, *supra*.

[75] Section 33(1). It is interesting to observe that the Act contains no mechanism that would be available to a subcontractor to force the issuance of a certificate of completion with respect to his subcontract. The *Report of the Attorney General's Advisory Committee on the Draft Construction Lien Act* (April 1982), at 83-84, commented on this issue as follows:

> The Committee is of the opinion that a mandatory scheme for the certification of the completion of subcontracts is not practical. In most cases, it is very difficult to determine the date of such completion with accuracy. Furthermore, a mandatory scheme of certification would be an extremely expensive burden for the industry to bear. To make the system work, it would be necessary for the owner or payment certifier to be familiar with the terms of all subcontracts. Given the fact that there may be seventy or more subcontracts in the construction of even a small apartment building, this would not be practical.

[76] Unlike the certification of substantial performance of a contract, which is expressed in mandatory terms ("shall determine"/"shall certify": see s. 32(1) 1), certification of completion of a particular subcontract is expressed in permissive terms ("may determine"/"may certify": see s. 33(1)).

[77] Section 33(1).

[78] Section 33(2).

Within seven days of the date of certification of the subcontract, the payment certifier, or the owner and the contractor, as the case may be, must give[79] a copy of the certificate to the subcontractor whose sub-contract has been certified as complete, and, where certification is by the payment certifier, to the owner and the contractor.[80] The provision of the certificate enables all parties to determine when part of the holdback may be released,[81] and assists the subcontractor in ascertaining the date his lien rights expire, if not preserved.[82]

It may be that a subcontract is certified complete, for the sake of expediency, when in point of fact there is some minor work left to be done. A typical instance might involve a situation where, for example, the heating, air-conditioning and ventilation subcontract has been com-pleted, but the subcontract calls for the staging of preliminary tests before actual start-up. For that type of case, the Act provides that services or materials supplied after the date of certification of the subcontract are deemed to have been supplied on the date of certification.[83] In this way, the holdback relating to the completed subcontract may be released[84] without jeopardy at any earlier date, without having to await the comple-tion of testing. However, that provision cuts both ways since the sub-contractor's lien rights could potentially expire before the testing has been completed.

B. PRESERVATION OF LIEN

(i) Generally

A person's lien rights will expire unless they are "preserved" within the time limits[85] and in accordance with the procedures[86] set forth in the Act.

A person who wishes to preserve a lien which "attaches to the premises"[87] must register a claim for lien[88] in the proper land registry

---

[79] See s. 89(1).
[80] Section 33(4).
[81] See s. 25.
[82] See ss. 31(3)(a)(iii) and 31(3)(b)(ii).
[83] Section 33(3).
[84] See s. 25.
[85] See s. 31.
[86] See s. 34.
[87] Contrast the provisions of s. 14(1) with those of s. 16(3).
[88] See Form 8 prescribed by O. Reg. 159/83 filed March 18, 1983, under the *Construction Lien Act, 1983*, as well as s. 34(5), which sets out the requisite contents of a claim for lien.

office[89] against the title to those premises.[90] Registration may be effected "during the supplying of services or materials or at any time before it (the lien) expires."[91]

The claim for lien is to contain much the same information[92] as that prescribed under the *Mechanics' Lien Act*, with two main exceptions:

(i) it must contain reference to "the contract price or subcontract price;"[93] and

(ii) it ought not to contain reference to the date of expiry of any period of credit,[94] since that information appears to be no longer relevant.

Under the *Construction Lien Act, 1983,* although the "giving of time for the payment" of any claim "does not in itself merge, waive, pay, satisfy, prejudice or destroy a lien,"[95] the provision of a period of credit does not extend the time for or dispense with the requirement for the preservation or perfection of a lien.[96]

Once the lien is preserved by registration, the lien claimant is deemed to be a purchaser to the extent of his lien[97] within the provisions of the *Registry Act*[98] and the *Land Titles Act.*[99] Consequently, once preserved, the lien may not be defeated by the owner conveying the premises to a purchaser who purports not to have knowledge or notice of the lien.[100]

Where the lien does not attach to the premises (such as where the provincial Crown is the owner of the premises,[101] or where the premises is either a public street or highway owned by a municipality,[102] or a railway right-of-way)[103] a claim for lien ought not to be registered.[104]

---

[89] Although the curative provision of the *Mechanics' Lien Act* (*i.e.,* s. 19(1)) protected the validity of a lien registered against the wrong property or in the wrong land registry office (see, for example, *Nor-Min Supplies Ltd. v. C.N.R.* (1979), 27 O.R. (2d) 390, 106 D.L.R. (3d) 325, 10 R.P.R. 62 (C.A.); and *Bolger Const. Inc. v. Labombarda et al.* (1982), 43 C.B.R. (N.S.) 226), the curative provision contained in the *Construction Lien Act, 1983* (s. 6) has no application in validating any claim for lien which was improperly registered.

[90] Section 34(1)(a).

[91] Section 34(1).

[92] See s. 34(5).

[93] Section 34(5)(c). Also see s. 1(1) 20.

[94] Contrast with s. 17(1)(e) of the *Mechanics' Lien Act.*

[95] Section 77(1).

[96] Section 77(3). Contrast with s. 26 of the *Mechanics' Lien Act.*

[97] Section 78.

[98] R.S.O. 1980, c. 445.

[99] R.SO. 1980, c. 230.

[100] See ss. 80(1) and (6).

[101] See. s. 16(3).

[102] See s. 16(3)(a).

[103] See s. 16(3)(b).

[104] See s. 34(1)(b).

Rather, a person seeking to preserve the lien must give[105] a copy of the claim for lien, together with an affidavit of verification,[106] to the clerk of the municipality, in the case of a municipally-owned public street or highway,[107] to the manager or any person apparently in charge of any office of the railway in Ontario, in the case of railway right-of-way,[108] or to the office prescribed by regulation,[109] or where no office has been prescribed, to the appropriate ministry or provincial Crown agency, in circumstances where the owner of the premises is the provincial Crown.[110]

(ii) Affidavit of Verification

Without exception, every claim for lien, whether required to be registered or not, must be verified by an affidavit[111] of the person claiming the lien,[112] or of an agent or assignee[113] of that person.[114] In the latter instance, the affidavit may be based upon the information and belief of the deponent.[115]

Where more than one person has a lien upon the same premises, all of them may unite in one claim for lien.[116] However, each person's lien must be similarly verified by a separate affidavit.[117]

It is important to note, by way of contrast with the *Mechanics' Lien Act,*[118] that the curative section[119] of the *Construction Lien Act, 1983* provides no relief to persons who neglect to verify their claims for lien by affidavit. If the affidavit is missing, or in any way does not comply with the requirements of the Act, then the claim for lien would be invalidated.[120]

---

[105] See s. 89(1).

[106] See Form 9 prescribed by O. Reg. 159/83 filed March 18, 1983, under the *Construction Lien Act, 1983,* and s. 34(6).

[107] Section 34(2).

[108] Section 34(4).

[109] See s. 1 of O. Reg. 159/83 filed March 18, 1983, under the *Construction Lien Act, 1983.*

[110] Section 34(3).

[111] See Form 9 prescribed by O. Reg. 159/83 filed March 18, 1983, under the *Construction Lien Act, 1983.*

[112] An affidavit of verification would be required from a trustee of a workers' trust fund, where applicable: s. 34(6).

[113] See s. 75.

[114] Section 34(6).

[115] *Ibid.* Contrast with s. 17(2) of the *Mechanics' Lien Act,* which required an agent or assignee to attest to having "personal knowledge of the matters required to be verified."

[116] Section 34(8).

[117] *Ibid.*

[118] See s. 19 of the *Mechanics' Lien Act.*

[119] Section 6.

[120] The *Report of the Attorney General's Advisory Committee on the Draft Construction Lien Act* (April 1982) contained the following comments (at 94):
> The committee is strongly of the view that an affidavit of verification should be mandatory, in the hope that this will help to prevent spurious and exaggerated claims that prejudice all persons on a project.

However, this would not invalidate the liens of those persons who might have validly perfected their liens by sheltering under an invalidated lien.[121]

Any person who, by affidavit, has verified a claim for lien that has been preserved is liable to be cross-examined on the claim for lien without an order at any time, irrespective of whether an action has been commenced.[122]

(iii) Preservation of a General Lien

A person having a general lien[123] is entitled to preserve it against each of the premises referred to in the contract, if so desired, and the claim against each premises may be for the price of services or materials supplied to all the premises.[124]

If it is determined that the general lien is valid against five premises, but invalid against three others which were sold to purchasers before the lien was preserved, the claimant may enforce his full lien, for supplying services or materials to eight premises, against each of the five premises validly liened.

Similarly, if a claimant agrees to discharge his general lien against one of the premises that is subject to it in consideration for a payment of less than one hundred percent of the price of the services or materials supplied to all of the premises, he may include the deficiency when attempting to enforce his general lien against the remaining premises in respect of which the general lien was not discharged.[125]

C. LIABILITY FOR EXAGGERATED LIEN OR LIEN KNOWN TO BE OUT OF TIME

In order to discourage the preservation of frivolous liens, s. 35 of the Act creates a civil cause of action in favour of any person who suffers damages as a result[126] of a person preserving or giving written notice of a lien which is for an amount which he knows or "ought to know" is "grossly in excess" of the amount which he is owed,[127] or where he knows or

---

[121] Section 36(4) 2.
[122] Section 40. By way of contrast, under the *Mechanics' Lien Act* no cross-examination could take place until an action had been commenced: see *Re Pecco Cranes (Can.) Ltd. et al.*, [1973] 3 O.R. 737 (M.C.); and the right to cross-examine was subject to obtaining an order for directions: s. 42(10), *Mechanics' Lien Act*.
[123] See s. 20 and "The General Lien" (heading C of Chapter 2).
[124] Section 34(7).
[125] Section 42.
[126] See. s. 1(1) 24.
[127] Section 35(a).

"ought to know" that he does not have a lien.[128] The phrases enclosed by quotation marks in the preceding sentence appear to allow for a wide range of judicial interpretation.[129] This exposure to liability would be "in addition to any other ground on which he may be liable."[130]

Any damage claim arising out of s. 35 may be asserted either in a separate action, or as a counterclaim in the lien action.[131]

D. EXPIRY OF LIEN BY FAILURE TO PRESERVE IT

(i) Generally

Under the *Mechanics' Lien Act,* the liens of contractors and subcontractors alike generally[132] expired 37 days after the "completion" (defined as "substantial performance") or abandonment of the contract or subcontract, as the case may have been.[133] The *Construction Lien Act, 1983,* though, has increased the 37-day period to 45 days;[134] has specifically distinguished between the expiry dates of the liens of contractors and those of "other persons" (*i.e.,* subcontractors, "workers,"[135] and trustees of "workers' trust funds");[136] and has created a rather complicated scheme for ascertainment of when the 45-day period is to commence to run, which depends upon the facts of each different situation.

---

[128] Section 35(b).
[129] For example, when does the amount of a claim transcend the point of being merely excessive, and become "grossly in excess of the amount . . . owed"? Similarly, suppose an engineer prepares preliminary design drawings with respect to a planned improvement, and the engineer is then summarily dismissed on the basis that his work product is defective and unsatisfactory. Does the preservation or the giving of written notice of a lien by the engineer expose him to a possible claim for damages, where he knew or ought to have known that he did not have a lien by virtue of the fact that his drawings could not possibly have "enhance[d] the value of the owner's interest in the land" (see s. 1(1) 25, ii)? It appears that the answer would be in the affirmative, although the issues of imputed knowledge and enhancement of value would be questions of fact to be determined by the court.
[130] Section 35. Other bases of liability might include, for example, slander of title, defamation, inducing breach of contract, interference with economic or contractual relations, or fraudulent misrepresentation.
[131] Section 57(2)(a). Also see ss. 53 and 52(3) relating to the jurisdiction of the "court" and the "master/appointed local master", respectively, to deal with any damage claim, arising from s. 35, in the context of the lien action.
[132] Liens for the supply of materials only and for wages received separate attention: See ss. 22(2) and (4), *Mechanics' Lien Act.*
[133] Section 22(1), *Mechanics' Lien Act.*
[134] See s. 31.
[135] See s. 1(1) 27.
[136] See s. 1(1) 28.

(ii) Expiry of Contractor's Lien Rights

Unless preserved in accordance with the Act, the lien rights of a contractor expire as follows:

(a) Where services or materials are supplied to an improvement *on or before* the date certified or declared to be the date of substantial performance of the contract, the contractor's lien rights expire 45 days after the earlier of (i) the date of publication of a copy of the certificate or declaration of substantial performance of the contract, or (ii) the date the contract is completed or abandoned.[137] This can perhaps be illustrated as follows:

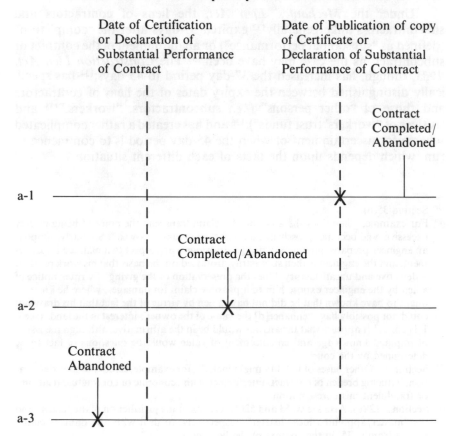

Date of Certification or Declaration of Substantial Performance of Contract

Date of Publication of copy of Certificate or Declaration of Substantial Performance of Contract

Contract Completed/Abandoned

a-1

Contract Completed/Abandoned

a-2

Contract Abandoned

a-3

Each of the lines marked "a-1" through "a-3" represent a time continuum in the life of a construction project, beginning chronologically

---

[137] Section 31(2)(a). Also see s. 2(3).

at the left-hand side of the page. The point *x* in each continuum is where the contractor's 45-day period commences to run.

In situation "a-1", the contractor's rights will expire 45 days after the date of publication of a copy of the certificate or declaration of substantial performance of the contract, inasmuch as it occurs earlier than the date the contract is completed or abandoned.

In situation "a-2", the contractor's lien rights will expire 45 days after the date of completion or abandonment of the contract, since that event precedes the date of publication of a copy of the certificate or declaration of substantial performance of the contract.

In situation "a-3", the contractor's lien rights will expire 45 days after the date of contract was abandoned, since that particular contract will never be certified or declared substantially performed by virtue of the contractor's premature abandonment.

Section 31(4) provides for two separate liens in circumstances where there is an ongoing supply of services or materials before and after the date of certification or declaration of substantial performance of the contract. The section indicates that the lien for services or materials supplied by the contractor before the date of substantial performance expires "without affecting any lien he may have for the supply of services or materials after that date". Therefore, although the contractor's lien rights in situation "a-1" above expire 45 days after the date of publication of a copy of the certificate or declaration of the substantial performance of the contract, this would be without prejudice to any lien rights which the contractor might have for the supply of services or materials after the date of substantial performance, which would expire as provided for in s. 31(2)(b).

(b) Where services or materials are supplied to an improvement *after* the date certified or declared to be the date of substantial performance of the contract, the contractor's lien rights expire 45 days after the date the contract is completed or abandoned, whichever occurs first.[138] The 45-day period commences to run from the same date in circumstances where there is no certification or declaration of substantial performance of the contract[139] (*e.g.,* where there is no payment certifier and the owner and the contractor have refused or neglected to provide the requisite certification; and where, notwithstanding the foregoing, no one has seen fit to apply to the court for a declaration of substantial performance).

Section 38 of the Act provides, though, that the expiry of lien rights under the Act is without prejudice to any other legal or equitable right or

---

[138] Section 31(2)(b). Also see s. 2(3).
[139] *Ibid.*

remedy otherwise available. Accordingly, the person who has lost his lien rights may sue for breach of contract and, if appropriate, for breach of trust.

(iii) Expiry of Lien Rights of Subcontractors and "Other Persons"

Unless preserved in accordance with the Act, the lien rights of subcontractors (and "other persons," such as "workers,"[140] and trustees of "workers' trust funds")[141] expire as follows:

(a) Where services or materials are supplied to an improvement *on or before* the date certified or declared to be the date of substantial performance of the contract, the subcontractor's lien rights expire 45 days after the earlier of (i) the date of publication of a copy of the certificate or declaration of substantial performance of the contract, or (ii) the date of his last supply of services or materials, or (iii) the date his contract is certified complete.[142] For example:

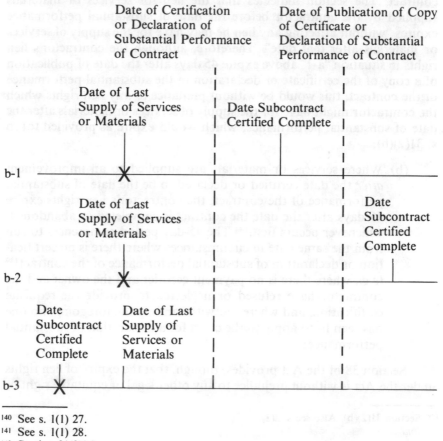

---

[140] See s. 1(1) 27.
[141] See s. 1(1) 28.
[142] Section 31(3)(a).

Each of the lines marked "b-1" through "b-3" represent a time continuum in the life of a construction project, beginning chronologically at the left-hand side of the page. The point x in each continuum is where the subcontractor's 45-day lien period commences to run.

In situation "b-1", the subcontractor's lien rights will expire 45 days after the date of last supply of services or materials, since that event precedes both the date the subcontract was certified complete and the date of publication of a copy of the certificate or declaration of substantial performance of the contract.

In situation "b-2", the subcontractor's lien rights will expire 45 days after the date of last supply of services or materials, based on the same rationale as in the preceding paragraph.

In situation "b-3", it appears that services or materials were supplied *subsequent* to the date of certification of completion of the subcontract. However, those services or materials are deemed to have been supplied on the date of certification.[143] In any event, the subcontractor's lien rights will expire 45 days after the date of certification of completion of the subcontract, particularly since that date is deemed to coincide with the date of last supply of services or materials.

Section 31(4) provides for two separate liens where there is an ongoing supply of services or materials both before and after the date of certification or declaration of substantial performance of the contract. The lien for services or materials supplied by a subcontractor (or "other person") before the date of substantial performance expires "without affecting any lien he may have for the supply of service or materials after that date." The following example, situation "b-4", may assist in understanding this notion:

Date of Certification or Declaration of Substantial Performance of Contract		Date of Publication of Copy of Certificate or Declaration of Substantial Performance of Contract		
Supply No. 1	Supply No. 2	Supply No. 3	Supply No. 4	Date Subcontract Certified Complete

Here, the subcontractor has supplied services or materials on four separate occasions. His lien rights for supply no. 1 and supply no. 2 expire

---

143 Section 33(3).

without prejudice to his lien rights for supply no. 3 and supply no. 4;[144] and therefore his first set of lien rights (*i.e.*, those contemplated by s. 31(3)(a)), with respect to supply no. 1 and supply no. 2, will expire 45 days after the date of supply no. 2. As will be seen below, his second set of lien rights (*i.e.*, those contemplated by s. 31(3)(b)), with respect to supply no. 3 and supply no. 4, will expire 45 days after the date of supply no. 4, since it precedes the date of certification of completion of his subcontract, and since no other date is relevant under s. 31(3)(b).

> (b) Where services or materials are supplied to an improvement *after* the date certified or declared to be the date of substantial performance of the contract, the subcontractor's (or "other person"'s) lien rights expire 45 days after (i) the date he last supplied services or materials, or (ii) the date his subcontract is certified complete, whichever occurs first.[145] The 45-day period commences to run from the same date where there is no certification or declaration of substantial performance of the contract.[146]

Section 38 of the Act provides, though, that the expiry of lien rights under the Act is without prejudice to any other legal or equitable right or remedy otherwise available. Accordingly, the person who has lost his lien rights may sue for breach of contract and, if appropriate, breach of trust.

E. PERFECTION OF LIEN

(i) Generally

Unless a lien has been preserved within the time periods set forth in s. 31 of the Act, it will be deemed to have expired,[147] and therefore may not be perfected.[148]

On the other hand, if the lien has been properly preserved, it becomes perfected where an "action"[149] to enforce the lien has been commenced[150] and a certificate of action[151] is registered against the title to the premises.[152]

---

[144] Section 31(4).
[145] Section 31(3)(b).
[146] *Ibid.*
[147] Section 31(1).
[148] Section 36(1).
[149] An "action" is defined to mean only an action under Part VIII of the Act: s. 1(1) 1.
[150] See s. 55(1).
[151] See Form 10 prescribed by O. Reg. 159/83 filed March 18, 1983, under the *Construction Lien Act, 1983*.
[152] Section 36(3)(a). It is to be noted that the proposed *Construction Lien Amendment Act, 1983*, which is expected to receive First Reading in October of 1983 and which will

The requirement for registering a certificate of action, though, is dispensed with if an order is obtained vacating the registration of the claim for lien on the basis of a payment into court or the posting of security in lieu thereof.[153]

Where the lien does not attach to the premises (such as where the provincial Crown is the owner of the premises, or where the premises is a municipally owned public street or highway, or a railway right-of-way),[154] an action must be commenced, but a certificate of action would not be required to be registered.[155]

A preserved lien may be perfected in an alternative fashion where it "shelters" under a lien perfected by another lien claimant.[156] The sheltering rules contained in the Act are discussed in the next section.

The commencement of an action, and the registration of a certificate of action (if it is required[157] or has not been dispensed with),[158] must be completed "prior to the end of the forty-five day period next following the last day, under section 31, on which the lien could have been preserved"[159] if the lien is to be perfected. Otherwise it expires,[160] and, upon motion,[161] the court is obliged to make a declaration to this effect and, if required, to order that the registration of the claim for lien be vacated.[162]

Consider the following example: A contract is certified to have been substantially performed on May 1. Publication of a copy of the certificate in a construction trade newspaper takes place on May 12, and the contract is finally completed on May 31. Under s. 31, the contractor's lien rights would expire 45 days after May 12 (the date of publication),[163] specifically on June 26. However, due to circumstances, the contractor decided to register his claim for lien on June 1, since he anticipated that he might not get paid. Under s. 36(2), that lien would expire unless it were perfected by

---

be deemed to have come into force on April 2, 1983, purports to amend s. 36 of the Act by adding thereto the following subsection:

A person who has preserved a lien, but who has extended a period of credit for the payment of the amount to which the lien relates, may commence an action for the purpose of perfecting his lien even though the period of credit has not at the time expired, but where the action is so commenced, the action is stayed until the expiration of the period of credit, unless the court is satisfied that the stay is unfair in the circumstances and orders that the action proceed.

[153] See s. 44 generally, and s. 44(9) 1 in particular.
[154] See s. 16(3).
[155] See s. 36(3)(b).
[156] See s. 36(4).
[157] See ss. 36(3)(a) and (b).
[158] See s. 44(9) 1.
[159] Section 36(2).
[160] *Ibid.*
[161] See s. 45.
[162] *Ibid.*
[163] Section 31(2)(a)(i).

August 10 (assuming that it is not sheltering under the perfected lien of another lien claimant), which is 45 days "next following the *last* day, under section 31, on which the lien *could have been* preserved [namely, June 26]." Simply stated, if an unpreserved lien will expire unless it is preserved by, say, June 26, but it is actually preserved earlier, on June 1, the 45-day period for perfecting that lien will commence to run on June 26.

(ii) Sheltering

Section 33(5) of the *Mechanics' Lien Act* provided that all lien claimants served with a notice of trial were deemed for all purposes to be parties to the action; and s. 34 of the same Act provided:

> 34. Any number of lien claimants claiming liens on the same land may join in an action, and an action brought by a lien claimant shall be deemed to be brought on behalf of himself and all other lien claimants.

These sections established the doctrine of "sheltering," pursuant to which a lien claimant, in certain circumstances,[164] could be said to have perfected his lien, without either commencing a separate action or registering a certificate of action, by sheltering under the certificate of action of another lien claimant.

The intent of ss. 33(5) and 34 of the *Mechanics' Lien Act* has been carried through into the *Construction Lien Act, 1983*,[165] although the latter Act omits the clause, contained in the above quotation, to the effect that a lien action is deemed to be, in effect, a class action ("brought on behalf of himself and all other lien claimants"). The *Construction Lien Act, 1983* does not deal with the doctrine of sheltering by implication, but rather establishes a set of concise rules[166] which essentially define its application:

1. A lien may not be perfected unless it has been preserved. Under Rule 1 of s. 36(4), the preserved lien of a lien claimant ("X") is perfected by sheltering under the perfected lien of another lien claimant ("Y") in respect of the same premises where:

   (a) Y's lien was a "subsisting perfected lien" at the time when X's lien was preserved; or
   (b) Y's lien is perfected between the time when X's lien was preserved and the time that X's lien would have expired, had it not been otherwise perfected (under s. 36(3)).

---

164 See, for example and clarification, *Brousseau et al. v. Muircrest Invts. Ltd. et al.* (1977), 15 O.R. (2d) 145, 75 D.L.R. (3d) 161; revd. 15 O.R. (2d) 155, 75 D.L.R. (3d) 171 (C.A.).
165 See ss. 59(1) and 50(3).
166 Section 36(4).

In the situation contemplated by (b) above, Y's lien has to have been perfected "in accordance with clause (3)(a) or (b)"[167] of s. 36. If, for example, another claimant ("Z") perfected his lien on day one, Y sheltered under Z's lien on day two, and Z settled his claim and discharged his lien on day three; and, assuming Y's lien nevertheless continued to be subsisting and perfected as at day four, which is the date when X preserved his lien; X would not be permitted to shelter under Z's lien (since it was not subsisting at the date X's lien was preserved) or under Y's lien (since Y's lien was not perfected in accordance with s. 36(3)(a) or (b)).

2. Under Rule 2 of s. 36(4), "[t]he validity of the perfection of a sheltered lien does not depend upon the validity, proper preservation or perfection of the lien under which it is sheltered." This rule is intended to protect the sheltered lien in the event that the perfected lien, under which it has sheltered, is defective. As stated by the Attorney General's Advisory Committee on the Draft *Construction Lien Act,*

> . . . a person who perfects his lien by sheltering cannot realistically be expected to investigate the merits of the lien claim under which he has sheltered, nor to determine whether that lien was preserved or perfected within the time allowed under the Act.[168]

3. Rule 3 circumscribes the ambit of the sheltered lien by providing that it is perfected "only as to the defendants and the nature of the relief claimed in the statement of claim under which it is sheltered." Again, the Attorney General's Advisory Committee commented that,

> . . . sheltering should not apply to protect claims underlying a sheltered lien where the claim is wholly different in nature to the claims in the action under which it is sheltered. To permit wholly different claims to be sheltered would be prejudicial to the defendants. If a person wishes to bring an entirely different claim, he should commence a separate action which may then be joined with the other actions. In this way pleadings will be delivered in respect of his claims, and defendants will be in a better position to determine whether they need to seek discovery against him.[169]

The problem posed by Rule 3, though, is that lien claimants will have to search title in order to review the certificate of action registered by the lien claimant under whose perfected lien they wish to shelter, so as to ascertain which defendants have been named. The lien claimants will also have to obtain the relevant Supreme Court action number from the certificate of action; and they will then have to obtain a copy of the statement of claim, by which the action was commenced, in order to review the allegations

---

[167] Section 36(4) 1, ii.
[168] *Report of the Attorney General's Advisory Committee on the Draft Construction Lien Act* (April 1982), at 101.
[169] *Ibid.*, at 101-102.

contained in it to satisfy themselves that they would be prepared to limit the scope of their claim to the nature of the relief claimed in the statement of claim. Furthermore, if no certificate of action was registered by virtue of the fact that money was paid into court to vacate the lien before it was subsequently perfected (by simply commencing an action), then it might be difficult for the sheltering lien claimant to locate and obtain a copy of the statement of claim for review. All things considered, it might be more prudent for a lien claimant not to shelter at all by reason of the potential limitations posed by Rule 3, but rather to commence his own action and register his own certificate of action. In due course, all lien actions would probably be consolidated[170] in any event.

4. Under Rule 4 of s. 36(4), a defendant may give[171] notice[172] to require a sheltering lien claimant to provide further particulars of his claim or of any fact alleged in his claim for lien. This rule will no doubt assist the defendant in clarifying factual matters, particularly to assist him in his defence of the action, without putting him to the expense of having his solicitor conduct a cross-examination of the lien claimant.[173]

(iii) Perfecting the General Lien

A preserved general lien,[174] that attaches to the premises, must be perfected against each of the premises to which the person having the lien desires the lien to continue to apply.[175]

F. EXPIRY OF PERFECTED LIEN

Section 62 of the Act authorizes any party to the action to make a motion to the court to have a day, time and place fixed for the trial of the lien action. If no trial date is obtained, or if the lien action is not set down for trial, within two years of "the date of the commencement of the action which perfected that lien,"[176] then the perfected lien expires,[177] and the

---

[170] See s. 61(2).

[171] See s. 89(1).

[172] See Form 11 prescribed by O. Reg. 159/83 filed March 18, 1983, under the *Construction Lien Act, 1983.*

[173] See s. 40.

[174] See ss. 20 and 34(7), and "The General Lien" (heading C of Chapter 2).

[175] Section 36(5). It is to be noted that s. 36(5) is subject to the provisions of s. 44(4) dealing with apportionment of a general lien where there is a payment into court.

[176] Section 37(1). The quoted reference makes it clear that, if X's lien was perfected by sheltering under Y's perfected lien, then the two-year period commences to run from the date Y commenced his action. Given the fact that the lien of X is entitled to shelter under Y's lien even though Y's lien was perfected before X's lien was preserved (by s. 36(4) 1, i), X's lien could possibly expire well in advance of a period of two years from the date X perfected, or even preserved, his lien.

[177] Section 37(1).

court, upon the motion of "any person," must make a declaration to that effect, and must order that the action be dismissed and the registration of the claim for lien and certificate of action be vacated.[178]

It is to be noted, though, that the expiry of a perfected lien will not affect any other rights and remedies available to the person whose lien expired.[179] Accordingly, that person may pursue, for example, an action for breach of trust or an ordinary collection action commenced by writ of summons.

---

[178] Sections 37(2) and 46 and Precedent Nos. 29, 30 and 31.
[179] Section 38.

Chapter 5

The Trust Fund

A. THE NATURE OF THE TRUST

Part II of the *Construction Lien Act, 1983* creates a "statutory" trust, which is distinct from trusts created by persons expressly (*e.g., inter vivos*, testamentary) or impliedly (*e.g.*, precatory), or those imposed by equity (*e.g.*, constructive). Although, as with the other types of trusts, the Part II statutory trust creates a fiduciary relationship between the trustee (*i.e.*, the owner, contractor or subcontractor, as the case may be) and the beneficiaries (*i.e.*, persons who have supplied services or materials to a particular construction project), all of the relevant rights and duties derive exclusively from Part II. Furthermore, Part II specifically characterizes the trust property and establishes the point in time when the trust is created.

Essentially, the trust provisions of the Act are meant to extend protection to the trades who have supplied services or materials but who have neglected to preserve and perfect their lien rights (although lien claimants are certainly also entitled to obtain the benefit of these provisions). The protection afforded by the trust provisions becomes particularly relevant in circumstances where a person, upon whom there are trust obligations, becomes bankrupt, in which case the trust monies do not fall into the bankrupt's estate and the beneficiaries of the trust are entitled to share in the trust fund to the exclusion of the bankrupt's other creditors.

B. TYPES OF TRUST FUNDS

(i) The "Mortgage Trust"

Section 7(1) creates what might be referred to as the "mortgage trust." It provides that all monies received by an owner[1] which are to be

---

[1] Section 7(1) expressly excludes "the Crown or a municipality", in respect of which the section has no application.

used in the financing of an improvement, such as an advance under a building mortgage, constitute a trust fund for the benefit of the contractor. However, the trust created by this section is "subject to the payment of the purchase price of the land[2] and prior encumbrances,"[3] meaning that the owner may use the borrowed funds to pay for the land[4] and to discharge prior mortgages without breaching the trust. It is significant to note that the trust arises when the owner "receives" the advance. This is a question of fact and has been the subject of litigation.[5]

(ii) The "Certificate Trust"

Section 7(2) creates the "certificate trust." On many construction projects, the owner usually engages the services of an architect or an engineer to prepare plans and specifications and to supervise construction. In order to facilitate the flow of payments down the construction pyramid and to assist the owner in dealing with his mortgage lender, the architect/engineer may issue certificates from time to time, certifying that a certain portion of the contractor's work has been completed and placing the dollar value on it. The amount so certified, where it is actually in the owner's hands or is received by him at any time after certification, constitutes a trust fund for the benefit of the contractor. This trust is intended to comprehend those situations where the owner may be using his own rather than borrowed funds to finance the improvement.

(iii) The "Substantial Performance Trust"

Pursuant to s. 7(3), where substantial performance of the contract has been certified,[6] but the owner has only made part payment of the authorized amount to the contractor, an amount equal to the unpaid price of the substantially performed portion of the contract that is in the owner's hands, or that he subsequently receives, is impressed with a trust for the benefit of the contractor.

Where there has been a failure or refusal to certify substantial performance, any person may apply to the court for a declaration of substantial performance.[7] Inasmuch as s. 32(1) 7 provides that "the

---

[2] "Land" is defined to include "any building, structure or works affixed to the land, or an appurtenance to any of them, but does not include the improvement": s. 1(1) 10.

[3] Section 7(1).

[4] See note 2, *supra*.

[5] See, for example, *Andrea Schmidt Const. Ltd. v. Glatt et al.* (1979), 25 O.R. (2d) 567, 104 D.L.R. (3d) 130, affd. 28 O.R. (2d) 672n, 112 D.L.R. (3d) 371n (C.A.); and *Minneapolis-Honeywell Regulator Co. Ltd. v. Empire Brass Mfg. Co. Ltd.,* [1955] S.C.R. 694 (particularly at 697), [1955] 3 D.L.R. 561 (at 563).

[6] See s. 32(1).

[7] Section 32(1)7.

declaration has the same force and effect as a certificate of substantial performance of the contract," the "substantial performance trust," as contemplated by s. 7(3), would arise.

This trust provision is designed to deal with those situations where the contract may not have provided for the issuance of progress certificates from time to time, and the owner may have made payments to the contractor totalling something less than the amount ultimately certified or declared to be due and owing as at the date of substantial performance.

(iv) The "Draws Trust"

Section 8(1) creates the "draws trust". It provides that any monies which are received[8] by, or owing to (whether or not due or payable),[9] a contractor or a subcontractor, on account of the contract or subcontract price, constitute a trust fund for the benefit of all unpaid persons who have supplied services or materials to the improvement.

If, for example, a contractor becomes bankrupt at a time when monies are in his hands which he received on account of the contract price, those monies do not fall into the estate of the bankrupt contractor but are to be distributed by the trustee in bankruptcy to all trust fund beneficiaries. Only if there are surplus funds does the trustee in bankruptcy become entitled to receive them.

The rationale for including the caveat in s. 8(1)(a) that the monies, although owing, need not be due or payable obviously is directed at prohibiting the payer from converting or making unauthorized use of trust funds during the period of credit which the trades customarily provide.

Under the *Mechanics' Lien Act,* an owner was also a beneficiary of the draws trust.[10] If, for example, a contractor misappropriated trust money and, as a result, one of the unpaid subcontractors registered a lien against the owner's interest in the property, the *Mechanics' Lien Act* afforded a cause of action to the owner. The *Discussion Paper on the Draft Construction Lien Act* (November 1980) also contained a similar provision.[11] However, the *Construction Lien Act, 1983* did not carry this provision through:

> The Committee decided that there is no benefit to be derived from making a payer on a contract or subcontract who has paid money down to the construction

---

[8] As with the "mortgage trust", it is a question of fact when the "draws trust" monies are "received" by the contractor or subcontractor.

[9] To the extent that s. 8(1)(a) clarifies the time when the trust arises, it was inspired by the Supreme Court of Canada decision in *Minneapolis-Honeywell Regulator Co. v. Empire Brass Mfg. Co., supra,* note 5.

[10] See the *Mechanics' Lien Act,* R.S.O. 1980, c. 261, s. 3(1).

[11] See (draft) s. 8(1) at 39.

pyramid a beneficiary of the trust imposed upon the recipient of that money as a result of that payment. . . . Those paying money under the Act have sufficient opportunity to determine what amount to pay out, as well as other remedies in contract law.[12]

(v) The "Vendor's Trust"

Typically in situations involving the construction of a new house, it is not uncommon for a developer-owner to conclude a sale of the property before all his trades have completed their work and before they have been paid.

If a deed evidencing the sale has been registered before any of the trades has registered a claim for lien, then generally, under the *Mechanics' Lien Act*, the purchaser would not have come within the definition of "owner,"[13] no "request" for the improvement having been made, and the subsequent registration of a claim for lien would therefore have been improper.

If, however, a "request" on the part of the purchaser could be implied, such as where the purchaser has given the trades assurances of payment,[14] or where a purchaser has purchased a house built in accordance with a sample or model,[15] then an argument could have been advanced to the effect that the purchaser was a statutory owner.[16]

Therefore, unless a request could be implied from the surrounding circumstances, the unpaid trades lost their lien rights upon the sale of the property, and their only recourse was a personal action against the developer-owner. This was an illusory remedy, though, inasmuch as most developer-owners are shell corporations which have been established solely to undertake a particular construction project. Furthermore, the sale proceeds received by the developer-owner could be used to retire bank or other indebtedness without the risk of incurring any form of liability[17] since, under the *Mechanics' Lien Act,* those proceeds were not impressed with a trust.

---

[12] *Report of the Attorney General's Advisory Committee on the Draft Construction Lien Act* (April 1982), at 38.

[13] See the *Mechanics' Lien Act*, s. 1(1)(f).

[14] See, for example, *John C. Love Lbr. Co. Ltd. v. Moore,* [1963] 1 O.R. 245, 36 D.L.R. (2d) 609 (C.A.); *Conrad v. Kaplan,* 24 Man. R. 368, 6 W.W.R. 1061, [1914] 18 D.L.R. 37 (C.A.).

[15] See, for example, *Watt Milling Co. (Trustee of) v. Jackson,* [1951] O.W.N. 841 (H.C.); *Reggin v. Manes* (1892), 22 O.R. 443 (C.D.); *Freedman v. Guaranty Trust Co.,* 64 O.L.R. 200, [1929] 4 D.L.R. 32 (C.A.).

[16] See "The Purchaser as Owner" (heading B(v) of Chapter 2).

[17] Save and except potential liability for preferences as contemplated by the *Bankruptcy Act,* R.S.C. 1970, c. B-3 (see ss. 73–75), and the *Assignments and Preferences Act,* R.S.O. 1980, c. 33 (see s. 4).

The definition of "owner" under the *Construction Lien Act, 1983*[18] is sufficiently broad to permit the same arguments, regarding the purchaser as statutory owner, to be advanced. However, the inequities which might arise as a result of the failure of those arguments, as described above, have been remedied by virtue of the establishment of the "vendor's trust". Pursuant to s. 9(1), where an owner sells his interest in the premises, the sale proceeds ("the consideration") received by him as a result of the sale, less the reasonable expenses arising from the sale and the amount, if any, paid by him to discharge any existing mortgage indebtedness on the premises, constitute a trust fund for the benefit of the contractor. As a result, the contractor, who is the beneficiary of that trust property, is entitled to trace, if necessary, and to assert a claim against it.

C. TRUST OBLIGATIONS OF OWNER

Once an owner receives or has possession of trust monies, specific trust obligations arise. Basically the owner is precluded from appropriating or converting all or part of those monies to his own use, or to any use not consistent with his statutory trust obligations.[19] The Act, however, affords complete protection to an owner where "the contractor is paid all amounts related to the improvement owed to him by the owner",[20] subject to the owner's right of set-off[21] as contained in s. 12. Once the owner renders payment in full to the contractor, the owner's trust obligations and liabilities are discharged.[22] If only a partial payment is made, then the owner's trust obligations and liabilities are only discharged to the extent of the payment made.[23]

Examples of an owner's breach of his trust obligations would be:

(a) where an owner uses monies advanced under a building mortgage on Project "A" to pay trades working on Project "B"; or
(b) where the owner uses trust monies to reduce his bank indebtedness.

The latter example is subject, however, to the qualification that an owner is legitimately entitled to use trust funds to repay non-trust money loaned to him so long as the non-trust money was applied toward payment for the supply of services or materials to the improvement.[24]

---

[18] See s. 1(1) 15.
[19] Section 7(4).
[20] *Ibid.*
[21] See "Set-Off Against Trust Funds" (heading E of this chapter, *infra*).
[22] Section 10.
[23] *Ibid.*
[24] Section 11(2).

In an analogous way, if an owner retains trust funds so as to repay himself for non-trust monies which he has laid out to pay for services or materials, he will not incur any liability for breach of trust.[25]

D. TRUST OBLIGATIONS OF CONTRACTORS AND SUBCONTRACTORS

Where a contractor or a subcontractor receives or has possession of funds impressed with the "draws trust," he will not breach the trust so long as he pays all subcontractors and other persons who have supplied services or materials to the improvement all amounts which he owes them.[26] Once any such payment is made, the contractor or subcontractor, as trustee, is discharged from his trust obligations, and from liability as trustee to all beneficiaries of the trust, to the extent of the payment made,[27] subject of course to his holdback obligation.[28]

Furthermore, a contractor or a subcontractor is entitled to use trust funds to repay non-trust money loaned to him[29] so long as the non-trust money was applied toward payment for the supply of services or materials to the improvement.

Similarly, if a contractor or a subcontractor retains trust funds so as to repay himself for non-trust monies which he has laid out to pay for services or materials, he will not incur any liability for breach of trust.[30]

E. SET-OFF AGAINST TRUST FUNDS

While s. 30 effectively prohibits any set-off against holdback[31] (until all liens that may be claimed against that holdback have either expired[32] or have been satisfied,[33] discharged[34] or vacated)[35] s. 12 makes it clear that an owner, a contractor or a subcontractor, *qua* trustee, is entitled to assert a set-off claim against trust monies without incurring any liability for

---

[25] Section 11(1).
[26] Section 8(2).
[27] Section 10.
[28] See Part IV of the Act ("Holdbacks").
[29] Section 11(2).
[30] Section 11(1).
[31] See "No Set-Off Against Holdback" (heading E of Chapter 3).
[32] See ss. 31, 45, 46 and 47 (1)(c).
[32] See ss. 31, 45, 46 and 47 (1)(c).
[33] See ss. 41 and 42.
[34] *Ibid.* Also see s. 47(1)(a).
[35] See ss. 44, 45(1), 46(1) and 47(1)(b).

breach of trust. Any such set-off claim may be comprised of "the balance in the trustee's favour of all outstanding debts, claims or damages, whether or not related to the improvement."[36]

For example, if a subcontractor's work is defective or incomplete and the contractor incurs damages in rectifying the defect or completing the work, the contractor is entitled to set off the amount of his damages against the monies comprising the "draws trust" without breaching the trust.

More significantly, if a contractor has a claim against his subcontractor for defective work on Project "A", and if he employs that same subcontractor on Project "B", the contractor would be entitled to set off the Project "A" claim against (trust) monies owing to the subcontractor for work done on Project "B", without incurring liability for breach of trust.[37]

F. ASSIGNMENT OF MONIES IMPRESSED WITH A TRUST

Consider the following scenario:

G.C. Ltd., a general contractor, may be working on several projects (Projects "X", "Y" and "Z") at the same time. Its business is financed by means of a line of credit with the bank, in consideration for which it has given the bank several types of security, including the personal guarantee of its president as well as an assignment of book debts.

G.C. Ltd. encounters cash flow problems and, as a result of making payments to some of its trades on Projects "Y" and "Z", its bank account goes into an overdraft position. Most of the trades working on Project "X" in particular have not been paid, although none of them has as yet registered a lien.

Upon receiving the next progress payment from the owner of Project "X", G.C. Ltd. deposits the money in its bank account with the supposed intention of drawing further progress cheques in favour of the trades on Project "X". However, as soon as the money is deposited, the bank promptly debits the account so as to bring both the overdraft and the debt owing under the line of credit into good standing.

G.C. Ltd. is of course concerned that the Project "X" trades may now not get paid out of this advance, and the liens that will inevitably be registered will no doubt bring Project "X" to a halt. On the other hand,

---

[36] Section 12.

[37] The fact that the contractor's set-off claim does not necessarily have to be related to the improvement may give rise to situations where the essential facts and issues relating to the improvement will be unduly complicated by extraneous issues requiring, in effect, separate trials for set-off claims.

the president of G.C. Ltd. may be privately pleased that the bank has seized the funds since it reduces his exposure on his personal guarantee.

Out of his hypothetical situation, which is not at all uncommon, will often arise an action by the Project "X" trades against the bank for breach of trust.

Under the *Mechanics' Lien Act*, the action was difficult to maintain successfully, since the plaintiff(s) had to prove that the monies debited by the bank from the contractor's bank account were impressed with a trust, and, more importantly, that the bank, in debiting the account, knowingly participated in a breach of trust.[38]

In these types of cases, the bank would take the position that it had no obligation to, and in fact did not, investigate whether the trades employed by its customer had been paid, and had no reason to believe that its customer was in financial difficulty. It was merely dealing with its customer's deposit in the ordinary course of business, pursuant to the banker-customer relationship. The trades, on the other hand, would argue that the existence of the overdraft and the other outstanding indebtedness constituted sufficient evidence to put the bank on notice that its customer may have been encountering financial problems and that the bank, in failing to investigate, was not acting in good faith. Furthermore, if the bank knew detailed particulars of its customer's receivables and payables, on a project-by-project basis, which is often the case, the bank should have easily been able to determine that certain receivables constituted, say, holdback on a particular project which obviously was not enough to cover the payables (*i.e.,* the trades) on the same project.

Many subcontractors, however, have been reluctant to incur the time and expense of a breach of trust action, particularly after considering the difficult onus of proof; the risk, insofar as costs are concerned, of being unsuccessful; the intimidating prospect of suing a major financial institution; and the potential recovery which might be insubstantial.

Section 12 of the *Discussion Paper on the Draft Construction Lien Act* (November 1980) purported to attempt to protect the trades in these situations by providing that:

Where a right to any payment which upon receipt by the assignor [*i.e.,* G.C. Ltd.] would be subject to a trust under this Part is assigned [by means of an assignment of

---

[38] See, for example, *Fonthill Lbr. Ltd. v. Bank of Montreal,* [1959] O.R. 461, 19 D.L.R. (2d) 618, 38 C.B.R. 72 (C.A.); revg. [1959] O.R. 451, 16 D.L.R. (2d) 746, 38 C.B.R. 68; *John M. M. Troup Ltd. v. Royal Bank,* [1962] S.C.R. 487, 34 D.L.R. (2d) 556, 3 C.B.R. (N.S.) 224; affg. [1961] O.R. 455, 28 D.L.R. (2d) 257, 2 C.B.R. (N.S.) 191; affg. [1960] O.W.N. 350, 24 D.L.R. (2d) 460; *Clarkson Co. Ltd. v. Can. Bank of Commerce,* [1966] S.C.R. 513, 57 D.L.R. (2d) 193, 8 C.B.R. (N.S.) 280; revg. [1965] 1 O.R. 197, 47 D.L.R. (2d) 289, 6 C.B.R. (N.S.) 312 (*sub nom. John Ritchie Ltd. v. Can. Bank of Commerce;* revg. [1963] 2 O.R. 116, 38 D.L.R. (2d) 546, 5 C.B.R. (N.S.) 28; and *Perlmutter Shore Ltd. v. Bank of Montreal* (1982), 34 O.R. (2d) 577, 40 C.B.R. (N.S.) 1, 22 R.P.R. 204 (H.C.).

book debts], the moneys received by the assignee [*i.e.,* the bank, for example] are subject to the trust.

However, in the opinion of the Attorney General's Advisory Committee on the Draft *Construction Lien Act*, "such a declaratory provision is unnecessary, and might lead to confusion. For this reason, Section 12 [was] deleted."[39]

It is clear, though, that, in the above scenario, the monies received by G.C. Ltd. would be impressed with a "draws trust" pursuant to s. 8(1), as being monies received on account of the contract price. Where these (trust) monies are assigned by G.C. Ltd. to the bank, they nevertheless continue to be subject to the trust. The bank would be unable to contract out of,[40] or in any way avoid, the effect of this, although the bank would be entitled to raise the same arguments, by way of defence, as it might have raised in a breach of trust action under the *Mechanics' Lien Act.*

Accordingly, the existing jurisprudence dealing with breach of trust actions against banks and other moneylenders will no doubt continue to be relevant in respect of those types of actions commenced pursuant to the *Construction Lien Act, 1983.*

G. LIABILITY FOR BREACH OF TRUST

(i) Who is Liable?

In cases where there has been a breach of trust by a corporation ostensibly having limited liability, ss. 13(1) and (2) permit the court to pierce the corporate veil and to impose liability upon every director, officer, employee or agent of the corporation, and upon any person having effective control of the corporation or its relevant activities.[41] Accordingly, since a corporation does not act or make decisions on its own, a trust fund beneficiary might be well advised to name, as defendants in an action for breach of trust, the persons "behind" the corporation who may have caused the corporation to deal with trust funds in a manner not authorized by the trust.

What must be demonstrated is that those persons assented to or acquiesced in conduct which they knew or reasonably ought to have

---

[39] *Report of the Attorney General's Advisory Committee on the Draft Construction Lien Act* (April 1982), at 43.

[40] Section 4.

[41] This provision carries through the basic approach which was taken, without the benefit of a specific statutory provision, under the *Mechanics' Lien Act.* See, for example, *Andrea Schmidt Const. Ltd. v. Glatt et al., supra,* note 5. Also see *Scott v. Riehl et al.* (1958), 15 D.L.R. (2d) 67, 25 W.W.R. 525 (B.C.S.C.); and *Horsman Bros. Holdings Ltd. et al. v. Panton et al.,* [1976] 3 W.W.R. 745 (B.C.S.C.).

known amounted to a breach of trust by the corporation. The issues of "assent," "acquiescence" and "effective control" are ones of fact, and, at least with respect to "effective control," "the court may disregard the form of any transaction and the separate corporate existence of any participant."[42]

The extension of civil liability contemplated by s. 13 is meant to replace the quasi-criminal sanctions[43] contained in the *Mechanics' Lien Act*.[44] At least part of the rationale for this is that the penal provisions are unnecessary, given s. 296 of the *Criminal Code*,[45] which establishes the conversion of trust funds, with an intent to defraud,[46] as an indictable offence punishable by imprisonment for up to 14 years, or, in the case of a corporation, to a fine that is in discretion of the court, in lieu of imprisonment.[47]

(ii) Apportionment of Liability

By virtue of s. 13(3), all persons who are found liable or have admitted liability for a particular breach of trust are deemed to be jointly and severally liable.

Those persons, however, are entitled to contribution as between themselves "in such amount as will result in equal contribution by all parties liable for the breach."[48] If the court considers equal apportionment not to be fair, it has authority to "direct such contribution or indemnity as [it] considers appropriate in the circumstances."[49]

(iii) Limitation Period

Under the *Mechanics' Lien Act* an action against a "lender of money" generally had to be brought within nine months of substantial performance or abandonment of the contract or subcontract.[50]

---

42 Section 13(2).
43 $5,000 maximum fine and/or two years' maximum imprisonment.
44 The *Mechanics' Lien Act*, s. 2(7).
45 The *Criminal Code*, R.S.C. 1970, c. C-34 provides:
    296. Every one who, being a trustee of anything for the use or benefit, whether in whole or in part, of another person, or for a public or charitable purpose, converts, with intent to defraud and in violation of his trust, that thing or any part of it to a use that is not authorized by the trust is guilty of an indictable offence and is liable to imprisonment for fourteen years.
46 Regarding "intent to defraud," see *R. v. Petricia*, [1974] 4 W.W.R. 425, 17 C.C.C. (2d) 27 (B.C.C.A.) leave to appeal to S.C.C. dismissed June 3, 1974, 17 C.C.C. (2d) 27n. According to this decision, the "intent to defraud" in s. 296 of the *Criminal Code*, when read in its context, is a limited intent directed to the trust duties.
47 See s. 647(a) of the *Criminal Code*.
48 Section 13(4).
49 *Ibid*. Also see *Ben Plastering Ltd. v. Global Dixie Ltd. et al.* (1981), 33 C.B.R. (N.S.) 253, 14 R.P.R. 161 (Ont. S.C.).
50 See the *Mechanics' Lien Act*, ss. 3(a), 1(1)(a) and 1(3).

However, the *Mechanics' Lien Act* contained no specific limitation provision with respect to other potential defendants in a breach of trust action, and therefore the general legal principles relating to the limitation of actions for breach of trust applied.[51]

Section 14 of the *Discussion Paper on the Draft Construction Lien Act* (November 1980) purported to deal with this issue by providing that:

> No proceeding to assert a claim to any trust fund shall be brought later than one year after the payment upon which the claim is made became due.[52]

The *Construction Lien Act, 1983,* however, contains no limitation provision regarding any breach of trust claim, and it therefore appears that the general legal principles relating to limitation of actions for breach of trust will henceforth apply to every situation.[53]

It is interesting to note that the Attorney General's Advisory Committee on the Draft *Construction Lien Act* was of the view that:

> . . . no claim arising from a breach of trust should be barred by a special limitation period. The ordinary limitation periods, as well as the equitable doctrine of laches, should apply to such claims. In the circumstances, there should be no special exemption for banks and other financial institutions.[54]

H. ACTION FOR BREACH OF TRUST

Section 50(2) provides that a trust claim shall not be joined with a lien claim, but may be brought in any court of competent jurisdiction.[55] According to the Attorney General's Advisory Committee:

> While the principles of joining these different claims is attractive in theory, in practice the joining of these different types of claims likely would result in hardship for many lien claimants. The issues as well as the parties would often be very different in a claim for lien as opposed to a trust claim. The avoidances of undue delay in the resolution of lien claims should be the primary purpose of the Act.[56]

I. PRIORITIES AS BETWEEN TRUST FUND BENEFICIARIES AND OTHER CLAIMANTS

See Chapter 10: Priorities

J. DISTRIBUTION OF A TRUST FUND

See Chapter 10: Priorities

---

[51] See J.S. Williams, *Limitation of Actions in Canada,* 2nd ed. (1980), at 145–152.
[52] See *Discussion Paper on the Draft Construction Lien Act* (November 1980), at 44.
[53] See note 51, *supra.*
[54] *Report of the Attorney General's Advisory Committee on the Draft Construction Lien Act* (April 1982), at 47.
[55] See Precedent Nos. 64 and 65.
[56] *Report of the Attorney General's Advisory Committee on the Draft Construction Lien Act* (April 1982), at 128.

Chapter 6

Right to Information

A. COMPETING INTERESTS

In dealing with the issue of access to information as it relates to construction lien claims, the Legislature was called upon to balance two competing legitimate interests:

(1) Any legislative provisions requiring the disclosure of information ought neither to compromise the confidentiality of business dealings nor to be unduly onerous;

(2) On the other hand, access to information ought to be sufficiently liberal, both qualitatively and quantitatively, so as to facilitate the enforcement of rights under the Act.

B. ACCESS TO INFORMATION[1]

(i) Information Regarding the Contract or a Subcontract

Under the *Mechanics' Lien Act*, any "lien claimant"[2] was entitled to demand, in writing and at any time, that either the owner or his "agent" (*e.g.*, the architect) produce for inspection the written agreement with the

---

[1] In addition to the information referred to under this heading, it is to be noted that the proposed *Construction Lien Amendment Act, 1983*, which is expected to receive First Reading in October of 1983 and which will be deemed to have come into force on April 2, 1983, purports to amend s. 39(1) of the Act by adding thereto the following paragraph:

> 3. By an owner who is selling his interest in a premises that is a home, with,
>   i. a copy of the agreement of purchase and sale, and
>   ii. the date on which a permit authorizing occupancy or a certificate of completion and possession has been issued.

The amending legislation eliminates "home buyer" from the definition of "owner" under the Act, and adds definitions for "home buyer" and "home" (see "Amendments to the Construction Lien Act" (heading D of chapter 1)).

In its Comments on the Discussion Draft of the proposed amending legislation, the Ministry of the Attorney General stated that,

contractor regarding a particular construction project.[3] If the agreement was not in writing, the lien claimant was entitled to particulars of the terms of any oral agreement.[4] Furthermore, the lien claimant could demand information as to the state of accounts between the owner and the contractor, particularly the amount due and unpaid.[5] If the owner or his agent, either through refusal or neglect, did not comply with any such demand within a reasonable period of time, or if he knowingly falsified his reply, he was liable to the lien claimant for any loss suffered as a result.[6]

The obvious rationale for this provision was to permit the lien claimant access to important information relating to, *inter alia,* holdback and trust funds.

This right of access to information has been carried through into the *Construction Lien Act, 1983,*[7] but with the following modifications, which serve to take into account the competing principles of disclosure and confidentiality referred to above:

(a) The right of access to information has been expanded so as to permit "any person having a lien[8] or who is the beneficiary of a trust under Part II or who is a mortgagee"[9] to submit a request;

(b) The request for information may be made not only upon the owner, but upon the contractor or a subcontractor as well;[10]

(c) The "reasonable time" within which there must be compliance with any request for information is specified to mean not more than 21 days;[11]

(d) Where the request for information relates to the contract, the recipient of the request (*i.e.*, the owner or the contractor) need

---

In new home construction, activity on the site increases to ready the home for occupancy just prior to closing. Those on or near the site will be aware of when a home sale is about to close. However, some suppliers of services and materials would find it useful to determine whether a purchaser is a home buyer, when the sale is likely to be closed, and when the home is ready for occupancy. The provision will allow them to obtain this information.

[2] Although this term is not defined in the *Mechanics' Lien Act,* R.S.O. 1980, c. 261, it presumably refers only to a person who actually registered a claim for lien and not to a person merely entitled to a lien.

[3] The *Mechanics' Lien Act,* R.S.O. 1980, c. 261, s. 32(1).

[4] *Ibid.*

[5] *Ibid.*

[6] *Ibid.*

[7] See S.O. 1983, c. 6, s. 39(1).

[8] "Person having a lien" is defined to include "both a lien claimant [*i.e.,* "a person having a preserved or perfected lien": s. 1(1) 11] and a person with an unpreserved lien": s. 1(1) 18.

[9] Section 39(1).

[10] *Ibid.*

[11] *Ibid.*

only respond by supplying the names of the parties to the contract,[12] the contract price,[13] and the state of accounts between the owner and the contractor,[14] and is not obliged to produce the contract for inspection;

(e) Where the request for information relates to a particular subcontract, the recipient of the request (*i.e.,* the contractor or the subcontractor) need only respond by supplying the names of the parties to the subcontract,[15] the state of accounts between the contracting parties,[16] a statement as to whether the subcontract provides for it to be certified on completion,[17] and a statement as to whether or not it has in fact been certified as complete.[18] The subcontract need not be produced for inspection; and

(f) The recipient of the request, whether it be in respect of the contract or a subcontract, must not only disclose the existence of a labour and material payment bond, but is also obliged to produce a copy of it for inspection.[19]

If the person who is obliged to supply the requested information fails to do so, or if he "knowingly or negligently"[20] mis-states that information, he is liable to the person who requested the information for any damages which result as a consequence.[21]

In any event, the person entitled to access to information may bring a motion[22] to the court[23] at any time, irrespective of whether or not an action[24] has been commenced, for an order enforcing compliance.[25] If the

---

[12] Section 39(1) 1, i.

[13] Section 39(1) 1, ii. It is to be noted that s. 1(1) 20 defines "price" to mean
"the contract . . . price,
   i. agreed upon between the parties, or
   ii. where no specific price has been agreed upon between them, the actual value of the services or materials that have been supplied to the improvement under the contract. . .;

[14] Section 39(1) 1, iii.

[15] Section 39(1) 2, i.

[16] Section 39(1) 2, ii.

[17] Section 39(1) 2, iii.

[18] Section 39(1) 2, iv.

[19] Section 39(1) 1, iv and 39(1) 2, v.

[20] In both the *Mechanics' Lien Act* and the *Construction Lien Act, 1983,* a person who "knowingly" supplies false information is exposed to civil liability. Under the *Construction Lien Act, 1983,* though, there is an extended duty to ensure that the information supplied is in fact accurate, since negligent mis-statement also attracts liability.

[21] Section 39(5).

[22] See Precedent Nos. 9, 10 and 11.

[23] Section 52(1) dictates whether the motion should be brought before the master, the appointed local master or a local judge.

[24] "Action" means "an action under Part VII." of the Act: s. 1(1) 1.

[25] Section 39(6).

application is successful, depending upon the circumstances, the court might be inclined to award costs of the motion on a solicitor-and-client basis, given the concluding words of legislative direction in s. 39(6).

(ii) Information Regarding Substantial Performance of the Contract

Under s. 32, the contractor is obliged to publish a copy of the certificate of substantial performance once in a construction trade newspaper.[26] The actual date of publication is significant for some subcontractors, since it might possibly represent the commencement date of their 45-day lien period.[27]

In order to ensure, therefore, that information relating to the publication of the certificate is accessible, the Act provides that "any person"[28] may, in writing, request that the contractor provide advice as to the date of publication and the name of the construction trade newspaper.[29] The contractor's reply must be furnished in writing, and within a "reasonable time" of the request.[30]

Non-compliance with the request, either by refusal or neglect or by "knowingly or negligently" mis-stating information, exposes the contractor to liability to the person who requested the information for any damages which result as a consequence.[31]

In any event, the person entitled to receive the information may bring a motion[32] to the court[33] at any time, irrespective of whether or not an action has been commenced, for an order enforcing compliance.[34]

(iii) Information Regarding Payroll Records of Beneficiaries of a Workers' Trust Fund

A "workers' trust fund" is defined by the Act to mean "any trust fund maintained in whole or in part on behalf of any worker[35] on an improve-

---

[26] Section 32(1) 5.

[27] See s. 31(3)(a).

[28] It is to be noted that this right to information is available to "any person," and not only to any "person having a lien," as defined in s. 1(1) 18. A mortgagee or other encumbrancer, who is concerned about the priority of his security in relation to the liens of the trades, would therefore be entitled to the information so that he would be able to assess his position. Similarly, a bonding company might want to ascertain the lien entitlement of a particular subcontractor before honouring a claim made by that subcontractor under a labour and material payment bond.

[29] Section 39(4).

[30] *Ibid.*

[31] Section 39(5).

[32] See Precedent Nos. 6, 7 and 8.

[33] See *supra,* note 23.

[34] Section 39(6).

[35] "Worker" is defined to mean "a person employed for wages in any kind of labour": s. 1(1) 27; and "wages" are defined to mean "the money earned by a worker for work done

ment and into which any monetary supplementary benefit is payable as wages for work done by the worker in respect of the improvement."[36] "Monetary supplementary benefits" would include, for example, vacation and statutory holiday pay, supplementary unemployment benefits, welfare and training fund benefits, and pensions; and apparently could constitute as much as 30 percent of the "wages"[37] of a construction worker.[38] Therefore, "[i]t is vitally important that these interests be protected."[39]

Where, as is often the case, these benefits are payable to a workers' trust fund instead of to the construction worker directly, the trustee of the fund is subrogated to the rights of the worker with respect to those benefits.[40] Accordingly, situations will arise where the trustee will be in the position of having to pursue subrogated lien rights to protect the benefits which are payable to the fund.

So as to ensure that, in these circumstances, the trustee would have access to sufficient information to permit him to enforce his lien rights, the Act provides that he may, at any time by written request, require any contractor or subcontractor, *qua* employer, to permit him to examine the payroll records of all workers (i) who are the beneficiaries of the fund; (ii) who have supplied labour to the making of the improvement; and (iii) who are employed by the contractor or the subcontractor.[41] In this way, the trustee will be able to establish the name of each worker, the amount of time spent by each worker on a project-by-project basis, and the monetary supplementary benefits owing to each worker with respect to each "improvement" or project.

After receiving the trustee's request for information, the contractor or subcontractor is obliged to make the relevant payroll records available for inspection within a "reasonable time," which is not to exceed 21 days.[42] Presumably this would give the trustee sufficient time to collect the information required to prepare and register a claim for lien.

If the contractor or the subcontractor fails to comply with the trustee's request, the trustee is entitled to bring a motion[43] to the court[44] at any time, irrespective of whether or not an action has been commenced,

---

by time or as piece work, and includes all monetary supplementary benefits, whether provided for by statute, contract or collective bargaining agreement": s. 1(1) 26.
[36] Section 1(1) 28.
[37] See *supra*, note 35, which sets out the definition of "wages" found in s. 1(1) 25.
[38] *Report of the Attorney General's Advisory Committee on the Draft Construction Lien Act* (April 1982), at 108.
[39] *Ibid.*
[40] Section 83(2).
[41] Section 39(3).
[42] *Ibid.*
[43] See Precedent Nos. 15, 16 and 17.
[44] See *supra*, note 23.

for an order enforcing compliance.[45] Obviously such an application could possibly delay the trustee's access to the payroll records beyond the point where he could register a timely claim for lien. Accordingly, the Act also provides that non-compliance with the trustee's request, either by refusal or neglect or by "knowingly or negligently" mis-stating information, exposes the contractor or the subcontractor to liability to the trustee for any damages which result as a consequence.[46]

(iv) Information Regarding Mortgages and Vendor's Liens

Part XI of the Act establishes a scheme of priorities as between lien claimants and other encumbrancers. Under s. 80(2), the lien is given priority over a "building mortgage" (*i.e.,* a mortgage intended to secure the financing of an improvement), irrespective of when that mortgage is registered, but only to the extent of any deficiency in the holdbacks which are required to be retained by the owner. Essentially, the thrust of this provision is to secure the holdback as an interest in the premises, and to prevent that interest from being eroded by the interest charges accruing under the mortgage.

In this regard, the Attorney General's Advisory Committee commented that

> ... building mortgages enjoy the benefit of the lien claimant's work: as a result of the improvement, the mortgagee's interest will usually be secured against a property which has been enhanced in value. Therefore, it is only fair that the mortgagee's interest be partly subordinated to the liens of the suppliers to the improvement, to ensure that there will be money available to pay them for the work that they have done.[47]

A different scheme of priorities exists under the Act as between liens and non-building mortgages. Consequently, in the context of competing priorities, it is relevant to know whether or not the mortgage registered on title is a building mortgage, as well as particulars of advances and interest arrears.

Under s. 39(2), "any person having a lien[48] or any beneficiary of a trust under Part II" may, at any time by written request, require a mortgagee to provide him with

> (i) sufficient details concerning any mortgage so as to enable him to ascertain whether or not the mortgage was taken by the mort-

---

[45] Section 39(6).
[46] Section 39(5).
[47] *Report of Attorney General's Advisory Committee on the Draft Construction Lien Act* (April 1982), at 179–180.
[48] See ss. 1(1) 18 and 1(1) 11.

gagee[49] for the purposes of financing the making of the improvement;[50] and

(ii) a mortgage statement setting forth the dates and amounts of all
advances under the mortgage and the amount of the arrears in
payment, including interest arrears.[51]

In a similar fashion, an unpaid vendor may be required to provide
the person requesting the information with a statement showing the
amount secured under the agreement of purchase and sale, as well as any
arrears in payment, including interest arrears.[52]

The rationale for obliging an unpaid vendor to provide the requested
information derives from the fact that, to all intents and purposes, the
effect of a vendor's lien is the same as that of a mortgage.[53] Furthermore,
since an amount equal to the value of the consideration received by an
owner as a result of a sale constitutes trust property,[54] the information
required to be supplied by an unpaid vendor would no doubt be of interest
to a Part II trust beneficiary.

After receiving a request for information, the mortgagee or unpaid
vendor is obliged to respond within a "reasonable time," which is not to
exceed 21 days.[55] If the mortgagee or unpaid vendor refuses or neglects to
provide the requested information, or "knowingly or negligently" mis-
states that information, he would be liable to the person who made the
request for any damages which may be incurred as a result.[56]

It is to be noted, though, that the person requesting the information

---

[49] In passing, it should be noted that "subsection 2 [of s. 80] gives the lien claimants
priority only where the mortgage is taken *by the mortgagee* to secure the financing of
the improvement. Thus it is the intention of the mortgagee which is relevant in determining whether a mortgage is a building mortgage": *Report of the Attorney General's
Advisory Committee on the Draft Construction Lien Act* (April 1982), at 180 (emphasis
added).

[50] Section 39(2)(a).

[51] Section 39(2)(b).

[52] Section 39(2)(c).

[53] Section 8(6) of the *Mechanics' Lien Act* deemed an unpaid vendor, under a registered
agreement for the sale and purchase of land, to be a mortgagee for all purposes under
that Act. Although the *Construction Lien Act, 1983* does not contain a similar deeming
provision, s. 80(1) does provide that ". . . the liens arising from an improvement have
priority over all conveyances, mortgages *or other agreements affecting the owner's
interest in the premises*" (emphasis added). Furthermore, "other agreements affecting
the owner's interest in the premises" are treated in the same way, from the point of view
of priorities, as mortgages in ss. 80(3), (4) and (6), which sections, according to the
marginal notes, purport to deal respectively with "prior mortgages, prior advances,"
"prior mortgages, subsequent advances," and "general priority against subsequent
mortgages."

[54] Section 9(1).

[55] Section 39(2).

[56] Section 39(5).

is entitled to bring a motion[57] to the court[58] at any time, irrespective of whether or not an action has been commenced, for an order enforcing compliance.[59]

C. CROSS-EXAMINATION ON CLAIM FOR LIEN

As indicated above, the Act prescribes the mechanics for a person having a lien and a Part II trust beneficiary to obtain access to sufficient information to enable them to enforce their rights.

Concomitantly, an owner, a contractor, the payer of the lien claimant, and any other person named in a claim for lien[60] has the right to obtain information from the lien claimant by participating in a cross-examination of the person who verified the claim for lien[61] (*i.e.*, the person who deposed the affidavit of verification).[62]

Any such cross-examination would serve the following purposes:

(a) To support a motion[63] for an order vacating the registration of a preserved or perfected lien, and any certificate of action in respect of that lien, by the payment into court of an amount which is less than the full amount claimed as owing in the claim for lien;[64]

(b) To support a motion for an order reducing the amount paid into court previously;[65]

(c) To support a motion for an order vacating the registration of a claim for lien on the basis that the lien was not perfected within the time allowed for doing so, and that it has therefore expired;[66]

(d) To support a motion for an order vacating the registration of a claim for lien or a certificate of action, or dismissing the lien action, "upon any proper ground";[67]

(e) To establish the basis for a counterclaim[68] against the lien

---

[57] See Precedent Nos. 12, 13 and 14.

[58] See *supra*, note 23.

[59] Section 39(6).

[60] Unlike s. 42(10) of the *Mechanics' Lien Act*, which permits "[a]ny party to an action . . . or any other interested person" to apply to the court for an order authorizing a cross-examination, the *Construction Lien Act, 1983* does not expressly stipulate who would be entitled to conduct such a cross-examination.

[61] Section 40.

[62] See s. 34(6).

[63] See Precedent Nos. 20, 21 and 22.

[64] See s. 44(2).

[65] See s. 44(5).

[66] See s. 45(1).

[67] See s. 47(1).

claimant for preserving a lien which he knew or ought to have known he did not have, or which he knew or ought to have known was grossly in excess of the amount which he is actually owed;[69]

(f) To enable the owner and the contractor to obtain information which might assist them in the preparation of their defence to the action. For example, the deponent, in his testimony, might confirm that the claim for lien was registered out of time, or might acknowledge that a portion of the lien claimant's work was defective;

(g) From a tactical perspective, to enable the persons who are or will be defendants in the lien action to obtain information under oath from the lien claimant at an early stage, without exposing them to an examination of any sort; and

(h) To narrow the issues in dispute, thereby promoting a full or partial settlement.

By way of contrast with the procedures laid down under the *Mechanics' Lien Act,* the cross-examination may take place at any time,[70] irrespective of whether an action has been commenced,[71] and no authorizing order need be obtained.[72]

Only one cross-examination is permitted, but the contractor, the payer of the lien claimant, and every person named in the claim for lien who has an interest in the premises are entitled to participate in it.[73] Accordingly, the person intending to conduct the cross-examination[74] is

---

[68] See s. 57(2)(a).

[69] See s. 35.

[70] Section 40(1). By way of comparison, see *Re Pecco Cranes (Canada) Ltd. et al.,* [1973] 3 O.R. 737 (M.C.), which held that, under the *Mechanics' Lien Act,* the master had no jurisdiction to compel the deponent of an affidavit verifying a claim for lien to submit to cross-examination under the affidavit prior to an action being commenced or a reference being ordered.

[71] *Ibid.*

[72] Section 40(1). By way of comparison, see s. 42(10) of the *Mechanics' Lien Act.*

[73] Section 40(2). Presumably this is to avoid multiple cross-examinations of a single deponent, thereby preserving the spirit of the legislation of attempting to provide an inexpensive and expedient remedy. *Quaere* whether a subcontractor, who is not the payer of the lien claimant, who has failed to preserve his lien within the time for so doing, but who is named in the claim for lien registered by his sub-subcontractor, is entitled to participate in the cross-examination of the lien claimant, given the fact that he, the subcontractor, would not have an "interest in the premises."

[74] In some cases, the mortgagee would not be named in a claim for lien, but might nevertheless be named as a defendant in the lien action. If, in those instances, the owner wishes to conduct a cross-examination, he, the owner, is not obliged to serve notice upon the mortgagee (see s. 40(3)), and the mortgagee is apparently not entitled to participate in the cross-examination (see s. 40(2)).

obliged to give at least seven days' notice, presumably by means of a special examiner's appointment,[75] to:

    (i) the person to be examined or his solicitor;[76]

    (ii) every other person named in the claim for lien as having an interest in the premises;[77]

    (iii) the contractor;[78] and

    (iv) the payer of the lien claimant.[79]

Section 40(4) provides that the Supreme Court Rules of Practice pertaining to examinations apply, with necessary modifications, to cross-examinations.[80]

---

[75] See s. 40(4).

[76] Section 40(3)(a).

[77] Section 40(3)(b).

[78] Section 40(3)(c).

[79] Section 40(3)(d).

[80] See Rules 326 through 345 of the Supreme Court of Ontario Rules of Practice, R.R.O. 1980, Reg. 540, as amended.

Chapter 7

Discharge of Preserved or Perfected Liens

A. DISTINCTION BETWEEN "DISCHARGING" AND "VACATING" A LIEN

Bulletin No. 82029, which was issued on December 31, 1982 by the Property Rights Division, Legal and Survey Standards Branch, of the Ministry of Consumer and Commercial Relations, instructs all Land Registrars in Ontario to note the distinction between "discharging" and "vacating" a lien.

A lien is "discharged" only when the lien claimant's claim has been satisfied, whereas a lien is "vacated" (*i.e.,* the registration of the claim for lien is vacated) usually where the lien is intended to survive, but no longer as a charge against the premises.

For a subsequent purchaser, it is of no consequence whether a lien has been discharged or vacated, since either will serve to eliminate the encumbrance from title.

If the registration of a claim for lien is vacated, say, by reason of a payment into court, the lien claimant would nevertheless still be entitled to notice of any subsequent proceedings[1] in respect of the premises. On the other hand, if a lien is discharged, the lien claimant would have no further interest in the premises since his claim has presumably been satisfied, and he would therefore not be entitled to notice of further court proceedings.

B. DISCHARGING A LIEN

A preserved or perfected lien, where it attaches to the premises, may be discharged by the registration of a release,[2] in the prescribed form,[3] against the title to the premises.[4]

---

[1] *E.g.,* notice of settlement meeting (see s. 62(2)); notice of trial (see s. 62(4)).

[2] By way of comparison, under the *Mechanics' Lien Act,* R.S.O. 1980, c. 261, a claim for lien could be discharged by the registration of a "receipt acknowledging payment" (s. 29(1)), generally referred to as a "Discharge of Lien."

[3] See Form 14 prescribed by O. Reg. 159/83 filed March 18, 1983, under the *Construction Lien Act, 1983.* It is to be noted that, where the lien claimant is not a corporation, the release must be verified by an affidavit of a subscribing witness

A general lien,[5] which has been preserved[6] or perfected,[7] may be discharged against any one or more of the premises that are subject to it, without affecting its application to any other premises to which it applies, by registering an appropriately drawn release only against the title to the premises being released.[8] For example, if a claim for a general lien is registered against the title to five lots, and the owner wishes to sell one of the lots, he would attempt to solicit a release from the lien claimant with respect to that particular lot, in exchange for payment of a portion of the monies owing. On closing, the owner/vendor might direct the purchaser to present two certified cheques — one drawn to the order of the lien claimant, which would be exchanged for a release, in registrable form, with respect to that lot; and the second drawn to the order of the owner/vendor, representing the balance of the sale proceeds.

A lien may also be discharged by court order, "upon any proper ground and subject to any terms and conditions that the court considers appropriate in the circumstances."[9] Any such order would have to include a description of the premises sufficient for registration purposes, and a reference to the registration number of the lien being discharged.[10] Once the order has been obtained, a certified copy of it may be registered on the title to the premises.[11]

The discharge of any lien, whether by release or court order, is irrevocable and the discharged lien can not be revived.[12] However, if the lien claimant whose lien was discharged continues to supply services or materials to the improvement after the date of preservation of his

---

(s. 41(1)(a)). Where the lien claimant is a corporation, *quaere* whether the release must be sealed with the corporate seal. Neither the Act nor Form 14 makes any reference to the requirement of a seal. By way of comparison, s. 29(1)(b) of the *Mechanics' Lien Act* expressly required the affixation of a corporate seal to the "receipt acknowledging payment." In practical terms, one should expect that Land Registrars will probably not be prepared to accept unsealed releases of corporate lien claimants for registration.

[4] Section 41(1)(a).
[5] See s. 20.
[6] See s. 34(7).
[7] See s. 36(5).
[8] Section 42.
[9] Section 47(1)(a). It is unclear when one would apply for a discharging order under s. 47(1)(a), and when one would apply for a vacating order under s. 47(1)(b). Presumably payment to the lien claimant would not be made unless there were reciprocal arrangements to secure a release in exchange. However, a situation may exist where the lien claimant's claim would be satisfied by his successful pursuit of ordinary collection proceedings concurrently with his prosecution of the lien action. In that situation, since the lien claimant's claim would have been satisfied, an order discharging the lien would be more appropriate than an order vacating the registration of the claim for lien.
[10] Section 49.
[11] *Ibid.*
[12] Section 48.

discharged lien, he would be entitled to preserve a fresh lien for that additional supply.[13]

C. WITHDRAWING A NOTICE OF LIEN

So long as he has not received a written notice of a lien,[14] a payer[15] may, without jeopardy, make payment, on account of his contract or subcontract, to the extent of 90 percent of the price[16] of the services or materials that have been supplied under that contract or subcontract.[17] Once he has received a written notice of lien, though, he must retain an amount sufficient to satisfy the lien, in addition to the holdbacks required by Part IV of the Act.[18]

If the claimant sees fit not to pursue his lien (*e.g.,* where he receives payment of the amount owing to him), he may voluntarily withdraw his claim by giving a withdrawal in writing[19] to the person to whom the written notice of a lien was given. Where this occurs, the payer given the written withdrawal would no longer be required to retain an amount sufficient to satisfy that lien,[20] although his holdback obligations would in no way be affected.

If the claimant does not gratuitously withdraw his notice of lien, and it is clear that he has failed to preserve his lien rights in time or that he is not entitled to a lien, a motion may be brought[21] for a declaration that the lien has expired, or that the written notice of the lien shall no longer bind the person to whom it was given.[22]

D. POSTPONEMENT OF LIEN

A preserved or a perfected lien may be postponed to the interest of another encumbrancer, such as a mortgagee, by the registration on the

---

[13] *Ibid.* This is consistent with the provision, contained in s. 34(5)(d), to the effect that a claim for lien shall set out only "the amount claimed in respect of services or materials *that have been supplied*" (emphasis added). If the preserved lien which was discharged only claimed an amount for services or materials supplied to the date of preservation, then it seems appropriate that a lien claimant should be entitled to preserve a fresh lien for services or materials supplied after the date of preservation of the original lien.

[14] See s. 1(1) 29 and Precedent No. 18.

[15] See s. 1(1) 16.

[16] See s. 1(1) 20.

[17] Section 24(1).

[18] Section 24(2).

[19] Section 41(2).

[20] *Ibid.*

[21] Section 52(1) dictates whether the motion is brought before a master, a local master or a local judge.

[22] Section 47(1)(c).

title to the premises of a notice of postponement[23] in the prescribed form.[24]

This will serve to facilitate the flow of funds on a construction project when further mortgage advances are intended to be made, or when re-financing is required.

In exchange for the postponement, the lien claimant may possibly be paid a portion of his claim out of the advance or the monies received on a re-financing, particularly where the reason for non-payment related to cash flow problems rather than to defective work.

The encumbrancer in whose favour the postponement is made will generally[25] have priority over the postponed lien,[26] and, where an advance is made and no written notice of a lien has been received, over any unpreserved lien.[27]

E. VACATING A LIEN

(i) Vacating a Lien By Payment into Court

Circumstances may arise where an owner wishes to remove the claims for liens registered against the title to his property so as to pave the way for a mortgage advance, or perhaps to facilitate a sale of the premises. Without admitting any liability, and without acknowledging the validity of those liens, he is entitled[28] to obtain a court order vacating the registration of all claims for liens by making a payment into court or by posting security in lieu thereof.

Where such an order is obtained, the liens would cease to attach to the premises, the holdbacks and any other amounts subject to a charge under s. 21 of the Act, and would instead become a charge against the amount paid into court or the security posted.[29] In effect, the monies paid in or the security posted would take the place of the premises.

As a result, the owner would be in a better position to deal with the premises in the manner in which he wishes, and the flow of funds down the construction pyramid to the trades could continue, without prejudice to the lien claimant's right to realize upon his claim.

Under the *Mechanics' Lien Act*,[30] the amount that a lien claimant

---

[23] Section 43.
[24] See Form 15 prescribed by O. Reg. 159/83 filed March 18, 1983, under the *Construction Lien Act, 1983.*
[25] This statement is qualified by the provision contained in s. 80(8) that "nothing in this subsection affects the priority of the liens under subsections (2) and (5)".
[26] Section 80(8)(a).
[27] Section 80(8)(b).
[28] Section 44(1) is expressed in mandatory, and not permissive, terms.
[29] Section 44(6).
[30] R.S.O. 1980, c. 261.

was entitled to recover for the costs of an action was limited to a maximum of 25 percent of the total amount found to be due and owing to him.[31] Accordingly, when an owner sought to vacate the registration of a claim for lien by a payment into court,[32] the common practice was for him to pay in the amount of the claim of the lien claimant plus 25 percent for costs.

The same type of provision, with some minor differences, is contained in the *Construction Lien Act, 1983*.[33] Where a lien attaches to the premises, any person may bring a motion[34] to the court,[35] without notice to any other person, for an order vacating the registration of a claim for lien and any certificate of action in respect of that lien. The person bringing the motion must pay into court, or must post security[36] in an amount equal to, the total of the full amount claimed as owing in the claim for lien;[37] plus the lesser of $50,000, or 25 percent of the amount claimed,[38] for costs.[39] If, in a specific instance, that amount is felt to be unreasonable (*i.e.,* excessive), the motion may be framed so as to request leave for the payment into court or the posting of security in an amount "that the court determines to be reasonable in the circumstances to satisfy the lien."[40]

Where there is a general lien[41] registered against several lots, and the owner wishes to vacate the lien with respect to one lot only (*i.e.,* to facilitate a sale), the court may apportion the general lien between the various lots, and may permit the owner to make a payment into court or to post security in an amount which is less than "the full amount claimed as owing in the claim for lien" (as contemplated by s. 44(1)(c)).[42]

Where more than one motion to vacate is made, the court may consolidate all of them, and may require that the amount paid into court

---

[31] *Ibid.,* s. 49(2).

[32] *Ibid.,* s. 29(2)(a).

[33] See s. 44(1).

[34] See Precedent Nos. 20, 21 and 22.

[35] Section 52(1) dictates whether the motion is brought to a master, a local master or a local judge.

[36] *E.g.,* letter of credit or bond. It is to be noted that the security which is to be posted with the court must be payable to the order of the Accountant of the Supreme Court of Ontario, and must be irrevocable. If the security purports to be valid for a period of one year from its date (which is often the case with letters of credit issued by chartered banks), it must contain a provision for annual automatic renewals. See Precedent No. 19 for a sample letter of credit.

[37] The amount claimed as owing in the claim for lien is limited to "the amount claimed in respect of services or materials that have been supplied" (s. 34(5)(d)), and is not to include any component for interest (s. 14(2)).

[38] *Ibid.*

[39] Section 44(1).

[40] Section 44(2).

[41] See s. 20.

[42] Section 44(4).

or the security posted be adequate to satisfy all the liens that are the subject of each of the motions.[43]

The following step-by-step procedure for obtaining a vacating order in the Judicial District of York is generally observed in the other counties and districts in Ontario as well:

1. After the requisite documents are prepared,[44] an application is made to the *ex parte*[45] master in Toronto, who will review the affidavit of search and the certified cheque or the security which is to be posted. If money is to be paid in, the cheque should be made payable to the order of "The Canadian Imperial Bank of Commerce." If a bond or letter of credit is to be posted, it should be made payable to "The Accountant of the Supreme Court of Ontario." If everything is in order, the master will execute a "fiat," authorizing the Accountant to accept the payment in or the security.

2. The applicant would then attend at the office of the Accountant,[46] file the fiat, post the security, and obtain the Accountant's receipt. If money is to be paid in, the Accountant would provide the applicant with a three-part Direction, which is to be taken to the Accountant's bank,[47] along with the certified cheque. The bank teller would then stamp the third part of the Direction, thereby acknowledging receipt.

3. The applicant would then return to the master and arrange to have the master sign an Order vacating the registration of the claim(s) for lien(s) and certificate(s) of action, if any.

4. The Order, having been signed, would be entered, and a certified copy of it would then be registered against the title to the premises.[48]

Where an order is obtained vacating the registration of a claim for lien before that lien is perfected, the lien claimant may nevertheless

---

[43] Section 44(8).

[44] See Precedent Nos. 20, 21 and 22.

[45] Where security is to be posted, the practice in the master's office in Toronto is to require the motion to be brought on notice to the lien claimant. The rationale is that, if a bond or a letter of credit is to replace the lien claimant's interest in the land, he should at least have the opportunity to make representations as to the form and substance of the replacement security.

[46] 123 Edward Street, 2nd Floor, Toronto, Ontario.

[47] In Toronto, it is the head office of the Canadian Imperial Bank of Commerce (as at the date of this writing).

[48] Section 49.

proceed with his action[49] to enforce his claim against the amount paid into court or the security posted, but he need not register a certificate of action.[50]

The amount paid into court or the security posted is subject to the claims of all persons having a lien,[51] and shall be distributed among all lien claimants[52] in accordance with the priorities created by s. 82 of the Act.[53] No person having a lien is entitled to a "first charge,"[54] or to any priority whatever, over another member of the same class.[55]

Any amount that is realized in a lien action (*e.g.*, the net proceeds realized upon a sale of all or part of the owner's interest in the premises; and rental payments received by a court-appointed trustee) are to be pooled into a common fund with any amount paid into court or any security posted, and is to be distributed among all lien claimants in accordance with the priorities created by s. 82.[56]

If it appears at some stage of the action that the money or the security standing in court to the credit of the lien action is more than is required (perhaps, for example, due to the fact that a settlement with one of several

---

[49] Despite the fact that his lien is vacated by, say, a payment into court, a lien claimant must nevertheless perfect his lien within the time prescribed for doing so. As s. 36(3)(a) provides (emphasis added):

    36(3) A lien claimant perfects his preserved lien,

      (a) where the lien attaches to the premises, when he commences an action to enforce his lien and, *except where an order to vacate the registration of his lien is made,* he registers a certificate of action in the prescribed form on the title of the premises;

[50] Sections 36(3)(a) and 44(9) 1.

[51] "Person having a lien" is defined to include both a "lien claimant" and a person with an unpreserved lien: s. 1(1) 18. Persons with unpreserved liens would lose their interest in the amount paid into court or the security posted, though, if they were to fail to preserve and perfect their liens within the time for doing so.

[52] "Lien claimant" is defined to mean a person having a preserved or perfected lien: s. 1(1) 11.

[53] Section 44(9) 2.

[54] Reference to a "first charge" derives from s. 29(4) of the *Mechanics' Lien Act,* R.S.O. 1980, c. 261, which provides (emphasis added):

    29(4) Any money so paid into court, or any bond or other security for securing the like amount and satisfactory to the judge or officer, takes the place of the property discharged and is subject to the claims of every person who has at the time of the application a subsisting claim for lien or given notice of the claim under subsection 12(7) or section 15 to the same extent as if the money, bond or other security was realized by a sale of the property in an action to enforce the lien, *but such amount as the judge or officer finds to be owing to the person whose lien has been so vacated is a first charge upon the money, bond or other security.*

Also see Kenneth Prehogan, "Distribution of Monies Paid Into Court in Mechanics' Lien Actions" (1979-81), 2 *Advocates' Quarterly* 131.

[55] Section 82(1)(a). Also see s. 81.

[56] Section 44(9) 3.

lien claimants has been concluded), a motion may be brought, upon notice to such persons as the court may require,[57] for an order reducing the amount paid into court and providing that a portion of the monies in court be paid out of court to the person entitled;[58] or alternatively for an order reducing the amount of security posted with the court and providing that the security be delivered up to the person who posted it for cancellation or substitution.[59]

(ii) Vacating a Lien Which Was Not Preserved in Time

Section 31 of the Act sets out the relevant time periods within which a lien must be preserved. Where a lien claimant fails to preserve his lien within the time allowed for doing so, his lien will expire.[60] The registration of his claim for lien, though, would not be expunged automatically from the title to the premises. In these circumstances, any person[61] may bring a motion[62] to the court,[63] without notice to any other person, for an order declaring that the lien has expired and that the registration of the claim for lien be vacated.[64]

---

[57] All persons having an interest in either the premises or the money/security in court should be served with notice, since their interests may be affected. In most circumstances, it would be prudent to serve all persons who would ordinarily be served with a notice of settlement meeting or a notice of trial (see ss. 62(2) and (4)). Section 44(5) does not specify whether the notice must be "served" or "given". If the latter were to be the case, then presumably the notice may be sent by certified or registered mail in accordance with s. 89(1). Upon the return of the motion, though, the court may see fit to adjourn the matter so as to permit personal service or service upon a solicitor of record, as the case may be. Inasmuch as a person with an unpreserved lien would have an interest in any monies paid into court or any security posted (see s. 44(9) 2), and since those persons would be difficult to ascertain, a court might be particularly cautious in ordering a reduction of the monies or security standing in court.

[58] Section 44(5)(a).

[59] Section 44(5)(b).

[60] Section 31(1).

[61] Presumably the reference to "any person" in s. 45(1)(a) is not limited to those persons who would have an interest in the premises. A contractor, for example, might be inclined to seek a vacating order with respect to the lien of a subcontractor so as to attempt to free up the flow of funds down the construction pyramid. The registration of the subcontractor's claim for lien might have prevented the owner from making any further payments to the contractor, and the order declaring that the lien has expired and that its registration be vacated would be sufficient to provide justification to the owner to release further funds.

[62] See Precedent Nos. 23, 24 and 25.

[63] Section 52(1) dictates whether the motion is made to a master, a local master or a local judge.

[64] Section 45(1).

Such an order will be granted[65] upon proof[66] that the lien has not been preserved within the time allowed,[67] and upon production of,

(a) a certificate of search under the *Land Titles Act,*[68]
(b) a registrar's abstract under the *Registry Act,*

together with a certified copy of the claim for lien.[69]

Where the court declares that the lien has expired, it will also order that any monies which were paid into court, in respect of that lien, be returned to the person who made the payment in,[70] or, where applicable, that any security which was posted be cancelled.[71]

(iii) Vacating a Lien Which Was Not Perfected in Time or At All

The wording of s. 45(1) is ambiguous in that it refers simply to a lien which is not perfected within the time allowed for doing so. For the purposes of bringing a motion for a vacating order, a distinction should be drawn between a lien which is never perfected, and one which is perfected late.

Where a lien is preserved but not perfected, a motion to vacate the lien would be brought pursuant to the authority contained in s. 45(1).[72] As may be noted, that section refers only to the vacating of the registration of a claim for lien, and makes no reference to any certificate of action which may be registered in respect of that lien. The inference to be drawn

---

65 Section 45(1) is expressed in mandatory, rather than permissive, terms. However, the fact that the court must be given "proof" that the lien has not been preserved within the time allowed would seem to imply a measure of discretion.

66 Proof could take the form of affidavits by persons who could testify as to facts which would demonstrate that the lien was not preserved in time. For example, the construction site superintendent or the architect might be sufficiently familiar with the lien claimant's work schedule and attendances at the site to be able to state that the lien was preserved after the expiry of the 45-day lien period. Even better proof might be in the form of admissions made by the lien claimant upon his being cross-examined under oath on his claim for lien (see s. 40(1)). The transcript of the cross-examination may be filed with the court and read in on the motion.

67 Section 45(1)(b).

68 R.S.O. 1980, c. 230. According to inquiries made with the Registrar of Land Titles in Toronto, a "certificate of search" is a certified copy of the title abstract.

69 Section 45(1)(c).

70 Section 45(3)(a).

71 Section 45(3)(b).

72 For a review of the procedure and sample precedents regarding motions brought pursuant to s. 45(1), see the previous sub-heading in this chapter, "Vacating a Lien Which Was Not Preserved in Time."

from this is that s. 45(1) has no application where the lien claimant purports to perfect his lien after the time for doing so has expired.

Where a lien is perfected out of time (*i.e.,* late), the authority for vacating its registration is contained in s. 47(1)(b), "upon any proper ground,"[73] which section clearly provides for the vacating of the registration of both the claim for lien and certificate of action.

(iv) Vacating a Lien "Upon Any Proper Ground"

Section 47(1) of the Act authorizes the court,[74] upon motion,[75] to exercise its discretion[76] in ordering that the registration of a claim for lien and/or a certificate of action be vacated,[77] and that the lien action be dismissed,[78] "upon any proper ground and subject to any terms and conditions that the court considers appropriate in the circumstances."[79]

Obvious examples where the court would grant a vacating order would be in circumstances where the claim being asserted is not the proper subject-matter of a lien (*e.g.,* where the claim can not be said to relate to the supply of services or materials to an improvement),[80] or where the claimant is clearly not entitled to a lien (*e.g.,* an architect).[81] However, unless the issue of entitlement is clear and unequivocal, it is doubtful that the court would grant the order. Rather, the determination of the issue would most likely be adjourned so that it could be dealt with at trial.

In addition to the foregoing examples, it is suggested that the court may also grant a vacating order where a lien claimant purports to perfect his lien after the time for doing so has expired.[82] However, since s. 47(1) affords wide discretion in dealing with these matters, one would expect that the court would be reluctant to grant a vacating order and to dismiss an action, and thereby try the action on its merits at an interlocutory stage,

---

[73] For a review of the procedure and sample precedents regarding motions brought pursuant to s. 47(1)(b), see the next sub-heading in this chapter, "Vacating a Lien 'Upon Any Proper Ground.' "

[74] Section 52(1) dictates whether the motion is made to a master, a local master or a local judge.

[75] See Precedent Nos. 26, 27 and 28.

[76] Section 47(1) is expressed in permissive, rather than mandatory, terms. This is to be contrasted with the mandatory direction contained in s. 45(1). See, however, note 65, *supra.*

[77] Section 47(1)(b).

[78] Section 47(1)(d).

[79] Section 47(1).

[80] See s. 14(1).

[81] See s. 3(3).

[82] See the previous sub-heading in this chapter, "Vacating a Lien Which Was Not Perfected In Time or At All," for a discussion of this point.

unless the evidence that the lien was perfected out of time was over-whelming.

On any motion to vacate, the court would no doubt have to give full consideration to the view that affidavit evidence and examination transcripts, characteristically relied upon on motions, are less persuasive than the *viva voce* testimony given at trial, and that an order before trial, which finally disposes of the action on its merits, would deprive the lien claimant of his day in court.

Where a court does see fit to vacate the registration of a certificate of action, and where there are other liens sheltering under it, the court shall give directions in respect of the continuation of the lien action.[83] In this regard, it is to be noted that the validity of the perfection of a sheltered lien does not depend upon the validity, proper preservation or perfection of the lien under which it is sheltered;[84] although the sheltered lien claimant would be entitled to continue the action only as against the defendants named, and only for the relief claimed, in the statement of claim under which it is sheltered.[85]

(v) Vacating a Perfected Lien for Want of Prosecution

At any time after all statements of defence have been delivered, or the time for their delivery has expired, any party to the lien action may bring a motion to have a day, time and place fixed for the trial of the action.[86]

If no trial date is fixed or if the lien action is not set down for trial within two years of the date of the commencement of the action which perfected that lien,[87] the lien would expire.[88]

As the Attorney General's Advisory Committee on the Draft *Construction Lien Act* commented,

> The Committee believes that it is not unreasonable to require lien claimants to proceed expeditiously with their actions. The two year period provided under this section is a reasonable balancing of interests. It provides lien claimants with sufficient time to prepare their actions and bring them to trial. At the same time, it protects the interests of owners from stale lien claims that are registered on the title to their property. It must be remembered that the lien encumbers the title of the owner's property. Such an encumbrance may be a great burden to him.[89]

---

[83] Section 47(2).

[84] Section 36(4) 2.

[85] Section 36(4) 3.

[86] Section 62(1).

[87] If A's lien was perfected by sheltering under the statement of claim of another lien claimant, B, then the two-year period would obviously commence to run from the date of the commencement of B's action.

[88] Section 37(1).

[89] *Report of the Attorney General's Advisory Committee on the Draft Construction Lien Act* (April 1982), at 102-103.

Where a perfected lien has expired for want of prosecution, any person may bring a motion[90] to the court,[91] without notice to any other person,[92] for an order declaring that the lien has expired, dismissing the lien action without costs,[93] and vacating the registration of both the claim for lien and certificate of action.

If the court dismisses the lien action, it will also order that any monies which were paid into court, in respect of that action, be returned to the person who made the payment in,[94] or, where applicable, that any security which was posted be cancelled.[95]

(vi) Registration of Vacating Order

Any order declaring that a lien has expired, or vacating the registration of a claim for lien or certificate of action, would have to include a description of the premises sufficient for registration purposes and a reference to the registration number of every instrument being vacated.[96] Once the order has been obtained, a certified copy of it may be registered on the title to the premises.[97]

It might be noted, in passing, that an application under the *Land Titles Act* to amend the register should be made in Form 15, O. Reg. 75/82, and an affidavit that the order is in full force and effect and that it affects the land, as required by s. 15(2) of the regulation, together with a copy of the order, should accompany the application.[98]

---

[90] See Precedent Nos. 29, 30 and 31.

[91] Section 52(1) dictates whether the motion is made to a master, a local master or a local judge.

[92] Section 46(3).

[93] Section 46(3) provides:

> 46(3) A motion under subsection (1) or (2) may be brought without notice, but no order as to costs in the action may be made upon the motion unless notice of that motion was given to the person against whom the order for costs is sought.

[94] Section 46(4)(a).

[95] Section 46(4)(b).

[96] Section 49.

[97] *Ibid.*

[98] See Bulletin No. 82029 (December 31, 1982), issued by the Property Rights Division, Legal and Survey Standards Branch, Ministry of Consumer and Commercial Relations.

Chapter 8
Extraordinary Remedies

A. APPOINTMENT OF TRUSTEE

(i) Generally

Inasmuch as persons who supply services or materials to a construction project are entitled to a lien upon the interest of the owner in the premises,[1] it would be in their best interests to ensure that the premises are protected, physically and otherwise, in the event that the owner should abandon his obligations.

The typical problem arises where, due to cost overruns or inadequate financing, the owner sees fit to abandon the project prior to completion, to the prejudice of the mortgage lender and the trades. No further mortgage funds are advanced, the owner is nowhere to be found, and all work comes to an immediate halt. If the winter season is approaching, the elements would pose a serious threat to the physical integrity of the partially constructed and perhaps unheated premises. Exposed foundation walls could crack, or, assuming a more advanced state of construction, the heating and plumbing system could be seriously damaged, thereby diminishing the value of the premises and concurrently increasing the costs of completion.

Furthermore, partially constructed vacant buildings tend to attract vandals and must be protected against theft and damage. Consideration must also be given to insurance coverage, since the owner's failure to provide for adequate and continuous coverage could cause the mortgagee and the lien claimants to lose a substantial part of their security.[2]

Part IX of the Act is meant to deal with those types of potential problems referred to above by providing the machinery for the appointment of a trustee to secure, protect and perhaps even sell the premises.

Under s. 70, "[a]ny person having a lien,[3] or any other person having

---

[1] Section 14.
[2] Section 85 deals with the distribution of insurance proceeds where the premises are destroyed in whole or in part, and provides that those proceeds "shall take the place of the premises so destroyed."
[3] A "person having a lien" is defined so as to include "both a lien claimant [*i.e.*, "a person having a preserved or perfected lien": s. 1(1) 11] and a person with an unpreserved lien": s. 1(1) 18.

an interest in the premises"[4] is given the right to apply[5] to the court,[6] at any time,[7] for the appointment of a trustee. The court may, but does not usually, require a trustee to post security; but would no doubt set financial and other parameters within which the trustee would be bound to act.[8] The fact of court supervision would ensure that the actions of the trustee would be for the benefit of all parties, and, more significantly, would protect both the trades and the trustee from any subsequent claim by the owner that, for example, the preservation costs were excessive, or that there had been an improvident sale.

(ii) Powers of Trustee

"Subject to the supervision and direction of the court,"[9] the trustee has authority:

(a) to act as a receiver and manager,[10] with power to collect rents and profits;[11]

(b) to mortgage, sell[12] or lease all or part of the premises,[13] subject to the *Planning Act*[14] and the approval of the court;[15]

---

[4] Persons having an interest in the premises would include, *inter alia,* mortgagees, persons who have registered a Notice of Security Interest under the *Personal Property Security Act,* R.S.O. 1980, c. 375, a purchaser under an agreement of purchase and sale, an execution creditor of the owner, etc. Section 1(1) 9 of the Act defines "interest in the premises" to mean:

. . . an estate or interest of any nature, and includes a statutory right given or reserved to the Crown to enter any lands or premises belonging to any person or public authority for the purpose of doing any work, construction, repair or maintenance in, upon, through, over or under any lands or premises;

[5] See Precedent Nos. 32, 33 and 34. It is to be noted that under the Act an "application" has been differentiated from a "motion" (see ss. 52(1) and (2)(c)). In this regard, see "Originating Applications;" "Interlocutory Motions Made Prior to the Commencement of an Action;" and "Interlocutory Motions Made Subsequent to the Commencement of an Action" (headings F(ii), (iii) and (iv) respectively of Chapter 9).

[6] It appears that an application for the appointment of a trustee is an originating application and may only be made to a Justice of the Supreme Court or a local judge: s. 52(2)(c).

[7] The fact that a person with an unpreserved lien is given the right to apply for the appointment of a trustee would imply that the application may be made at any time.

[8] Section 70(2) provides that the specified powers of the trustee are "[s]ubject to the supervision and direction of the court."

[9] Section 70(2).

[10] Section 70(2)(a).

[11] The Attorney General's Advisory Committee was of the view that the power of a receiver to collect rents and profits is included within the power of the trustee to "manage" the premises: see *Report of the Attorney General's Advisory Committee on the Draft Construction Lien Act* (April 1982), at 166–167.

[12] Section 70(4) provides that the court may direct that any interest in the premises may be offered by the trustee for sale subject to any mortgage, charge, interest or other encum-

(c) to complete or partially complete construction;[16]

(d) to take appropriate steps for the preservation of the premises,[17] such as, for example, posting a security guard to protect against vandalism, and ensuring that the premises are heated during the winter months; and

(e) to take such other steps as are appropriate in the circumstances.[18]

In order to carry out his authority, especially if he intends to secure the premises or to complete construction, the trustee may be required to borrow funds and may be obliged to provide the lender with some form of security such as an additional mortgage against the title to the premises. So as to facilitate these borrowings and to protect the lender's security, the Act provides that the interest in the premises acquired by the lender (*i.e.*, the mortgage) takes full priority, to the extent of the amount advanced, over every lien existing[19] at the date of the trustee's appointment.[20] In addition, "the amount received is not subject to any lien existing at the date of the trustee's appointment,"[21] since the reason for granting such a mortgage would be to acquire the funds necessary to complete the improvement.[22] Since the date of the trustee's appointment appears to be pivotal insofar as this priority issue is concerned, the lender would no doubt want to subsearch the title to the premises at the time of the advance to ensure that no liens were registered at any time after the date the trustee was appointed which might take priority over the mortgage.

All liens constitute a charge against any monies recovered by the trustee in the exercise of his powers (*i.e.*, rents, profits, and sale proceeds).[23] However, that charge is subject to the priority of the security

---

brance. This means that the trustee may petition the court for approval of a sale subject to existing financing, or financing that was put in place by the trustee for the purpose of funding completion of the improvement, or new financing arranged by either the trustee or the purchaser.

[13] Section 70(5) provides that the court may make any order that may be required in order to complete any mortgage, lease or sale transaction entered into by the trustee. See Precedent No. 35 by way of example.

[14] R.S.O. 1980, c. 379. Particular reference should be made to s. 29 of the *Planning Act*.

[15] Section 70(2)(a).

[16] Section 70(2)(b).

[17] Section 70(2)(c).

[18] Section 70(2)(d).

[19] It is to be noted that a person's lien comes into existence, or "arises," and takes effect when he first supplies services or materials to the improvement: s. 15.

[20] Section 80(7)(a).

[21] Section 80(7)(b).

[22] See *Report of the Attorney General's Advisory Committee on the Draft Construction Lien Act* (April 1982), at 186.

[23] Section 70(3).

granted to the lender, in the circumstances referred to in the preceding paragraph, as well as the trustee's reasonable business expenses and management costs.[24]

B. LABOUR AND MATERIAL PAYMENT BONDS

(i) Generally

The rather substantial financial risks inherent at every level in the construction industry are intended to be minimized by the use of bonds. Bonds are commonly entered into for the purpose of providing financial security for tender bids (bid bonds); to protect an owner in the event of default by the contractor (performance bonds); or to secure payment to the trades (labour and material payment bonds).[25]

The fundamental obligation embodied in a labour and material payment bond is that, if the person primarily liable (*i.e.,* the "principal") to pay the trades for labour and materials fails to do so, the bonding company (*i.e.,* the "surety") will entertain claims made on the bond. This general statement, though, is subject to three important qualifications:

1. A labour and material payment bond is a bilateral contract of surety-ship between the principal and the surety; and the trades, who are the potential claimants and the intended beneficiaries, are not parties to it. That being the case, the rather important issue arises as to whether unpaid trades have a cause of action against the surety for payment under the bond to which they are not privy.

Under the authority of a number of English and Canadian cases,[26] it can generally be stated that only the parties to a contract may sue upon it, even though, in the facts under consideration here, the trades, as third party beneficiaries, would have a direct interest in the performance of the contract.[27]

Courts have attempted to deal with this problem by construing the contract as creating a trust, and by then permitting the third party beneficiary, as *cestui que trust*, to sue.[28] Such an approach was recently

---

[24] *Ibid.*

[25] See Precedent No. 66.

[26] *Dunlop Pneumatic Tyre Co. Ltd. v. Selfridge & Co. Ltd.,* [1915] A.C. 847, [1914–15] All E.R. Rep. 333 (H.L.); *Scruttons Ltd. v. Midland Silicones Ltd.,* [1962] A.C. 446, [1962] 1 All E.R. 1; *Greenwood Shopping Plaza Ltd. v. Beattie et al.,* [1980] 2 S.C.R. 228, 39 N.S.R. (2d) 119, 71 A.P.R. 119, 111 D.L.R. (3d) 257, 32 N.R. 163, 10 B.L.R. 236, [1980] I.L.R. 4732.

[27] As will be noted later in this chapter, s. 71 purports to remedy this problem by creating a cause of action for payment on the bond.

applied by Mr. Justice R.E. Holland in a 1980 decision of the Supreme Court of Ontario in *Johns-Manville Can. Inc. et al. v. John Carlo Ltd. et al.*[29] That action was based upon a claim for payment by a subcontractor against both the contractor, on the subcontract, and the surety, on the labour and material payment bond. The headnote of the trial decision speaks for itself:

> A labour and material [payment] bond giving rights in certain circumstances to unpaid suppliers of labour and materials to a construction project, and providing that a claimant may sue on the bond "as a beneficiary of the trust herein provided for", evinces a sufficient intention to create a trust entitling an unpaid claimant to sue on the bond even though not a party to it.[30]

In that case, the bond itself spoke in terms of the claimant being a "beneficiary of the trust" which allowed the court to come to the decision that it did. However, that wording is not found in all such bonds (particularly those entered into after the *Johns-Manville* decision was handed down), and it is therefore doubtful that that decision can be categorically relied upon in every instance. Accordingly, it remains to be a question of fact and construction as to whether a particular labour and material payment bond creates a trust.

Despite the fact that legal arguments do exist which would support a surety's assertion that coverage ought to be denied, sureties do in fact appear to honour their obligations notwithstanding, so long as there has been compliance with all of the terms and conditions set forth in the bond. If they were to do otherwise, their industry would lose its credibility, and labour and material payment bonds, if unenforceable, would become a thing of the past. So of course would the bond premiums. A view on the reliability of sureties in honouring these bonds was expressed by Donald A. Keith (now a Supernumerary Justice of the High Court of the Supreme Court of Ontario) in the Law Society Special Lectures for 1962:

> . . . I am not aware of any case in which a surety who has entered into a contract bond for the benefit of third parties, namely, suppliers of labour and material who correctly fall within the terms and conditions of the bond, has refused to honour its obligation on the basis that the contract is unenforceable. There is no reason to doubt that this demonstration of commercial morality has a strong foundation in practical economics. However strong such foundation, one can be equally sure that it will not be strong enough to resist the impact of an extraordinarily heavy loss and if, as and when the question of the enforceability of such bonds comes

---

28 See *Les Affréteurs Réunis Société Anonyme v. Leopold Walford (London) Ltd.*, [1919] A.C. 801, 121 L.T. 393 (H.L.); *Vandepitte v. Preferred Accident Ins. Corp. of New York*, [1933] A.C. 70, [1932] 3 W.W.R. 573, [1933] 1 D.L.R. 289 (P.C.).

29 29 O.R. (2d) 592, 113 D.L.R. (3d) 686, 12 B.L.R. 80; affd. 32 O.R. (2d) 697n, 123 D.L.R. (3d) 763n; affd. unreported, May 17, 1983 (*sub. nom. Citadel General Assur. Co. v. Johns-Manville Can. Inc. et al.*) (S.C.C.).

30 *Ibid.*, 29 O.R. at 592.

before the court in an actual case, it may very well be that substantial hardship will ensue.[31]

2. The second qualification is that a surety will require that all of the specified terms and conditions of the bond have been met, failing which there may be a denial of coverage.

Most bonds have strict notice provisions, similar to the following:

> No suit or action shall be commenced hereunder by any Claimant unless such Claimant shall have given written notice within the time limits hereinafter set forth to each of the Principal, the Surety and the Obligee, stating with substantial accuracy the amount claimed. Such notice shall be served by mailing the same by registered mail to the Principal, the Surety and the Obligee, at any place where an office is regularly maintained for the transaction of business by such persons or served in any manner in which legal process may be served in the Province or other part of Canada in which the subject matter of the Contract is located. Such notice shall be given (1) in respect of any claim for the amount or any portion thereof, required to be held back from the Claimant by the Principal, under either the terms of the Claimant's contract with the Principal, or under the Mechanics' Liens Legislation applicable to the Claimant's contract with the Principal, whichever is the greater, within one hundred and twenty (120) days after such Claimant should have been paid in full under the Claimant's contract with the Principal; (2) in respect of any claim other than for the holdback, or portion thereof, referred to above, within one hundred and twenty (120) days after the date upon which such Claimant did, or performed, the last of the work or labour or furnished the last of the materials for which such claim is made, under the Claimant's contract with the Principal;[32]

Unless this notice provision is complied with, the claimant may be disentitled to any recovery under the bond.[33]

Similarly, most if not all labour and material payment bonds contain a limitation provision, such as the following:

> No suit or action shall be commenced hereunder by any Claimant . . . after the expiration of one (1) year following the date on which the Principal ceased work on the Contract, including work performed under the guarantees provided in the Contract;[34]

Unless an action is commenced within the required period, the surety will no doubt avail itself of the limitation period defence.

In many cases, the trades, not being parties to the bond, may not know of its existence, and may therefore be prejudiced to the extent that their lack of information may prevent them from giving the requisite

---

[31] Donald A. Keith, "Performance Bonds," *Special Lectures of the Law Society of Upper Canada (1962)*, 311 at 320.

[32] See Precedent No. 66, para. 3(a).

[33] But see unreported decision of the Supreme Court of Canada in *Johns-Manville, supra,* note 29.

[34] See Precedent No. 66, para. 3(b).

notice within the 120-day period, or from commencing an action within the specified limitation period.[35] As a result, there is a question as to whether or not the surety or the principal has any positive obligation to inform them. The court was called upon to deal with this issue in *Dominion Bridge Co. Ltd. v. Marla Const. Co. Ltd. et al.,*[36] a 1970 County Court decision of His Honour Judge Grossberg:

> Counsel for the plaintiff [the claimant] as I understand his contention puts his case against Sun Oil [the Principal] as follows: He submits that there was a duty on the part of Sun Oil because it was a trustee, to notify the plaintiff of the Labour and Material Payment Bond, ex. 4. . . . I asked in argument: when did the duty arise? at what point of time? what exactly was that duty? must Sun Oil embark upon inquiries who were the labourers? who were the creditors? who were the suppliers? Must Sun Oil seek out the creditors and suppliers? If the contention of counsel for the plaintiff be upheld, Sun Oil would be obliged to acquire knowledge of all materials purchased, all labourers on the job from day to day and to keep a constant surveillance. The consequence of the submission must be that Sun Oil must seek out material, men, suppliers, labourers, subcontractors, etc., of Marla and acquaint each that there was a bond in existence. No such duty is imposed by the bond itself. In the absence of applicable authority I would not imply such duty in law.[37]

3. The third qualification to which a labour and material payment bond is subject relates to the definition of "claimant". In most cases, a "claimant" is defined in the bond as one who has direct contractual dealings with the principal for all labour and material used, or reasonably required for use, in the performance of the contract.[38] Assuming that the principal is the contractor, the bond will serve to secure payment *only* to those subcontractors who have contracted directly with the contractor. If those subcontractors have in turn subcontracted part of their work to sub-subcontractors, the latter will be afforded no protection at all by the existence of the bond. As will be seen, there is nothing in the *Construction Lien Act, 1983* which would alter this situation.

The purpose of the labour and material payment bond is to ensure that work proceeds smoothly by providing for the payment of the accounts of those who have supplied labour or materials to the improvement. Given the problems and obstacles relative to notice, limitation periods, disclosure and status to claim and to sue, as discussed above, which have hitherto affected bond claims, the potential impact of

---

[35] Section 39(1) provides that any potential claimant under a labour and material payment bond may require the owner, the contractor, or a subcontractor, as the case may be, to produce for inspection a copy of any such bond, if there is one. This right may be enforced by court order (s. 39(6)). Furthermore, failure to comply with a request for production exposes the person, who is obliged to comply, to liability for damages sustained as a result (s. 39(5)).

[36] [1970] 3 O.R. 125, 12 D.L.R. (3d) 453.

[37] *Ibid.*, at O.R. 129.

[38] See Precedent No. 66, para. 1.

bonding, as a remedial and protective feature in the construction industry, has been considerably diluted.

(ii) Right of Action against Surety on Labour and Material Payment Bond

In its 1966 *Report on Proposed Extension of Guarantor's Liability on Construction Bonds,* the Ontario Law Reform Commission put forward the view that,

> . . . where a surety performance bond[39] on a construction contract has been taken out and default has been made on the construction contract, the subcontractors, material men and wage earners should have the right to assert a claim directly against the surety. Those who have contributed to the performance of the contract without having been paid for materials supplied or services rendered should have a first claim on the bond and not be left to rank with ordinary creditors of the defaulting contractor or to rely entirely on Mechanics' Lien procedure.[40]

Having said this, the Commission went on to recommend legislation creating a civil cause of action by a third party beneficiary against a surety under a labour and material payment bond.[41] The suggested legislation,

---

[39] This was an unfortunate choice of words since it is important to distinguish between the concepts contained in, and the relief afforded by, performance bonds as contrasted with labour and material payment bonds. Given the context, and the thrust of the proposed amendment, it is suggested that the Commission was intending to deal only with the latter type of bond.

[40] *Report on Proposed Extension of Guarantor's Liability on Construction Bonds* (1966), at 4.

[41] Section 49, contained in the *Report on Proposed Extension of Guarantor's Liability on Construction Bonds* (1966), provides:

> (1). A claimant under a labour and material payment bond that guarantees payment to the claimant as defined therein and subject to the terms and conditions contained therein shall have a cause of action against the surety named in such bond in the event that the principal named in the bond defaults in any obligation with respect to payment to such claimant. Such action shall be on his own behalf and on behalf of all other claimants to recover the amount of the claim or claims and any moneys recovered shall be solely for the benefit of the claimants.
>
> (2). In an action against a surety under this section the Judge may give judgment in favour of each claimant who is entitled to recover under the bond and subject to the provisions of subsection (3) of this section all moneys recovered under the judgment shall be distributed pro rata among the claimants in whose favour the judgment is given.
>
> (3). Nothing in this section makes the surety liable for an amount in excess of the amount which he undertakes to pay under the bond and the surety's liability under the bond shall be reduced by and to the extent of any payment made in good faith to claimants either before or after judgment is obtained against the surety.
>
> (4). Every principal named in a payment bond shall display and keep displayed in a conspicuous place on the work site a notice giving information to the effect that a payment bond has been provided, the name and address of the principal, surety and obligee and the requirements for asserting such cause of action against the surety.

although drafted as an amendment to the *Mechanics' Lien Act*,[42] was not intended by the Commission to be incorporated into the Act, but rather to be the subject of separate legislation.[43] Until the proclamation of the *Construction Lien Act, 1983,* though, the Commission's recommendation was not pursued, and the fact that the subcontractor had no clear legal right to sue the surety meant that any claim which would be made on the bond would be subject to the discretion and good faith of the surety.

Under s. 71(1) of the Act, though, any person,[44] whose payment is guaranteed by a labour and material payment bond, has a direct right of action against the surety for payment, "in accordance with the terms and conditions of the bond,"[45] where the principal defaults in making the payment guaranteed by the bond.

The extent of the surety's liability is made clear by s. 71(2), which limits the surety's exposure to the amount which he undertook to pay under the bond. That liability is further reduced to the extent of any payment made by the surety in good faith.[46] If, for example, the surety made a payment in good faith to a claimant which subsequently turned out to be excessive, the surety would be protected by this section from any direct or subrogated claims which may be asserted by the principal, or any one claiming through the principal (*e.g.,* a guarantor of the principal's liability to the surety). In all probability, though, notwithstanding this protection, a surety would attempt to obtain the approval of the principal before compromising any claims made on the bond. If the principal were not available for one reason or another, the claimants would nevertheless be able to recover payment on the bond on the argument that the surety would incur no liability in making the payment.

(iii) Surety's Right of Subrogation

By s. 71(3), once the surety satisfies its obligations under the bond to a particular person, he, the surety, is subrogated to all of the rights of that person.

---

(5). A person who fails to comply with subsection (4) is guilty of an offence and on summary conviction is liable to a fine of not less than $10.00 and not more than $100.00 for each day during which default continues.

(6). The surety, upon satisfaction of its obligation to any claimant under the payment bond, shall be subrogated to all rights of such claimant.

[42] R.S.O. 1960, c. 233, as amended.

[43] *Report on Proposed Extension of Guarantor's Liability on Construction Bonds* (1966), at 4.

[44] This would generally apply only to subcontractors, and not to sub-subcontractors, for the reasons set forth in the third qualification in the preceding section of this chapter.

[45] Given the provisions of s. 4, it is doubtful whether the surety would be entitled to contract out of this section of the Act by amending the usual "terms and conditions of the bond."

[46] See Precedent No. 66, para. 6.

Simply stated, this would mean that the claim which the surety has satisfied is "assigned" to the surety, who may then recover a like amount from the principal. The surety usually may also look to collateral personal guarantees in addition to the covenant of the principal, and the rights of subrogation set forth in the Act, the bond and any indemnity agreement would crystallize the claim of the surety for indemnification.

Chapter 9

Jurisdiction, Practice and Procedure

A. COMMENCING THE CONSTRUCTION LIEN ACTION

Civil proceedings are generally commenced by a writ of summons,[1] an originating notice of motion,[2] or a petition.[3] The *Judicature Act*[4] defines "action" to mean "a civil proceeding commenced by writ or in such other manner as is prescribed by the rules."[5] Under the *Construction Lien Act, 1983*, however, an "action" is defined to mean "an action under Part VIII,"[6] and is commenced by the filing of a statement of claim[7] in the office of the registrar or local registrar of the Supreme Court of Ontario in the county or district in which the premises or a part thereof[8] are situate.[9]

Unlike the other types of civil proceedings referred to above, only the Supreme Court has the subject-matter jurisdiction to entertain an action to enforce a lien claim,[10] even where the amount of the claim would otherwise be less than the Supreme Court's minimum monetary jurisdiction.

When a lien claimant files his statement of claim, he will usually arrange concurrently to have the registrar or local registrar issue a

---

[1] See Rule 4 of the Rules of Practice of the Supreme Court of Ontario.

[2] See, for example, Rules 607-614 of the Rules of Practice of the Supreme Court of Ontario.

[3] See Rule 787 of the Rules of Practice of the Supreme Court of Ontario.

[4] R.S.O. 1980, c. 223.

[5] *Ibid.*, s. 1(1)(a).

[6] Section 1(1) 1.

[7] See Precedent No. 39.

[8] Where the premises or a part thereof are situate in more than one county or district, an action may be tried by any judge or local judge in *any* one of the counties or districts in which the premises are situate: s. 51(3). Notwithstanding the foregoing, where the premises (or a part thereof) are situate in more than one county or district, a lien claimant would be remiss if he did not perfect his lien claim by registering a certificate of action against the title to the *entire* premises. If, for example, a county line divides the premises into two parts, a lien claimant will have to register both his claim for lien and certificate of action in two registry offices in order to preserve and perfect his lien. However, s. 51(3) permits him to commence his action in *either* county.

[9] Section 55(1).

[10] See ss. 50(1) and 1(1) 5.

certificate of action,[11] which would then be registered against the title to the premises. No certificate of action is required, though, in the following instances:

(a) where, although the lien attaches to the premises, an order vacating the registration of the claim for lien has been obtained,[12] as would be the case where, for example, monies had previously been paid into court;[13] and

(b) where the lien does not attach to the premises,[14] which situation would obtain where the provincial Crown is the owner of the premises,[15] or where the premises is either a municipally-owned public street or highway,[16] or a railway right-of-way.[17]

If a lien claimant purports to perfect his lien by sheltering,[18] he need neither commence an action nor obtain nor register a certificate of action. His lien would be perfected subject to, and so long as it was in compliance with, the sheltering rules contained in s. 36(4). However, given the limitations of those rules,[19] a lien claimant would probably be well advised to commence his own action.

Lien actions are akin to "class actions,"[20] and any number of lien claimants, whose liens are in respect of the same statutory owner and the same premises, may join in the same action.[21]

Under the *Mechanics' Lien Act,* the scope of claims which could properly have been asserted in a lien action was unclear. This problem has been rectified by the *Construction Lien Act, 1983,* which clearly provides that a plaintiff may join with his lien claim a claim for breach of his contract or subcontract.[22] As a result, he is potentially entitled to recover a personal judgment[23] plus interest[24] in respect of the personal contractual claims.[25] The Act, though, does not permit a plaintiff to join a breach of

---

[11] See Form 10 prescribed by O. Reg. 159/83 filed March 18, 1983, under the *Construction Lien Act, 1983.*

[12] See s. 36(3)(a).

[13] See s. 44(1)(a).

[14] See s. 36(3)(b).

[15] See s. 16(3).

[16] See s. 16(3)(a).

[17] See s. 16(3)(b).

[18] See s. 36(4).

[19] See "Sheltering" (heading E(ii) of Chapter 4).

[20] Support for this statement may be found in ss. 36(4), 59(1), 61(2), 81 and 82.

[21] Section 50(3).

[22] Section 57(1).

[23] Section 65.

[24] Section 14(2).

[25] *Quaere* whether a breach of contract claim can properly be delegated to a master under s. 60 of the Act. See "Constitutional Validity of References to the Master," *infra,* in this chapter.

trust claim with a lien claim.[26] Trust claims which arise under the Act "may be brought in any court of competent jurisdiction."[27]

Inasmuch as the Act provides for the noting of pleadings closed against a defendant who defaults in the delivery of a statement of defence,[28] s. 56(5) provides that every statement of claim must include the following warning:

> WARNING: If you wish to defend against this claim, you are required to deliver a statement of defence within twenty days. Should you fail to deliver a statement of defence as required, pleadings may be noted closed against you, and you shall be deemed to admit all allegations of fact contained in this claim, and you shall not be entitled to notice of or to participate in the trial or any proceeding in respect of this claim and judgment may be given against you.[29]

Once the action has been commenced, the statement of claim must be served[30] upon the defendants within 90 days thereafter.[31] The time for service may be extended by the court,[32] though, upon a motion made either before or after the expiration of the 90-day period.[33]

B. PARTIES TO THE ACTION

All persons against whom a plaintiff would have any claim should be named as defendants in the lien action.

---

[26] Section 50(2).

[27] *Ibid.* The idea of a separate action for breach of trust may only serve to create a multiplicity of proceedings. Where such an action is commenced, it is suggested that an application be brought for an order to have it tried, together with the lien action, by a judge. In this situation, a motion under s. 60(1), to refer the lien action to the master for trial, ought not to be brought.

[28] See s. 56(2).

[29] Section 56(5).

[30] Section 89(3) requires that a statement of claim be served "in the manner provided in the Rules of the Supreme Court for service of a writ of summons". In this regard, reference is made to Rule 16, which provides that, if a defendant's solicitor does not accept service (in accordance with Rule 15), every writ of summons shall be served personally. The Rule goes on to provide that, if it appears that the plaintiff is unable to effect prompt personal service, substituted service, by advertisement or otherwise, may be ordered. Furthermore, Rule 23(3) provides:
> (3) Any other corporation [other than a municipal corporation, or a railway, telegraph or express corporation] may be served with a writ of summons by delivering a copy to the president or other head officer, vice-president, secretary, treasurer, director, or any agent thereof, or the manager or person in charge of any branch or agency thereof in Ontario and any person who, within Ontario, transacts or carries on any business of, or any business for, a corporation whose chief place of business is out of Ontario shall, for the purpose of being served as aforesaid, be deemed to be the agent thereof.

[31] Section 55(2).

[32] Section 52(1) dictates whether the motion is made to a master, a local master or a local judge.

[33] Section 55(2).

In addition to the person having privity of contract with the plaintiff, any person who might be holding unreleased holdback funds for the benefit of the plaintiff ought to be a party defendant. To that end, the plaintiff should name both the contractor and all subcontractors under whom the plaintiff's claim is derived.

Furthermore, irrespective of whether or not the statutory owner has met all of his obligations under the Act, he nevertheless is a necessary and proper party and must be named as a defendant. Failure to sue the statutory owner may mean that the lien has not been properly perfected, and the plaintiff may be precluded from adding him as a party at a later date.[34]

Finally, the plaintiff should name as a defendant any person holding a prior mortgage,[35] or other prior registered instrument (such as a conditional vendor who has registered a Notice of Security Interest under the *Personal Property Security Act*),[36] over which priority is claimed.

A subsequent mortgagee[37] or encumbrancer is not a necessary defendant, but is deemed to become a party to the action upon being served with a notice of trial.[38] The same applies to execution creditors of the statutory owner and to other lien claimants, all of whom, as will be seen below, must be served with notice of trial.

If the plaintiff neglects to sue a particular person who ought to have been sued, a motion may be brought at any time to add or join any person as a party to the action.[39] The court's discretion in this regard, though, is subject to, among other things, the jurisprudence[40] and the comments made above regarding the adding of a statutory owner as a defendant after the date when the lien was supposedly perfected.

C. CONSIDERATIONS REGARDING A BANKRUPT DEFENDANT

Lien rights are often pursued in circumstances where a person in the construction pyramid becomes bankrupt. Section 49(1) of the *Bankruptcy Act*[41] provides:

---

[34] See *Arnold Lbr. Ltd. v. Vodouris et al.,* [1968] 2 O.R. 478 (M.C.); *Rocca Steel Ltd. v. Tower Hill Apts. Ltd.,* [1968] 2 O.R. 701 (M.C.); and *G. Newman Aluminum Sales Ltd. v. Snowking Enterprises Inc.* (1980), 13 R.P.R. 275 (Ont. S.C.). But see *Fairy v. Doner et al.,* [1947] O.W.N. 217 (H.C.); *Re M & S Roofing and Sheet Metal Ltd. and G.B.S. Const. (Eastern) Ltd.,* [1979] 2 A.C.W.S. 291 (Ont. Co. Ct.). Also see s. 59(2).

[35] See ss. 80(3) and (4).

[36] R.S.O. 1980, c. 375, s. 54.

[37] See s. 80(6).

[38] Section 59(1).

[39] Section 59(2).

[40] See note 34, *supra.*

[41] R.S.C. 1970, c. B-3.

49(1) Upon the filing of a proposal made by an insolvent person or upon the bankruptcy of any debtor, no creditor with a claim provable in bankruptcy shall have any remedy against the debtor or his property or shall commence or continue any action, execution or other proceedings for the recovery of a claim provable in bankruptcy until the trustee has been discharged or until the proposal has been refused, unless with the leave of the court and on such terms as the court may impose.

However, Section 49(2) goes on to provide, in part:

49(2) Subject to section 57 and sections 98 to 105, a secured creditor may realize or otherwise deal with his security in the same manner as he would have been entitled to realize or deal with it if this section had not been passed, unless the court otherwise orders . . .

A lien claimant who holds a lien against the title to the premises of an owner who has become bankrupt is a "secured creditor"[42] under the *Bankruptcy Act*. As such, he may proceed to realize upon his security, by commencing and continuing a lien action, without being required to obtain leave under s. 49(1) of the *Bankruptcy Act*. However, without obtaining leave, he would not be entitled to a personal judgment against the bankrupt.[43]

There are two major reasons why a lien claimant would want to seek leave:

(a) If he intends to file a proof of claim in the bankruptcy, he might want to obtain a court determination as to the precise amount owing to him by the bankrupt. This is especially the case where he expects in due course to recover a portion of the debt out of the proceeds realized from a judicial sale of the bankrupt's interest in the premises pursuant to judgment in the lien action. The typical order giving leave to proceed[44] ordinarily provides,

(i) that the time for filing a declaration under s. 99(1) of the *Bankruptcy Act,* whereby the lien claimant would purport to value his security in circumstances where he has neither realized upon nor surrendered his security, is extended for a period of thirty days following the completion of the judicial sale; and

(ii) that the time for the lien claimant to file his proof of claim, as an *un*secured creditor, for the balance of his claim (if any), is extended until after it has been asserted what amount he will receive pursuant to the judicial sale.[45]

---

[42] *Re Rockland Cocoa and Chocolate Co., Ltd.* (1921), 50 O.L.R. 66, 61 D.L.R. 363, 1 C.B.R. 452 (S.C.).

[43] *Ibid., Imperial Lbr. Co., Ltd. v. Johnson,* 19 Alta. L.R. 292, [1923] 1 W.W.R. 920, [1923] 1 D.L.R. 1125, 3 C.B.R. 707 (C.A.).

[44] See Precedent No. 48.

[45] See s. 67(5).

(b) The lien claimant would want to apply for leave to continue the lien action if there is important documentation or information relating to his claim, such as the amount of the holdback or the disposition of trust funds, which can best be obtained through the discovery process.

If leave to continue the action is required, the trustee in bankruptcy would usually be prepared to consent[46] to be made a party defendant, and the order to proceed would be obtained on application to the bankruptcy court.

D. DEFENDING THE ACTION

Upon being served with a statement of claim, a defendant must deliver[47] his statement of defence[48] within 20 days,[49] failing which pleadings may be noted closed against him.[50]

Where pleadings have been noted closed against a defendant, he will not be permitted to contest the claim or to file a statement of defence, except with leave of the court.[51] Leave will only be granted where the court is satisfied that there is evidence to support a defence, in which case the court has discretion to make an order on terms as to costs, and to give directions as to the subsequent conduct of the action.[52]

Except where leave to defend has been granted, a person against whom pleadings have been noted closed is deemed to admit all the allegations of fact made in the statement of claim,[53] and shall not be entitled to notice of or to participate in the trial or any aspect of the action.[54] Furthermore, judgment may be given against him in his absence.[55] All of this is set forth in the warning,[56] referred to above, which must be included in the statement of claim.

The statement of claim would ordinarily contain sufficient particulars to enable a defendant to respond to it. However, in preparing his

---

[46] See Precedent No. 49.
[47] Although the Act deals with the manner in which documents or notices may be "given" (s. 89(1)) or "served" (s. 89(3)), no reference is made to the "delivery" of a statement of defence. Under the Rules of Practice, however, "delivery" is meant to consist of filing and serving, and there is no "delivery" of pleadings until these two acts are completed: See *DeForest v. Saunders*, [1960] O.W.N. 111 (H.C.).
[48] See Precedent No. 40.
[49] Section 56(1).
[50] Section 56(2).
[51] Section 56(3).
[52] *Ibid.*
[53] Section 56(4).
[54] *Ibid.*
[55] *Ibid.*
[56] See s. 56(5).

statement of defence, a defendant may require particulars of the claims of other lien claimants whose liens are sheltered under that statement of claim. In these circumstances, a defendant is entitled to give[57] notice[58] to any sheltering lien claimant requiring him to provide further particulars of his claim or of any fact alleged in his claim for lien.[59]

In addition to defending the action, a defendant may assert three types of claims in response to the plaintiff's action:

(i) COUNTERCLAIM — A defendant may counterclaim "against the person who named him as a defendant"[60] in respect of any claim against that person, "whether or not that claim is related to the making of the improvement."[61] It therefore appears that the potential scope of the counterclaim is considerably wider than that of the plaintiff's claim.[62]

Since the Act provides for the noting of pleadings closed against "a person against whom a claim is made in a ... counterclaim,"[63] the warning which must be included in a statement of claim must also be set out in the counterclaim.[64]

The defendant's counterclaim must accompany his statement of defence,[65] and must therefore be delivered[66] within 20 days of his being served with the statement of claim.[67] On motion, however, the court[68] may grant leave to deliver a counterclaim after this time, and, in so doing, may

---

[57] See s. 89(1).

[58] See Form 11 prescribed by O. Reg. 159/83 filed March 18, 1983, under the *Construction Lien Act, 1983*.

[59] Section 36(4) 4.

[60] Section 57(2)(a). *Quaere* whether this provision may properly be construed so as to permit a defendant to assert a counterclaim against a lien claimant whose lien is sheltered under the statement of claim. If not, then perhaps the defendant's recourse would be to add that lien claimant as a "defendant added by counterclaim", assuming this recourse is available.

[61] *Ibid.* Section 17(3) permits a payer to set off "all outstanding debts, claims or damages, whether or not related to the improvement," from the amount owing to the person he is liable to pay. Section 57(2)(a), though, takes this a step further by permitting a defendant (not necessarily a payer) to counterclaim against the "person who named him as a defendant" (not necessarily the person the defendant is liable to pay) in respect of *any claim*, "whether or not that claim is related to the making of the improvement." Furthermore, there is nothing in the Act which would preclude the defendant from defending the action on the basis of an allegation of legal or equitable set-off.

[62] Compare ss. 57(1) and 50(2), on the one hand, with s. 57(2)(a) on the other.

[63] Section 56(2).

[64] Section 56(5).

[65] Section 55(3). See Precedent No. 42.

[66] See note 47, *supra*.

[67] Section 56(1).

[68] Section 52(1) dictates whether the motion is made to a master, a local master or a local judge.

make any order as to costs as it considers appropriate, and may give directions as to the conduct of the action.[69]

The Act makes no provision for the assertion of a counterclaim against a non-party, and the issue may therefore arise as to whether or not this procedure is available in a lien action. One might argue that, since the Act is silent on this matter, the right would not be available, particularly in light of the fact that, by way of analogy, the Legislature saw fit to permit expressly the institution of third party proceedings against a non-party.[70] The response to this argument, though, would be that the purpose of third party proceedings is to permit a defendant to claim only contribution or indemnity from the third party in respect of the plaintiff's claim, which is fundamentally different in concept from a counterclaim.

It is clear that the court has authority to try the action, including any counterclaim "and all questions that arise therein or that are necessary to be tried in order to dispose completely of the action."[71] Furthermore, "[e]xcept where inconsistent with [the] Act, . . . the *Judicature Act* and the Supreme Court Rules of Practice apply to pleadings and proceedings under [the] Act."[72] On these bases, it is suggested that an argument can be made that a counterclaim against a non-party would be permissible.[73] This would be consistent with an objective of the legislation in authorizing the court to "do all things necessary to dispose finally of the action and all matters, questions and accounts arising therein,"[74] provided that the proceedings shall be of a summary character[75] aimed at expediting the resolution of the issues in dispute.[76]

Under Ontario's Rules of Practice, "[w]here a defendant sets up a counter-claim which raises questions between himself and the plaintiff and any other person, he shall add a second style of cause in which he is described as 'Plaintiff by Counter-claim' and the plaintiff and such other

---

[69] Section 55(3).
[70] See s. 58.
[71] Section 53(a).
[72] Section 69(3).
[73] See *obiter dicta* of Blair L.J.S.C. in *Anchor Shoring Ltd. v. Halton Region Conservation Authority et al.; Dufferin Materials and Const. Ltd. v. Halton Region Conservation Authority* (1977), 15 O.R. (2d) 599 at 602-3, 3 C.P.C. 153 (S.C.):

> It may be observed that the instances in which third party proceedings would be proper under the Rules with respect to issues normally raised in a mechanics' lien action, must surely be uncommon. There may, however, be circumstances frequently in which a third party should be added as a defendant in a counterclaim and, in my opinion, such a party may be added as a defendant where there is a proper counterclaim against the plaintiff and that party jointly in accordance with Rule 114. . . .

[74] Section 53(b).
[75] Section 69(1).
[76] Section 69(2).

person are described as 'Defendants by Counter-claim'. "[77] Furthermore, the defendant would be obliged to issue a Summons to Defendant Added by Counter-claim[78] with the court and to serve it, along with his statement of defence and counterclaim, "upon any party to the counter-claim who is not a plaintiff in the original action."[79]

(ii) CROSSCLAIM — A defendant may crossclaim against a co-defendant in respect of any claim that he may be entitled to make against that person relating to the making of the improvement.[80] The scope of a crossclaim is more limited than that of a counterclaim, since the former must be related to the making of the improvement. In a lien action by a subcontractor, one might expect, for example, a crossclaim by the contractor against the owner for non-payment under the contract; or a crossclaim by the owner against the contractor for defective work.

Since the Act provides for the noting of pleadings closed against "a person against whom a claim is made in a . . . crossclaim,"[81] the warning which must be included in a statement of claim must also be set out in the crossclaim.[82]

The defendant's crossclaim must accompany his statement of defence,[83] and must therefore be delivered[84] within 20 days of his being served with the statement of claim.[85] On motion, however, the court[86] may grant leave to deliver a crossclaim after this time, and, in so doing, may make any order as to costs as it considers appropriate, and may give directions as to the conduct of the action.[87]

(iii) THIRD PARTY PROCEEDINGS — Under the *Mechanics Lien Act,* a defendant was precluded from taking third party proceedings[88] on the basis that proceedings under that Act were purely statutory and their scope was limited to the realization of liens. Furthermore, the courts held that it would be unjust to deprive the third party, in the proposed third party proceedings, of those rights to which it would otherwise be entitled

---

[77] Rule 114, Supreme Court of Ontario Rules of Practice.

[78] See Form 26, Appendix of Forms, Supreme Court of Ontario Rules of Practice.

[79] Rule 45, Supreme Court of Ontario Rules of Practice.

[80] Section 57(2)(b).

[81] Section 56(2).

[82] Section 56(5).

[83] Section 55(3). See Precedent No. 41.

[84] See note 47, *supra.*

[85] Section 56(1).

[86] Section 52(1) dictates whether the motion is made to a master, a local master or a local judge.

[87] Section 55(3).

[88] *Caruso v. Campanile et al.,* [1972] 1 O.R. 437, 23 D.L.R. (3d) 285 (M.C.); *Anchor Shoring Ltd. v. Halton Region Conservation Authority et al., supra,* note 73.

if the action were tried in the ordinary way, such as discovery, production, and trial by a Judge of the Supreme Court,[89] with or without a jury. The determination of issues extraneous to the lien claim was therefore discouraged. In the circumstances, the only recourse which was available to a defendant in a lien action was to commence an ordinary action in the Supreme Court[90] against the third party, and then to apply to the court for an order that both actions be tried together.[91]

There are situations, though, where a claim for contribution or indemnity is intimately related to the evidence in a lien action. The prospect of prohibiting a defendant in those instances from commencing third party proceedings would serve only to increase costs and to promote a multiplicity of proceedings.

As a result, the *Construction Lien Act, 1983* authorizes the taking of third party proceedings, but only in accordance with strict rules.[92] Under the Act, a defendant may join a person who is not a party[93] to the action as a third party for the purpose of claiming contribution or indemnity[94] in respect of the plaintiff's claim.[95] However, a person may only be joined as a third party with leave of the court,[96] upon a motion[97] made with notice[98]

---

[89] See *Caruso v. Campanile et al., ibid.*

[90] If the ordinary action is commenced in the county court by virtue of the fact that the amount in issue is not within the monetary jurisdiction of the Supreme Court of Ontario, then the two actions could not be tried together. *Quaere* whether the defendant (being the "third party" in the ordinary action) would be entitled to take the benefit of the provisions of Rule 656 of the Supreme Court of Ontario Rules of Practice, where the amount recovered is less than the minimum monetary jurisdiction of the Supreme Court of Ontario.

[91] See, for example, *Anchor Shoring Ltd. v. Halton Region Conservation Authority et al., supra,* note 73.

[92] See s. 58.

[93] Third party proceedings under the Act appear to be limited to claims against *non-parties* (compare with Rule 172 of the Supreme Court of Ontario Rules of Practice). If a defendant intends to claim contribution or indemnity from a co-defendant or from the plaintiff, he presumably would do so by crossclaim or counterclaim, respectively. This is reminiscent of the provisions contained in the *Negligence Act,* R.S.O. 1980, c. 315 (see ss. 2, 4 and 5).

[94] By way of comparison, Rule 167 of the Supreme Court of Ontario Rules of Practice permits a defendant to take third party proceedings for "contribution or indemnity *or any other relief over*" (emphasis added).

[95] Section 58, 1. *Quaere* whether a defendant may commence third party proceedings in respect of the claim of a lien claimant who is sheltering under the plaintiff's lien.

[96] Section 52(1) dictates whether the motion is made to a master, a local master or a local judge. The Act contains no provision as to when the leave application must be made, and presumably it may therefore be made at any reasonable time up until the trial. If the application is made late in the day, though, it is doubtful whether leave will be granted since the delay in initiating the third party claim may prejudice the ability of the third party to conduct a full defence before trial (see s. 58, 2, i) or may delay or complicate the resolution of the lien claim (see s. 58, 2, ii).

[97] See Precedent Nos. 44, 45 and 46.

[98] It is suggested that notice would be given in accordance with s. 89(1).

to the statutory owner and to all persons having subsisting[99] preserved or perfected liens at the time of the motion.[100] The court may not grant the requisite leave unless it is satisfied that the trial of the third party claim will not "unduly prejudice the ability of the third party or of any lien claimant or defendant to prosecute his claim or conduct his defence,"[101] or "unduly delay or complicate the resolution of the lien action."[102] In this regard, the court has wide discretion to give directions in respect of the third party proceedings,[103] which would no doubt include directions as to pleadings, discovery, production and so on. Given that leave to assert a third party claim is required, the Rules of Practice relating to the commencement of proceedings, particularly with respect to the issuance of a Third Party Notice,[104] would not apply. Once leave has been obtained, the defendant would be permitted to deliver his third party claim[105] in accordance with the court's directions.

Since the Act provides for the noting of pleadings closed against "a person against whom a claim is made in a . . . third party claim,"[106] the warning which must be included in the statement of claim must also be set out in the third party claim.[107]

Inasmuch as the Act creates a right of action to recover payment under a labour and material payment bond,[108] surety companies may find that attempts will be made to join them as third parties in lien actions. Suppose, for example, the obligor under a bond is the contractor, who has become insolvent or bankrupt. A subcontractor would in most cases be entitled to assert a claim under the bond. However, under the terms and conditions of most bonds, a sub-subcontractor would ordinarily not have that right. In a lien action by a sub-subcontractor against the subcontractor, contractor and owner, the subcontractor, who has a statutory right of action, might see fit to attempt to join the surety as a third party. In most cases, the surety would simply honour the subcontractor' claim, assuming it was valid and timely, and the flow of funds would then permit

---

99 The inclusion of the word "subsisting" in s. 58, 2 is unfortunate. On the one hand, one might suggest that the omission of a comma after it, is a typographical error, and that it modifies the word "liens." This view does not entirely make sense, through, because on any large project it would be virtually impossible to ascertain all those persons who would have subsisting liens for the purpose of serving them with notice under the section. The better view, it is suggested, is that the word is in fact superfluous, and that it is there to modify the words "preserved or perfected" rather than the word "liens."

100 Section 58, 2.

101 Section 58, 2, i.

102 Section 58, 2, ii.

103 Section 58, 3.

104 See Rule 167(1) of the Rules of Practice of the Supreme Court of Ontario.

105 See Precedent No. 47.

106 Section 56(2).

107 Section 56(5). See Precedent No. 47.

108 Section 71(1).

the subcontractor to pay his sub-subcontractor. However, it is always open to the surety to disallow the claim of the subcontractor, in which case the issue of entitlement to recover under the bond may now be resolved in the context of the lien action.

E. DEFENDING THE COUNTERCLAIM, CROSSCLAIM OR THIRD PARTY CLAIM

The time for delivering[109] a statement of defence to a counterclaim,[110] a crossclaim[111] or a third party claim[112] is 20 days.[113]

Where a person neglects to deliver his statement of defence within the required time, pleadings may be noted closed against him[114] in respect of that claim, in which case he shall not be permitted to contest the claim or to file a statement of defence except with leave of the court.[115] Leave will only be granted where the court is satisfied that there is evidence[116] to support a defence, in which case the court has discretion to make an order on terms as to costs, and to give directions as to the subsequent conduct of the action.[117]

Except where leave to defend has been granted, a person against whom pleadings have been noted closed is deemed to admit all the allegations of fact contained in the counterclaim, crossclaim or third party claim.[118] Furthermore, he shall not be entitled to notice of or to participate in the trial or any aspect of the action.[119] Judgment may be given against him in his absence.[120] The foregoing implications of failing to defend are spelled out clearly in the warning[121] which is required to be included in every counterclaim, crossclaim and third party claim.

---

[109] See note 47, *supra.*

[110] See Precedent No. 43.

[111] See Precedent No. 41.

[112] See Precedent No. 47.

[113] Section 56. *Quaere* whether an order may be obtained pursuant to Rule 178 enlarging the 20-day period, if necessary, by virtue of s. 69(3). *Quaere,* also, whether a court would have jurisdiction under the Rules, which are nothing more than regulations under the *Judicature Act,* to extend the time set out in a statute despite the provisions of s. 69(3).

[114] Section 56(2).

[115] Section 56(3).

[116] *Quaere* whether the use of the word "evidence", rather than the word "facts", heightens or otherwise affects the onus upon the applicant seeking leave to set aside the noting of pleadings closed and to deliver a statement of defence.

[117] Section 56(3).

[118] Section 56(4).

[119] *Ibid.*

[120] *Ibid.*

[121] See s. 56(5).

In addition to delivering a statement of defence, any person against whom a claim is made in a counterclaim, a crossclaim or a third party claim may join a person who is not a party to the action as a third party (or a "fourth party," in a case of third party proceedings being pursued by an existing third party) for the purpose of claiming contribution or indemnity in respect of that claim.[122] See the discussion of the rules which govern third party proceedings, which appears earlier in this chapter.

F. MOTIONS

(i) Jurisdiction

Where all or part of the premises are situated in the Judicial District of York, the master has jurisdiction to hear and dispose of any motion,[123] with the exception of those specifically designated in s. 52(2), referred to below. The master's jurisdiction extends to motions brought prior to the commencement of a lien action,[124] as well as to all motions relating to the conduct of an action or reference under the Act.[125]

Where all or part of the premises are situated outside of the Judicial District of York, the appointed local master[126] for, or a master assigned to, the particular county or district has the same jurisdiction regarding the hearing of motions as the master in the Judicial District of York.[127]

Where an order of a local judge has been made pursuant to s. 51(2)(c), for the trial of an action by a Supreme Court judge at the regular sittings of the court in the county or district in which all or part of the premises are situated, the local judge would have the same jurisdiction regarding the hearing of motions as the master in the Judicial District of York.[128] His jurisdiction, though, is not subject to the same exceptions as those to which the master's jurisdiction is subject.[129]

Section 52(2) purports to limit the jurisdiction of the master or appointed local master by providing that they shall not hear or dispose of:

---

[122] Section 58, 1.

[123] Section 52(1)(a).

[124] Section 52(1). Also see s. 69(6).

[125] Section 52(1).

[126] "An 'appointed local master' is one who has been specifically appointed as such under subsection 101(1) of the *Judicature Act,* and should be distinguished from a county court judge who may act as a local master under subsection 101(2) of that Act": *Report of the Attorney General's Advisory Committee on the Draft Construction Lien Act* (April 1982), at 131.

[127] Section 52(1)(b).

[128] Section 52(1)(c).

[129] Section 52(2).

(a) a motion for the trial of the action by a judge under clause 51(2)(c);
(b) a motion for the reference of an action to a master or appointed local master for trial;
(c) an originating application; or
(d) a motion in respect of an appeal.

(ii) Originating Applications

As indicated above, a master and an appointed local master do not have jurisdiction to entertain "an originating application."[130] The application must therefore be made to a Supreme Court judge, in the Judicial District of York, or to a local judge, outside of the Judicial District of York.

Although the Act is not clear on the point, it appears that "originating applications" are distinguishable from "motions." It is suggested that an originating application is contemplated where a section provides that, in certain circumstances, a person may "apply" to the court for a particular order; and a motion is contemplated where the section expressly provides for the making of a motion. Part of the reason for the confusion relates to the unresolved questions as to whether there is a distinction to be drawn between an "application" and an "originating application," and whether an application brought after an action has been commenced is "originating." Furthermore, the marginal notes opposite those sections which deal with some types of motions make confusing reference to the fact that those sections supposedly deal with "applications."[131]

Examples of originating applications would include:

— an application for a declaration of substantial performance of the contract, pursuant to s. 32(1) 7;

— an application for directions, pursuant to s. 68, in circumstances where a person has in his possession an amount that may be subject to a Part II trust;

— an application for the appointment of a trustee, pursuant to s. 70(1).

(iii) Interlocutory Motions Made Prior to the Commencement of an Action

Section 69(6) of the Act provides that any motion may be made to the court regardless of whether or not an action has been commenced at the time the motion is made; and s. 52(1) dictates which judicial officer has jurisdiction to hear the majority of motions brought under the Act, "including a motion brought prior to the commencement of an action."

---

[130] See s. 52(2)(c).
[131] See, for example, the marginal notes opposite ss. 60(3) and 62(1).

Examples of motions brought prior to the commencement of an action would include:

— a motion for an order requiring a person to comply with a request for information, pursuant to s. 39(6);

— a motion for an order vacating the registration of a claim for lien upon the making of a payment into court, pursuant to s. 44(1);

— a motion pursuant to s. 45(1) for a declaration that a lien, which was not preserved or perfected within the time allowed for doing so, has expired, and for an order that the registration of the claim for lien be vacated;

— a motion for an order discharging a lien, or vacating the registration of a claim for lien, "upon any proper ground", pursuant to s. 47(1).

It is important to note that no appeal lies from an interlocutory order made by the court.[132]

(iv) Interlocutory Motions Made Subsequent to the Commencement of an Action

Section 52(1) dictates which judicial officer has jurisdiction to deal with motions, including "all motions relating to the conduct of an action or reference under this Act."

The Act directs that a "motion may be made in the manner provided for in the Supreme Court Rules of Practice for the making of interlocutory motions,"[133] which would involve the service of a notice of motion,[134] in the form prescribed,[135] along with supporting affidavit material (if required),[136] upon all persons who would be affected by the order sought.[137]

Examples of motions brought subsequent to the commencement of an action would include:

— a motion for an order extending the time for service of a statement of claim, pursuant to s. 55(2);

— a motion for an order permitting substitutional service of a statement of claim, pursuant to s. 89(3);

---

[132] Section 73(3).

[133] Section 69(6).

[134] Rule 215 of the Rules of Practice of the Supreme Court of Ontario.

[135] Form 39 of the Appendix of Forms to the Rules of Practice of the Supreme Court of Ontario. Also see Rule 220.

[136] Rule 228 of the Rules of Practice of the Supreme Court of Ontario.

[137] Rule 215 of the Rules of Practice of the Supreme Court of Ontario.

— a motion for an order for leave to amend any pleading, pursuant to s. 52(3);[138]

— a motion to add a party to the action, pursuant to s. 59(2);

— a motion for an order setting aside the noting of pleadings closed, with leave to a defendant to file a statement of defence, pursuant to s. 56(3);

— a motion for leave to join a person, who is not a party to the action, as a third party, pursuant to s. 58, 2;

— a motion to have a day, time and place fixed for the trial of the lien action, pursuant to s. 62(1);

— a motion for a declaration that a perfected lien has expired under s. 37 (where an action is not set down for trial within two years of the date the action, which perfected the lien, was commenced), and for an order dismissing the lien action and vacating the registration of a claim for lien and certificate of action, pursuant to s. 46(1);

— a motion for the giving of directions to a trustee appointed by the court, pursuant to s. 52(3).[139]

Generally, courts in the past have been reluctant to dismiss a lien claimant's action on a summary motion before trial.[140]

From another perspective, courts have also tended to refrain from granting an interlocutory judgment to a lien claimant prior to trial for default of defence.[141]

The Act contains a proscription to the effect that interlocutory proceedings, other than those provided for in the Act,[142] are not to be taken without the consent[143] of the court, obtained upon proof that the

---

[138] A motion for leave to amend any pleading is properly returnable before a master: s. 52(3).

[139] A motion for the giving of directions to a court-appointed trustee is properly returnable before a master: s. 52(3).

[140] See, for example, *Brant Transit Mix Ltd. v. Carriage Lane Estates Ltd. et al.*, [1971] 3 O.R. 82 (H.C.); *Re Boulay et al. and Seeh,* [1970] 2 O.R. 313 (H.C.); and *Re Ellwood Robinson Ltd. and Ohio Dev. Co. Ltd.* (1975), 7 O.R. (2d) 556 (Dist. Ct.). But see *McMurray v. Parsons,* [1953] O.W.N. 414 (H.C.); and *Patsis et al. v. 75-89 Gosford Ltd. et al.; Papas et al. v. Patsis et al.,* [1973] 1 O.R. 629, 32 D.L.R. (3d) 31 (H.C.).

[141] See, for example, *Kennedy Glass Ltd. v. Jeskay Const. Ltd. et al.,* [1973] 3 O.R. 493, 37 D.L.R. (3d) 321 (Div. Ct.) and *D. & M. Bldg. Supplies Ltd. v. Stravalis Holdings Ltd. et al.* (1976), 13 O.R. (2d) 443, 71 D.L.R. (3d) 328, 24 C.B.R. (N.S.) 53, 2 C.P.C. 343 (H.C.).

[142] By way of comparison, s. 42(10) of the *Mechanics' Lien Act,* R.S.O. 1980, c. 261 required an application for directions "as to pleadings, discovery, production or any other matter relating to the action or reference."

[143] *Quaere* why the word "consent" rather than "leave" or "directions", was used in s. 69(2).

proceedings are necessary or would expedite the resolution of the issues in dispute.[144]

No appeal lies from an interlocutory order made by the court.[145]

G. THE CONCURRENT MAINTENANCE OF A LIEN ACTION AND AN ORDINARY ACTION FOR THE SAME CLAIM[146]

There is a question as to whether or not a lien claimant is entitled to initiate lien proceedings concurrently with an action commenced by a writ of summons for the same claim.

The advantages of registering a lien are obvious. However, in many instances, lien proceedings are complicated by issues relating to priority, by the owner's or contractor's bankruptcy, by the commencement of foreclosure or power of sale proceedings by a mortgagee, by the occasional difficulties encountered in determining the value of the work and the proper holdback amount, and so on. Furthermore, it may be a number of months before a settlement meeting[147] is held, and at least several more months before the actual trial takes place.

By way of comparison, in an action commenced by specially endorsed writ, a plaintiff may obtain default judgment, or may move for judgment, within as short a period as 15 days from the date of service of the writ.[148]

Consequently, in order for the plaintiff to secure his rights both expeditiously and comprehensively, he may be well advised to initiate both construction lien and ordinary proceedings at or around the same time. If default judgment is obtained in the ordinary proceedings, there may be no need for the plaintiff to pursue the lien action if the judgment is satisfied. On the other hand, if it is not satisfied, the plaintiff may nevertheless pursue the lien action with a view to possibly recovering at least his *pro rata* share of the holdback.

In these situations, the defendant in both actions would attempt to argue that one or the other of the two actions ought to be stayed on the basis that a multiplicity of proceedings constitutes an abuse of process.

---

[144] Section 69(2).

[145] Section 73(3)(b).

[146] See Harvey J. Kirsh, "The Concurrent Maintenance of a Mechanics' Lien Action and an Action Commenced by a Writ for the same Claim" (1979), 2 *Advocates' Quarterly* 107, and Harvey J. Kirsh, "The Concurrent Maintenance of a Mechanics' Lien Action and an Action Commenced by a Writ for the Same Claim — A Further Comment" (1981), 3 *Advocates' Quarterly* 118.

[147] See s. 63.

[148] See Rules 35(1), 42 and 51 of the Rules of Practice of the Supreme Court of Ontario.

In *Rockwall Concrete Forming Ltd. v. Robintide Invts. Ltd.,*[149] the plaintiff commenced an action for recovery of a debt, by way of specially endorsed writ, subsequent to the commencement of a mechanics' lien action which dealt with the same alleged indebtedness. Before the commencement of the second action, the defendant paid into court the full amount of the mechanics' lien claim plus costs so that the money would stand in place of the land, enabling the registration of the claim for lien to be vacated. The defendant then applied to the court to stay the second action on the basis that it was an abuse of process to allow both actions to proceed. Weatherston J. agreed and stayed the second action, holding that, if the plaintiff were to obtain judgment in the ordinary action, he would be entitled to enforce the judgment even though the defendant had already paid money into court with respect to the same debt pending the outcome of the mechanics' lien action. The court looked at the prejudice which would be suffered by the defendant if the second action were allowed to proceed.

Weatherston J. did however make reference to s. 26(1) of the *Mechanics' Lien Act*[150] which provided, in part, that:

> . . . the taking of any proceedings for the recovery, or the recovery of a personal judgment for the claim, does not merge, waive, pay, satisfy, prejudice or destroy the lien unless the lien claimant agrees in writing that it has that effect.

Weatherston J. saw a distinction between a situation where a plaintiff registers a lien first, subsequently starting an ordinary action; and a situation where a plaintiff commences an ordinary action first and registers a lien afterwards; and concluded that the latter procedure would allow the plaintiff to proceed on both fronts, whereas the former procedure may in fact prejudice a defendant and may create a situation where the defendant would be entitled to apply to the court for a stay of the subsequent action.

As an aside, it is to be noted that s. 77(1) of the *Construction Lien Act, 1983* is substantially the same as s. 26(1) of the *Mechanics' Lien Act,* quoted above.

In *Standard Industs. Ltd. v. E-F Wood Specialties Inc.,*[151] which was decided only three months after the *Rockwall Concrete Forming* case, Maloney J. was called upon to deal with an action where a defendant was similarly bringing an application to the court for an order staying the ordinary action until the lien action had been disposed of. There, the lien was registered in December of 1976, and an action was commenced, by way of specially endorsed writ, in February of 1977 for the same debt. The

---

[149] (1977), 15 O.R. (2d) 422, 3 C.P.C. 224 (H.C.).
[150] R.S.O. 1970, c. 267.
[151] (1977), 16 O.R. (2d) 398, 78 D.L.R. (3d) 280, 4 C.P.C. 226 (H.C.).

court held that the presence of s. 26(1) in the *Mechanics' Lien Act* indicated that the Legislature contemplated the bringing of a mechanics' lien action contemporaneously with an ordinary action in respect of the same subject matter. This was qualified, though, by the pronouncement that there may in fact be circumstances where a stay of one or the other of such actions would be justified (as in the *Rockwall Concrete Forming* case where there would be real prejudice to the defendant which could not be compensated by costs). In effect, the *Standard Industs.* case indicates that the pivotal reason the court in the *Rockwall Concrete Forming* case held as it did was due to the fact that the plaintiff had paid monies into court in the lien action.

The next case to address this issue was *Pioneer Weather Systems Ltd. v. 349207 Ont. Ltd.; Pioneer Weather Systems Ltd. v. Hunting Wood Homes Ltd.*[152] a March 22, 1978 decision of His Honour Judge Borins, sitting as a local judge of the Supreme Court. In his decision, Judge Borins followed the reasoning in the *Standard Industs.* case.

At the date of this writing, the most recent decision in this area is that of Hollingworth J. in *Markus Bldrs. Supply (Can.) Ltd. v. Allied Drywall Ltd.*[153] There, a mechanics' lien action was commenced prior to an ordinary action for the same debt. The defendant in both actions succeeded in obtaining an order from His Honour Judge Winter staying the ordinary action. The plaintiff appealed this order, basing its submission upon the *Standard Industs.* case. Essentially, it was the plaintiff's position that the presence of s. 26(1) of the *Mechanics' Lien Act* indicated that the Legislature contemplated the bringing of a mechanics' lien action contemporaneously with an ordinary action in respect of the same debt, and that it should be of no consequence which action is commenced first so long as the defendant is not prejudiced. By way of reply, the defendant argued that the chronology of events is significant and that, since the lien action was commenced first and the ordinary action second, the order staying the ordinary action ought to be upheld. Although the defendant relied upon the *Rockwall Concrete Forming* case, it is suggested that that case does not, in fact, stand for the proposition put forward by the defendant, but, rather, correctly analyzes the issue in terms of prejudice to the defendant. In the facts of that particular case, it was appropriate for the court to stay the ordinary action.

In the *Markus Bldrs.* case, however, the defendant did not appear to have argued that it had been prejudiced. Rather, the argument was advanced that, if the lien was ultimately held to be invalid, the plaintiff might nevertheless obtain a personal judgment in the lien action thereby making the ordinary action superfluous.

---

[152] (1978), 5 C.P.C. 202 (Ont. H.C.).
[153] (1980), 30 O.R. (2d) 144, 116 D.L.R. (3d) 190 (H.C.).

In deciding the issue under appeal, Hollingworth J. accepted the defendant's argument, stating:

> It may well be that some other Court will have to decide which approach is the one that should be taken. I must confess that I find [the defendant's] argument more attractive and consequently I am going to dismiss [the plaintiff's] application.[154]

It is regrettable that this decision serves only to add to the confusion relating to the issue under consideration. While acknowledging the discretion available to His Lordship, it is suggested that the ordinary action ought not to have been stayed, and the plaintiff's appeal ought to have been granted, for the following reasons:

1. No reference was made to the decision of His Honour Judge Borins, sitting as a local judge of the Supreme Court, in the *Pioneer Weather Systems* case, which was decided subsequent to the *Standard Industs.* and *Rockwall Concrete Forming* cases, and in which Judge Borins adopted the following reasons of Maloney J. in the *Standard Industs.* case:

> Notwithstanding s. 40, I have already stated that the presence of s. 26(1) in the Act indicates that the Legislature contemplated the bringing of a mechanics' lien action contemporaneously with an ordinary action in respect of the same subject-matter (although, obviously, a plaintiff may only execute on one judgment). I can see no reason why, as a general rule, a plaintiff should be restricted to one course of action only; he may thereby be deprived of an expeditious resolution of his claim which may have been available had he been allowed to proceed with the other course of action as well.[155]

Although Hollingworth J. alluded to s. 26(1) of the *Mechanics' Lien Act,* no attempt was made to put it in any form of context or to determine what effect it ought to have on the concurrent maintenance of the two actions.

2. His Lordship accepted the defendant's argument that, if the plaintiff's lien is held to be invalid, the plaintiff may nevertheless obtain a personal judgment in the lien action. However, His Lordship did not advert to the potential prejudice to the plaintiff. For example, there is a line of authority which indicates that a plaintiff, who fails to prove his lien but nevertheless recovers a personal judgment, may be deprived of his costs.[156]

---

[154] *Ibid.,* O.R. at 146, D.L.R. at 191-2.

[155] See note 152, *supra,* at 208.

[156] *D. Faga Const. Co. Ltd. v. Havenbrook Const. Co. Ltd.,* [1968] 2 O.R. 800 (M.C.). But see *A.J. (Archie) Goodale Ltd. v. Risidore Bros. Ltd.* (1975), 8 O.R. (2d) 427, 58 D.L.R. (3d) 203 (C.A.). But see *Condotta c.o.b. A.C. Construction Co. v. Thomson,* not yet reported, Oct. 19, 1983 (Ont. S.C.).

3. His Lordship did not deal with the issue of prejudice to the defendant, but simply relied upon the fact that the ordinary action ought to have been stayed since it was commenced after the lien action. Although the remedy of staying an action is discretionary, it is trite to say that discretion ought not to be exercised in a vacuum and that reasonable grounds ought to exist.

On the basis of the foregoing analysis, it does not appear to be improper to commence an ordinary action, by way of writ of summons, contemporaneously with the initiation of lien proceedings. The court will reserve its right, though, to determine whether or not a defendant is prejudiced, as he most certainly was in the *Rockwall Concrete Forming* case, in deciding whether or not to stay one or the other action. Following the reasoning of Weatherston J. in the *Rockwall Concrete Forming* case, it is suggested that it would be prudent for a plaintiff to initiate an ordinary action by way of writ *before* the actual registration of a claim for lien, if possible. In that way, even if the defendant does in fact pay money into court in the lien action, the plaintiff can make the argument that the monies were so paid into court with the knowledge that the plaintiff could obtain a speedy judgment in the ordinary action and could take immediate steps to issue execution.

H. THE TRIAL OF A LIEN ACTION

(i) Jurisdiction in the Judicial District of York

Where all or part of a premises is situated in the Judicial District of York, the lien action is to be tried by a judge of the Supreme Court.[157]

However, upon motion[158] made after the delivery[159] of all statements of defence,[160] or after the time for their delivery has expired, a Supreme Court judge[161] may order that the whole action be referred to a master for

---

[157] Section 51(1).

[158] See Precedent Nos. 50, 51 and 52. It is to be noted that the current practice is for the "judgment," referring the trial of the action to the master, to be obtained on the written consent of all parties, without the necessity of a formal court appearance.

[159] See note 47, *supra*.

[160] Section 60(1) refers to "all statements of defence, or the statements of defence to all crossclaims, counterclaims, or third party claims, if any".

[161] See s. 52(2)(b) which provides, *inter alia*, that a master has no jurisdiction to dispose of "a motion for the reference of an action to a master . . . for trial".

trial[162] under s. 71 of the *Judicature Act*.[163] Where this occurs, any person who subsequently becomes a party to the action may bring a motion[164] to the judge who directed the reference to set aside the judgment directing the reference.[165] If no such motion is brought, or if the motion is dismissed, the person who subsequently became a party to the action is bound by the judgment directing the reference.[166]

Alternatively, the Supreme Court judge at trial may direct a reference to a master under s. 70[167] or 71[168] of the *Judicature Act*.[169]

Where a reference has been directed, a master has all the jurisdiction, powers and authority of the court to try and completely dispose of the action and all matters and questions arising in connection with the action.[170] He would therefore enjoy all the powers of the court set out in s. 53 of the Act, which authorizes him to "try the action, including any set-off, crossclaim, counterclaim, and, subject to section 58, third party claim, and all questions that arise therein or that are necessary to be tried in order to dispose completely of the action and to adjust the rights and liabilities of the persons appearing before [him] or upon whom notice of trial has been served;" and to "take all accounts, make all inquiries, give all

---

[162] Section 60(1)(a).
[163] Section 71 of the *Judicature Act*, R.S.O. 1980, c. 223 provides:
   71. In an action,
    (a) if all the parties interested who are not under disability consent, and, where there are parties under disability, the judge is of opinion that the reference should be made and the other parties interested consent; or
    (b) where a prolonged examination of documents or a scientific or local investigation is required that cannot, in the opinion of a court or a judge, conveniently be made before a jury or conducted by the court directly; or
    (c) where the question in dispute consists wholly or partly of matters of account,
   a judge of the High Court may at any time refer the whole action or any question or issue of fact arising therein or question of account either to an official referee or to a special referee agreed upon by the parties.
   But see *V.K. Mason Const. Ltd. v. Courtot Invts. Ltd. et al.* (1975), 9 O.R. (2d) 325 (H.C.).
[164] See Precedent Nos. 53, 54 and 55.
[165] Section 60(3).
[166] Section 60(4).
[167] Section 70 of the *Judicature Act*, R.S.O. 1980, c. 223 provides:
   70(1) Subject to the rules and to a right to have particular cases tried by a jury, a judge of the High Court may refer a question arising in an action for inquiry and report either to an official referee or to a special referee agreed upon by the parties.
   (2) Subsection (1) does not, unless with the consent of the Crown, authorize the reference to an official referee of an action to which the Crown is a party or of a question or issue therein.
[168] See note 163, *supra*.
[169] Section 60(2)(a).
[170] Section 52(3).

directions and do all things necessary to dispose finally of the action and all matters, questions and accounts arising therein or at the trial and to adjust the rights and liabilities of, and give all necessary relief to, all parties to the action."

(ii) Jurisdiction outside the Judicial District of York

Where the premises are situated outside of the Judicial District of York, the lien action is ordinarily to be tried by the appropriate county court judge who would be sitting as a local judge of the Supreme Court.[171]

Where the consent of all persons to whom a notice of trial must be given[172] is obtained, though, a local judge, who would otherwise have jurisdiction over the action, may order that the action be tried by a local judge of another county or district (other than the Judicial District of York).[173] Presumably, such an order would be sought when the balance of convenience favoured a change of venue.

In the alternative to the two preceding options, a local judge, who would otherwise have jurisdiction over the action, may order that the action be tried by a Supreme Court judge on assizes "at the regular sittings of the court for the trial of actions in the county or district in which the premises or a part thereof are situate."[174]

Where the premises are situate in, say, two counties (*i.e.,* where the county line intersects the premises), the lien action may be tried by a local judge of either county.[175]

After all statements of defence[176] have been delivered,[177] or the time for their delivery has expired, a local judge may order[178] that the whole action be referred to a local master[179] for trial[180] under s. 71 of the *Judicature Act.*[181]

Where this occurs, any person who subsequently becomes a party to the action may bring a motion[182] to the local judge who directed the reference to set aside the judgment directing the reference.[183] If no such

---

[171] Section 51(2)(a).

[172] See ss. 62(4) and (2).

[173] Section 51(2)(b).

[174] Section 51(2)(c).

[175] Section 51(3).

[176] See note 160, *supra.*

[177] See note 47, *supra.*

[178] See Precedent Nos. 50, 51 and 52.

[179] i.e., "a master assigned to, or a local master appointed for, the county or district in which the trial is to take place": s. 60(1)(b).

[180] Section 60(1)(b).

[181] See note 163, *supra.*

[182] See Precedent Nos. 53, 54 and 55.

[183] Section 60(3).

motion is brought, or if the motion is dismissed, the person who subsequently became a party to the action is bound by the judgment directing the reference.[184]

Alternatively, a local judge at trial may direct a reference to a local master under s. 70[185] or 71[186] of the *Judicature Act*.[187]

Where a reference has been directed, a local master has all the jurisdiction, powers and authority of the court to try and completely dispose of the action and all matters and questions arising in connection with the action.[188] He would therefore enjoy all the powers of the court set out in s. 53 of the Act.

(iii) Constitutional Validity of References to the Master

Despite the fact that mechanics' lien trials in Toronto have commonly been tried by masters since 1916,[189] the issue as to whether a lien action may be referred to a master for trial is open to dispute. Are ss. 60(1), 52(3) and 53 of the Act *ultra vires* the legislature, to the extent that those sections purport to confer delegated judicial authority upon the master?

Section 96 of the *Constitution Act, 1867* (formerly known as the *British North America Act, 1867*)[190] has traditionally been interpreted as disallowing a provincial legislature the power to confer jurisdiction upon provincially-appointed officers (such as masters) similar to that exercised by federally-appointed "Judges of the Superior, District and County Courts in each Province."

The first inquiry into the constitutional validity of the master's jurisdiction in mechanics' lien references came in 1918 in *Johnson & Carey Co. v. Can. Northern Ry. Co.*[191] There, the Ontario Court of Appeal was asked, "Are the provisions of the said Mechanics and Wage-Earners Lien Act [sic], conferring jurisdiction on the special officers referred to in sec. 33 of the said Act, *intra vires?*" Riddell J. disposed of the issue without analysis:

As at present advised, however, I have no scintilla of doubt of the validity of the legislation of the Province, in view of the British North America Act, sec. 92(14) and sec. 96.[192]

---

[184] Section 60(4).

[185] See note 167, *supra*.

[186] See note 163, *supra*.

[187] Section 60(2)(b).

[188] Section 52(3).

[189] See *An Act to amend The Mechanics' and Wage Earners' Lien Act*, S.O. 1916, c. 30, ss. 1 and 2.

[190] (U.K.), 30-31 Vict., c. 3.

[191] (1918), 43 O.L.R. 10 at 11, 14 O.W.N. 159; vard. 44 O.L.R. 533, 15 O.W.N. 279, 47 D.L.R. 75, 24 C.R.C. 294 (C.A.).

[192] *Ibid.*, 44 O.L.R. at 544, D.L.R. at 85.

In 1950, the Manitoba Court of Appeal, in *C. Huebert Ltd. v. Sharman et al.*[193] was called upon to assess the constitutional validity of s. 56 of the *Mechanics' Lien Act,* R.S.M. 1940, c. 129. That section allowed a county court judge, who was a federal appointee, to refer the lien action to a referee, who was an appointee of the Lieutenant Governor in Council. The referee was "thereupon [to] have the same powers and jurisdiction to hear and dispose of the action and all matters and questions therein involved as a judge would have under this Act."[194]

The issue, as phrased by the court, was whether the jurisdiction conferred on the referee conformed to the jurisdiction exercised by Superior, District or County Courts. After reviewing the history of the legislation; the powers and rights of the master thereunder; and s. 96 of the *British North America Act, 1867*, the court concluded that,

> Mechanics' lien trials are important judicial proceedings and in that class of cases invariably heard by a Judge of a Superior, District or County Court. The conclusion must be that the jurisdiction conferred on the Referee by reference under the order appealed from broadly conforms "to the type of jurisdiction exercised by the Superior, District or County Courts," and usually exclusively within the jurisdiction of Superior Courts.[195]

The authority of the *Sharman* decision was accepted by both the Ontario Court of Appeal and the Supreme Court of Canada in *Display Service Co. Ltd. v. Victoria Medical Bldg. Ltd. et al.*[196] The Court of Appeal in that case held that s. 31(1) of the *Mechanics' Lien Act,*[197] which provided for the trial of a lien action by a master where the land was wholly situated in the County of York, was *ultra vires* the province because it offended against s. 96 of the *British North America Act, 1867*. In rendering the judgment of the court, Schroeder J.A. stated:

> It cannot be doubted that the power to be exercised by the master or assistant master of the Supreme Court under s. 31(1) of the Mechanics' Lien Act, is judicial power.[198]

> . . .

> It requires no more than a superficial examination of the sections of the Mechanics' Lien Act to which I have referred to compel the conviction that in enacting the provisions of s. 31(1) the legislature has purported to vest in an officer of the Supreme Court of Ontario, judicial power which can be validly exercised only by a superior, District, or County Court or by a tribunal analogous thereto. In my opinion this legislation purports to confer upon the master or assistant master a jurisdiction which broadly conforms to the type of jurisdiction exercised by such

---

193 58 Man. R. 1, [1950] 1 W.W.R. 682, [1950] 2 D.L.R. 344 (C.A.).
194 *Mechanics' Lien Act,* R.S.M. 1940, c. 129, s. 56.
195 Note 193, *supra,* at W.W.R. 688 (per Adamson J.A.).
196 [1958] O.R. 759, 16 D.L.R. (2d) 1; affd. [1960] S.C.R. 32, 21 D.L.R. (2d) 97.
197 R.S.O. 1950, c. 227, as amended by S.O. 1953, c. 61, s. 2(1).
198 Note 196, *supra,* O.R. at 769, 16 D.L.R. (2d) at 10.

Courts. As the masters and assistant masters are appointed by the Lieutenant-Governor in Council and not by the Governor General of Canada, the legislation plainly constitutes a violation of s. 96 of the British North America Act and must be held invalid as being legislation which is beyond the competency of the provincial legislature to enact.[199]

. . .

Finally, we are urged that the authority of the master having been recognized in mechanics' lien cases for such a long period of time, this Court ought not to disturb a practice which has been proven to be so highly advantageous in York County. I cannot give effect to that argument. The question of the validity of this legislation has been squarely and authoritatively raised in the case before us, and if the view is taken that this legislation is invalid on constitutional grounds, this Court has no alternative but to make the declaration for which the appellant asks.[200]

The Supreme Court of Canada upheld the decision of the Court of Appeal, on the basis that the assignment of the power of final adjudication to the master went beyond matters of mere procedure and was tantamount to an appointment of a judge under s. 96 of the *British North America Act, 1867*.

In response to this decision, the Ontario Legislature quickly repealed and re-enacted s. 31 in 1960[201] in an attempt to circumvent the constitutional problem. Section 31(3), as re-enacted, provided that, in the County of York (as it then was), a lien action was to be tried by a judge of the Supreme Court; but, on motion, a judge of the Supreme Court could refer the whole action to the master for trial pursuant to s. 68 (now s. 71) of the *Judicature Act*.[202] Alternatively, the Supreme Court judge at trial was entitled to direct a reference to the master under ss. 67 or 68 (now ss. 70 or 71) of the *Judicature Act*.[203] These provisions formed part of Ontario's mechanics lien legislation for the next 23 years, and are substantially the same as those contained in ss. 51(1), 60(1) and (2) of the *Construction Lien Act, 1983*.

Furthermore, the 1960 legislative amendment also provided that, where the action was referred to the master, he would have "all the jurisdiction, powers and authority of the Supreme Court to try and completely dispose of the action and questions arising therein".[204] Again, the thrust and spirit, if not the precise words, of this provision were carried through the next 23 years of lien legislation, and have found their way into ss. 52(3) and 53 of the *Construction Lien Act, 1983*.

Presumably, the Attorney General had advised the Legislature in

---

[199] *Ibid.*, O.R. at 774, 16 D.L.R. (2d) at 15.
[200] *Ibid.*, O.R. at 784, 16 D.L.R. (2d) at 25.
[201] See *An Act to amend The Mechanics' Lien Act*, S.O. 1960, c. 65, s. 7.
[202] *Ibid.*
[203] *Ibid.*
[204] *Ibid.*, at s. 8(1). Also see *ibid.*, at s. 10(1).

1960 that the constitutional problem created by *Display Service Co. Ltd. v. Victoria Medical Bldg. Ltd. et al.*[205] could be remedied by simply positing the judicial power to try lien actions in a Supreme Court judge, and then giving that judge the authority to delegate the totality of his judicial function to a master. The fact that the master embodied his decision in a "report" rather than a "judgment,"[206] which was deemed to have been confirmed subsequently by a Supreme Court judge,[207] purported to lend legitimacy to the new procedure.

Currently, under the *Construction Lien Act, 1983*, the jurisdiction of the master to hear lien actions is not "original," since the jurisdiction is delegated to him by a Supreme Court judge whose "original" jurisdiction derives from s. 51(1). However, the functions performed by the master in trying lien actions go far beyond those ordinarily dealt with by such judicial officers on references.[208]

Under s. 71 of the *Judicature Act*, which authorizes references contemplated by ss. 60(1) and (2) of the *Construction Lien Act, 1983*, a Supreme Court judge "may at any time refer the whole action or any question or issue of fact arising therein or question of account to an official referee[209] or to a special referee agreed upon by the parties." However, this power to delegate only exists,

(i) where all parties consent to the reference;[210] or
(ii) where a prolonged examination of documents or a scientific or local investigation is required;[211] or

---

205 Note 196, *supra*.

206 Section 35(4)(c)(ii), as re-enacted by *An Act to amend The Mechanics' Lien Act, supra*, note 201.

207 Section 40(3), as re-enacted by *An Act to amend The Mechanics' Lien Act, supra*, note 201.

208 For example, *Union Elec. Supply Co. Ltd. v. Joice Sweanor Elec. Ltd. et al.* (1974), 5 O.R. (2d) 457 (C.A.) indicates that the power of the master to grant leave to amend any pleadings in a lien action is not limited to the correction of palpable errors or to matters of form, but includes the power to permit amendments of substance. By way of comparison, *Russel Timber Co. Ltd. v. Kallio*, [1937] O.W.N. 12, [1937] 2 D.L.R. 257 (S.C.) appears to provide that, once there is a judgment directing a reference, the matter is referred on the pleadings as they exist at the time of the judgment, and not on the basis that new or modified issues are contemplated. Therefore, the referee would have no authority to grant leave to amend the pleadings.

209 Section 95(1) of the *Judicature Act*, R.S.O. 1980, c. 223, provides, *inter alia*, that masters and local masters are official referees for the trial of such questions as are directed to be tried by an official referee.

210 Section 71(a) of the *Judicature Act*. It should be noted that, in most cases, all parties to a construction lien action do not expressly consent to a reference. Rather, the motion for judgment directing the reference is usually unopposed.

211 Section 71(b) of the *Judicature Act*. The likelihood of there being a "prolonged examination of documents" is no greater in a construction lien trial than in any civil trial involving a commercial dispute.

(iii) where the question in dispute consists wholly or partly of matters of account.[212]

Where none of these conditions is satisfied, the action must be tried by a Supreme Court judge.[213]

The authority for referring most mechanics' lien actions to a master for trial has generally derived from subpara. (iii). Clearly, though, lien actions may involve significant issues which transcend "matters of account." Issues of liability as well as damages[214] are determined. Breach of contract claims, in addition to lien claims, may be entertained.[215] The master at trial may be called upon to make a decision as to the competing priorities claimed by the various persons having an interest in the premises. Personal judgment may be granted.[216] The owner's interest in the premises may be ordered sold.[217] Surely what is involved exceeds mere matters of account.

Aside from these comments, the following factors should be considered:

(a) The judgment directing the reference is generally obtained on *praecipe,* in circumstances where there is no inquiry whatever by a Supreme Court judge as to the issues in dispute; and

(b) In almost every case, the master's report is deemed to have been confirmed without any involvement by a Supreme Court judge.

The scheme which has been developed to avoid constitutional problems clearly contains many fictions.

The foregoing analysis leads one to conclude that, despite the legislative attempt to legitimize lien references, a compelling argument can be made that ss. 60(1), 52(3) and 53 of the *Construction Lien Act, 1983*, to the extent that they relate to the master's trial jurisdiction, are *ultra vires.*

(iv) Obtaining Order for Settlement Meeting and Trial

At any time after the delivery[218] of all statements of defence,[219] or after the time for their delivery has expired, any party to the action may

---

[212] Section 71(c) of the *Judicature Act.*

[213] *V.K. Mason Const. Ltd. v. Courtot Invts. Ltd. et al.* (1975), 9 O.R. (2d) 325 (H.C.).

[214] *Quaere* whether the ascertainment of unliquidated damages for breach of a construction contract arises out of an inquiry into "matters of account."

[215] See s. 57(1).

[216] Section 65.

[217] See ss. 64(5) and 67.

[218] See note 47, *supra.*

[219] Section 62(1) refers to "the statements of defence or the statements of defence to all crossclaims, counterclaims or third party claims, if any, where the plaintiff's claim is disputed."

bring a motion[220] to the court, without notice to any other person, for an order fixing the day, time and place for the trial of the action, and/or for the holding of a settlement meeting.[221]

In the Judicial District of York, the motion is made to the master after the usual judgment has been obtained, pursuant to s. 60(1), referring the action to the master for trial.

Outside of the Judicial District of York, the motion is made to the local judge, unless the local judge had previously ordered,

    (a) that the action be tried by a local judge in another county or district,[222] or

    (b) that the action be tried by a Supreme Court judge on assizes;[223] or

    (c) that the action be referred to the local master for trial.[224]

The judicial officer who fixes the day, time and place of the trial or the settlement meeting does not, by so doing, necessarily become seized of the action.[225]

Where a settlement meeting has been ordered, the party who obtained the appointment must serve[226] a notice thereof[227] at least 10 days in advance of the meeting.[228] The notice must be served upon every person who was, on the 12th day before the meeting date,

    (a) a statutory owner;[229]

    (b) a person named as a defendant in any statement of claim in respect of the action;[230]

---

[220] See Precedent Nos. 56, 57 and 58. Although the motion may be brought "without notice to any other person," the court will usually require the filing of a notice of motion in any event.

[221] Section 62(1).

[222] See s. 51(2)(b).

[223] See s. 51(2)(c).

[224] See s. 60(1)(b).

[225] Section 54.

[226] Section 89(3) 2 requires that, unless otherwise ordered by the court, a notice of trial or settlement meeting may not be mailed, but must be served personally, in the same manner provided for the service of a writ of summons under the Rules of Practice. *Quaere* whether a solicitor may properly accept service on behalf of one of the persons mentioned in s. 62(2).

[227] See Form 18 prescribed by O. Reg. 159/83 filed March 18, 1983, under the *Construction Lien Act, 1983*.

[228] Section 62(2).

[229] Section 62(2)(a). Also see s. 1(1) 15. It is to be noted that a notice of settlement meeting need not be served upon the statutory owner where pleadings have been noted closed against him: see ss. 56(2) and (4).

[230] Section 62(2)(a). To ascertain the names of "every other person named as a defendant in every statement of claim in respect of the action" could be a difficult task. As Master D.D. MacRae (as he then was) wrote,

    The first group of persons named includes the owner and every person named as

(c) a registered encumbrancer,[231]

(d) an execution creditor of the statutory owner(s);[232]

(e) a person having a preserved or perfected lien;[233]

(f) a person who was joined as a third party under s. 58.[234]

In practical terms, this would mean that the person serving the notice must up-date all real estate, Supreme Court office and execution searches no more than 12 days prior to the settlement meeting so as to ensure that all persons mentioned in s. 62(2) have been ascertained and served.

When a trial date has been fixed, the party who obtained the appointment must serve[235] a notice of trial,[236] at least ten days before trial, upon all persons referred to above who would otherwise be entitled to a notice of settlement meeting. Notice of trial need not be served, though, upon any person against whom pleadings have been noted closed.[237]

The person serving the notice of trial and all persons who are served with it, are deemed to be parties to the action.[238]

(v) The Settlement Meeting

In the Judicial District of York (and in numerous other counties), an informal pre-trial system has developed over the years. Although pre-

---

a defendant in every Statement of Claim in respect of the action. Ascertaining who such defendants are will be difficult. It will require the institution of a whole range of inquiries to find out who else has commenced action, which of the defendants in the other actions have been served, when and where, which defendants are in default etc. It is often found at the pre-trial [under the Mechanics' Lien Act procedure] that some of the lien claimants have commenced action but have not served any of the defendants.

(See MacRae, "The Jurisdiction of the Master," in The New Construction Lien Act — Bill 139 (materials distributed at conference sponsored by Oyez Limited, October 7 and 8, 1982, Toronto), at 18.)

It therefore appears that the party, who is obliged to serve notice of the settlement meeting, must conduct a search at the Supreme Court office of all statements of claim relative to the action so as to ensure that *all* defendants have been ascertained and served. This, though, is subject to the proviso that notice need not be served upon any defendant against whom pleadings have been noted closed (see ss. 56(2) and (4)).

[231] Section 62(2)(b). This section provides that notice need only be served upon registered encumbrancers, however, "where the lien attaches to the premises" (see s. 16 (3)).

[232] Section 62(2)(c). This section provides that notice need only be served upon execution creditors, however, "where the lien attaches to the premises" (see s. 16(3)).

[233] Section 62(2)(d).

[234] Section 62(2)(e).

[235] See s. 89(3) 2, and note 226, *supra*.

[236] See Form 17 prescribed by O. Reg. 159/83 filed March 18, 1983, under the *Construction Lien Act, 1983*.

[237] Section 62(4) provides that it is subject to s. 56, which deals with the noting of pleadings closed for default of defence.

[238] Section 59(1).

trials were never sanctioned by the mechanics' lien legislation, their use was well established and almost institutionalized. The fact that they were not "trials,"[239] as such, did not detract from their value.

One would expect that the settlement meeting procedure contemplated by the *Construction Lien Act, 1983* may replace the pre-trial system, so that, if the action is not settled at the settlement meeting stage, the parties would proceed directly to trial.[240] Presumably any party wishing to obtain an order for production and discovery could do so by bringing the appropriate motion at any time after the exchange of pleadings, pursuant to the authority contained in s. 52(3). Most likely, the parties would simply consent to such an order at the settlement meeting, or would obtain the requisite order under s. 63(5)(d) once the statement of settlement has been filed with the court.

The stated purpose of the settlement meeting procedure is to resolve or narrow any issues to be tried in the action.[241] For example, it may be alleged that certain liens were preserved out of time. Alternatively, the amount of the statutory owner's holdback obligation may be in dispute. The settlement meeting will serve to underscore the areas requiring judicial intervention. The issues not in dispute may be agreed upon, thereby narrowing the scope of the trial and significantly reducing the amount of trial time required.

Section 63(2) provides that the settlement meeting should be conducted by either a person selected by the majority of the persons present at the meeting, or, where no person is selected, by the party who obtained the appointment.

The results of the settlement meeting are to be embodied in a "statement of settlement," setting out those issues of fact and law to which the parties have agreed.[242] In an abundance of caution, the statement ought to be clear and unambiguous, and ought to be executed by all parties present who are sought to be bound by it.

The statement shall then be filed with the court as part of the record.[243] Once filed, the settlement shall be binding upon all persons served with notice of the settlement meeting (whether or not they were in

---

[239] See *Kennedy Glass Ltd. v. Jeskay Const. Ltd. et al.,* [1973] 3 O.R. 493, 37 D.L.R. (3d) 321 (Div. Ct.).

[240] This view may not be shared by Master D.D. MacRae (as he then was), who commented that,

> it is my opinion that the pre-trial system as presently [sic] constituted, although not recognized in the legislation, represents a more practical solution [than the settlement meeting procedure] and will continue, particularly in those jurisdictions where the court takes an active part in the pre-trial.

(See MacRae, "The Jurisdiction of the Master," *supra,* note 230, at 22.)

[241] Section 63(2).

[242] Section 63(3).

[243] Section 63(4).

attendance), and upon all defendants against whom pleadings have been noted closed.[244] If any person wishes to seek relief against the binding effect of the statement of settlement, though, a motion may be made to the court[245] for an order varying it or setting it aside, on terms.[246]

Upon the filing of the statement of settlement with the court, the court may,

(a) declare a non-contentious lien valid and give judgment accordingly;[247]

(b) enter a judgment or make a report, on consent, with respect to the issues which have been settled by the parties;[248]

(c) make any order that is necessary to give effect to any judgment or report of the court under (a) or (b) above;[249] and

(d) make any order that will serve to expedite the conduct of the trial.[250]

A motion for an order for a settlement meeting ought not to be automatic, but should be brought only after due consideration of the prospects of a full or partial settlement. As Master D. D. MacRae (formerly the mechanics' lien master in the Judicial District of York) cautioned,

> I would be afraid that if a settlement meeting was held which did not result in any substantial reduction of the trial time it might be contended that because the least expensive course had not been taken[251] no costs should be allowed in respect of it.[252]

(vi) The Trial

The trial of a lien action, whether it be held before a judge or a master, is essentially no different than the trial of any other action. The rules of evidence and the usual formalities involved in the presentation

---

[244] *Ibid.*

[245] Section 52(1) dictates which judicial officer has jurisdiction to entertain such a motion.

[246] Section 63(4). It is to be noted that the court's discretion in varying or setting aside a statement of settlement is subject to s. 56(3). Therefore, if, for example, a defendant, against whom pleadings have been noted closed, wishes to vary or set aside a statement of settlement, he will probably have to satisfy the court that there is evidence to support a defence to the plaintiff's action and that he should also be given leave to defend (on terms).

[247] Section 63(5)(a).

[248] Section 63(5)(b).

[249] Section 63(5)(c).

[250] Section 63(5)(d).

[251] See s. 88(2).

[252] MacRae, "The Jurisdiction of the Master," *supra,* note 230, at 21.

and proof of the case, for example, are generally observed. As s. 69(1) provides, the *Judicature Act*[253] and the Supreme Court Rules of Practice apply to construction lien proceedings.

At the opening of trial, where there is more than one lien action being prosecuted, the court may order that all of the various actions be consolidated into one action,[254] and may award carriage of the action to one of the claimants (most often the one having the largest claim) who has a perfected lien.[255] The solicitor representing the lien claimant having carriage would then be instrumental in organizing and presenting the plaintiffs' case(s).

If no preliminary filings were made at the pre-trial, the solicitor having carriage would file the following documents with the court at the opening of the trial:

1. a duplicate original claim for lien;
2. a certified copy of the abstract of title to the premises;
3. an execution certificate with respect to the statutory owner;
4. the original order appointing the date, time and place for trial;
5. a notice of trial, with proof of service.

If any person having a perfected lien is not served with a notice of trial, he may nevertheless be "let in" at trial to prove his claim at any time before the amount realized in the lien action has been distributed.[256] The same right extends to a person having a perfected lien, whose action was stayed pending compulsory arbitration.[257]

Although an individual is entitled to represent himself at trial, the

---

[253] R.S.O. 1980, c. 223.

[254] Section 61(2)(a). Also see Precedent No. 59.

[255] Section 61(2)(b). Also see Precedent No. 59. It should be noted that the court may make an order *at any time* awarding carriage of the action to any person who has a perfected lien: s. 61(1). The following note of caution to solicitors undertaking the carriage of a consolidated lien action was contained in "The Advisor" (No. 4, April 1983), which is published by The Practice Advisory Service of the Law Society of Upper Canada:

> Practitioners handling cases falling under the new *Construction Lien Act, 1983* must be wary of orders consolidating actions and appointing themselves as solicitors with carriage. The concept of carriage of consolidated actions is preserved in the new Act (s. 61); however, once such an order is made, that solicitor may then be taken to have "knowingly participated in the preservation and perfection" of all liens involved in the consolidated actions and may therefore have consequential exposure as to costs under s. 88, at least to the extent that procedures are taken after the order of consolidation. Either a waiver of the benefit of s. 88 or an indemnity in favour of the solicitor having carriage should be executed with respect to all procedures taken after the order for carriage and consolidation being made, all in consideration of the solicitor having undertaken carriage of the consolidated action.

[256] Section 64(6)(a).

[257] Section 64(6)(b).

weight of authority appears to hold that a corporate party should be represented by counsel.[258] However, where a claim is for an amount which is within the monetary jurisdiction of a small claims court,[259] a lien claimant, corporate or otherwise, may be represented by an agent who is a non-lawyer.[260]

Inasmuch as construction disputes are sometimes technical in nature, the Act provides wide discretion to the court to permit the appointment of an independent architect, engineer, building contractor, or other person to assist the court in determining any fact in issue.[261] The court may fix the cost of such technical assistance and may direct any of the parties to pay it.[262]

Once the evidence is in, the court will assess the validity of all liens, in terms of timeliness and quantum; will determine the proper holdback amount which ought to have been retained by the owner; will balance and adjudicate upon the competing claims for priority; and will deliver judgment accordingly. Although breach of trust claims are not within the purview of the court hearing the lien action,[263] nevertheless the court will entertain an application for directions[264] by a person who has in his possession what might be trust funds, "and the court may give any direction or make any order that the court considers appropriate in the circumstances."[265]

(vii) Judgment After Trial

The results of trial held before a judge or a local judge are to be embodied in a "judgment,"[266] in the prescribed form.[267] Where the trial is

---

258   *Scriven v. Jescott* (1908), 126 L.T. Jour. 100; *Re Arbitration between London County Council etc.* (1897), 13 T.L.R. 254. But see *Northern Homes Ltd. v Steel-Space Industs. Ltd. et al.,* [1975] 5 W.W.R. 115, 57 D.L.R. (3d) 309 (N.W.T.S.C.); *Re Canron Ltd. and Can. Wkrs. Union et al.* (1976), 12 O.R. (2d) 765, 70 D.L.R. (3d) 198 (H.C.); and *Bural et al. v. Thomas Custom Brokers Ltd. et al.* (1978), 20 O.R. (2d) 600, 7 C.P.C. 90 (H.C.).

259   At the date of this writing, the monetary jurisdiction of most small claims courts in Ontario does not exceed $1,000 (see the *Small Claims Courts Act,* R.S.O. 1980, c. 476, s. 55). However, the maximum monetary jurisdiction of the small claims courts comprising the Provincial Court (Civil Division) of the Municipality of Metropolitan Toronto is $3,000 (see the *Provincial Court (Civil Division) Project Act,* R.S.O. 1980, c. 397, s. 6(1)), and may soon be increased to $7,500.

260   Section 69(5).

261   Section 69(4).

262   *Ibid.*

263   Section 50(2).

264   See Precedent Nos. 36, 37 and 38.

265   Section 68.

266   Section 64(1)(a).

267   Forms 19 and 20 prescribed by O. Reg. 159/83 filed March 18, 1983, under the *Construction Lien Act, 1983.*

conducted by a master or a local master on a reference, the results are embodied in a "report,"[268] in the prescribed form.[269]

It is to be noted, though, that the prescribed form of judgment or report may be modified by the court in order to accommodate particular circumstances.[270]

Furthermore, where a lien claimant is "let in" to prove his claim after the judgment or report has been settled but before the amount realized in the action has been distributed, the judgment or report may be amended to include his claim.[271]

The judgment or report generally contains the following types of provisions:

(a) a declaration as to the validity and entitlement of each claim for lien;

(b) a declaration identifying the statutory owner;

(c) an adjudication as to the amount owing to each lien claimant;

(d) a declaration identifying the "primary debtor"[272] of each lien claimant (*i.e.*, the person against whom each lien claimant would be seeking a personal judgment);[273]

(e) a declaration as to the entitlement of certain persons to a charge or an encumbrance, other than a lien, on the interest of the statutory owner (*e.g.*, mortgagees, judgment credtiors, *etc.*);

(f) an adjudication as to the amount of holdback payable by the statutory owner to each lien claimant;

(g) an order fixing the amount that the statutory owner must pay into court in order to discharge all liens;

(h) an order authorizing the sale of the statutory owner's interest in the premises,[274] in the event that the payment into court is not made;

(i) an order that either the monies paid into court by the statutory owner, or the proceeds of sale of the statutory owner's interest in the premises, be paid to those persons entitled to a lien;

(j) a personal judgment in favour of each lien claimant against his "prime debtor" for any deficiency owing, plus interest,[275] once

---

[268] Section 64(1)(b).

[269] Forms 21 and 22 prescribed by O. Reg. 159/83 filed March 18, 1983, under the *Construction Lien Act, 1983*.

[270] Section 64(2).

[271] Section 64(6).

[272] Although the Act makes no specific reference to the term "primary debtor", the prescribed forms of judgment and report do.

[273] See s. 65.

[274] This would obtain only where the lien attaches to the premises.

[275] See s. 14(2).

the amount of the payment contemplated by subpara. (i) above
has been determined;

(k) a personal judgment in favour of each lien claimant, who fails to
establish a lien, against his "primary debtor"; and

(l) an adjudication as to any priority claims in issue.

As indicated above, the court may award any lien claimant a
personal judgment, whether he proves his lien or not, against any party to
the action.[276] It is to be noted, though, that, with respect to a sheltered
claim for lien, the scope of a personal judgment is limited to the defendants and the nature of the relief claimed in the statement of claim
under which it is sheltered.[277]

By virtue of its derivative nature, a "report," as distinguished from a
"judgment," would ordinarily have to be confirmed by a Supreme Court
judge before it takes effect. However, a report is *deemed* to be confirmed
after the expiry of 15 days from the date notice of filing the report[278]
with the court is given[279] to all parties, unless a notice of appeal is served[280]
within that time.[281]

Where a judgment directs that any payment be made, execution may
be issued immediately.[282] In the case of a report, however, the issuance of
execution must await confirmation.[283]

(viii) Judicial Sale

A judgment or report generally provides that, if a statutory owner
refuses or neglects to pay into court the amount for which he is found by
the court to be liable, his interest in the premises may be ordered sold.[284]

Such a sale would take place under the court's supervision and
subject to its approval. The sale procedure, whether it be by listing with an
agent, by the solicitation of bids, by auction, or otherwise, would have to
be authorized by the court. Similarly, the court would provide directions
regarding the nature and extent of advertising required, and would be
responsible for approving the acceptance of any offers, or for establishing
a reserve bid, as the case may be.

Further, the court would make all orders necessary for the com-

---

[276] Section 65.
[277] See ss. 65 and 36(4) 3.
[278] See Precedent No. 60.
[279] See s. 89(1).
[280] See s. 89(3) 3.
[281] Section 64(3).
[282] Section 64(4)(a).
[283] Section 64(4)(b).
[284] Section 64(5).

pletion of a sale, including an order vesting an interest in the premises in the purchaser.[285]

Where there is a judicial sale pursuant to a judgment or a report, or where a trustee appointed under Part IX of the Act sells an interest in the premises in pursuance of his authority,[286] the sale proceeds are to be paid into court to the credit of the lien action.[287]

The court would then direct payment of the sale proceeds in accordance with priorities established by the Act.[288] In this regard, it should be noted that the party having carriage of the sale proceedings is entitled to add to his claim his fees and actual disbursements incurred in connection with the sale.[289]

A person with a perfected lien is entitled to share in the proceeds of sale, in respect of the amount owing to him, despite the fact that that amount was not payable to him at the time of the commencement of the action, or at the time of the distribution of the proceeds.[290] This serves to protect the lien claimant by permitting him to share in the distribution, notwithstanding that he may have granted an extended period of credit to the statutory owner. As the Attorney General's Advisory Committee on the Draft *Construction Lien Act* commented,

> [T]he claims of all persons who have a right to claim against [the owner's] interest [in the premises] must be disposed of in a single proceeding. If a person who was entitled to a lien were not allowed to realize upon that lien at the same time as the other claimants, his lien right would be lost.[291]

Where the sale proceeds are insufficient to satisfy the judgment and costs, the court will ascertain the amount of the deficiency and will grant

---

[285] Section 67(1). Also see Precedent No. 63.

[286] Section 70(2)(a) authorizes a court-appointed trustee, *inter alia*, to sell the premises, or any part thereof, subject to the approval of the court and the *Planning Act*, R.S.O. 1980, c. 379.

[287] Section 67(2).

[288] Section 67(4).

[289] Section 67(3). In actions under the *Mechanics' Lien Act*, R.S.O. 1980, c. 261, the party having carriage of the sale proceedings was generally entitled to treat his "salvage costs", which were the fees and disbursements incurred in connection with the sale, as a first charge on the sale proceeds. This was a fair approach, since the party having carriage was in fact acting for the benefit and in the interest of all parties. Section 67(3), however, clouds this issue, and appears to provide that the party having carriage is merely entitled to add his salvage costs to his claim. If all claimants ultimately receive, say, 50 cents on the dollar, the party having carriage will have incurred an additional unrecoverable expense that none of the other claimants incurred. For this reason, no party may be willing to undertake carriage, unless of course his fees and disbursements are protected. Presumably, though, the court can make the necessary order to avoid this problem, under the authority of s. 67(1). Section 67(3), it should be noted, is permissive, and not mandatory.

[290] Section 66.

[291] *Report of the Attorney General's Advisory Committee on the Draft Construction Lien Act* (April 1982), at 154.

personal judgment to each claimant for that amount against each person who is found to be liable to him.[292]

(ix) Costs

Under the *Mechanics' Lien Act,* there was a 25 percent ceiling on the amount of costs recoverable both by and against the plaintiff and other persons claiming liens. This limitation has not been carried forward into the *Construction Lien Act, 1983.*

As with ordinary actions, costs continue to be in the complete discretion of the court. The Act, however, contains references to costs which may serve as a suggestion or an implicit direction in certain circumstances.

According to s. 88(1), costs may be awarded against,

(a) any party to the action;[293] or

(b) the solicitor or agent of any party to the action, where that person has prejudiced or delayed the conduct of the action, or has knowingly participated in the preservation or perfection of a lien that is without foundation, or is for a grossly excessive amount, or that has expired.[294]

Section 88(1) further provides that "the order may be made on a solicitor-and-client basis." The court would have the authority to do this without legislative enactment. One might therefore infer that this provision is meant to be a direction to the court that the "wrongful" conduct referred to above will be met with relatively severe consequences.

From another perspective, if a successful party, who is entitled to an award of costs, imprudently does not take the least expensive course in proceeding to trial, his costs award will be adjusted (downward) accordingly.[295]

I. APPEALS

(i) Stated Case

Where in the course of an action a question of law arises, the court may state the question in the form of a stated case for the opinion of the Divisional Court.[296] Once the stated case is set down to be heard, the party

---

[292] Section 67(5).
[293] Section 88(1)(a).
[294] Section 88(1)(b).
[295] Section 88(2).
[296] Section 72(1).

setting down the matter is obliged to serve[297] notice of the hearing upon all parties concerned.[298] The stated case shall set forth those facts material to the determination of the question of law raised.[299]

(ii) Appeal from Judgment or Report

So long as the amount in issue is more than $1,000,[300] an appeal lies from a judgment or a report to the Divisional Court.[301]

The Rules of Practice of the Supreme Court of Ontario govern any such appeal proceeding.[302]

Where the appeal is in respect of a report, the appellant must file and serve[303] his notice of appeal[304] prior to the confirmation of the report,[305] which, as indicated in s. 64(3), is deemed to occur 15 days after notice of filing the report[306] with the court is given[307] to all parties.

Where the appeal is in respect of a judgment, the appellant shall file and serve[308] his notice of appeal[309] within 15 days of the date of judgment.[310]

In either instance, the time for filing or serving the notice of appeal may be extended by the written consent of all parties, or by a single judge of the Divisional Court where the extension can be shown to be justified.[311]

(iii) Appeal from Interlocutory Order

The Act dictates that the procedure in a lien action shall be as far as possible of a summary character.[312] Generally speaking, interlocutory proceedings are discouraged and, except for those specifically provided

---

[297] See s. 89(3) 3. *Quaere* whether a notice of hearing of a stated case must be served in the same manner as a notice of appeal.
[298] Section 72(1).
[299] Section 72(2).
[300] Section 73(3)(a).
[301] Section 73(1).
[302] Section 69(3).
[303] See s. 89(3) 3.
[304] See Precedent No. 61.
[305] Section 73(2)(a).
[306] See Precedent No. 60.
[307] See s. 89(1).
[308] See s. 89(3) 3.
[309] See Precedent No. 62.
[310] Section 73(2)(b).
[311] Section 73(2).
[312] Section 69(1).

for in the Act, are not to be taken without the consent of the court.[313] To obtain such consent, it must be demonstrated that the proceedings are necessary or would expedite the resolution of the issues in dispute.[314]

Consistent with the foregoing theory, s. 73(3)(b) provides that no appeal lies from an interlocutory order made by the court. Interlocutory orders, by definition, do not finally dispose of an action on its merits.

(iv) Costs of Appeal

Where the amount involved in an appeal is within the proper competence of the county court,[315] the costs of the appeal shall be on the county court scale, "except where otherwise ordered."[316]

Where the amount involved exceeds the monetary jurisdiction of the county court, the costs of the appeal shall be on the Supreme Court scale, "except where otherwise ordered."[317]

---

[313] Section 69(2).
[314] *Ibid.*
[315] See the *County Courts Act,* R.S.O. 1980, c. 100, s. 14(1), as amended by S.O. 1981, c. 24, s. 1.
[316] Section 88(3).
[317] *Ibid.*

Chapter 10

Priorities

A. SETTING THE STAGE

Many lien disputes which are litigated are not between the construction trades, on the one hand, and the general contractor or the project owner, on the other. Rather, where a general contractor or an owner becomes insolvent or bankrupt, as appears to have become an unfortunate trend in Ontario over the last few years, the trades may be obliged to do legal battle with the mortgage lender who financed construction. The ensuing litigation often revolves around the competing claims to a finite and usually inadequate source of funds and assets. It is in this context that the priority provisions of the *Construction Lien Act, 1983* become extremely important.

A lien claimant may legitimately argue that his supply of services and materials has increased the value of the property being improved, thereby enhancing the mortgage security held by the lender who financed construction. However, the failure of that lien claimant to establish the priority of his claim over that of the lender may result, in practical terms, in his lien remedy becoming entirely nugatory.

The mortgage lender has another perspective. He claims to be entitled to complete and unassailable security for the monies lent because of the financial risks he has assumed, and because those monies grease the wheels of construction and have made it possible for the owner to be able to afford to provide employment for the construction trades.

If the security created by a mortgage were to be placed in jeopardy by virtue of the competing claims of lien claimants, lenders would likely respond by establishing a new framework of stringent lending guidelines. This would create concerns among borrowers regarding the feasibility of undertaking new construction projects, and would impact significantly upon the entire industry and the consumer public.

In addition to dealing with the competing claims of mortgage lenders and lien claimants, the *Construction Lien Act, 1983* also establishes a set scheme of priorities amongst different "classes"[1] of lien claimants, and between lien claimants, execution creditors, and trust fund beneficiaries.

---

[1] See ss. 81 and 82.

Aside from the statutory provisions contained in the Act, there are also equitable principles of law, as well as other legislation, which may be relevant in a priority dispute. For example, in certain circumstances mortgage security could be attacked, pursuant to the provisions of the *Bankruptcy Act,*[2] the *Assignments and Preferences Act*[3] or the *Fraudulent Conveyances Act,*[4] on the basis that one creditor may have received preferential treatment over that given to other creditors. What must usually be proved is that the mortgage was given by the owner with the intention of hindering, delaying, defeating, defrauding or otherwise prejudicing the claims of lien claimants.

In the same vein, where, for example, the principal of a corporation, which owns a construction project, causes the corporation to grant a non-arm's length mortgage to the principal's wife, allegedly as security for what turns out to be a non-existent shareholder's loan, the mortgage could be set aside as a sham.[5]

Furthermore, assuming all of the relevant factors are present, the lien claimants may be entitled to petition the court to invoke the doctrine of marshalling, in order to oblige the mortgagee to realize upon other pledged security before realizing upon the security which he has in the property in which the lien claimants also have an interest.[6]

B. COMPETING PRIORITIES AS BETWEEN LIENS AND MORTGAGES

(i) Introduction

The value of the security held by a mortgage lender is fundamentally dependent upon and directly related to the extent of the priority of his interest in the secured lands over the interests of others in those same lands. As will be seen, that is one of the reasons why building mortgages are advanced in stages as construction progresses.

Subject to the provisions of the *Construction Lien Act, 1983,* which will be discussed below, the value of a lender's secured interest ordinarily extends to, and is limited by, the amount of monies actually advanced,

---

[2] R.S.C. 1970, c. B-3 (see ss. 73-75).

[3] R.S.O. 1980, c. 33 (see s. 4).

[4] R.S.O. 1980, c. 176.

[5] See, for example, *Hart Hotel & Restaurant Equipment Inc. v. Carfa et al.* (1982), 34 O.R. (2d) 760, 126 D.L.R. (3d) 95 (S.C.).

[6] For a discussion of the doctrines of marshalling and subrogation, see Samuel L. Phillips, *A Treatise on the Law of Mechanics' Liens on Real and Personal Property,* 3rd ed. (1893), at 455ff.

plus interest thereon,[7] irrespective of the face amount of the mortgage instrument registered on title.

The value of the security which the Act provides to the construction trades is governed by analogous principles. A person's construction lien arises and takes effect when he first supplies services or materials to a project.[8] The lien will continue to exist until it either expires,[9] or is formally preserved[10] and perfected.[11] Once his lien is preserved by registration, a lien claimant is deemed by s. 78 of the Act to be a "purchaser," to the extent of his lien, within the provisions of the *Registry Act*[12] and the *Land Titles Act*.[13] This means that, once registered, a lien will have priority over any subsequent interest in the premises, other than another lien in respect of the same improvement.[14] By way of analogy to mortgage advances, the lien is limited in amount to the price[15] of the services or materials that have actually been supplied,[16] irrespective of the face amount of the contract or subcontract giving rise to the lien, and irrespective of any damage claim which the lien claimant might be entitled to assert.

As the work proceeds, progress invoices are usually rendered. So long as regular payments on account are received, and funds (with the exception of holdback) are transmitted down the construction pyramid, no resort would be had to the lien remedy, and priority issues would not arise.

While seeking to protect their individual interests, all parties must maintain an equilibrium in the financial aspects of construction by ensuring the continuation of a smooth and regular flow of both mortgage draws and progress payments. If that equilibrium is upset by the mortgagee's refusal to advance further funds or by the registration of a claim for lien, construction could be brought to a standstill while all parties assess the potential impact of the scheme of priorities established by the Act upon their secured interests in the property.

(ii) Securing the Holdbacks

The concept of a "holdback" was established in order to provide

---

[7] See *Sullivan (M.) & Son Ltd. v. Rideau Carleton Raceway Holdings Ltd.,* [1971] S.C.R. 2, 12 D.L.R. (3d) 662.
[8] Section 15.
[9] See s. 31.
[10] See s. 34.
[11] See s. 36.
[12] R.S.O. 1980, c. 445.
[13] R.S.O. 1980, c. 230.
[14] See *Report of the Attorney General's Advisory Committee on the Draft Construction Lien Act* (April 1982), at 177.
[15] See s. 1(1) 20.
[16] See ss. 14, 17(1) and 34(5)(d).

some financial protection for those persons who have worked on or have supplied materials to a construction project, thereby enhancing its value, but who would not otherwise be entitled to assert any direct claim against the owner since they had no privity of contract with him. Theoretically, according to the Act, the trades should always be able to look to the holdback funds as providing them with a modicum of security in the event that, for whatever reason, there is an interruption in the downward flow of payments.

The holdback, however, is only a notional concept. Under the *Mechanics' Lien Act*,[17] the holdback scheme essentially provided the owner with an additional form of construction financing, at the expense of the trades, since he was not required either to establish a holdback fund, or to release the 15 percent holdback amount until after the expiry of the lien period. If the owner became insolvent or bankrupt, and defaulted on the mortgage which was granted to a lender to secure construction financing, what invariably happened was that the interest which accrued on the mortgage, as well as the insurance premiums and other charges which were added to the mortgage debt, diminished the equity in the property, to the prejudice of the lien claimants. In almost every such case, the owner would not have set aside a separate and identifiable holdback fund. As a result, there would be neither a holdback fund nor any equity in the property to which the lien claimants could look for satisfaction of their claims.

The Attorney General's Advisory Committee on the Draft *Construction Lien Act* considered a variety of options in an attempt to ensure that the new legislation would properly secure the statutory holdbacks for the benefit of the lien claimants. The Council of Ontario Contractors Associations recommended to the Committee that, when progress payments are made, the holdback should be paid into a bank account in the joint names of the owner and the general contractor. This would have served to create an actual, interest-bearing holdback fund. This proposal, though, was rejected as being administratively unwieldy. Moreover, it was noted that the majority of construction projects are completed and payment is made without incident, so that the necessity for requiring a joint trust account for every project, regardless of its size or other characteristics, would be unnecessarily expensive and burdensome.

In addition, the prospect of bonding the holdbacks was considered but rejected, essentially on the basis that it would be unduly expensive and would tend to discriminate against smaller contractors who might have difficulty qualifying for bonds.

Ultimately, the Committee decided that the best method to secure the holdback was to create a new scheme of priorities which would

---

[17] R.S.O. 1980, c. 261.

effectively put a heavier responsibility on the mortgage lender, who usually controls the flow of funds, and whose position is often bolstered by collateral security.

Section 80 of the Act contains a comprehensive code for determining priorities. That section is introduced with the basic premise that, "[e]*xcept as provided in this section*, the liens arising from any improvement have priority over all conveyances, mortgages or other agreements affecting the owner's interest in the premises."[18] The balance of that section purports to dictate and clarify the exceptions to the stated rule.

The Act distinguishes between three different classes of mortgages which may be registered against the title to a construction project:

1. building mortgages;
2. non-building mortgages registered *after* the time the first lien arises; and
3. non-building mortgages registered *before* the time the first lien arises.

(iii) The "Building Mortgage" (Section 80(2))

A "building mortgage" is one which is taken "with the intention to secure the financing of an improvement."[19] The relevant "intention" is that of the lender, and not of the borrower.[20]

Whether or not a particular mortgage is a building mortgage is a question of fact. In this regard, it should be noted that s. 39(2) of the Act authorizes any person having a lien, or any beneficiary of a trust under Part II, to require a mortgagee to provide "sufficient details concerning any mortgage on the premises to enable the person who requests the information to determine whether the mortgage was taken by the mortgagee for the purposes of financing the making of the improvement." Further evidence may be garnered from the original mortgage application documentation, as well as the mortgagee's commitment letter.

Section 80(2) provides that liens have priority over a building mortgage, regardless of when it is registered, to the extent of any deficiency in the holdback monies required to be retained by the owner under the Act. That subsection, though, applies only to mortgages that were registered on or after April 2, 1983.[21]

By way of illustration, suppose an owner grants a building mortgage to a lender, and then engages a general contractor to commence con-

---

[18] Section 80(1); emphasis added.
[19] Section 80(2).
[20] Section 80(2) is introduced with the words, "Where a *mortgagee* takes a mortgage with the intention to secure the financing of an improvement . . ." (emphasis added).
[21] Section 80(9).

struction. If the owner were to become insolvent or bankrupt subsequently, it would be likely that, despite his statutory obligation to hold back, say, $100,000, no actual fund would be available for distribution to lien claimants. In this situation, the liens would have priority over the building mortgage to the full extent of $100,000. In this way, although no holdback fund as such exists, the accruing interest on the building mortgage would not detrimentally affect the lien claimants.

It is to be noted that the priority of the lien, as discussed above, is only with respect to such deficiency in the holdback as may exist, and is not necessarily for the full amount of the required holdback.[22] If, for example, the owner was obliged to hold back $100,000, but in fact only retained $95,000, the extent of the priority of the lien over the building mortgage would be limited to the difference, namely $5,000.

It should further be noted that a "takeout" mortgage, which replaces a building mortgage upon the completion of construction, will be subject to the same loss of priority in favour of the lien claimants as the building mortgage which it is designed to replace.[23]

(iv) Non-Building Mortgages Registered After the Time the First Lien Arises (Section 80(5))

A person's lien "arises" and takes effect when he first supplies services or materials to an improvement.[24] The determination of that point in time, as well as the dates a mortgage is registered and advanced, are pivotal in terms of analyzing the competing priority claims of lien claimants and mortgage lenders.

It is not uncommon for a lender to register a collateral mortgage against the title to a property after construction has already commenced but before any lien claims are registered. Before the enactment of the *Construction Lien Act, 1983*, such a collateral mortgage had full priority over any subsequently registered claim for lien, irrespective of when the mortgage monies were actually advanced, and irrespective of whether or not they were used to improve the property.

Dorbern Invts. Ltd. v. Unity Bank of Can. et al.,[25] which was decided before the enactment of the *Construction Lien Act, 1983*, may serve to illustrate an aspect of this point. There, the owners of a property in St. Catharines, Ontario, namely Frank Lentini and Tony Caparello, engaged Dorbern Investments Ltd. to re-construct and renovate an old clothing

---

[22] Section 80(2).

[23] *Ibid.*

[24] Section 15.

[25] (1977), 20 O.R. (2d) 137, 86 D.L.R. (3d) 739, 29 C.B.R. (N.S.) 30 (Div. Ct.); affd. (1980), 23 O.R. (2d) 649, 97 D.L.R. (3d) 576 (C.A.); affd. [1981] 1 S.C.R. 459, 37 N.R. 74, 122 D.L.R. (3d) 197, 18 R.P.R. 145.

store into a modern restaurant. On September 11, 1972, the initial work of gutting the interior of the building began. In April 1973, the Unity Bank of Canada agreed to loan money to Messrs. Lentini and Caparello to finance this work, and apparently advanced the sum of $245,000 between April 5 and June 15, 1973. Mortgage security was given to the bank on other property, but was apparently considered to be inadequate. Consequently, further security, by way of a collateral mortgage on the subject property, was given by the owners to the bank. The collateral mortgage, which purported to secure the principal sum of $175,000, was dated July 12, 1973 and was registered July 30, 1973. On August 1, 1973, two days after the registration of the collateral mortgage, Dorbern registered its claim for lien.

One of the issues in the case was whether Dorbern's claim for lien had priority over the bank's collateral mortgage. At trial, the court (per Scott Co. Ct. J.) held that the lien took priority over the bank's mortgage, presumably on the dual bases that the bank had knowledge that work was going on at the mortgaged premises and therefore had actual notice of Dorbern's lien,[26] and that the monies advanced by the bank were not "advances made on account of . . . [the] mortgage."[27] The Divisional Court (per Weatherston J.), in allowing the bank's appeal, held that a registered mortgage takes priority over a prior unregistered claim for a mechanics' lien, in accordance with ss. 69(1) and 70 of the *Registry Act*,[28] which provided that priority of registration prevails in the absence of actual notice of prior unregistered claims. Dorbern's appeal to the Ontario Court of Appeal was dismissed without written or recorded reasons, but leave to appeal to the Supreme Court of Canada was granted shortly thereafter. On May 28, 1981, the Supreme Court of Canada (per Laskin C.J.C., Ritchie, Beetz, Estey and McIntyre JJ. concurring) dismissed Dorbern's appeal, holding that the *Mechanics' Lien Act* afforded no protection to an unregistered lien claimant, and accordingly the case must be decided on priority of registration. As the Chief Justice stated:

I do not think that any supportable distinction can be drawn between a collateral

---

[26] Section 14(1) of the *Mechanics' Lien Act*, R.S.O. 1970, c. 267, which was then in effect, provided as follows (emphasis added):

14(1) The lien has priority over all judgments, executions, assignments, attachments, garnishments and receiving orders recovered, issued or made *after the lien arises, and over all payments or advances made on account of any conveyance or mortgage after notice in writing of the lien has been given to the person making such payments* or after registration of a claim for the lien as hereinafter provided, and, in the absence of such notice in writing or the registration of a claim for lien, all such payments or advances have priority over any such lien.

[27] *Ibid.*

[28] R.S.O. 1970, c. 409.

mortgage which, as here, was given as additional security for a previous advance made to finance construction on the land on which a lien is claimed and a collateral mortgage given as additional security for an advance not related to construction on the particular land. It was pointed out by counsel for the respondent and conceded by counsel for the appellant that the *Mechanics' Lien Act* does not purport to control the destination of advances made on security of land on which a lien arises. They may be put to uses other than for construction and improvement of the mortgaged land, save as the mortgage itself, through the requirement of progress certificates to support further advances as stipulated in the mortgage, provides some control. In the present case, therefore, I find no basis upon which the collateral mortgage, by reason only of being collateral, may be subordinated to an unregistered or later registered lien claim of which the mortgagee had no previous notice.

. . .

In short, the difficulty with the appellant's position lies in its attempt to found its priority on an unregistered lien claim. The statute gives no support to this, and I see no escape from the conclusion that the present case must be decided on priority of registration.[29]

Given what was felt to be a "major inequity in the law"[30] resulting from this decision, the Legislature, in enacting s. 80(5) of the *Construction Lien Act, 1983,* saw fit to provide that, where any mortgage[31] is registered after the first lien arose, the liens arising from the improvement would have priority over the mortgage to the extent of any deficiency in the holdback monies required to be retained by the owner. That subsection, though, applies only to mortgages that were registered on or after April 2, 1983.[32]

As the Attorney General's Advisory Committee on the Draft *Construction Lien Act* commented in its Report,

> While the Committee does not disagree with the Supreme Court's decision as an application of the existing law, in the opinion of the Committee, to permit a subsequent collateral mortgage to take full priority over the liens is unjust. A subsequent collateral mortgage may provide no additional funds to enable the

---

[29] (1981), 37 N.R. 74 at 79-80.

[30] *Report of the Attorney General's Advisory Committee on the Draft Construction Lien Act* (April 1982), at 183.

[31] It is to be noted that the proposed *Construction Lien Amendment Act, 1983,* which is expected to receive First Reading in October of 1983 and which will be deemed to have come into force on April 2, 1983, purports to change the introductory words of s. 80(5) from:

> (5) Where any mortgage is registered after the time when the first lien arose in respect of an improvement . . .

to:

> Where a mortgage affecting the owner's interest in the premises is registered after the time when the first lien arose in respect of an improvement . . .

This proposed change is intended to make it clear that a mortgage of the interest in the premises of a person who is not a statutory owner is not affected by the priority of liens.

[32] Section 80(9).

owner to pay for the work that has been done on its property. At the same time it reduces the value of the owner's interest in the premises, and thereby reduces the equity available to satisfy the lien claimants should the owner subsequently become insolvent. It should be noted that the value of the property will usually increase as a result of the improvement, and that the mortgagee will enjoy greater security than if the improvement had not been made. If there is a sale under the mortgage, the price received will reflect the improved value of the premises. Since the mortgagee will enjoy the benefit of the improvement, it is unfair for the lien claimants to suffer as a result of the reduction in the owner's equity. The liens should have priority to the extent of any deficiency in the holdback that the owner is required to retain. Providing the lien claimants with this priority protects their rights from total eradication by the registration of a subsequent collateral mortgage.[33]

The priority of the lien over a mortgage, as contemplated by s. 80(5), is not affected by the knowledge (or lack of knowledge) on the part of the mortgagee as to the making of the improvement:

The effect of the improvement will almost always be to enhance the value of the premises. As a person holding a security interest in the premises, the mortgagee will enjoy the benefit of this enhancement, irrespective of his knowledge of its making.[34]

Subject to the rather significant qualification contained in s. 80(5), advances under a mortgage that is registered after the time the first lien arises have priority over any lien, unless (a) at the time when the mortgage advance was made, a claim for lien had been preserved or perfected,[35] or (b) prior to any such advance, the mortgagee received written notice of a lien.[36]

The foregoing priority principles may be illustrated by the use of the following example. Suppose a person's lien arises on June 1. Written notice of the lien is given to the owner and the mortgagee on July 1, and the lien is preserved and perfected on July 5 and 30, respectively. If a (non-building) mortgage had been registered prior to June 1, then s. 80(5) would not apply. If the mortgage had been registered on June 2, though, it would ordinarily have priority, pursuant to s. 80(6), with respect to all advances made up to July 1 (*i.e.*, the date on which the mortgagee received written notice of the lien); but any advances made subsequent to July 1 would be subordinate to the lien. However, the priority of the mortgage may only be sustained if the owner has properly complied with his holdback obligations under the Act. If he has not, then, pursuant to s. 80(5), the liens would have priority over all advances to the extent of any deficiency in the holdback monies required to be retained by the owner.

It therefore becomes apparent that there is a heavy onus on the

---

[33] *Report of the Attorney General's Advisory Committee on the Draft Construction Lien Act* (April 1982), at 184.
[34] *Ibid.*, at 185.
[35] Section 80(6)(a).
[36] Section 80(6)(b). Also see Precedent No. 18.

mortgage lender to protect the security of the holdback, and his failure to do so could prejudice or diminish the extent of his security.

(v) Section 80(5) Priority and New Home Purchases[37]

On May 20, 1983, the Attorney General for Ontario made the following statement in the Legislature:

> Mr. Speaker, on January 25th, 1983, the House gave 2nd and 3rd Reading to Bill 216, the Construction Lien Act, 1983. The Act came into force on April 2nd. Some members of the Legislature and others have raised a problem that is causing hardship to new home purchasers. I have been asked to intervene to redress the problem. It is my intention to do so.
>
>   . . .
>
> The problem raised by the Member for Oshawa relates particularly to subsection 80(5), dealing with the priority of liens over mortgages registered subsequent to the commencement of an improvement.
>
> When a purchaser of a new home who has not had the house built for him or her and, therefore, is not an "owner" under the Act, closes the transaction, advances the purchase price and receives a conveyance from the builder, it is clear that if no liens are registered at the time and the purchaser has no written notice of a lien, the interest of the purchaser has priority over any lien. That is the effect of subsection 80(6).
>
> It has long been, and in my opinion, is now the law, that a mortgage arranged by the purchaser, who is not an owner, advanced and registered at closing also has priority over liens which have not been registered.
>
> It was not our intention to confiscate part of the interest of mortgagees lending to purchasers. The lien is a right over the interest in the property of the person who had the improvement made.
>
> While several highly regarded lawyers have given the same opinion as I have just expressed, doubt remains in the mind of some lenders.
>
> They have not been advancing 10 or more percent of the price on closing. Some purchasers of new homes have been forced to arrange interim financing for a period of up to sixty days from closing. Not only could this be harmful to the individual purchaser, but it also could put a cloud over purchasing a home and might thereby harm the construction industry which is important to the economic health of the province.
>
> I could refer the interpretation of the subsection to the courts and wait for clarification. However, that would not be the desire of the Government or of Members opposite.
>
> While I had hoped to wait for at least a year before making amendments to the Act, I believe that there should be amendments in the near future to clarify the intention of the legislation.
>
> The effect of the amendments that I will bring forward will be to make it clear that a mortgage of a purchaser's interest in a new home is not subject to the priorities of subsections 80(2) or of 80(5). These amendments will be retroactive to April 2nd when the Act came into force.
>
> In addition, the conveyancing Bar has requested that there be legislative clarifi-

---

[37] See generally "Amendments to the Construction Lien Act" (heading D of Chapter 1). Also see note 31, *supra*.

cation of when a purchaser of a new home becomes an owner, and thereby becomes responsible for holdback. The amendments will clarify this issue.

Mr. Speaker, I trust that the lenders in the province will act on this statement of intention to bring forward legislation. It is not necessary, and it is undesirable, for a lender to a purchaser to be concerned about the priority of liens under subsections 80(2) or 80(5).[38]

Further to this statement, the Ministry of the Attorney General proposed the enactment of the *Construction Lien Amendment Act, 1983,* which is expected to receive First Reading in October of 1983 and which will be deemed to have come into force on April 2, 1983. One of the proposed amendments involves the addition of the words "but does not include a home buyer" to the end of the definition of "owner." "Home buyer" is defined in the amending legislation to mean "a person who buys the interest of an owner in a premises that is a home, whether built or not at the time the agreement of purchase and sale in respect thereof is entered into, where not more than 20 percent of the purchase price is paid prior to the conveyance and where the home is not conveyed until it is ready for occupancy, evidenced in the case of a new home by the issuance under the *Building Code Act* of a permit authorizing occupancy or the issuance under the *Ontario New Home Warranties Plan Act* of a certificate of completion and possession". Furthermore, "home" is defined to mean,

i. a self-contained one-family dwelling, detached or attached to one or more others by common wall,
ii. a building composed of more than one and not more than two self-contained, one-family dwellings under one ownership, or
iii. a condominium dwelling unit, including the common elements,
and includes any structure or works used in conjunction therewith.

Section 5 of the *Construction Lien Act, 1983* would also be amended by the addition of the following subsection:

Without restricting the generality of subsection (1), an agreement of purchase and sale that provides for the making or completion of an improvement shall, where the purchaser is an owner, be deemed to provide for the retention of a holdback by the purchaser, and tender by the purchaser on closing is not defective by reason only that the purchaser does not tender the amount of the holdback.

Finally, s. 80 would be amended by the addition of the following subsection:

(11) Subsections (2) and (5) do not apply to a mortgage given or assumed by a home buyer.

---

[38] May 20, 1983 *Statement by The Honourable R. Roy McMurtry, Attorney General for Ontario.*

(vi) Non-Building Mortgages Registered Before the Time the First Lien Arises (Sections 80(3) and (4))

As noted above, a person's lien "arises" and takes effect when he first supplies services or materials to the construction project.[39]

Sections 80(3) and (4) deal with "prior mortgages" (*i.e.*, mortgages which are registered before any lien arises). Generally, mortgages that are registered prior to the first supply of services or materials to the project, have priority over all liens which subsequently may arise. However, under the Act, that priority is limited to the *lesser* of (a) the actual value of the premises at the time when the first lien arose,[40] and (b) the total amount of all advances made up to the time when the first lien arose.[41]

If, for example, the actual value of the premises at the time the first lien arose was $100,000, but only $80,000 had been advanced at that time, the mortgage would have priority over the lien to the extent of $80,000. This surely makes sense since only $80,000 had been advanced. However, if the numbers were to be reversed, and if the actual value of the property at the time the first lien arose was $80,000, but $100,000 had been advanced, the mortgage would have priority only to the extent of $80,000, and would be subordinate to the lien in respect of the $20,000 balance. This latter example is unlikely to occur, though, unless there is non-institutional mortgage financing, where appraisals are not obtained, or unless real estate values are falling rapidly.

Advances will usually continue to be made under a prior mortgage after the first lien arises. Each "subsequent advance" would have priority over any liens, unless (a) at the time the advance was made, there was a preserved or perfected lien against the premises,[42] or (b) prior to the advance, the lender received written notice of a lien.[43] Suffice it to say that, if a lien is preserved or perfected or the mortgagee receives written notice of a lien, the advance ought not to be made.

---

[39] Section 15.
[40] Section 80(3)(a). This provision is similar to s. 8(3) of the *Mechanics' Lien Act*, R.S.O. 1980, c. 261. The jurisprudence appears to indicate that the onus of proving the "actual value of the premises" is on the mortgagee: see *Dominion Lbr. and Fuel Co., Ltd. v. Paskov et al.*, 29 Man. R. 325, [1919] 1 W.W.R. 657 (K.B.). However, where the lien claimant's priority depends upon an *increased* value of the property, the onus of proof is on the lien claimant: see *Independent Lbr. Co. v. Bocz et al.* (1911), 4 Sask. L.R. 103, 16 W.L.R. 316 (C.A.).
[41] Section 80(3)(b)(i). This provision is similar to s. 15(1) of the *Mechanics' Lien Act*, R.S.O. 1980, c. 261. The *Mechanics' Lien Act* provision spoke in terms of "advances made *on account of* any ... mortgage," whereas the current provision deals with "the total of all amounts ... advanced *in the case of* a mortgage." One might speculate that this change in wording was effected in order to clarify that no distinction ought to be drawn in the case of a collateral mortgage.
[42] Section 80(4).
[43] Section 80(5).

(vii) Priority Problems and the Use of Bonding

Where an owner of a construction project goes into default under his mortgage, the lender may wish to take power of sale proceedings. However, if a lien claimant has claimed priority over the mortgage, a prospective purchaser may be unwilling to complete the sale transaction due to his concern as to whether the mortgagee/vendor is capable of conveying title to the property free of the priority of the liens.

In these circumstances, the mortgagee would be able to facilitate the sale of the property by obtaining a Financial Guarantee Bond, in a form prescribed by the regulations.[44] The principal of the bond (*i.e.,* the party primarily obliged to pay) would be the mortgagee, and the obligees (*i.e.,* the persons who are guaranteed payment) would be "all persons having liens whose liens are entitled to priority over the interest of the principal under subsection 80(2) or (5) of the Act."[45] The surety who issues the bond would be responsible for paying the obligees only in the event that the principal defaults in so doing.

Once the bond is registered against the title to the premises, a purchaser would take title from the mortgagee free of the priority of the liens created by ss. 80(2) or (5), and the bond would take the place of the priority created by those subsections,[46] thereby providing alternative security for the lien claimants. Persons who have proved liens have a statutory right of action, as obligees, against the surety on the bond.[47]

The prescribed form of bond provides that the surety is not liable to pay more than a total maximum amount equivalent to 20 percent of the contract price.[48] The rationale for a 20 percent ceiling is unclear, though,

---

[44] Form 23 prescribed by O. Reg. 159/83 filed March 18, 1983, under the *Construction Lien Act, 1983*. It is to be noted that the proposed *Construction Lien Amendment Act, 1983*, which is expected to receive First Reading in October of 1983 and which will be deemed to have come into force on April 2, 1983, purports to repeal s. 80(10) and substitute the following, in part, therefor:

> (10) A purchaser who takes title from a mortgagee takes title to the premises free of the priority of the liens created by subsections (2) and (5) where,
>> (a) a financial guarantee bond; or
>> (b) a letter of credit or a letter of guarantee from a Canadian chartered bank,
> in a form prescribed is registered on the title to the premises and the security of the bond, letter of credit or letter of guarantee thereupon takes the place of the priority created by those subsections, and persons who have proved liens have a right of action against the surety on the bond or the issuer on the letter of credit or letter of guarantee.

[45] See the preamble of Form 23 prescribed by O. Reg. 159/83 filed March 18, 1983, under the *Construction Lien Act, 1983*.

[46] Section 80(10).

[47] *Ibid.*

[48] The "contract price" referred to in the prescribed form of bond (see clause 2) is that amount which the mortgagee believes to be the contract price, based upon information obtained from the contractor and the owner.

particularly since the mortgagee's maximum exposure to the lien claimants under ss. 80(2) and (5) would be the amount of the holdbacks
required to be retained by the owner under Part IV of the Act, namely 10
percent of the contract price.

In addition to the Financial Guarantee Bond which is prescribed by
the Act, insurers have developed new products in response to the priority
problems created by the legislation. The Mortgage Insurance Company
of Canada, for example, has created two forms of Lien Holdback
Deficiency Bonds: (a) the individual bond, which covers individual
properties and projects involving the smaller builder;[49] and (b) the blanket
or income property bond, which covers the larger builder of tract housing
and income properties.[50]

For a discussion of the Lien Holdback Deficiency Bond, see J.
Donald Bergeron, "The Construction Lien Holdback Deficiency Bond
and Mortgage Priorities Under The Construction Lien Act (Ontario)."[51]

(viii) Some General Recommendations to Mortgage Lenders[52]

1. It would be prudent for lenders to obtain personal guarantees and
other collateral security, or to receive increased compensation, from the
borrower for the increased risk associated with the *Construction Lien
Act's* new priority provisions. Lenders might also consider requiring a
borrower to inject more of his own funds into a construction project in
order to increase the equity cushion which would be available to satisfy
any holdback deficiency.

2. Lenders may wish to adopt the practice of ensuring that every
borrower makes a written declaration as to his intended use of the funds
to be advanced. Although an argument could be advanced that mortgage
lenders might be better off not inquiring as to the intended use of funds, a
mortgagee would be better able to assess and to protect his security by
demanding full disclosure before he is committed by having already
advanced funds.

3. If the loan being advanced is not intended to finance an improvement, then an acknowledgement ought to be included in the mortgage
instrument to this effect. Although such an acknowledgement would not

---

[49] See sample form of individual bond at Precedent No. 67.
[50] See sample form of blanket bond at Precedent No. 68.
[51] (1983), 1 C.L.R. 11.
[52] Also see, generally, Harvey J. Kirsh, "The Impact of the Construction Lien Act upon
     Mortgage Lenders" (1983), 4 *Advocates' Quarterly* 211.

be dispositive of the issue, nevertheless it would serve to evidence the mortgagee's intention.

4. Both the commitment letter and the mortgage instrument should authorize the lender to add the cost of obtaining a Financial Guarantee Bond or a Lien Holdback Deficiency Bond to the mortgage debt.

5. Lenders may want to provide in the mortgage documentation that a portion of each mortgage advance, equal to 10 percent of the value of services or materials supplied under a contract, may be withheld until such time as all liens that may be claimed against the holdback have expired, or have been satisfied, discharged or vacated. This recommendation takes on added importance if the lender sees fit *not* to obtain a Financial Guarantee Bond or a Lien Holdback Deficiency Bond. The mortgage documentation could also authorize the lender to establish a bank account and to deposit into such account the holdback funds withheld from each advance. By maintaining this account, the lender will always be cognizant of the amount of the holdback, and will be able to determine whether sufficient funds are being held to satisfy the requirements of the Act.

6. Loan commitments, with respect to building mortgages, ought to call for the production of a true copy of all construction documents relative to the project being financed. These documents should then be reviewed by the lender in order to determine what amounts should be maintained for holdback purposes. The commitment should also oblige the borrower to advise the lender forthwith as to any construction extras, and should provide authority to the borrower to increase the holdback fund so as to accommodate those extras.

7. At the time of each advance, the lender should consider obtaining a certificate of value from an independent architect to ensure that the loan is not being overadvanced when considered in the context of the value of the property comprising the security.

8. With respect to non-building mortgages, it is now prudent for mortgage lenders to conduct an inspection of the mortgaged premises immediately prior to the registration of the mortgage in order to ensure that there is no construction under way which could give rise to the registration of a valid claim for lien at a time subsequent to the registration of the mortgage. Previously, it was ordinarily sufficient for the mortgagee to instruct its solicitor to conduct a search of title in order to reveal any registered lien claims. Now, though, an inspection may be required in order to avoid the mortgage becoming subordinate to subsequently registered lien claims to the extent of any deficiency in the holdback, pursuant to s. 80(5) of the Act.

(ix) Mortgage Advances to a Trustee Appointed under the Act

As indicated in Chapter 8, circumstances may arise requiring the making of an application to the court for the appointment of a trustee to secure, protect and perhaps even sell the premises.[53] Subject to the supervision and direction of the court, a trustee has authority, *inter alia*, to complete or partially complete construction,[54] and to take appropriate steps for the preservation of the premises,[55] such as, for example, posting a security guard to protect against vandalism, and ensuring that the premises are heated during the winter months.

In order to carry out his authority, particularly if he intends to complete construction or to secure the premises, the trustee may be required to borrow funds and to provide the lender with mortgage security. So as to facilitate these borrowings and to protect the lender's security, s. 80(7) of the Act provides that the interest in the premises acquired by the lender (*i.e.*, the mortgage) takes full priority, to the extent of the amount advanced, over every lien existing[56] at the date of the trustee's appointment.[57] In addition, "the amount received is not subject to any lien existing at the date of the trustee's appointment,"[58] since the reason for granting such a mortgage would be to acquire the funds necessary to complete the improvement.[59] Since the date of the trustee's appointment appears to be pivotal insofar as this priority issue is concerned, the lender would no doubt want to subsearch the title to the premises at the time of the advance to ensure that no liens were registered at any time after the date the trustee was appointed which might take priority over the mortgage.

All liens constitute a charge against any monies recovered by the trustee in the exercise of his powers (*i.e.*, rents, profits, and sale proceeds).[60] However, that charge is subject to the priority of the mortgage granted to the lender, in the circumstances referred to above, as well as the trustee's reasonable business expenses and management costs.[61]

---

[53] Section 70.
[54] Section 70(2)(b).
[55] Section 70(2)(c).
[56] It is to be noted that a person's lien comes into existence, or "arises" and takes effect, when he first supplies services or materials to the improvement: s. 15.
[57] Section 80(7)(a).
[58] Section 80(7)(b).
[59] See *Report of the Attorney General's Advisory Committee on the Draft Construction Lien Act* (April 1982), at 186.
[60] Section 70(3).
[61] *Ibid.*

(x) Priority Over Postponed Liens

As indicated in Chapter 7, a preserved or a perfected lien may be postponed to the interest of another encumbrancer, such as a mortgagee, by the registration on the title to the premises of a notice of postponement[62] in the prescribed form.[63] This will serve to facilitate the flow of funds on a construction project when further mortgage advances are intended to be made, or when re-financing is required.

In exchange for the postponement, the lien claimant may possibly be paid a portion of his claim out of the advance or the monies received on a re-financing, particularly where the reason for non-payment related to cash flow problems rather than to defective work.

The encumbrancer in whose favour the postponement is made will generally[64] have priority over the postponed lien,[65] and, where an advance is made and no written notice of a lien has been received, over any unpreserved lien.[66]

C. COMPETING PRIORITY CLAIMS AS AMONGST PERSONS HAVING LIENS

(i) Introduction

In any lien action, there is usually a contest amongst the various lien claimants for the right to share, albeit *pro rata*, in the distribution of a finite fund.

One lien claimant may be inclined to challenge the timeliness or the quantum of the lien of another lien claimant. To the extent that this challenge is successful, the *pro rata* share ultimately earmarked for the challenging lien claimant could increase.

In addition to the foregoing, the *pro rata* distribution of monies to persons having liens is governed by the principles of priority established by the Act. Although all persons having a lien who have supplied services or materials to the same payer comprise a "class,"[67] the fact that some of the persons in a particular class may not have preserved and perfected

---

62 Section 43.
63 See Form 15 prescribed by O. Reg. 159/83 filed March 18, 1983, under the *Construction Lien Act, 1983*.
64 This statement is qualified by the provision contained in s. 80(8) that "nothing in this subsection affects the priority of the liens under subsections (2) and (5)."
65 Section 80(8)(a).
66 Section 80(8)(b).
67 See s. 81.

their lien rights would certainly affect any distribution made within that class.

In all of this, it is important to note that "person having a lien" is defined in the Act to include both a "lien claimant" (defined to mean "a person having a preserved or perfected lien")[68] and a person with an unpreserved lien.[69]

(ii) Priority Between and Within Classes of Persons Having Liens

All persons having a lien,[70] who have supplied services or materials to the same payer,[71] comprise a class.[72] Where a person supplies services or materials to more than one payer (as where, for example, a person contracts with the contractor for part of the work, and with the owner for the balance), he may be a member of more than one class, but only to the extent to which his lien relates to a particular class.[73]

Subject to special priority rules respecting workers' liens and general liens, which are discussed below, the following principles establish the priorities between and within classes:

(a) No person who has a lien is entitled to any priority over another member of the same class.[74] Those whose lien rights have expired, however, would not be entitled to share in the distribution of hold-back monies.[75] Furthermore, in circumstances where a payer becomes insolvent, the trust fund of which that payer is trustee is to be distributed so that priority over all others is given to a beneficiary of that trust who has proved a lien.[76]

(b) All amounts available to satisfy the liens in respect of an improvement are to be distributed *pro rata* among all members of each class.[77] For example, suppose:

   (i) that subcontractors A, B and C comprise a class, in that they are all looking to the contractor for payment;

  (ii) that the contractor owes $5,000 to subcontractor A, $15,000 to subcontractor B, and $10,000 to subcontractor C; and

  (iii) that the contractor has only $10,000 available for distribution.

In these circumstances, subcontractors A, B and C would share the

---

[68] Section 1(1) 11.
[69] Section 1(1) 18.
[70] See *ibid.*
[71] See s. 1(1) 16.
[72] Section 81.
[73] *Ibid.*
[74] Section 82(1)(a).
[75] See ss. 26 and 27.
[76] Section 87(1).
[77] Section 82(1)(b).

$10,000 on a *pro rata* basis, each getting approximately 33 cents on the dollar, and would recover a personal judgment against the contractor for the balance.

(c) The lien of every member of a class has priority over the lien of the payer of that class.[78] This can be analogized to a water glass which receives a flow of water from above, but fills up from the bottom. Similarly, although the flow of funds down the construction pyramid emanates from above (*i.e.*, from the owner who is at the apex), s. 80(1)(c) makes it clear that the persons at the lower levels of the pyramid are to receive payment before the persons who are obliged to pay them. The example in the preceding paragraph can be expanded to illustrate and clarify this point:

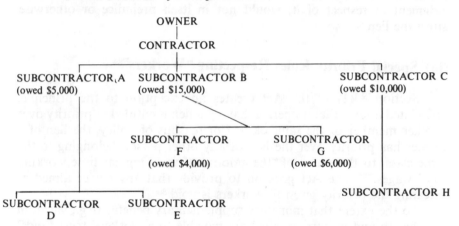

In the above diagram, subcontractors A, B and C comprise a class, since they each contracted with the contractor. Since there is only $10,000 available for distribution to them in total, subcontractor B, for example, will recover $5,000 and a personal judgment against the contractor for $10,000. Subcontractor B's $5,000 share would be distributed *pro rata* to subcontractors F and G, who comprise their own separate class, and their recovery would be $2,000 and $3,000 respectively (*i.e.*, $5,000 distributed amongst $10,000 in claims). Additionally, subcontractors F and G would recover personal judgments against subcontractor B for the balance, namely $2,000 and $3,000 respectively.

A person who has a lien is entitled to assert his claim to priority, as a member of a particular class, despite the non-completion or abandonment of the contract or a subcontract by any other person.[79]

Furthermore, the fact that lien rights may have been assigned, or may have devolved (in the case of the death of the person having the lien),

---

[78] Section 82(1)(c).
[79] Section 74.

would not affect the claim to priority asserted by the assignee or personal representative, as the case may be.[80]

Finally, a lien claimant is precluded from attempting to enhance his priority position by accepting, for example, a mortgage, in respect of the premises to which he supplied services or materials, in payment or as security for his claim.[81] Any such mortgage, whether given before or after the lien arises, would be void as against other persons who are entitled to liens on the premises.[82] On the other hand, it is always open for a person having a lien to obtain a mortgage, as security for his claim, against property other than the premises to which he supplied services or materials. In this latter case, the acceptance of such a mortgage, and indeed the initiation of enforcement proceedings or the recovery of a personal judgment in respect of it, would not in itself prejudice or otherwise affect the lien.[83]

(iii) Special Priority Rules Respecting "Workers"[84]

Section 83(1) of the Act creates an exception to the principle, articulated above, that no person having a lien is entitled to priority over another member of the same class. For reasons of policy, the lien of a worker has priority over the lien of any other person belonging to the same class, to the extent of "the amount of forty regular-time working days' wages."[85] The Act goes on to provide that any device aimed at defeating the priority given to workers is void.[86]

To the extent that monetary supplementary benefits (*e.g.*, vacation pay, health and welfare benefits) are payable to a workers' trust fund[87] instead of to a worker, the trustee of the fund is subrogated to the rights of the worker under the Act with respect to those benefits.[88]

(iv) Special Priority Rules Respecting General Liens

Section 84 of the Act deals with the issue of priority as between a general lien claim and other lien claims registered against a particular premises. If, for example, a subcontractor supplies $3,000 worth of

---

[80] Section 75.
[81] Section 82(2).
[82] *Ibid.*
[83] Section 77(1).
[84] A "worker" is defined to mean "a person employed for wages in any kind of labour;": s. 1(1) 27.
[85] Section 83(1).
[86] Section 83(3).
[87] See s. 1(1) 28.
[88] Section 83(2).

drywall and insulation materials to each of 15 premises, he would be entitled to register a $45,000 general lien claim against the title to each of the premises.[89] A plumbing subcontractor of the same class,[90] though, may only have liened premises no. 4 for $5,000. The abstract of title for premises no. 4 would reveal the registration of two lien claims in the respective sums of $45,000 and $5,000.

In the circumstances, since the drywall subcontractor supplied only $3,000 worth of services and materials to premises no. 4, it would be inequitable to permit him to recover nine times the amount which would ordinarily be recovered by the plumbing subcontractor on a *pro rata* distribution.

Accordingly, s. 84 sets forth a formula which deals with the relative priorities of the two lien claims. Under the formula,

(a) the general lien shall rank with the other liens according to the rules of priority set out in section 82 only to the extent of,
  (i) the total value of the general lien,
divided by,
  (ii) the total number of premises to which the person having the general lien supplied services or materials under his contract or subcontract.

Section 84(b) goes on to provide that,

in respect of the balance of the general lien, it shall rank next in priority to all other liens against the premises, whether or not of the same class.

Therefore, if $4,000 in equity were realized upon the judicial sale of premises no. 4, it would be distributed rateably[91] as between the two subcontractors, in which case the drywall subcontractor would recover $1,500, *i.e.,* $\dfrac{\$3,000}{(\$3,000 + \$5,000)} \times \$4,000$, and the plumbing subcontractor would recover $2,500, *i.e.,* $\dfrac{\$5,000}{(\$3,000 + \$5,000)} \times \$4,000$. If, on the other hand, $8,500 of sale proceeds were realized, the drywall subcontractor would receive $3,000, the plumbing subcontractor $5,000, and, assuming there were no other lien claimants, the balance of $500 would go to the drywall subcontractor on account of his general lien.

(v) Priorities Amongst Trust Fund Claimants

In circumstances where a payer becomes insolvent,[92] the trust fund of

---

[89] Section 20.
[90] See s. 81.
[91] Section 82.
[92] The Act does not define the word "insolvent." *Stroud's Judicial Dictionary*, 4th ed. (1973) provides that an "insolvent" is a person who can not pay his debts (vol. 3, p.

which that payer is trustee is to be distributed so that priority over all
others is given to a beneficiary of that trust[93] who has proved a lien.[94] This
constitutes a second exception to the principle contained in s. 82(1)(a) to
the effect that no person who has a lien is entitled to any priority over
another member of the same class. It is also an exception to the normal
rules of equity, which require a trustee to distribute trust monies *pro rata*
among all beneficiaries of the trust.

Priority in the distribution of funds amongst persons who *have* liens
is to be in accordance with Part XI.[95] The balance of trust funds, however,
are to be distributed among the remaining trust beneficiaries, who do *not*
have liens, in accordance with s. 87(3) which provides:

> (3) The remaining trust funds shall be distributed among the beneficiaries of
> that trust and the beneficiaries of trusts created by section 8 that are derived from
> that trust, whose liens have not been proved, in accordance with the respective
> priorities to which those liens would have been entitled as set out in this Part, had
> those liens been proved.

This section is a departure from the former scheme of distribution of trust
monies.[96] As the Attorney General's Advisory Committee on the Draft
Construction Lien Act commented,

> [Section 87(3) applies to] the general scheme of priority in the distribution of trust
> funds, even among trust beneficiaries whose liens have expired. In the opinion of the
> Committee, the same considerations which militate in favour of granting priority to
> a particular type of lien claimant are no less cogent where a person of that type
> makes a claim as a trust beneficiary.[97]

D. COMPETING PRIORITIES AS BETWEEN LIENS AND EXECUTIONS

Section 79 of the Act provides:

1380). Further, the *Bankruptcy Act*, R.S.C. 1970, c. B-3, defines "insolvent person"
in terms of that person's inability to meet his obligations as they generally become
due.

[93] It is to be noted that s. 87(1) refers not only to the beneficiary of the trust, but also to
"a beneficiary of a trust created by section 8 that is derived from that trust."

[94] Section 87(1).

[95] Section 87(2).

[96] See Richard D. Howell, "How is a Section 2 Fund Distributed," p. 16ff. of a paper
entitled "Trust Funds — Mechanics' Lien Act" delivered at a continuing legal
education conference entitled "Bailing Out: A Guided Tour Through the Law
Relating to Bankruptcy and Insolvency," sponsored by the Canadian Bar Association (Ont.), November 20, 1978, Toronto.

[97] *Report of the Attorney General's Advisory Committee on the Draft Construction
Lien Act* (April 1982), at 202.

79. The liens arising from an improvement have priority over all judgments, executions, assignments, attachments, garnishments and receiving orders except those executed or recovered upon before the time when the first lien arose[98] in respect of the improvement.

If, for example, a creditor seizes the premises in executing or recovering upon a judgment before any work commences in respect of an improvement (*i.e.*, before the time when the first lien arose), the claim of that creditor would have priority over any lien which may subsequently arise. However, if a lien arises before the judgment is "executed or recovered upon," the lien would take priority.

The establishment of this priority concept was premised upon the fact that "[t]he essential purpose of the lien created by the Act is to ensure that those who have contributed their services or materials towards the improvement of a premises will be entitled to claim against that premises in priority to the general creditors of the owner."[99]

Furthermore, since a lien is a charge against the monies required to be retained by the owner under the Act,[100] and given the trust rights provided to suppliers of services or materials under Part II, it is consistent for the lien also to take priority over all "assignments, attachments, garnishments and receiving orders." This would be subject, though, to the stated qualification that the lien must arise before the premises are seized (*i.e.*, "executed or recovered upon") by the competing creditor.

E. APPLICATION OF INSURANCE PROCEEDS

Where a premises is totally or partially destroyed, any insurance monies received by the owner or a mortgagee "shall take the place of the premises so destroyed and shall be distributed in accordance with the priorities set out in this Part."[101] Unlike s. 9 of the *Mechanics' Lien Act*,[102]

---

[98] See s. 15.

[99] *Report of the Attorney General's Advisory Committee on the Draft Construction Lien Act* (April 1982), at 177.

[100] Section 21.

[101] Section 85.

[102] Section 9 of the *Mechanics' Lien Act*, R.S.O. 1980, c. 261 provides (emphasis added):
9. Where any of the property upon which a lien attaches is wholly or partly destroyed *by fire*, any money received by reason of any insurance thereon by an owner or prior mortgagee or chargee shall take the place of the property so destroyed and is, after satisfying any prior mortgage or charge in the manner and to the extent set out in subsection 8(3), subject to the claims of all persons for liens to the same extent as if the money had been realized by a sale of the property in an action to enforce the lien.

which contemplated only fire insurance coverage, s. 85 of the *Construction Lien Act, 1983* makes no specific mention of a particular hazard and refers to "*any* insurance on the premises."

The interests of an owner and a mortgagee in a premises are generally protected by insurance. Where construction is to take place, the contractor would often contract to receive the benefit of insurance coverage in order to secure payment of the contract monies owing to him in the event that the premises are destroyed. Despite the placement of such coverage, though, the contractor would nevertheless continue to enjoy the full benefit of his lien rights.[103] The insurance coverage available to him would be additional security of the kind contemplated by s. 77(1) of the Act.[104]

In the event that a premises is destroyed, all insurance monies payable to the owner shall, if the mortgagee so requires, be applied by the owner in making good the loss or damage.[105] Alternatively, the mortgagee may require the owner to apply the insurance proceeds to reduce the mortgage debt.[106] If the owner neglects to consult the mortgagee, and simply proceeds to engage a contractor to effect repairs, one would expect that a priority dispute would arise between the mortgagee and the contractor with respect to the insurance monies. In these circumstances, it has been held that it would be inequitable for the mortgagee to have its security restored and also to get the value of the repairs, to the detriment of the contractor who did the work.[107]

F. DISTRIBUTION OF PROCEEDS OF SALE

As indicated in Chapter 9, a judgment or report generally provides that, if a statutory owner refuses or neglects to pay into court the amount for which he is found by the court to be liable, his interest in the premises may be ordered sold.[108] Such a sale would take place under the court's supervision and subject to its approval.

Where there is a judicial sale, or where a trustee appointed under Part IX of the Act sells an interest in the premises in pursuance of his

---

[103] *W.J.C. Kaufmann Co. Ltd. v. Berberi* (1982), 36 O.R. (2d) 774, 135 D.L.R. (3d) 442 (H.C.).

[104] *Ibid.*

[105] *Mortgages Act*, R.S.O. 1980, c. 296, s. 6(1).

[106] *Ibid.*, s. 6(2).

[107] *First City Savings and Trust Co. v. Jovanovich et al.* (1983), 40 O.R. (2d) 161, 142 D.L.R. (3d) 602, 27 R.P.R. 16 (H.C.). It might be noted that, in this case, the court also held that s. 3 of the *Mechanics' Lien Act* impressed the insurance fund with a trust in favour of the contractor. By way of comparison, s. 8(1) of the *Construction Lien Act, 1983* provides that the "draws trust" is only "for the benefit of the subcontractors and other persons who have supplied services or materials to the improvement who are owed amounts by the contractor or subcontractor."

[108] Section 64(5).

authority,[109] the sale proceeds are to be paid into court to the credit of the lien action.[110]

The court would then direct payment of the sale proceeds in accordance with the priorities established by the Act.[111] Section 86 provides that,

> 86. Where an interest in the premises is sold or leased under an order of the court or by a trustee appointed under Part IX, the proceeds received as a result of that disposition, together with any amount paid into court under subsection 67(2), shall be distributed in accordance with the priorities set out in this Part.

It should be noted that the party having carriage of the sale proceedings is entitled to add to his claim his fees and actual disbursements incurred in connection with the sale.[112]

A person with a perfected lien is entitled to share in the proceeds of sale, in respect of the amount owing to him, despite the fact that that amount was not payable to him at the time of the commencement of the action, or at the time of the distribution of the proceeds.[113] This serves to protect the lien claimant by permitting him to share in the distribution, notwithstanding that he may have granted an extended period of credit to the statutory owner. As the Attorney General's Advisory Committee on the Draft *Construction Lien Act* commented,

> [T]he claims of all persons who have a right to claim against [the owner's] interest [in the premises] must be disposed of in a single proceeding. If a person who was entitled to a lien were not allowed to realize upon that lien at the same time as the other claimants, his lien right would be lost.[114]

---

[109] Section 72(2)(a) authorizes a court-appointed trustee, *inter alia,* to sell the premises, or any part thereof, subject to the approval of the court and the *Planning Act,* R.S.O. 1980, c. 379.

[110] Section 67(2).

[111] Section 67(4).

[112] Section 67(3).

[113] Section 66.

[114] *Report of the Attorney General's Advisory Committee on the Draft Construction Lien Act* (April 1982), at 154.

Chapter 11

Crown Lands, Municipally-Owned Public Streets and Highways, and Railway Rights-Of-Way

A. INTRODUCTION

The purpose of this chapter is to highlight the procedural and substantive differences which must be noted in circumstances where a lien may not be transformed, by registration, into a proprietary interest[1] in, or an encumbrance against, the lands in respect of which services or materials have been supplied.

Section 16(3) of the Act provides:

> (3) Where the Crown[2] is the owner[3] of a premises[4] within the meaning of this Act, or where the premises is,
>   (a) a public street or highway owned by a municipality;[5] or
>   (b) a railway right-of-way,
> the lien does not attach to the premises but constitutes a charge as provided in section 21, and the provisions of this Act shall have effect without requiring the registration of a claim for lien against the premises.

In the situations contemplated by s. 16(3), public policy dictates that the ultimate remedy provided by the Act, that of being able to force a sale of the owner's interest in the premises,[6] ought not to be available. As the Attorney General's Advisory Committee on the Draft *Construction Lien Act* stated in its Report,[7]

> the Committee is of the view that the lien should not attach to the interest of the Crown in a premises in any event. Nor should it attach to municipal street (sic) or to

---

[1] See s. 78.
[2] See s. 1(1) 6.
[3] See s. 1(1) 15.
[4] See s. 1(1) 19.
[5] See s. 1(1) 14.
[6] See s. 64(5).
[7] *Report of the Attorney General's Advisory Committee on the Draft Construction Lien Act* (April 1982).

a railway right-of-way. The attachment of the lien to a municipal road or to a railway is impractical. The attachment of a lien to Crown land is theoretically absurd since the Crown is the source of property rights. Furthermore, it is unnecessary. Section 26 of the Proceedings Against The Crown Act[8] requires the Crown to pay all final judgments against it.[9]

Although liens may not attach to premises in those instances under discussion, lien claimants are not deprived of their remedies. They may still pursue their lien rights in the manner as set forth in the Act. The only difference is that their liens would not encumber the title to the premises, but would rather create "a system of charges equivalent in value to a lien against land."[10]

Except where modified by the commentary contained in this chapter, all other aspects of the law and procedures relating to construction liens, as are discussed elsewhere in this book, apply to (provincial) Crown lands, municipally-owned public streets and highways, and railway rights-of-way.

B. APPLICATION OF THE ACT TO THE CROWN

(i) Provincial Crown v. Federal Crown

Provincial legislation dealing with mechanics' liens, including the *Construction Lien Act, 1983,* does not apply to the federal Crown. Various reasons, other than the obvious constitutional one, have been given by the courts. In *Bain v. The Director, Veterans' Land Act et al.,*[11] for example, the issue arose at the opening of trial as to whether the remedies created by the mechanics' lien legislation then in force were available against the Director of the federal *Veterans' Land Act.* In addressing the issue, Assistant Master Marriott stated,

> The next question to be considered is whether the rights and privileges of the Dominion Crown prevent the plaintiff maintaining this action. . . . The substance of the enactment [The Mechanics' Lien Act] is the sale of the land: per Meredith C.J.C.P. in *Crawford v. Tilden et al.* (1907), 14 O.L.R. 572 at 577. How can that relief be enforced as against the Dominion Crown? The Ontario Courts have no power to order the sale of property owned by the Crown, and I have found the Director to be an emanation or agent of the Crown. In another aspect of the matter the plaintiff is seeking to reach, by a judgment of this Court, revenue or property which in substance is that of the Dominion Crown, and this of course he cannot

---

[8] R.S.O. 1980, c. 393.
[9] *Report of the Attorney General's Advisory Committee on the Draft Construction Lien Act* (April 1982), at 50.
[10] *Ibid.*
[11] [1947] O.W.N. 917 (H.C.).

do except by petition of right, as there appears to be nothing in The Veterans' Land Act which gives him this right either specifically or by implication.[12]

As a result, persons who supply labour or materials to a federal Crown construction project, such as the supply of building materials to a Canada Mortgage and Housing Corporation[13] housing project, or the construction of a building on an armed forces base such as Camp Borden, would not be entitled to a lien.

The term "Crown" is defined in the *Construction Lien Act, 1983,* to include "a Crown agency to which the *Crown Agency Act*[14] applies."[15] Section 1 of the *Crown Agency Act* defines "Crown agency" to mean "a board, commission, railway, public utility, university, manufactory, company or agency, owned, controlled or operated by Her Majesty in right of Ontario, or by the Government of Ontario, or under the authority of the Legislature or the Lieutenant Governor in Council."

Given the foregoing definition, it would appear that the applicability of the *Crown Agency Act* generally depends upon the facts of each case. For example, the Ontario Housing Corporation, which is a corporate body governed by the *Ontario Housing Corporation Act*[16] and whose directors are appointed by the Lieutenant Governor in Council,[17] has been held to be a Crown agency;[18] whereas the Ontario Food Terminal Board, which is a corporate body governed by the *Ontario Food Terminal Act*[19] and whose Board members are also appointed by the Lieutenant Governor in Council,[20] has been held not to be a Crown agency.[21]

There are very few reported cases dealing with the matter of Crown agencies, but one might expect that such entities as, for example, the University of Toronto,[22] Ontario Place,[23] the Art Gallery of Ontario[24] and

---

[12] *Ibid.,* at 918-19.

[13] See *Central Mortgage and Housing Corporation Act,* R.S.C. 1970, c. C-16, ss. 3 and 5. The Act was amended in 1979 to change the name of the corporation to "Canada Mortgage and Housing Corporation" (see S.C. 1978-79, c. 16, ss. 12 and 13).

[14] R.S.O. 1980, c. 106.

[15] Section 1(1) 6.

[16] R.S.O. 1980, c. 339.

[17] *Ibid.,* ss. 2(1) and 3(1).

[18] *R. v. O.L.R.B., ex parte Ont. Housing Corp.,* [1971] 2 O.R. 723, 19 D.L.R. (3d) 47 (H.C.); *Berardinelli v. Ont. Housing Corp. et al.* (1977), 15 O.R. (2d) 217, 75 D.L.R. (3d) 348; revd. on other grounds [1979] 1 S.C.R. 275, 90 D.L.R. (3d) 481, 23 N.R. 298, 8 C.P.C. 100.

[19] R.S.O. 1980, c. 334.

[20] *Ibid.,* s. 2(2).

[21] *R. v. O.L.R.B., ex parte Ont. Food Terminal Bd.,* [1962] O.R. 981, 35 D.L.R. (2d) 6; affd. [1963] 2 O.R. 91, 38 D.L.R. (2d) 530 (C.A.).

[22] Section 7 of the *University of Toronto Act,* S.O. 1971 (Vol. 1), c. 56, refers to the University of Toronto as a "provincial university".

[23] See *Ontario Place Corporation Act,* R.S.O. 1980, c. 353.

[24] See *Art Gallery of Ontario Act,* R.S.O. 1980, c. 28.

the Royal Ontario Museum[25] would come within the definition. Oddly enough, Massey-Ferguson Limited could possibly be regarded as a "Crown agency," since the Minister of Industry and Tourism, on behalf of the Province of Ontario, is authorized to purchase, hold and sell up to 37½ percent of the total aggregate number of a particular series of preferred shares of the corporation purchased at any time by the provincial and federal governments,[26] subject to certain limitations.[27] *Quaere* whether the ownership of these shares could be construed to mean that the Government of Ontario "owned, controlled or operated" the corporation.

Although Ontario Hydro is not affected by the *Crown Agency Act*[28] it is controlled by and accountable to the Lieutenant Governor in Council,[29] and would probably come within the definition of "Crown" in the *Construction Lien Act, 1983.*[30]

(ii) The Crown As Statutory Owner

Despite the fact that a lien does not attach to the interest of the Crown in a premises,[31] the *Construction Lien Act, 1983* nevertheless binds the Crown.[32]

The definition of "owner" in the Act expressly includes the Crown,[33] and "interest in the premises" is defined to include "a statutory right given or reserved to the Crown to enter any lands or premises belonging to any person or public authority for the purpose of doing any work, construction, repair or maintenance in, upon, through, over or under any lands or premises."[34]

Where the Crown is the statutory owner, a lien would not attach to the premises, but would constitute a charge, as provided in s. 21, upon, *inter alia,* the holdbacks required to be retained under the Act.[35] In these circumstances, the claim for lien need not be registered against the title to the premises,[36] but may be preserved in the manner set forth below.

---

[25] See *Royal Ontario Museum Act,* R.S.O. 1980, c. 458.

[26] See *An Act Respecting Massey-Ferguson Limited,* S.O. 1981, c. 3.

[27] *Ibid.,* ss. 2(2) and (3).

[28] See *Crown Agency Act,* R.S.O. 1980, c. 106, s. 3.

[29] See, for example, ss. 3, 9, 10, 22, 23, 24, 25 and 56 (as amended) of the *Power Corporation Act,* R.S.O. 1980, c. 384.

[30] It is to be noted that s. 1(1)6 of the Act, which defines the term "Crown," uses the word "includes" rather than the word "means."

[31] Section 16(1).

[32] Section 3(1).

[33] See s. 1(1) 15.

[34] Section 1(1) 9.

[35] Section 16(3).

[36] *Ibid.*

Where the Crown is not the statutory owner, but merely has an interest in the premises which are being improved, the lien may attach to the interest of any other person in that premises.[37]

(iii) Preservation of Lien Where Crown is Statutory Owner

The lien, where it does not attach to the premises, may be preserved by giving[38] the Crown a copy of the claim for lien,[39] together with an affidavit of verification.[40]

The office of the Crown to which a copy of the claim for lien must be given is as follows:

(a) where the contract is with a ministry of the Crown, the office of the Director of Legal Services of that ministry;[41]

(b) where the contract is with the Ontario Housing Corporation, the office of the Director of Legal Services of the Ministry of Municipal Affairs and Housing;[42]

(c) where the contract is with a college of applied arts and technology, the office of the president of the college;[43] and

(d) where the contract is with any other office of the Crown, the chief executive officer of that office.[44]

Notification of the Crown in the manner set forth above must be effected "during the supplying of services or materials or at any time before it [the lien] expires."[45]

---

[37] Section 16(2). By way of comparison, the *Mechanics' Lien Act*, R.S.O. 1980, c. 261 provided that a lien did not attach to the lands and premises comprising a "public work" (s. 6(2)), and defined "public work" to include "land in which the Crown has an estate or interest" (s. 1(1)(g)). Therefore, if Ontario Housing Corporation (for example) held a mortgage on a property, then presumably that property would be a "public work" under the *Mechanics' Lien Act* and a lien would not have attached. Under the *Construction Lien Act, 1983,* however, the fact that Ontario Housing Corporation may hold a mortgage and would thereby have an interest in the premises, would not preclude the registration of a claim for lien against the statutory owner's interest.

[38] See ss. 89(1), (2) and (4).

[39] See s. 34(5) and Form 8 prescribed by O. Reg. 159/83 filed March 18, 1983, under the *Construction Lien Act, 1983*. Where the lien does not attach to the premises, a claim for lien must set out "a description of the premises, ... being the address or other identification of the location of the premises" (s. 34(5)(e)(ii)).

[40] See s. 34(5) and Form 9 prescribed by O. Reg. 159/83 filed March 18, 1983, under the *Construction Lien Act, 1983*. Also, see "Affidavit of Verification" (heading B (ii) of chapter 4).

[41] O. Reg. 159/83, s. 1, 1.

[42] O. Reg. 159/83, s. 1, 2.

[43] O. Reg. 159/83, s. 1, 3.

[44] O. Reg. 159/83, s. 1, 4.

[45] Section 34(1). Also see s. 31.

(iv) Perfection of Lien Where Crown is Statutory Owner

Unless a lien has been preserved within the time periods set forth in s. 31 of the Act, it will be deemed to have expired,[46] and therefore may not be perfected.[47]

If it has been properly preserved, though, it becomes perfected when an action[48] to enforce the lien has been commenced.[49] Alternatively, a preserved lien may become perfected by sheltering under a lien perfected by another lien claimant.[50]

Section 7 of the *Proceedings Against the Crown Act*[51] does not apply to actions commenced against the Crown under the *Construction Lien Act, 1983*.[52] Accordingly, service of a notice upon the Crown is not a condition precedent to the commencement of an action.

Where the lien does not attach to the premises, a certificate of action need not be registered.[53] However, the lien action must be commenced "prior to the end of the forty-five day period next following the last day, under section 31, on which the lien could have been preserved"[54] if the lien is to be perfected. Otherwise it expires,[55] and upon motion,[56] the court is obliged to make a declaration to this effect.[57]

(v) Discharging or Vacating a Lien Where it does not Attach to the Premises

A preserved or perfected lien, where it does not attach to the premises, may be discharged by giving[58] a release in the prescribed form[59] to the Crown (where it is the statutory owner).[60] The release would be given to the same Crown office as that to which a copy of the claim for lien was given.[61]

A lien may also be discharged by court order, "upon any proper

---

[46] Section 31(1).
[47] Section 36(1).
[48] Section 1(1) 1 defines "action" to mean "an action under Part VIII."
[49] Section 36(3)(b).
[50] See s. 36(4).
[51] R.S.O. 1980, c. 393.
[52] Section 3(2).
[53] Section 36(3)(b).
[54] Section 36(2).
[55] *Ibid.*
[56] See Precedent Nos. 23, 24 and 25.
[57] Section 45(2).
[58] See s. 89(1).
[59] See Form 14 prescribed by O. Reg. 159/83 filed March 18, 1983, under the *Construction Lien Act, 1983*.
[60] Section 41(b).
[61] *Ibid.* Also see "Preservation of Lien Where Crown is Statutory Owner" (heading B (iii) of this chapter).

ground and subject to any terms and conditions that the court considers appropriate in the circumstances."[62]

The discharge of any lien, whether by release or court order, is irrevocable and the discharged lien can not be revived.[63] However, if the lien claimant whose lien was discharged continues to supply services or materials to the improvement after the date of preservation of his discharged lien, he would be entitled to preserve a fresh lien for that additional supply.[64]

Despite the fact that a lien does not attach to the premises, a court order may be obtained vacating a claim for lien upon a payment into court or the posting of security.[65] Such an order may be obtained upon the motion[66] of any person, without notice to any other person.[67]

Where a claim for lien is vacated by a payment into court or the posting of security, the lien ceases to attach to the holdbacks and other amounts subject to a charge under s. 21, and becomes a charge upon the monies paid into court or the security posted, as the case may be.[68]

For a general discussion of vacating a lien by payment into court, see heading E (i) of chapter 7.

Where a lien claimant, whose lien does not attach to the premises, fails to preserve or perfect his lien within the time allowed for doing so, his lien will expire.[69] In these circumstances, any person may bring a motion[70] to the court,[71] without notice to any other person, for an order declaring that the lien has expired.[72]

Where a perfected lien that does not attach to the premises has expired for want to prosecution,[73] any person may bring a motion[74] to the court,[75] without notice to any other person,[76] for an order declaring that the lien has expired and dismissing the lien action without costs.[77]

---

[62] Section 47(1)(a).
[63] Section 48.
[64] *Ibid.*
[65] See ss. 44(1)(b) and (3).
[66] See Precedent Nos. 20, 21 and 22.
[67] Section 44(1). But see note 45 of Chapter 7.
[68] Section 44(7).
[69] Sections 31(1) and 36(2).
[70] See Precedent Nos. 23, 24 and 25.
[71] Section 52(1) dictates whether the motion is made to a master, a local master or a local judge.
[72] Section 45(2).
[73] See s. 37.
[74] See Precedent Nos. 29, 30 and 31.
[75] Section 52(1) dictates whether the motion is made to a master, a local master or a local judge.
[76] Section 46(3).
[77] Section 46(3) provides:
    (3) A motion under subsection (1) or (2) may be brought without notice, but no order as to costs in the action may be made upon the motion unless notice of that motion was given to the person against whom the order for costs is sought.

Where the court declares that the lien has expired, it will also order that any monies which were paid into court, in respect of that lien, be returned to the person who made the payment in,[78] or, where applicable, that any security which was posted be cancelled.[79]

Finally, s. 47(1) of the Act authorizes the court,[80] upon motion,[81] to exercise its discretion in ordering that the lien action be dismissed,[82] "upon any proper ground and subject to any terms and conditions that the court considers appropriate in the circumstances."[83]

(vi) Reference to the Master

Upon motion[84] or at trial,[85] a judge may refer the whole lien action to the master for trial under s. 71 of the *Judicature Act*.[86]

Furthermore, at trial, a judge may direct a reference, having a more limited scope, to the master pursuant to s. 70 of the *Judicature Act*.[87] Section 70(1) contemplates the reference of "a question arising in an action for inquiry and report either to an official referee[88] or to a special referee[89] agreed upon by the parties."

However, it is to be noted that a judge has no authority to direct a reference to an official referee of an action, or any question or issue in an action, to which the Crown is a party, unless the consent of the Crown is obtained.[90]

(vii) Settlement Meeting

Where the court orders the holding of a settlement meeting,[91] the party who obtained the appointment date is obliged to serve a notice of

---

[78] See ss. 45(3)(a) and 46(4)(a).
[79] See ss. 45(3)(b) and 46(4)(b).
[80] Section 52(1) dictates whether the motion is made to a master, a local master or a local judge.
[81] See Precedent Nos. 26, 27 and 28.
[82] Section 47(1)(d).
[83] Section 47(1). Although the Act does not specifically provide for it, one would assume that, if a lien action were dismissed "upon any proper ground", one of the "terms and conditions" would be that any monies which were paid into court be returned to the person who made the payment in, or, where applicable, that any security which was posted be cancelled.
[84] See s. 60(1).
[85] See s. 60(2).
[86] R.S.O. 1980, c. 223.
[87] Section 60(2).
[88] See s. 95, *Judicature Act*, R.S.O. 1980, c. 223.
[89] See s. 73, *Judicature Act*.
[90] Section 70(2), *Judicature Act*.
[91] See s. 62 and "Obtaining Order for Settlement Meeting and Trial" (heading H (iv) of chapter 9).

settlement meeting[92] upon all parties to the action and all persons having an interest in the premises.[93]

However, where the lien does not attach to the premises, a search of title would not disclose the names of all lien claimants who must be served with the notice. Accordingly, s. 62(3) of the Act provides that, in these circumstances, the party who is obliged to serve the notice shall request information from the Crown, where it is the statutory owner, as to the identity of all persons having a preserved or a perfected lien against the premises.[94]

(viii) Form of Judgment or Report

Since, where the Crown is a statutory owner, the lien does not attach to the premises and the Crown's proprietary interest may not be sold, a different form of judgment or report is required. In this regard, reference is made to Forms 20 and 22 of O. Reg. 159/83.[95]

(ix) Breach of Trust Claim against Crown

Notwithstanding that lien rights exist with respect to the Crown, the "mortgage trust" provisions of the Act[96] expressly exempt the Crown from any obligations, *qua* trustee,[97] where the Crown is the statutory owner.[98]

However, the other trusts created by the Act (*i.e.*, the "certificate trust": s. 7(2); the "substantial performance trust": s. 7(3); the "draws trust": s. 8(1); and the "vendor's trust": s. 9(1)) do not appear to contain the same exemption.

To the extent that it may be possible to assert a breach of trust claim against the Crown, it is to be noted that a "trust claim shall not be joined with a lien claim but may be brought in any court of competent jurisdiction."[99]

---

[92] See Form 18 prescribed by O. Reg. 159/83 filed March 18, 1983, under the *Construction Lien Act, 1983*.

[93] Section 62(2).

[94] Section 62(3) contemplates a request for information only as to the "identity" of every person described in s. 62(2)(d). Although "identity" would not necessarily include more than the names of all lien claimants, one might expect that the Crown would also supply addresses and particulars of all claims for liens as well. However, the Act does not specifically oblige the Crown to comply with any request, and no penalty exists for non-compliance.

[95] See Appendix C.

[96] See s. 7(1).

[97] See s. 7(4).

[98] Section 7(1).

[99] Section 50(2).

Although s. 7 of the *Proceedings Against the Crown* Act[100] "does not apply in respect of an action[101] against the Crown under [the] Act,"[102] it would in fact apply in respect of a breach of trust claim which is asserted by a separate action.

As a result, it appears that the service of a notice upon the Crown[103] is a condition precedent to the commencement of a breach of trust action against it.[104]

In consequent proceedings, the Crown shall be designated "Her Majesty the Queen in right of Ontario."[105]

In proceedings against the Crown, the trial shall be without a jury.[106]

C. APPLICATION OF THE ACT TO MUNICIPALLY-OWNED[107] PUBLIC STREETS AND HIGHWAYS

(i) Ownership of Public Streets and Highways

The *Construction Lien Act, 1983* does not define "public street or highway". However, the *Municipal Act*[108] provides[109] that, except where they have been closed according to law, "common and public highways" include, *inter alia,* all roads dedicated by the owner of the land to public use, all highways[110] laid out or established under the authority of any statute, all road allowances made by Crown surveyors, all roads on which

---

100 R.S.O. 1980, c. 393.
101 Section 1(1) 1 defines "action" to mean "an action under Part VIII". Therefore, a breach of trust action is not an "action against the Crown under [the] Act" (s. 3(2)).
102 Section 3(2).
103 The notice shall be served "by leaving a copy with the Attorney General or Deputy Attorney General or any barrister or solicitor in the office of the Attorney General": s. 14, *Proceedings Against the Crown Act,* R.S.O. 1980, c. 393.
104 Section 7(1) of the *Proceedings Against the Crown Act* requires the claimant to serve a notice of the claim, "containing sufficient particulars to identify the occasion out of which the claim arose," upon the Crown at least 60 days before the commencement of the action.
105 Section 13, *Proceedings Against the Crown Act.*
106 Section 15, *Proceedings Against the Crown Act.*
107 Section 1(1) 14 defines "municipality" to mean "a municipality as defined in the *Municipal Affairs Act* or a metropolitan, regional or district municipality, or a local board thereof." The *Municipal Affairs Act,* R.S.O. 1980, c. 303, defines "municipality" to mean "the corporation of a county, city, town, village, township or improvement district and includes a local board thereof and a board, commission or other local authority exercising any power with respect to municipal affairs or purposes, including school purposes, in an unorganized township or unsurveyed territory" (s. 1(f)).
108 R.S.O. 1980, c. 302.
109 *Ibid.,* s. 257.
110 "Highway" is defined to mean "a common and public highway, and includes a street and a bridge forming part of a highway or on, over or across which a highway passes": *Municipal Act,* R.S.O. 1980, c. 302, s. 1, 9.

public money[111] has been spent for opening them, and all bridges[112] over such highways, roads and road allowances.

Furthermore, subject to statutory exceptions, the freehold of every highway[113] not owned by a company or an individual[114] is vested in the municipal corporation which has jurisdiction over it.[115]

Insofar as new residential subdivisions are concerned, when a plan of subdivision is registered, the land for public streets is usually dedicated[116] to the municipality. The subdivision agreement generally provides the requisite elements to establish a dedication, namely, an intention on the part of the owner of the land to dedicate, and an acceptance of the streets or roads by the municipality on behalf of the public.[117]

(ii) Construction, Maintenance and Repair of Municipally-Owned Public Streets and Highways

The council of every municipality has jurisdiction over all highways[118] and bridges[119] within the municipality[120] (with the exception of roads and bridges owned by companies or individuals).[121]

The municipal council may pass by-laws for establishing and laying out highways,[122] and for widening, altering or directing any highway.[123]

Additionally, a municipal corporation has a public duty to maintain every highway and bridge, over which its municipal council has jurisdiction, in a state of repair.[124]

(iii) Ministry of Transportation and Communications Creditors Payment Act

It is important to distinguish between public streets and highways owned by a municipality, to which the *Construction Lien Act, 1983*

---

111 See *R. v. Hall* (1866), 17 U.C.C.P. 282.
112 See, for example, *Alspan Wrecking Ltd. v. Dineen Const. Ltd.*, [1972] S.C.R. 829, 26 D.L.R. (3d) 238.
113 The definition of "highway" includes a "street": see s. 1, 9, *Municipal Act.*
114 See *Municipal Act*, s. 260.
115 *Ibid.*, s. 258(1).
116 "Dedication" is defined to mean "[t]he appropriation of land, or an easement therein, by the owner, for the use of the public, and accepted for such use by or on behalf of the public. Such dedication may be expressed where the appropriation is formally declared, or by implication arising by operation of law from the owner's conduct and the facts and circumstances of the case": *Black's Law Dictionary*, 5th ed. (1979).
117 *Reed v. Town of Lincoln* (1974), 6 O.R. (2d) 391, 53 D.L.R. (3d) 14 (C.A.).
118 See *Municipal Act*, s. 1, 9.
119 See *ibid.*, s. 1, 5.
120 *Ibid.*, s. 259.
121 *Ibid.*, s. 260.
122 *Ibid.*, s. 298(1)(a).
123 *Ibid.*, s. 298(1)(b).
124 *Ibid.*, s. 284(1).

applies, and those vested in the Crown to which the *Ministry of Transportation and Communications Creditors Payment Act*[125] applies.

Under the *Public Transportation and Highway Improvement Act*,[126] the Minister of Transportation and Communications is authorized to enter into agreements, on behalf of the Crown, an agency of the Crown, or Ontario Hydro,[127] with respect to the construction, maintenance and repair of roads and highways owned by the Crown.[128]

Where a "contractor"[129] on a Ministry of Transportation and Communications construction project does not pay one of his "creditors"[130] (*e.g.*, subcontractors, material suppliers) in accordance with his obligation to do so under his contract with the Minister, that creditor would not be entitled to avail himself of the remedies afforded by the *Construction Lien Act, 1983*.[131] Rather, the creditor may give[132] notice[133] to the appropriate office of the Ministry,[134] setting out the nature of his claim and the amount alleged to be due and owing.[135] The notice must be sent not later than 120 days after the last day on which labour, materials or services were provided.[136]

Upon receipt of the notice, the Minister, in an attempt to resolve the matter, would notify the contractor and, if appropriate, the bonding company which issued the performance and labour and material payment bonds.[137]

If the claim can be settled informally, the Minister has discretion to pay the claimant the amount settled upon and to deduct that amount from any monies due or that may become due to the contractor.[138] If the amount of the payment to the claimant exceeds the amount which would

---

[125] R.S.O. 1980, c. 290. See Appendix F.

[126] R.S.O. 1980, c. 421.

[127] *Ibid.*, s. 26(2).

[128] *Ibid.*, ss. 26 and 33(1).

[129] The *Ministry of Transportation and Communications Creditors Payment Act* defines "contractor" to mean "a person who enters into a contract with the Minister [of Transportation and Communications]": s. 1(c).

[130] The *Ministry of Transportation and Communications Creditors Payment Act* defines "creditor" to mean "a person who supplies labour, materials or services used or reasonably required for use in the performance of work as set out in a contract": s. 1(d).

[131] *Construction Lien Act*, S.O. 1983, c. 6, s. 3(1).

[132] The *Ministry of Transportation and Communications Creditors Payment Act* provides that notice is to be given by registered mail: s. 2(1).

[133] See Precedent No. 69.

[134] 1201 Wilson Avenue, Downsview, Ontario, M3M 1J8, or Queen's Park, Ferguson Block, 77 Wellesley Street, Toronto, Ontario, M7A 1Z8.

[135] *Ministry of Transportation and Communications Creditors Payment Act*, R.S.O. 1980, c. 290, s. 2(1).

[136] *Ibid.*

[137] *Ibid.*, s. 2(2).

[138] *Ibid.*

otherwise be payable to the contractor, the Minister would pursue his rights against the surety under the bond.[139]

In paying the claim, the Minister "may act upon any evidence that he considers sufficient and may compromise any disputed liability, and such payment is not open to dispute or question by the contractor or the surety, if any, but is final and binding upon them."[140]

In practice, if the claim can not be settled, and the Minister is not inclined or is not in a position to impose a compromise solution, the Minister will either hold back the amount of the claim or oblige the contractor to post security until such time as the matter has been disposed of by the court or otherwise resolved.

(iv) The Municipality as Statutory Owner

The definition of "owner" in the Act[141] comprehends a municipal corporation, despite the fact that, unlike the *Mechanics' Lien Act*,[142] no specific reference is made to a "municipal corporation" in that definition.[143]

Where a municipal corporation is the statutory owner of a public street or highway, a lien would not attach to the premises, but would constitute a charge, as provided in s. 21, upon, *inter alia,* the holdbacks required to be retained under the Act.[144] In these circumstances, the claim for lien need not be registered against the title to the premises,[145] but may be preserved in the manner set forth under the next sub-heading of this chapter.

---

[139] *Ibid.*

[140] *Ibid.*, s. 2(3). Under the predecessor legislation, the *Public Works Creditors Payment Act,* R.S.O. 1970, c. 394, which was repealed in 1975, a hearing was usually held before a referee, who would hear *viva voce* evidence under oath to determine the validity and amount of the claim and who would make a recommendation to the "Crown" or Ministry regarding payment. Despite the fact that the intent and the wording of ss. 2(3) of both Acts is the same, this procedure is apparently no longer available. *Quaere* whether a supposedly "final and binding" payment made by the Minister, under the *Ministry of Transportation and Communications Creditors Payment Act,* is open to judicial review under the *Statutory Powers Procedure Act,* R.S.O. 1980, c. 484.

[141] See s. 1(1) 15.

[142] See *Mechanics' Lien Act,* R.S.O. 1980, c. 261, s. 1(f).

[143] See the *Report of the Attorney General's Advisory Committee on the Draft Construction Lien Act* (April 1982), at 12, which provides:

> The reference to the Crown, municipal corporations and railways that was found in the earlier versions of this definition has been deleted as unnecessary. The Act expressly binds the Crown, and will automatically extend to railways and municipal corporations.

[144] Section 16(3).

[145] *Ibid.*

In the development of a residential subdivision, where privately-owned subdivision land is dedicated by a developer to a municipality for public streets, the municipality's ownership status may become unclear, particularly where the construction of roads and services is carried out by trades retained by the developer.

As the Attorney General's Advisory Committee on the Draft *Construction Lien Act* commented,

> When a plan of subdivision in a municipality is registered, the land for public streets is dedicated to the municipality. However, subdivision agreements often provide for the developer to build the roads to the municipality's specifications, but at the developer's own expense. If these improvements were made by the municipality itself, it would be liable as an owner to the builder's suppliers for the amounts justly owed to them for the services and materials supplied by them. Due to the sub-division agreement however, no claim can be made against the municipality, since it does not pay for the improvement and is therefore not an 'owner' within the meaning of the Draft Act.[146]

Section 17(4) of the Act, though, is designed to rectify this problem by making the municipality liable, on default by the developer, to persons who have supplied services or materials, to the extent of any deficiency in the holdbacks which ought to have been retained by the developer. The lien claimants could protect their rights in this regard by adopting the same procedure as for enforcing a claim for lien against a municipality in respect of a public street or highway.[147]

In order to protect against this kind of potential liability, a municipality will no doubt seek to extract a bond (*e.g.,* a lien holdback deficiency bond, discussed in chapter 10) from the developer.

(v) Preservation of Lien in Respect of Municipally-Owned Public Street or Highway

The lien, where it does not attach to the premises, may be preserved by giving[148] the clerk of the municipality[149] a copy of the claim for lien,[150] together with an affidavit of verification.[151]

Notification of the municipality in the manner set forth above must be effected "during the supplying of services or materials or at any time before it (the lien) expires."[152]

---

[146] *Report of the Attorney General's Advisory Committee on the Draft Construction Lien Act* (April 1982), at 54.

[147] See the next heading (C(v)) in this chapter, entitled "Preservation of Lien in Respect of Municipally-Owned Public Street or Highway."

[148] See ss. 89(1), (2) and (4).

[149] Section 34(2).

[150] See note 39, *supra.*

[151] See note 40, *supra.*

[152] Section 34(1). Also see s. 31.

It is important to note that, despite the fact that the construction of roads and services on a public street that has been dedicated to a municipality appears to "benefit" the abutting subdivision lots owned by a developer, a lien could not properly be preserved against those lots.[153]

(vi) Perfection of Lien in Respect of Municipally-Owned Public Street or Highway

Unless a lien has been preserved within the time periods set forth in s. 31 of the Act, it will be deemed to have expired,[154] and therefore may not be perfected.[155]

If it has been properly preserved, though, it becomes perfected when an action[156] to enforce the lien has been commenced.[157] Alternatively, a preserved lien may become perfected by sheltering under a lien which has been perfected by another lien claimant.[158]

Where the lien does not attach to the premises, a certificate of action need not be registered.[159] However, the lien action must be commenced "prior to the end of the forty-five day period next following the last day, under section 31, on which the lien could have been preserved"[160] if the lien is to be perfected. Otherwise, it expires,[161] and upon motion[162] the court is obliged to make a declaration to this effect.[163]

(vii) Discharging or Vacating a Lien Where it does not Attach to the Premises

For a discussion of this topic, see heading B(v) of this chapter.

(viii) Settlement Meeting

For a discussion of this topic, see heading B(vii) of this chapter.

---

[153] *George Wimpey Can. Ltd. v. Peelton Hills Ltd. et al.* (1981), 31 O.R. (2d) 563, 119 D.L.R. (3d) 408, 14 M.P.L.R. 1, 16 R.P.R. 222; affd. 35 O.R. 787, 132 D.L.R. (3d) 732, 42 C.B.R. (N.S.) 1, 18 M.P.L.R. 65, 23 R.P.R. 123; leave to appeal to S.C.C. refused (1982), 43 N.R. 618n. Also see note 13 of chapter 2.
[154] Section 31(1).
[155] Section 36(1).
[156] Section 1(1) 1 defines "action" to mean "an action under Part VIII."
[157] Section 36(3)(b).
[158] See s. 36(4).
[159] Section 36(3)(b).
[160] Section 36(2).
[161] *Ibid.*
[162] See Precedent Nos. 23, 24 and 25.
[163] Section 45(2).

(ix) Form of Judgment or Report

For a discussion of this topic, see heading B(viii) of this chapter.

(x) Breach of Trust Claim Against Municipality

The "mortgage trust" provisions of the Act[164] expressly exempt a municipality from any obligations, *qua* trustee,[165] where the municipality is a statutory owner. This is the case irrespective of whether the improvement being financed is a public street or highway, or another type of municipal project such as a sewage treatment plant.

The other trusts created by the Act, though, do not appear to contain the same exemption.

To the extent that it may be possible to assert a breach of trust claim against a municipality, it is to be noted that a "trust claim shall not be joined with a lien claim but may be brought in any court of competent jurisdiction."[166]

D. APPLICATION OF THE ACT TO RAILWAY RIGHTS-OF-WAY

(i) A Constitutional Issue

Railways are under the exclusive jurisdiction of the federal Parliament[167] and are generally considered to be works for the general advantage of Canada.

Section 2 of the *Railway Act*[168] defines "railway" to include, *inter alia,* "all branches, extensions, sidings, stations, depots, wharfs, rolling stock, equipment, stores, property real or personal and works connected therewith, and also any railway bridge, tunnel or other structure that the [railway] company is authorized to construct." Although "railway right-of-way" is not defined in either the *Railway Act* or the *Construction Lien Act, 1983,* presumably it would come within the ambit of the above definition.

The issue which then arises is whether a person who supplies services or materials in connection with construction on a railway right-of-way would be entitled to assert lien rights created by provincial legislation.

---

[164] See s. 7(1).
[165] See s. 7(4).
[166] Section 50(2).
[167] See *Railway Act,* R.S.C. 1970, c. R-2, as amended.
[168] *Ibid.*

Crawford v. Tilden et al.[169] is an Ontario Court of Appeal decision in an action commenced under the *Mechanics' and Wage-Earners' Lien Act*[170] to enforce a wage-earner's lien. The court there held that the lands of a railway company incorporated under a federal Act are not subject to a lien, and that the mechanics' lien legislation then in effect in Ontario did not create any enforceable lien rights in the circumstances.

The next time the issue was considered in Ontario was in the 1918 Court of Appeal decision in *Johnson & Carey Co. v. Can. Northern Ry. Co.*[171] The plaintiffs in that action were retained as principal contractors for the filling and construction of a new railway line at Rainy Lake, Ontario. Having supplied labour and materials under their contract, the plaintiffs registered a claim for lien against the lands comprising the railway line. In following the *Crawford v. Tilden* decision, the court held that a lien claimed under the *Mechanics' and Wage-Earners' Lien Act* does not exist and can not be enforced against the property of the Canadian Northern Railway Company, a Dominion corporation.

In both of the foregoing decisions, the courts observed that the substance of provincial legislation was to provide the claimant with an ultimate remedy of sale. Since a court would have no authority to order the sale of federally-controlled railway lands, the granting of a lien would be an illusory right.

Under the *Construction Lien Act, 1983,* where the premises is a railway right-of-way, the lien does not attach to the premises,[172] and accordingly the ultimate remedy of selling the statutory owner's interest in the premises is unavailable. One must therefore assume that this legislative change will avoid the constitutional problem discussed above.

(ii) The Railway Corporation as Statutory Owner

The definition of "owner" in the Act[173] includes a railway corporation, despite the fact that, unlike the *Mechanics' Lien Act*,[174] no specific reference is made to "railway company" in that definition.

As the Attorney General's Advisory Committee on the Draft *Construction Lien Act* commented:

> The meaning of the term "owner" has always been somewhat opaque. The Committee has redrafted the provision to clarify its meaning. The reference to the

---

[169] (1907), 14 O.L.R. 572, 6 C.R.C. 437 (C.A.); affg. (1906), 13 O.L.R. 169, 6 C.R.C. 300.
[170] R.S.O. 1897, c. 153.
[171] (1918), 44 O.L.R. 533, 15 O.W.N. 279, 47 D.L.R. 75, 24 C.R.C. 294 (C.A.) varg. 43 O.L.R. 10, 14 O.W.N. 159.
[172] Section 16(3).
[173] See s. 1(1) 15.
[174] See *Mechanics' Lien Act,* R.S.O. 1980, c. 261, s. 1(f).

Crown, municipal corporations and railways that was found in the earlier versions of this definition has been deleted as unnecessary. The Act expressly binds the Crown, and will automatically extend to railways and municipal corporations.[175]

(iii) Preservation of Lien in Respect of Railway Right-of-Way

Under the *Mechanics' Lien Act,* a claim for lien could be registered against the title to "the land of the railway company."[176] The *Construction Lien Act, 1983,* however, makes no general reference to railway lands, but purports to deal only with railway rights-of-way.

Where the premises being improved is a railway right-of-way, the lien does not attach to the premises, but rather constitutes a charge, as provided in s. 21, upon, *inter alia,* the holdbacks required to be retained under the Act.[177]

In these circumstances, the claim for lien need not be registered against the title to the premises,[178] but may be preserved by giving[179] the manager or any person apparently in charge of any office of the railway in Ontario[180] a copy of the claim for lien,[181] together with an affidavit of verification.[182]

Notification of the railway corporation in the manner set forth above must be effected "during the supplying of services or materials or at any time before it [the lien] expires."[183]

(iv) Perfection of Lien in Respect of Railway Right-of-Way

Unless a lien has been preserved within the time periods set forth in s. 31 of the *Construction Lien Act, 1983,* it will be deemed to have expired,[184] and therefore may not be perfected.[185]

If it has been properly preserved, though, it becomes perfected when an action[186] to enforce the lien has been commenced.[187] Alternatively, a

---

[175] *Report of the Attorney General's Advisory Committee on the Draft Construction Lien Act* (April 1982), at 12.
[176] *Mechanics' Lien Act,* R.S.O. 1980, c. 261, s. 17(3).
[177] Section 16(3).
[178] *Ibid.*
[179] See ss. 89(1), (2) and (4).
[180] Section 34(4).
[181] See note 39, *supra.*
[182] See note 40, *supra.*
[183] Section 34(1). Also see s. 31.
[184] Section 31(1).
[185] Section 36(1).
[186] Section 1(1) 1 defines "action" to mean "an action under Part VIII."
[187] Section 36(3)(b).

preserved lien may become perfected by sheltering under a lien which has been perfected by another lien claimant.[188]

Where the lien does not attach to the premises, a certificate of action need not be registered.[189] However, the lien action must be commenced "prior to the end of the forty-five day period next following the last day, under section 31, on which the lien could have been preserved"[190] if the lien is to be perfected. Otherwise it expires,[191] and upon motion,[192] the court is obliged to make a declaration to this effect.[193]

(v) Discharging or Vacating a Lien Where it does not Attach to the Premises

For a discussion of this topic, see heading B(v) of this chapter.

(vi) Settlement Meeting

For a discussion of this topic, see heading B(vii) of this chapter.

(vii) Form of Judgment or Report

For a discussion of this topic, see heading B(viii) of this chapter.

---

[188] See s. 36(4).
[189] Section 36(3)(b).
[190] Section 36(2).
[191] *Ibid.*
[192] See Precedent Nos. 23, 24 and 25.
[193] Section 45(2).

Appendix A

Precedent No. 1

STATUTORY DECLARATION

C A N A D A   In the matter of contract entered into with . . . .
              . . . ., Owner, by . . . .,
Province of   Contractor, ...
              At Project . . . . Contractor No. . . . .
              File No. . . . .

TO WIT:

    I, ... of the . . . .
of . . . . in the Province of . . . . do solemnly declare:

    1. That I am . . . .
               (President, Vice-President, Secretary, Treasurer, A Partner)
of . . . .
the contractor named in the contract above mentioned and as such have personal
knowledge of the facts hereunder declared.

    2. That all subcontractors, labour, and accounts for materials and equipment whatsoever entering into the construction of the project built under the said contract have been duly paid except for holdbacks on subcontracts.

    3. That the wages paid are in all cases the same as or above those set out in any applicable legislation.

AND I MAKE THIS SOLEMN DECLARATION conscientiously believing it to be true and knowing that it is of the same force and effect as if made under oath and by virtue of the *Canada Evidence Act.*

DECLARED before me at the . . . .)
of . . . . in the . . . .)
of . . . .)Signed: . . . .
this . . . . day of . . . ., 19 . . .)

A Commissioner for Oaths, Notary Public,
Justice of the Peace.

Precedent No. 2

CLA 1234/83

IN THE SUPREME COURT OF ONTARIO

IN THE MATTER OF the *Construction Lien Act*, S.O. 1983, c. 6

B E T W E E N:

SUBCONTRACTOR LTD.,

Plaintiff,

- and -

GENERAL CONTRACTOR LTD.,
OWNER LTD. and
MORTGAGEE LTD.,

Defendants.

NOTICE OF DIRECT PAYMENT TO PERSON HAVING LIEN UNDER SECTION 28

TO: GENERAL CONTRACTOR LTD.

TAKE NOTICE that on the 2nd day of December, 1983, pursuant to Section 28 of the *Construction Lien Act*, S.O. 1983, c. 6, Owner Ltd. paid to Subcontractor Ltd. the sum of $5,000, which payment will be applied by Owner Ltd. on its contract with you dated the 2nd day of April, 1983.

DATED at Toronto this 3rd day of December, 1983.

Precedent No. 3

IN THE SUPREME COURT OF ONTARIO

IN THE MATTER OF the *Construction
Lien Act*, S.O. 1983, c. 6

B E T W E E N:

GENERAL CONTRACTOR LTD.,

Applicant,

- and-

OWNER LTD.,

Respondent.

NOTICE OF MOTION

TAKE NOTICE that an application will be made to the Court on behalf of
the Applicant, General Contractor Ltd., at Osgoode Hall, Queen Street West,
Toronto, Ontario, on Monday, the 12th day of December, 1983 at 10:30 o'clock
in the forenoon, or so soon thereafter as Counsel can be heard, for a declaration,
pursuant to Section 32(1)7 of the *Construction Lien Act*, S.O. 1983, c. 6, that the
contract between the Applicant and the Respondent has been substantially
performed, or for such other declaration as to this Honourable Court may seem
just.

AND TAKE NOTICE that in support of such application will be filed the
Affidavit of Calvin Contractor, and such further and other material as Counsel
may advise.

DATED at Toronto this 3rd day of December, 1983.

PETERS & RICHARDS
Barristers and Solicitors
210 Bay Street
Toronto, Ontario

Solicitors for the Applicant,
General Contractor Ltd.

Precedent No. 4

IN THE SUPREME COURT OF ONTARIO

IN THE MATTER OF the *Construction Lien Act*, S.O. 1983, c. 6

B E T W E E N:

GENERAL CONTRACTOR LTD.,

Applicant,

- and -

OWNER LTD.,

Respondent.

A F F I D A V I T

I, CALVIN CONTRACTOR, of the Municipality of Metropolitan Toronto, in the Province of Ontario, Executive, MAKE OATH AND SAY AS FOLLOWS:

1. I am President of the Applicant, General Contractor Ltd., and as such have knowledge of the matters hereinafter deposed to.

2. On or about the 2nd day of April, 1983, the Applicant and the Respondent entered into a written contract whereby the Applicant agreed to provide general contracting services to the Respondent, in consideration for an agreed price of $500,000, with respect to the renovation of an industrial building situated on the lands referred to in Schedule A annexed hereto.

3. As at November 7, 1983, the renovations to the said industrial building were capable of completion at a cost of not more than $10,000, and the said industrial building was being used for the purposes intended. On the basis of the foregoing, I verily believe that the contract has been substantially performed, in accordance with the formula established by Section 2 of the *Construction Lien Act*.

4. More than three weeks ago, I applied to Owner Ltd. and its architect for a determination as to whether the contract had been substantially performed. However, as of the date of this my Affidavit, they have failed or refused to certify substantial performance of the contract.

5. This Affidavit is made in support of an application for a declaration that the said contract has been substantially performed, and for no improper purpose.

SWORN before me (etc.) . . . .   )
)
)
)
)   CALVIN CONTRACTOR
)

A Commissioner, etc.

Precedent No. 5

IN THE SUPREME COURT OF ONTARIO

IN THE MATTER OF the *Construction Lien Act,* S.O. 1983, c. 6

THE HONOURABLE	)	MONDAY, THE 12TH DAY OF
MR. JUSTICE	)	
	)	DECEMBER, 1983.

B E T W E E N:

GENERAL CONTRACTOR LTD.,

Applicant,

- and -

OWNER LTD.,

Respondent.

ORDER

UPON application made this day on behalf of the Applicant, General Contractor Ltd., for a declaration, pursuant to Section 32(1)7 of the *Construction Lien Act,* S.O. 1983, c. 6, that the contract between the Applicant and the Respondent dated the 2nd day of April, 1983, has been substantially performed in accordance with Section 2 of the *Construction Lien Act,* in the presence of Counsel for the Applicant and for the Respondent, Owner Ltd., upon reading the Affidavit of Calvin Contractor, filed, and upon hearing Counsel aforesaid:

1. IT IS HEREBY DECLARED that the contract between the Applicant and the Respondent dated the 2nd day of April, 1983, in respect of the renovation of a building located on the lands referred to in Schedule A annexed hereto, has been substantially performed.

Precedent No. 6

CLA 1234/83

IN THE SUPREME COURT OF ONTARIO

IN THE MATTER OF the *Construction Lien Act*, S.O. 1983, c. 6

B E T W E E N:

SUBCONTRACTOR LTD.,

Plaintiff,

- and -

GENERAL CONTRACTOR LTD.,
OWNER LTD. and
MORTGAGEE LTD.,

Defendants.

NOTICE OF MOTION

TAKE NOTICE that a motion will be made to the Master on behalf of the Plaintiff at 145 Queen Street West, Toronto, Ontario, on Monday, the 12th day of December, 1983, at the hour of 10:00 o'clock in the forenoon, or so soon thereafter as Counsel can be heard, for an Order, pursuant to Section 39(6) of the *Construction Lien Act*, S.O. 1983, c. 6, obliging General Contractor Ltd. to furnish in writing the date of publication and the name of the construction trade newspaper in which a copy of a certificate of substantial performance, in relation to the renovation of an industrial building on the lands referred to in Schedule A annexed hereto, has been published under Section 32(1) of the said Act, or for such other Order as to this Honourable Court may seem just.

AND TAKE NOTICE that in support of such motion will be filed the Affidavit of Stanley Subcontractor, and such further and other material as Counsel may advise.

DATED at Toronto this 3rd day of December, 1983.

KIRSH & KIRSH
Barristers and Solicitors
45 Bay Street
Toronto, Ontario

Solicitors for the Plaintiff,
Subcontractor Ltd.

Precedent No. 7

CLA 1234/83

IN THE SUPREME COURT OF ONTARIO

IN THE MATTER OF the *Construction Lien Act,* S.O. 1983, c. 6

B E T W E E N:

SUBCONTRACTOR LTD.,

Plaintiff,

- and -

GENERAL CONTRACTOR LTD.,
OWNER LTD. and
MORTGAGEE LTD.,

Defendants.

A F F I D A V I T

I, STANLEY SUBCONTRACTOR, of the Municipality of Metropolitan Toronto, in the Province of Ontario, Executive, MAKE OATH AND SAY AS FOLLOWS:

1. I am President of the Plaintiff, Subcontractor Ltd., and as such have knowledge of the matters hereinafter deposed to.

2. Pursuant to a written agreement between Subcontractor Ltd. and General Contractor Ltd., Subcontractor Ltd. supplied services and materials to General Contractor Ltd. in connection with the renovation of an industrial building on the lands referred to in Schedule A annexed hereto.

3. I am advised by Arnold Architect, who was the payment certifier in connection with the aforesaid construction project, and verily believe that the contract between General Contractor Ltd. and Owner Ltd. was certified as having been substantially performed many weeks ago.

4. By letter dated November 3, 1983, Subcontractor Ltd. requested General Contractor Ltd. to furnish in writing the date of publication and the name of the construction trade newspaper in which a copy of the certificate of substantial performance has been published. However, as of the date of this my Affidavit, General Contractor Ltd. has failed to comply with this request.

5. This Affidavit is made in support of a motion of an Order obliging

General Contractor Ltd. to comply with the said request, and for no improper purpose.

SWORN before me (etc.) . . . .)
)
)
)   _____
)   STANLEY SUBCONTRACTOR
)
)

A Commissioner, etc.

Precedent No. 8

CLA 1234/83

IN THE SUPREME COURT OF ONTARIO

IN THE MATTER OF the *Construction Lien Act*, S.O. 1983, c. 6

MASTER   )   MONDAY, THE 12TH DAY OF
)
)   DECEMBER, 1983.

B E T W E E N:

SUBCONTRACTOR LTD.,

Plaintiff,

- and -

GENERAL CONTRACTOR LTD.,
OWNER LTD. and
MORTGAGEE LTD.,

Defendants.

O R D E R

UPON motion made this day on behalf of the Plaintiff, Subcontractor Ltd., for an Order, pursuant to Section 39(6) of the *Construction Lien Act*, S.O. 1983, c. 6, obliging General Contractor Ltd. to furnish in writing the date of publication and the name of the construction trade newspaper in which a copy of a certificate of substantial performance, in relation to the renovation of an industrial building on the lands referred to in Schedule A annexed hereto, has been published under Section 32(1) of the said Act, in the presence of Counsel for the Defendant, General Contractor Ltd., and counsel for the Plaintiff, no one appearing for the Defendants, Owner Ltd. and Mortgagee Ltd., although duly served, upon reading the Affidavit of Stanley Subcontractor, filed, and upon hearing Counsel aforesaid:

1. IT IS ORDERED that, within ten days of the date of this Order, General Contractor Ltd. shall furnish particulars in writing to Subcontractor Ltd. as to the date of publication and the name of the construction trade newspaper in which a copy of the certificate of substantial performance, in relation to the renovation of an industrial building on the lands referred to in Schedule A annexed hereto, has been published.

Precedent No. 9

CLA 1234/83

IN THE SUPREME COURT OF ONTARIO

IN THE MATTER OF the *Construction Lien Act*, S.O. 1983, c. 6

B E T W E E N:

SUBCONTRACTOR LTD.,

Plaintiff,

- and -

GENERAL CONTRACTOR LTD.,
OWNER LTD. and
MORTGAGEE LTD.,

Defendants.

NOTICE OF MOTION

TAKE NOTICE that a motion will be made to the Master on behalf of the Plaintiff, Subcontractor Ltd., at 145 Queen Street West, Toronto, Ontario, on Monday, the 12th day of December, 1983, at the hour of 10:00 o'clock in the forenoon, or so soon thereafter as Counsel can be heard, for an Order, pursuant to Section 39(6) of the *Construction Lien Act*, S.O. 1983, c. 6, obliging General Contractor Ltd. to comply with the written request for information made by the Plaintiff, particulars of which are referred to in the Affidavit filed in support hereof, or for such other Order as to this Honourable Court may seem just.

AND TAKE NOTICE that in support of such motion will be filed the Affidavit of Stanley Subcontractor, or such further and other material as Counsel may advise.

DATED at Toronto this 3rd day of December, 1983.

KIRSH & KIRSH
Barristers and Solicitors
45 Bay Street
Toronto, Ontario

Solicitors for the Plaintiff,
Subcontractor Ltd.

Precedent No. 10

CLA 1234/83

IN THE SUPREME COURT OF ONTARIO

IN THE MATTER OF the *Construction Lien Act,* S.O. 1983, c. 6

B E T W E E N:

SUBCONTRACTOR LTD.,

Plaintiff,

- and -

GENERAL CONTRACTOR LTD.,
OWNER LTD. and
MORTGAGEE LTD.,

Defendants.

A F F I D A V I T

I, STANLEY SUBCONTRACTOR, of the Municipality of Metropolitan Toronto, in the Province of Ontario, Executive, MAKE OATH AND SAY AS FOLLOWS:

1. I am President of the Plaintiff, Subcontractor Ltd., and as such have knowledge of the matters hereinafter deposed to.

2. Subcontractor Ltd. supplied services and materials to General Contractor Ltd. in connection with the renovation of an industrial building on the lands referred to in Schedule A annexed hereto. By virtue of the foregoing, I verily believe that Subcontractor Ltd. has a lien against the title to the said lands in respect thereof.

3. By letter dated November 3, 1983, Subcontractor Ltd. requested information from General Contractor Ltd. as to:

(a) the contract price;
(b) the state of accounts between Owner Ltd. and General Contractor Ltd.;
(c) a copy of any labour and material payment bond in respect of the contract posted by General Contractor Ltd. with Owner Ltd.

However, as at the date of this my Affidavit, General Contractor Ltd. has failed to comply with the said request.

4. This Affidavit is made in support of a motion for an Order obliging General Contractor Ltd. to comply with the aforesaid request, and for no improper purpose.

SWORN before me (etc.) . . . .   )
)
)
)   STANLEY SUBCONTRACTOR
)
)

A Commissioner, etc.

Precedent No. 11

CLA 1234/83

IN THE SUPREME COURT OF ONTARIO

IN THE MATTER OF the *Construction
Lien Act*, S.O. 1983, c. 6

MASTER) MONDAY, THE 12TH DAY OF
)
) DECEMBER, 1983.

B E T W E E N:

SUBCONTRACTOR LTD.,

Plaintiff,

- and -

GENERAL CONTRACTOR LTD.,
OWNER LTD. and
MORTGAGEE LTD.,

Defendants.

O R D E R

UPON motion made this day on behalf of the Plaintiff, Subcontractor Ltd., for an Order, pursuant to Section 39(6) of the *Construction Lien Act*, S.O. 1983, c. 6, obliging General Contractor Ltd. to comply with the written request for information made by the Plaintiff, particulars of which are referred to in the Affidavit filed in support hereof, in the presence of Counsel for the Defendant, General Contractor Ltd., and Counsel for the Plaintiff, no one appearing for the Defendants, Owner Ltd. and Mortgagee Ltd., although duly served, upon reading the Affidavit of Stanley Subcontractor, filed, and upon hearing Counsel aforesaid:

1. IT IS ORDERED that, within ten days of the date of this Order, General Contractor Ltd. shall provide Subcontractor Ltd. with the following:

(a) the contract price;
(b) the state of accounts between Owner Ltd. and General Contractor Ltd.;

(c) a copy of any labour and material payment bond in respect of the contract posted by General Contractor Ltd. with Owner Ltd.,

relating to the renovation of an industrial building on the lands referred to in Schedule A annexed hereto.

IN THE SUPREME COURT OF ONTARIO

IN THE MATTER OF the Construction Lien Act, S.O. 1983, c. 6

B E T W E E N:

CORPORATION LTD.,

Plaintiff

- and -

GENERAL CONTRACTOR LTD.
BANK LTD.
CORPORATION LTD.

Defendant

NOTICE OF MOTION

TAKE NOTICE that a motion will be made on the day of 19 , at 10:00 a.m. or as soon thereafter as the motion can be heard before the presiding judge in Chambers at Osgoode Hall, Toronto, for an order pursuant to section of the Construction Lien Act, S.O. 1983, c. 6 compelling General Contractor Ltd. to comply with the written request for information wherein the exhibits, particulars of which are referred to in the Affidavit filed in support hereof, and for such further or other Order as to this Honourable Court may seem just.

AND TAKE NOTICE that in support of such motion will be filed the Affidavit of Smith, Subcontractor Ltd., and such further and other material as Counsel may advise.

DATED at Toronto this 3rd day of December, 1984.

LINOTEX LAWYER
Barristers and Solicitors
45 Bay Street
Toronto, Ontario

Solicitors for the Plaintiff,
Subcontractor Ltd.

Precedent No. 12

CLA 1234/83

IN THE SUPREME COURT OF ONTARIO

IN THE MATTER OF the *Construction Lien Act,* S.O. 1983, c. 6

B E T W E E N:

SUBCONTRACTOR LTD.,

Plaintiff,

- and -

GENERAL CONTRACTOR LTD.,
OWNER LTD. and
MORTGAGEE LTD.,

Defendants.

NOTICE OF MOTION

TAKE NOTICE that a motion will be made to the Master on behalf of the Plaintiff, Subcontractor Ltd., at 145 Queen Street West, Toronto, Ontario, on Monday, the 12th day of December, 1983, at the hour of 10:00 o'clock in the forenoon, or so soon thereafter as Counsel can be heard, for an Order, pursuant to Section 39(6) of the *Construction Lien Act,* S.O. 1983, c. 6, obliging Mortgagee Ltd. to comply with the written request for information made by the Plaintiff, particulars of which are referred to in the Affidavit filed in support hereof, or for such further or other Order as to this Honourable Court may seem just.

AND TAKE NOTICE that in support of such motion will be filed the Affidavit of Stanley Subcontractor, and such further and other material as Counsel made advise.

DATED at Toronto this 3rd day of December, 1983.

KIRSH & KIRSH
Barristers and Solicitors
45 Bay Street
Toronto, Ontario

Solicitors for the Plaintiff,
Subcontractor Ltd.

Precedent No. 13

CLA 1234/83

IN THE SUPREME COURT OF ONTARIO

IN THE MATTER OF the *Construction
Lien Act*, S.O. 1983, c. 6

B E T W E E N:

SUBCONTRACTOR LTD.,

Plaintiff,

- and -

GENERAL CONTRACTOR LTD.,
OWNER LTD. and
MORTGAGEE LTD.,

Defendants.

A F F I D A V I T

I, STANLEY SUBCONTRACTOR, of the Municipality of Metropolitan Toronto, in the Province of Ontario, Executive, MAKE OATH AND SAY AS FOLLOWS:

1. I am President of the Plaintiff, Subcontractor Ltd., and as such have knowledge of the matters hereinafter deposed to.

2. Subcontractor Ltd. supplied services and materials to General Contractor Ltd. in connection with the renovation of an industrial building on the lands referred to in Schedule "A" annexed hereto. By virtue of the foregoing, I verily believe that Subcontractor Ltd. has a lien against the title to the said lands in respect thereof.

3. By letter dated November 3, 1983, Subcontractor Ltd. requested from Mortgagee Ltd. the following:

(a) sufficient details concerning the mortgage held by Mortgagee Ltd. on the lands referred to in Schedule A annexed hereto to enable Subcontractor Ltd. to determine whether the said mortgage was taken by Mortgagee Ltd. for the purposes of financing the making of the improvement, including, without limitation, copies of the mortgage application documentation, Mortgagee Ltd.'s letter of commitment, all memos, correspondence and other documentation relative to the said

mortgage, and all cancelled cheques representing mortgage advances;
(b) a statement showing the amount(s) advanced under the said mortgage, the dates of those advances, and any arrears in payment including any arrears in the payment of interest.

However, as of the date of this my Affidavit, Mortgagee Ltd. has failed to provide the requested information and documentation.

4. This Affidavit is made in support of a motion for an Order obliging Mortgagee Ltd. to comply with the said request, and for no improper purpose.

SWORN before me (etc.) . . . .   )
)
)
)
)   **STANLEY SUBCONTRACTOR**
)

A Commissioner, etc.

Precedent No. 14

CLA 1234/83

IN THE SUPREME COURT OF ONTARIO

IN THE MATTER OF the *Construction Lien Act*, S.O. 1983, c. 6

MASTER	)	MONDAY, THE 12TH DAY OF
	)	
	)	DECEMBER, 1983.

B E T W E E N:

SUBCONTRACTOR LTD.,

Plaintiff,

- and -

GENERAL CONTRACTOR LTD.,
OWNER LTD. and
MORGAGEE LTD.,

Defendants.

O R D E R

UPON motion made this day on behalf of the Plaintiff, Subcontractor Ltd., for an Order, pursuant to Section 39(6) of the *Construction Lien Act*, S.O. 1983, c. 6, obliging Mortgagee Ltd. to comply with the written request for information made by the Plaintiff, particulars of which are referred to in the Affidavit filed in support hereof, in the presence of Counsel for the Defendant, Mortgagee Ltd., and Counsel for the Plaintiff, no one appearing for the Defendants, General Contractor Ltd. and Owner Ltd., although duly served, upon reading the Affidavit of Stanley Subcontractor, filed, and upon hearing Counsel aforesaid:

1. IT IS ORDERED that, within ten days of the date of this Order, Mortgagee Ltd. shall provide to Subcontractor Ltd. the following:

(a) sufficient details concerning the mortgage held by Mortgagee Ltd. on the lands referred to in Schedule A annexed hereto to enable Subcontractor Ltd. to determine whether the said mortgage was taken by Mortgagee Ltd. for the purposes of financing the making of the improvement, including, without limitation, copies of the mortgage application documentation, Mortgagee Ltd.'s letter of commitment, all memos, correspondence and other documentation relative to the said mortgage, and all cancelled cheques representing mortgage advances;

(b) a statement showing the amount(s) advanced under the said mortgage, the dates of those advances, and any arrears in payment including any arrears in the payment of interest.

Precedent No. 15

CLA 1235/83

IN THE SUPREME COURT OF ONTARIO

IN THE MATTER OF the *Construction Lien Act*, S.O. 1983, c. 6

B E T W E E N:

DAVID DUCT, Trustee,

Plaintiff,

- and -

GENERAL CONTRACTOR LTD.,
OWNER LTD. and
MORTGAGEE LTD.,

Defendants.

NOTICE OF MOTION

TAKE NOTICE that a motion will be made to the Master on behalf of the Plaintiff, David Duct, Trustee, at 145 Queen Street West, Toronto, Ontario, on Monday, the 12th day of December, 1983, at the hour of 10:00 o'clock in the forenoon, or so soon thereafter as Counsel can be heard, for an Order, pursuant to Section 39(6) of the *Construction Lien Act*, S.O. 1983, c. 6, obliging General Contractor Ltd. to comply with the written request for information made by the Plaintiff, particulars of which are referred to in the Affidavit filed in support hereof, or for such further or other Order as to this Honourable Court may seem just.

AND TAKE NOTICE that in support of such motion will be filed the Affidavit of David Duct, and such further and other material as Counsel may advise.

DATED at Toronto this 3rd day of December, 1983.

KIRSH & KIRSH
Barristers and Solicitors
45 Bay Street
Toronto, Ontario

Solicitors for the Plaintiff,
David Duct, Trustee.

Precedent No. 16

CLA 1235/83

IN THE SUPREME COURT OF ONTARIO

IN THE MATTER OF the *Construction
Lien Act*, S.O. 1983, c. 6

B E T W E E N:

DAVID DUCT, Trustee,

Plaintiff,

- and -

GENERAL CONTRACTOR LTD.,
OWNER LTD. and
MORTGAGEE LTD.,

Defendants.

A F F I D A V I T

I, DAVID DUCT, TRUSTEE, of the Municipality of Metropolitan Toronto, in the Province of Ontario, Executive, MAKE OATH AND SAY AS FOLLOWS:

1. I am the Trustee of Sheet Metal Workers' Trust Fund, which I verily believe is a "workers' trust fund" as defined by the *Construction Lien Act*.
2. By letter dated November 3, 1983, I requested General Contractor Ltd. to permit me to inspect the payroll records of all workers who are beneficiaries of the fund, who are employed by General Contractor Ltd., and who have supplied labour in connection with the renovation of an industrial building on the lands referred to in Schedule A annexed hereto. However, as of the date of this my Affidavit, General Contractor Ltd. has failed to permit me access to the said payroll records.
3. This Affidavit is made in support of a motion for an Order obliging General Contractor Ltd. to comply with the said request, and for no improper purpose.

SWORN before me (etc.) . . .   )
)
)
)   _____
)   DAVID DUCT, TRUSTEE
)
)

A Commissioner, etc.

Precedent No. 17

CLA 1235/83

IN THE SUPREME COURT OF ONTARIO

IN THE MATTER OF the *Construction Lien Act*, S.O. 1983, c. 6

MASTER   )   MONDAY, THE 12TH DAY OF
)
)   DECEMBER, 1983.

B E T W E E N:

DAVID DUCT, Trustee,

Plaintiff,

- and -

GENERAL CONTRACTOR LTD.,
OWNER LTD. and
MORTGAGEE LTD.,

Defendants.

O R D E R

UPON motion made this day on behalf of the Plaintiff, David Duct, Trustee, for an Order, pursuant to Section 39(6) of the *Construction Lien Act*, S.O. 1983, c. 6, obliging General Contractor Ltd. to comply with the written request for information made by the Plaintiff, particulars of which are referred to in the Affidavit filed in support hereof, in the presence of Counsel for the Defendant, General Contractor Ltd., and Counsel for the Plaintiff, no one appearing for the Defendants, Owner Ltd. and Mortgagee Ltd., although duly served, upon reading the Affidavit of David Duct, Trustee, filed, and upon hearing Counsel aforesaid:

1. IT IS ORDERED that, within ten days of the date of this Order, General Contractor Ltd. shall permit David Duct, Trustee, to inspect the payroll records of all workers who are beneficiaries of the Sheet Metal Workers' Trust Fund, who are employed by General Contractor Ltd., and who have supplied labour in connection with the renovation of an industrial building on the lands referred to in Schedule A annexed hereto.

Precedent No. 18

NOTICE OF LIEN

TAKE NOTICE that Subcontractor Ltd., of 206 Main Street, Toronto, Ontario, claims to be entitled to a lien under the *Construction Lien Act,* S.O. 1983, c. 6, upon the estate of Owner Ltd., of 123 Home Street, Toronto, Ontario, in the lands referred to in Schedule A annexed hereto.

The said lien is in respect of the supply of plumbing materials on the 3rd day of November, 1983 to General Contractor Ltd. of 99 Queen Street, Toronto, Ontario, in connection with the renovation of an industrial building on the lands referred to in the said Schedule A, which lands are owned by Owner Ltd.

The amount that has not been paid and is owing to Subcontractor Ltd. by General Contractor Ltd. is the sum of $75,000.

DATED at Toronto this 3rd day of December, 1983.

SUBCONTRACTOR LTD.

Per: _____

(signature of claimant or agent)

Precedent No. 19

SAMPLE LETTER OF CREDIT

Bank of Toronto
123 Ontario Street
Toronto, Ontario
December 12, 1983

Accountant
Supreme Court of Ontario
123 Edward Street
Toronto, Ontario

Dear Sir:

Re: Subcontractor Ltd. v. General Contractor Ltd.,
Owner Ltd. and Mortgagee Ltd.
Action No. CLA 1234/83

For good and valuable consideration, the Bank of Toronto hereby establishes an irrevocable letter of credit, and hereby undertakes and agrees to pay any sum of money, up to an aggregate amount of $93,750 (Canadian Funds), that Owner Ltd. may be called upon to pay pursuant to any judgment of the Supreme Court of Ontario in the above-captioned action.

This letter of credit will expire on December 11, 1984, and is subject to automatic renewal on an annual basis, unless you are notified in writing by the Bank of Toronto of its cancellation at least thirty days prior to the aforesaid expiry date.

The Bank of Toronto hereby agrees with the drawers, endorsers, and bona fide holders of drafts drawn under and in compliance with the terms of this credit, that such drafts will be duly honoured on due presentation to the drawees if negotiated on or before the expiration date of this letter or presented at the Bank of Toronto together with the letter of credit on or before that date.

Yours very truly,

Leonard Lender
Supervisor, Letters of Credit Dept.

Precedent No. 20

CLA 1234/83

IN THE SUPREME COURT OF ONTARIO

IN THE MATTER OF the *Construction Lien Act*, S.O. 1983, c. 6

B E T W E E N:

SUBCONTRACTOR LTD.,

Plaintiff,

- and -

GENERAL CONTRACTOR LTD.,
OWNER LTD. and
MORTGAGEE LTD.,

Defendants.

NOTICE OF MOTION

TAKE NOTICE that a motion will be made to the Master on behalf of the Defendant, Owner Ltd., at 145 Queen Street West, Toronto, Ontario, on Monday, the 12th day of December, 1983, at the hour of 10:00 o'clock in the forenoon, or so soon thereafter as Counsel can be heard, for an Order, pursuant to Section 44(1) of the *Construction Lien Act*, S.O. 1983, c. 6, vacating the registration of the Claim for Lien of the Plaintiff and the Certificate of Action in respect thereof against the title to the lands described in Schedule A annexed hereto upon the payment into court by the Defendant, Owner Ltd., of the sum of $75,000 claimed as owing by the Plaintiff in the aforesaid Claim for Lien, together with the sum of $18,750 as security for costs, or for such further or other Order as to this Honourable Court may seem just.

AND TAKE NOTICE that in support of such motion will be filed the Affidavit of Andrew Owner, and such further and other material as Counsel may advise.

DATED at Toronto this 3rd day of December, 1983.

STEPHENS & MITCHELL
Barristers and Solicitors
206 Torson Road
Toronto, Ontario

Solicitors for the Defendant,
Owner Ltd.

Precedent No. 21

CLA 1234/83

IN THE SUPREME COURT OF ONTARIO

IN THE MATTER OF the *Construction
Lien Act*, S.O. 1983, c. 6

B E T W E E N:

SUBCONTRACTOR LTD.,

Plaintiff,

- and -

GENERAL CONTRACTOR LTD.,
OWNER LTD. and
MORTGAGEE LTD.,

Defendants.

A F F I D A V I T

I, ANDREW OWNER, of the Municipality of Metropolitan Toronto, in the Province of Ontario, Executive, MAKE OATH AND SAY AS FOLLOWS:

1. I am President of the Defendant, Owner Ltd., and as such have knowledge of the matters hereinafter deposed to.

2. The Defendant, Owner Ltd., is the registered owner of the lands referred to in Schedule A annexed hereto (hereinafter referred to as the "Lands").

3. Attached hereto and marked as Exhibit 1 to this my Affidavit is a certified copy of the abstract of title in respect of the Lands.

4. As indicated by the said abstract of title, a Claim for Lien on behalf of the Plaintiff was registered against the title to the Lands on the 3rd day of November, 1983 as Instrument No. 1234567. Attached hereto and marked Exhibit 2 to this my Affidavit is a certified copy of the Plaintiff's Claim for Lien.

5. As also indicated by the said abstract of title, a Certificate of Action on behalf of the Plaintiff was registered against the title to the Lands on the 17th day of November, 1983 as Instrument No. 1234568. Attached hereto and marked Exhibit 3 to this my Affidavit is a certified copy of the Plaintiff's Certificate of Action.

6. As also indicated by the said abstract of title, there is no other Claim for Lien or Certificate of Action registered against the title to the Lands.

7. I am advised by Arnold Architect, being the supervising architect for the

construction upon the Lands, and verily believe that there are no unregistered liens.

8. This Affidavit is made in support of a motion for an Order vacating the registration of the Plaintiff's Claim for Lien and Certificate of Action upon a payment into court, and for no improper purpose.

SWORN before me (etc.) . . . .)
)
)
)   _____
)   ANDREW OWNER
)

A Commissioner, etc.

Precedent No. 22

CLA 1234/83

IN THE SUPREME COURT OF ONTARIO

IN THE MATTER OF the *Construction Lien Act,* S.O. 1983, c. 6

MASTER   )   MONDAY, THE 12TH DAY OF
)
)   DECEMBER, 1983.

B E T W E E N:

SUBCONTRACTOR LTD.,

Plaintiff,

- and -

GENERAL CONTRACTOR LTD.,
OWNER LTD. and
MORTGAGEE LTD.,

Defendants.

O R D E R

UPON motion made this day on behalf of the Defendant, Owner Ltd., for an Order, pursuant to Section 44(1) of the *Construction Lien Act,* S.O. 1983, c. 6, vacating the registration of the Claim for Lien of the Plaintiff and the Certificate of Action in respect thereof against the title to the lands referred to in Schedule A annexed to the Notice of Motion, in the presence of Counsel for the Defendant, Owner Ltd., upon reading the Affidavit of Andrew Owner, filed, and upon it appearing that the sum of $75,000, together with the sum of $18,750 as security for costs, have been paid into Court, upon hearing Counsel aforesaid:

1. IT IS ORDERED that the registration of the Claim for Lien of the Plaintiff, dated the 3rd day of November, 1983 and registered the same day against the title to the lands and premises described in Schedule A annexed hereto as Instrument No. 1234567, be and the same is hereby vacated.

2. AND IT IS ORDERED that the Certificate of Action of the Plaintiff, dated the 17th day of November, 1983 and registered the same day against the title to the lands described in Schedule A annexed hereto as Instrument No. 1234568, be and the same is hereby vacated.

Precedent No. 23

IN THE SUPREME COURT OF ONTARIO

IN THE MATTER OF the *Construction Lien Act*, S.O. 1983, c. 6

AND IN THE MATTER OF an intended action

B E T W E E N:

SUBCONTRACTOR LTD.,

Plaintiff,

- and -

GENERAL CONTRACTOR LTD.,
OWNER LTD. and
MORTGAGEE LTD.,

Defendants.

NOTICE OF MOTION

TAKE NOTICE that a motion will be made to the Master on behalf of the Defendant, Owner Ltd., at 145 Queen Street West, Toronto, Ontario, on Monday, the 12th day of December, 1983, at the hour of 10:00 o'clock in the forenoon, or so soon thereafter as Counsel can be heard, for an Order, pursuant to Section 45(1) of the *Construction Lien Act*, S.O. 1983, c. 6, declaring that the Plaintiff's lien has expired and vacating the registration of the Plaintiff's Claim for Lien against the title to the lands referred to in Schedule A annexed hereto, or for such further or other Order as to this Honourable Court may seem just.

AND TAKE NOTICE that in support of such motion will be filed the Affidavit of Arnold Architect, and such further and other material as Counsel may advise.

DATED at Toronto this 3rd day of December, 1983.

STEPHENS & MITCHELL
Barristers and Solicitors
206 Torson Avenue
Toronto, Ontario

Solicitors for the Defendant,
Owner Ltd.

Precedent No. 24

IN THE SUPREME COURT OF ONTARIO

IN THE MATTER OF the *Construction Lien Act*, S.O. 1983, c. 6

AND IN THE MATTER OF an intended action

B E T W E E N:

SUBCONTRACTOR LTD.,

Plaintiff,

- and -

GENERAL CONTRACTOR LTD.,
OWNER LTD. and
MORTGAGEE LTD.,

Defendants.

A F F I D A V I T

I, ARNOLD ARCHITECT, of the City of Toronto, in the Municipality of Metropolitan Toronto, Architect, MAKE OATH AND SAY AS FOLLOWS:

1. I was retained by Owner Ltd., the registered owner of the lands referred to in Schedule A annexed hereto (hereinafter referred to as the "Lands"), to provide architectural services in connection with the renovation of an industrial building situated on the Lands. By virtue of the foregoing, I have knowledge of the matters hereinafter deposed to.

2. One of my functions as architect was to coordinate the sub-trades and to ensure the timely and orderly progress of work.

3. Based upon my personal knowledge and my review of my daily log, which was prepared by me in the ordinary course of business, I verily believe that Subcontractor Ltd. failed to complete its contract and abandoned its work on the 30th day of August, 1983.

4. Attached hereto and marked as Exhibit A to this my Affidavit is a certified copy of the abstract of title to the Lands. As indicated, a Claim for Lien on behalf of Subcontractor Ltd. was registered against the title to the Lands on the 3rd day of November, 1983 as Instrument No. 1234567. Now shown to me and marked as Exhibit B to this my Affidavit is a certified copy of the Claim for Lien of Subcontractor Ltd. The Plaintiff's Claim for Lien acknowledges and

confirms that the date of most recent supply of services or materials by the Plaintiff was the 30th day of August, 1983.

5. In view of the fact that Subcontractor Ltd. abandoned its work on the 30th day of August, 1983, and did not register a Claim for Lien against the title to the Lands until the 3rd day of November, 1983, I verily believe that Subcontractor Ltd. has failed to preserve its lien within the time allowed for doing so under Section 31 of the Construction Lien Act, S.O. 1983, c. 6.

6. As appears from the abstract of title attached hereto as Exhibit A, there are no other Claims for Liens or Certificates of Action registered against the title to the Lands. I am not aware of any other unregistered liens.

7. This Affidavit is made in support of a motion for an Order declaring that the Plaintiff's lien has expired and vacating the registration of the Plaintiff's Claim for Lien against the title to the Lands, and for no improper purpose.

SWORN before me (etc.) . . . .   )
)
)
)   _____
)   ARNOLD ARCHITECT
)
)

A Commissioner, etc.

Precedent No. 25

IN THE SUPREME COURT OF ONTARIO

IN THE MATTER OF the *Construction Lien Act*, S.O. 1983, c. 6

AND IN THE MATTER OF an intended action

MASTER	)	MONDAY, THE 12TH DAY OF
	)	
	)	DECEMBER, 1983.

B E T W E E N:

SUBCONTRACTOR LTD.,

Plaintiff,

- and -

GENERAL CONTRACTOR LTD.,
OWNER LTD. and
MORTGAGEE LTD.,

Defendants.

O R D E R

UPON motion made this day on behalf of the Defendant, Owner Ltd., for an Order, pursuant to Section 45(1) of the *Construction Lien Act*, S.O. 1983, c. 6, declaring that the Plaintiff's lien has expired and vacating the registration of the Plaintiff's Claim for Lien against the title to the lands referred to in Schedule A annexed to the Notice of Motion herein, in the presence of Counsel for the Plaintiff and the Defendant, Owner Ltd., upon reading the Affidavit of Arnold Architect, filed, and upon hearing Counsel aforesaid:

1. IT IS HEREBY DECLARED that the Plaintiff's lien has expired.
2. AND IT IS ORDERED that the registration of the Plaintiff's Claim for Lien, dated the 3rd day of November, 1983 and registered the same day as Instrument No. 1234567 against the title to the lands referred to in Schedule A annexed hereto, be and the same is hereby vacated.

Precedent No. 26

CLA 1236/83

IN THE SUPREME COURT OF ONTARIO

IN THE MATTER OF the *Construction Lien Act,* S.O. 1983, c. 6

B E T W E E N:

ARNOLD ARCHITECT,

Plaintiff,

- and -

OWNER LTD. and MORTGAGEE LTD.,

Defendants.

NOTICE OF MOTION

TAKE NOTICE that a motion will be made to the Master on behalf of the Defendant, Owner Ltd., at 145 Queen Street West, Toronto, Ontario, on Monday, the 12th day of December, 1983, at the hour of 10:00 o'clock in the forenoon, or so soon thereafter as Counsel can be heard, for an Order, pursuant to Section 47(1) of the *Construction Lien Act*, S.O. 1983, c. 6, vacating the registration of the Plaintiff's Claim for Lien and Certificate of Action against the title to the lands described in Schedule A annexed hereto, and dismissing the Plaintiff's action herein with costs, or for such further or other Order as to this Honourable Court may seem just.

AND TAKE NOTICE that in support of such motion will be filed the Affidavit of Andrew Owner, and such further and other material as Counsel may advise.

DATED at Toronto this 3rd day of December, 1983.

STEPHENS & MITCHELL
Barristers and Solicitors
206 Torson Avenue
Toronto, Ontario

Solicitors for the Defendant,
Owner Ltd.

Precedent No. 27

CLA 1236/83

IN THE SUPREME COURT OF ONTARIO

IN THE MATTER OF the *Construction Lien Act*, S.O. 1983, c. 6

B E T W E E N:

ARNOLD ARCHITECT,

Plaintiff,

- and -

OWNER LTD. and MORTGAGEE LTD.,

Defendants.

A F F I D A V I T

I, ANDREW OWNER, of the City of Toronto, in the Municipality of Metropolitan Toronto, Executive, MAKE OATH AND SAY AS FOLLOWS:

1. I am President of Owner Ltd., and as such have knowledge of the matters hereinafter deposed to.

2. Owner Ltd. is the registered owner of the lands referred to in Schedule A annexed hereto (hereinafter referred to as the "Lands"). Attached hereto and marked as Exhibit 1 to this my Affidavit is a certified copy of the abstract of title in respect of the Lands.

3. The Plaintiff, Arnold Architect, was engaged by Owner Ltd. to provide architectural services in connection with the renovation of an industrial building situated on the Lands.

4. As indicated in the abstract of title, being Exhibit 1 hereto, the Plaintiff registered his Claim for Lien and Certificate of Action against the title to the Lands on November 3, 1983 and November 17, 1983, respectively, as Instrument Nos. 1234569 and 1234570. Now shown to me and marked as Exhibits 2 and 3 to this my Affidavit are certified copies of the Plaintiff's Claim for Lien and Certificate of Action respectively.

5. By virtue of Section 3(3) of the *Construction Lien Act*, S.O. 1983, c. 6, I verily believe that the Plaintiff does not have a lien.

6. As indicated by the aforesaid abstract of title attached hereto, there are no other Claims for Liens or Certificates of Action registered against the title to the

Lands. Furthermore, I verily believe that there are no unregistered liens in respect of the improvement.

7. This Affidavit is made in support of a motion for an Order vacating the registration of the Plaintiff's Claim for Lien and Certificate of Action and dismissing the within action with costs, and for no improper purpose.

SWORN before me (etc.) . . . .   )
)
)   _____
)   ANDREW OWNER
)
)

A Commissioner, etc.

Precedent No. 28

CLA 1236/83

IN THE SUPREME COURT OF ONTARIO

IN THE MATTER OF the *Construction Lien Act*, S.O. 1983, c. 6

MASTER   )   MONDAY, THE 12TH DAY OF
)
)   DECEMBER, 1983.

B E T W E E N:

ARNOLD ARCHITECT,

Plaintiff,

- and -

OWNER LTD. and MORTGAGEE LTD.,

Defendants.

O R D E R

UPON motion made this day on behalf of the Defendant, Owner Ltd., for an Order, pursuant to Section 47(1) of the *Construction Lien Act,* S.O. 1983, c. 6, vacating the registration of the Plaintiff's Claim for Lien and Certificate of Action against the title to the lands referred to in Schedule A annexed to the Notice of Motion herein, and dismissing the within action with costs, in the presence of Counsel for the Defendant, Owner Ltd., and Counsel for the Plaintiff, no one appearing for the Defendant, Mortgagee Ltd., although duly served, upon reading the Affidavit of Andrew Owner, filed, and upon hearing Counsel aforesaid:

1. IT IS ORDERED that the registration of the Plaintiff's Claim for Lien, dated the 3rd day of November, 1983 and registered the same day as Instrument No. 1234569 against the title to the lands referred to in Schedule A annexed hereto, be and the same is hereby vacated.

2. AND IT IS ORDERED that the registration of the Plaintiff's Certificate of Action, dated the 17th day of November, 1983, and registered the same day as Instrument No. 1234570 against the title to the lands referred to in Schedule A annexed hereto, be and the same is hereby vacated.

3. IT IS FURTHER ORDERED that the within action be and the same is hereby dismissed with costs to each of the Defendants, including the costs of this motion.

Precedent No. 29

CLA 1234/83

IN THE SUPREME COURT OF ONTARIO

IN THE MATTER OF the *Construction Lien Act*, S.O. 1983, c. 6

B E T W E E N:

SUBCONTRACTOR LTD.,

Plaintiff,

- and -

GENERAL CONTRACTOR LTD.,
OWNER LTD. and
MORTGAGEE LTD.,

Defendants.

NOTICE OF MOTION

TAKE NOTICE that a motion will be made to the Master on behalf of the Defendant, Owner Ltd., at 145 Queen Street West, Toronto, Ontario, on Thursday, the 12th day of December, 1985, at the hour of 10:00 o'clock in the forenoon, or so soon thereafter as Counsel can be heard, for an Order, pursuant to Sections 37 and 46(1) of the *Construction Lien Act*, S.O. 1983, c. 6:

(a) declaring that the Plaintiff's lien has expired;
(b) dismissing the Plaintiff's action with costs;
(c) vacating the registration of the Plaintiff's Claim for Lien and Certificate of Action from the title to the lands referred to in Schedule A annexed hereto;
(d) such further or other Order as to this Honourable Court may seem just.

AND TAKE NOTICE that in support of such motion will be read the Affidavit of Andrew Owner, and such further and other material as Counsel may advise.

DATED at Toronto this 3rd day of December, 1985.

STEPHENS & MITCHELL
Barristers and Solicitors
206 Torson Avenue
Toronto, Ontario

Solicitors for the Defendant,
Owner Ltd.

Precedent No. 30

CLA 1234/83

IN THE SUPREME COURT OF ONTARIO

IN THE MATTER OF the *Construction
Lien Act*, S.O. 1983, c. 6

B E T W E E N:

SUBCONTRACTOR LTD.,

Plaintiff,

- and -

GENERAL CONTRACTOR LTD.,
OWNER LTD. and
MORTGAGEE LTD.,

Defendants.

A F F I D A V I T

I, ANDREW OWNER, of the City of Toronto, in the Municipality of Metropolitan Toronto, Executive, MAKE OATH AND SAY AS FOLLOWS:

1. I am the President of the Defendant, Owner Ltd., and as such have knowledge of the matters hereinafter deposed to.

2. The Defendant, Owner Ltd., is the registered owner of the lands referred to in Schedule A annexed hereto (hereinafter referred to as the "Lands").

3. Attached hereto and marked as Exhibit 1 to this my Affidavit is a certified copy of the abstract of title in respect of the Lands.

4. As indicated by the said abstract of title, a Claim for Lien on behalf of the Plaintiff was registered against the title to the Lands on the 3rd day of November, 1983 as Instrument No. 1234567. Attached hereto and marked as Exhibit 2 to this my Affidavit is a certified copy of the Plaintiff's Claim for Lien.

5. As also indicated by the said abstract of title, a Certificate of Action on behalf of the Plaintiff was registered against the title to the Lands on the 17th day of November, 1983 as Instrument No. 1234568. Attached hereto and marked as Exhibit 3 to this my Affidavit is a certified copy of the Plaintiff's Certificate of Action.

6. I have conducted a search of the Supreme Court file with respect to this action, and have ascertained that the Plaintiff's action was commenced on November 17, 1983. My search of the Supreme Court file also disclosed that

neither the Plaintiff nor any of the other parties to this action have obtained a trial date, and that the lien action has not been set down for trial as of the date of this my Affidavit, namely December 3, 1985. Furthermore, neither Owner Ltd. nor its solicitors has been served with any Notice of Trial in respect of the within action.

7. As also indicated by the aforesaid abstract of title, there is no other Claim for Lien or Certificate of Action registered against the title to the Lands.

8. This Affidavit is made in support of a motion for an Order declaring that the Plaintiff's lien has expired, dismissing the Plaintiff's action with costs, and vacating the registration of the Plaintiff's Claim for Lien and Certificate of Action, and for no improper purpose.

SWORN before me (etc.) . . . .   )
)
)   _____
)   ANDREW OWNER
)
)

A Commissioner, etc.

Precedent No. 31

CLA 1234/83

IN THE SUPREME COURT OF ONTARIO

IN THE MATTER OF the *Construction Lien Act*, S.O. 1983, c. 6

MASTER   )   THURSDAY, THE 12TH DAY OF
)
)   DECEMBER, 1985.

B E T W E E N:

SUBCONTRACTOR LTD.,

Plaintiff,

- and -

GENERAL CONTRACTOR LTD.,
OWNER LTD. and
MORTGAGEE LTD.,

Defendants.

O R D E R

UPON motion made this day on behalf of the Defendant, Owner Ltd., for an Order, pursuant to Sections 37 and 46(1) of the *Construction Lien Act*, S.O. 1983, c. 6, declaring that the Plaintiff's lien has expired, dismissing the Plaintiff's action with costs, and vacating the registration of the Plaintiff's Claim for Lien and Certificate of Action registered against the title to the lands referred to in Schedule A annexed to the Notice of Motion herein, in the presence of Counsel for the Plaintiff and for the Defendant, Owner Ltd., no one appearing for the Defendants, General Contractor Ltd. and Mortgagee Ltd., although duly served, upon reading the Affidavit of Andrew Owner, filed, and upon hearing Counsel aforesaid:

1. IT IS HEREBY DECLARED that the Plaintiff's lien has expired.

2. AND IT IS ORDERED that the registration of the Claim for Lien of the Plaintiff, dated the 3rd day of November, 1983 and registered the same day against the title to the lands referred to in Schedule A annexed hereto as Instrument No. 1234567, be and the same is hereby vacated.

3. IT IS FURTHER ORDERED that the Certificate of Action of the

Plaintiff, dated the 17th day of November, 1983 and registered the same day against the title to the lands referred to in Schedule A annexed hereto as Instrument No. 1234568, be and the same is hereby vacated.

4. AND IT IS FURTHER ORDERED that the within action be and the same is hereby dismissed with costs to each of the Defendants, including the costs of this motion.

Precedent No. 32

CLA 1234/83

IN THE SUPREME COURT OF ONTARIO

IN THE MATTER OF the *Construction Lien Act*, S.O. 1983, c. 6

B E T W E E N:

SUBCONTRACTOR LTD.,

Plaintiff,

- and -

GENERAL CONTRACTOR LTD.,
OWNER LTD. and
MORTGAGEE LTD.,

Defendants.

NOTICE OF MOTION

TAKE NOTICE that an application will be made to the Court on behalf of the Plaintiff, Subcontractor Ltd., at Osgoode Hall, Queen Street West, Toronto, Ontario, on Monday, the 12th day of December, 1983, at the hour of 10:30 o'clock in the forenoon, or so soon thereafter as Counsel can be heard, for the appointment of a trustee to preserve and protect the premises referred to in Schedule A annexed hereto, and, subject to the approval of the Court, to take such steps as may be appropriate in the circumstances, or for such further or other Order as to this Honourable Court may seem just.

AND TAKE NOTICE that in support of such application will be filed the Affidavit of Stanley Subcontractor, the Consent of Timothy Trustee, and such further and other material as Counsel may advise.

DATED at Toronto this 3rd day of December, 1983.

KIRSH & KIRSH
Barristers and Solicitors
45 Bay Street
Toronto, Ontario

Solicitors for the Plaintiff.

Precedent No. 33

CLA 1234/83

IN THE SUPREME COURT OF ONTARIO

IN THE MATTER OF the *Construction Lien Act*, S.O. 1983, c. 6

B E T W E E N:

SUBCONTRACTOR LTD.,

Plaintiff,

- and -

GENERAL CONTRACTOR LTD.,
OWNER LTD. and
MORTGAGEE LTD.,

Defendants.

I, STANLEY SUBCONTRACTOR, of the Municipality of Metropolitan Toronto, in the Province of Ontario, Executive, MAKE OATH AND SAY AS FOLLOWS:

1. I am President of the Plaintiff, Subcontractor Ltd., and as such have knowledge of the matters hereinafter deposed to.

2. Subcontractor Ltd. supplied services and materials to General Contractor Ltd. in connection with the renovation of an industrial building on the lands referred to in Schedule A annexed hereto (hereinafter referred to as the "Lands"), which Lands are owned by the Defendant, Owner Ltd.

3. A Claim for Lien on behalf of the Plaintiff was registered against the title to the Lands on the 3rd day of November, 1983 as Instrument No. 1234567, and a Certificate of Action on behalf of the Plaintiff was registered against the title to the Lands on the 17th day of November, 1983 as Instrument No. 1234568.

4. On the 2nd day of December, 1983, I attended at the Lands to conduct an inspection of the industrial building under renovation, and ascertained that:

   (a) although construction had not as yet been completed, no work was being carried out;

   (b) the heating system did not appear to be operational, and, given the approaching winter season, there is an immediate threat to the physical integrity of the building;

   (c) no security guard had been posted to protect the premises;

(d) windows had been broken, and construction materials stored on the site had been stolen or damaged.

5. I verily believe that it is in the interest of all parties to this action that a trustee be appointed to preserve and protect the premises, and, subject to the approval of the Court, to complete construction and to sell the premises before they are damaged by the elements and by further vandalism.

6. Now shown to me and marked as Exhibit 1 to this my Affidavit is a true copy of the Consent of Timothy Trustee, a licensed trustee, to act in respect of this matter.

SWORN before me (etc.) . . . .   )
)
)
)   STANLEY SUBCONTRACTOR
)
)

A Commissioner, etc.

Precedent No. 34

CLA 1234/83

IN THE SUPREME COURT OF ONTARIO

IN THE MATTER OF the *Construction Lien Act*, S.O. 1983, c. 6

THE HONOURABLE	) MONDAY, THE 12TH DAY OF
MR. JUSTICE	)
	) DECEMBER, 1983.

B E T W E E N:

SUBCONTRACTOR LTD.,

Plaintiff,

- and -

GENERAL CONTRACTOR LTD.,
OWNER LTD. and
MORTGAGEE LTD.,

Defendants.

O R D E R

UPON application made this day on behalf of the Plaintiff, Subcontractor Ltd., pursuant to Section 70 of the *Construction Lien Act*, S.O. 1983, c. 6, for the appointment of a trustee to preserve and protect the premises referred to in Schedule A annexed to the Notice of Motion herein, in the presence of Counsel for all parties, upon reading the Affidavit of Stanley Subcontractor, filed, and the Consent of Timothy Trustee, and upon hearing Counsel aforesaid:

1. IT IS ORDERED that Timothy Trustee be and he is hereby appointed trustee of the lands and premises referred to in Schedule A annexed hereto, with power to manage and preserve the said lands and premises pending the determination of this action.

2. AND IT IS ORDERED that the said trustee may arrange for insurance coverage, may appoint a security guard and may take all necessary steps for the preservation and protection of the said lands and premises.

3. IT IS FURTHER ORDERED that the trustee's reasonable business

expenses and management costs incurred in the exercise of his powers shall be a first charge upon any amounts recovered by the trustee.

4. AND IT IS FURTHER ORDERED that the said trustee is not at this time required to deposit any security with this Court.

5. AND IT IS FURTHER ORDERED that the trustee, or any party to this action, may apply again to this Court at any time for further directions.

Precedent No. 35

CLA 1234/83

IN THE SUPREME COURT OF ONTARIO

IN THE MATTER OF the *Construction Lien Act*, S.O. 1983, c. 6

THE HONOURABLE	)	TUESDAY, THE 6TH DAY OF
MR. JUSTICE	)	
	)	JANUARY, 1984.

B E T W E E N:

SUBCONTRACTOR LTD.,

Plaintiff,

- and -

GENERAL CONTRACTOR LTD.,
OWNER LTD. and
MORTGAGEE LTD.,

Defendants.

O R D E R

UPON the application of Timothy Trustee, trustee appointed pursuant to the Order of this Court dated the 12th day of December, 1983, for an Order authorizing the sale of those lands and premises referred to in Schedule A annexed hereto, and for directions with respect to the acceptance of an offer to purchase the said lands and premises, in the presence of Counsel for the Applicant and for all parties to this action, upon reading the Affidavit of Timothy Trustee, filed, and upon hearing Counsel aforesaid:

1. IT IS ORDERED that Timothy Trustee be and he is hereby authorized to sell the lands and premises referred to in Schedule A annexed hereto, subject to existing financing now in place.
2. AND IT IS ORDERED that Timothy Trustee be and he is hereby authorized to accept the offer of Paula Purchaser to purchase the said lands and premises.

Precedent No. 36

CLA 1234/83

IN THE SUPREME COURT OF ONTARIO

IN THE MATTER OF the *Construction Lien Act*, S.O. 1983, c. 6

B E T W E E N:

SUBCONTRACTOR LTD.,

Plaintiff,

- and -

GENERAL CONTRACTOR LTD.,
OWNER LTD. and
MORTGAGEE LTD.,

Defendants.

NOTICE OF MOTION

TAKE NOTICE that an application will be made to the Court on behalf of the Defendant, Owner Ltd., at Osgoode Hall, Queen Street West, Toronto, Ontario, on Monday, the 12th day of December, 1983, at the hour of 10:30 o'clock in the forenoon, or so soon thereafter as Counsel can be heard, pursuant to Section 68 of the *Construction Lien Act*, S.O. 1983 c. 6, for directions with respect to funds in the possession of Owner Ltd. that may be subject to a trust under Part II of the said Act.

AND TAKE NOTICE that in support of such application will be filed the Affidavit of Andrew Owner, and such further and other material as Counsel may advise.

DATED at Toronto this 3rd day of December, 1983.

STEPHENS & MITCHELL
Barristers and Solicitors
206 Torson Avenue
Toronto, Ontario

Solicitors for the Defendant,
Owner Ltd.

Precedent No. 37

CLA 1234/83

IN THE SUPREME COURT OF ONTARIO

IN THE MATTER OF the *Construction Lien Act*, S.O. 1983, c. 6

B E T W E E N:

SUBCONTRACTOR LTD.,

Plaintiff,

- and -

GENERAL CONTRACTOR LTD.,
OWNER LTD. and
MORTGAGEE LTD.,

Defendants.

A F F I D A V I T

I, ANDREW OWNER, of the City of Toronto, in the Municipality of Metropolitan Toronto, Executive, MAKE OATH AND SAY AS FOLLOWS:

1. I am President of the Defendant, Owner Ltd., and as such have knowledge of the matters hereinafter deposed to.

2. On or about the 2nd day of April, 1983, Owner Ltd. retained General Contractor Ltd. to carry out certain renovation work to an industrial building on the lands referred to in Schedule A annexed hereto (hereinafter referred to as the "Lands").

3. Owner Ltd. arranged financing with the Bank of Toronto in connection with the aforesaid renovation work.

4. On the 3rd day of November, 1983, Owner Ltd. received an advance of $50,000 from the Bank of Toronto, but, as of the date of this my Affidavit, Owner Ltd. has not disbursed all or any portion of these funds.

5. I verily believe that the aforesaid $50,000 advance is impressed with a trust pursuant to the provisions of Section 7(1) of the *Construction Lien Act*.

6. This Affidavit is made in support of an application for directions with respect to the said funds, and for no improper purpose.

SWORN before me (etc.) . . . .   )
)
)   ————————————————
)   ANDREW OWNER
)
)

A Commissioner, etc.

Precedent No. 38

CLA 1234/83

IN THE SUPREME COURT OF ONTARIO

IN THE MATTER OF the *Construction Lien Act*, S.O. 1983, c. 6

THE HONOURABLE	)	MONDAY, THE 12TH DAY OF
MR. JUSTICE	)	
	)	DECEMBER, 1983.

B E T W E E N:

SUBCONTRACTOR LTD.,

Plaintiff,

- and -

GENERAL CONTRACTOR LTD.,
OWNER LTD. and
MORTGAGEE LTD.,

Defendants.

O R D E R

UPON application made this day on behalf of the Defendant, Owner Ltd., for directions, pursuant to Section 68 of the *Construction Lien Act*, S.O. 1983, c. 6, with respect to an amount in the possession of Owner Ltd. that may be subject to a trust under Part II of the said Act, in the presence of Counsel for all parties, upon reading the Affidavit of Andrew Owner, filed, and upon hearing Counsel aforesaid:

1. IT IS ORDERED that the sum of $50,000 currently in the possession of the Defendant, Owner Ltd., be paid into Court to the credit, and to abide the outcome, of this action.

Precedent No. 39

CLA 1234/83

IN THE SUPREME COURT OF ONTARIO

IN THE MATTER OF the *Construction Lien Act*, S.O. 1983, c. 6

B E T W E E N:

SUBCONTRACTOR LTD.,

Plaintiff,

- and -

GENERAL CONTRACTOR LTD.,
OWNER LTD. and
MORTGAGEE LTD.,

Defendants.

STATEMENT OF CLAIM

1. The Plaintiff is a corporation incorporated pursuant to the laws of the Province of Ontario, having its head office in the Municipality of Metropolitan Toronto, in the Province of Ontario.

2. The Defendant, General Contractor Ltd., is a corporation incorporated pursuant to the laws of the Province of Ontario, having its head office in the Municipality of Metropolitan Toronto, in the Province of Ontario.

3. The Defendant, Owner Ltd., is a corporation incorporated pursuant to the laws of the Province of Ontario, having its head office in the Municipality of Metropolitan Toronto, in the Province of Ontario. At all material times, the Defendant, Owner Ltd., was the registered owner of the lands referred to in Schedule A annexed hereto (hereinafter referred to as the "Lands").

4. The Defendant, Mortgagee Ltd., is a corporation incorporated pursuant to the laws of the Dominion of Canada, having its head office in the Municipality of Metropolitan Toronto, in the Province of Ontario.

5. On the 2nd day of April, 1983, the Plaintiff entered into a written agreement under seal with the Defendant, General Contractor Ltd., whereby the Plaintiff agreed to supply and install plumbing materials, in consideration for an agreed price, in connection with the renovation of an industrial building situated on the Lands, which building was being renovated for the Defendant, Owner Ltd. The Plaintiff has completed its obligations under its agreement with the Defendant, General Contractor Ltd., but the said Defendant has refused or neglected to pay the amount which is due and owing to the Plaintiff, namely the sum of $75,000 plus interest thereon.

6. By reason of supplying services and materials as aforesaid, the Plaintiff

is entitled to a lien upon the interest of the Defendant, Owner Ltd., in the Lands for the sum of $75,000, together with the costs of this action pursuant to the provisions of the *Construction Lien Act*, S.O. 1983, c. 6.

7. On the 3rd day of November, 1983, the Plaintiff caused to be registered the following Claim for Lien against the title to the Lands in the Land Registry Office for the Registry Division of Toronto:

"Name of Lien Claimant:	SUBCONTRACTOR LTD.
Address for Service:	206 Main Street, Toronto, Ontario
Name of Owner: Address:	OWNER LTD. 123 Home Street, Toronto, Ontario
Name of Person to Whom Lien Claimant Supplied Services or Materials:	GENERAL CONTRACTOR LTD.
Address:	99 Queen Street, Toronto, Ontario
Time Within Which Services or Materials Were Supplied:	from April 2, 1983 to November 2, 1983
Short Description of Services or Materials That Have Been Supplied:	Supply and installation of plumbing materials.
Contract Price or Subcontract Price:	$75,000
Amount Claimed as Owing in Respect of Services or Materials That Have Been Supplied:	$75,000
The Lien Claimant claims a lien against the interest of every person identified above as an owner of the premises described in Schedule A to this Claim for Lien.	
	SUBCONTRACTOR LTD.
DATE: November 3, 1983	Per: 'Stanley Subcontractor'
	(signature of claimant or agent)"

which Claim for Lien is verified by the Affidavit of Stanley Subcontractor, sworn before a Commissioner for Taking Oaths in the Province of Ontario.

8. The Lands described in Schedule A to the Claim for Lien hereinbefore

set forth were at all material times occupied by the Defendant, Owner Ltd., and are the Lands for which the Plaintiff supplied services and materials at the request, on behalf, with the consent, and for the direct benefit, of the Defendant, Owner Ltd., and accordingly the Defendant, Owner Ltd., is and was at all material times an owner within the meaning of the *Construction Lien Act.*

9. By Instrument No. A-987654 registered April 2, 1983, the Lands were mortgaged in favour of the Defendant, Mortgagee Ltd., for the sum of $500,000. The Plaintiff alleges that the said mortgage was taken by the Defendant, Mortgagee Ltd., with the intention to secure the financing of the improvement herein, and the Plaintiff therefore claims that its lien has full priority over the said mortgage to the extent of any deficiency in the holdbacks required to be retained by the Defendant, Owner Ltd. In the alternative, the Plaintiff claims that its lien has priority over the said mortgage to the extent that any portion of the mortgage advanced exceeded the actual value of the premises at the time when the first lien arose. In the further alternative, the Plaintiff claims that its lien has priority over the said mortgage to the extent of any unadvanced portions thereof.

10. The Plaintiff therefore claims as against the Defendants:

(a) payment of the sum of $75,000;

(b) as against only the Defendant, General Contractor Ltd., payment of interest on the said sum of $75,000 pursuant to the provisions of Section 36 of the *Judicature Act*, R.S.O. 1980, c. 223;

(c) the costs of this action;

(d) that, in default of payment of the said sum of $75,000 plus costs, all the estate and interest of the Defendant, Owner Ltd., in the Lands be sold and the proceeds applied toward payment of the Plaintiff's claim as aforesaid, pursuant to the provisions of the *Construction Lien Act;*

(e) full priority over the mortgage of the Defendant, Mortgagee Ltd., or alternatively priority over the said mortgage to the extent that any portion of the mortgage advanced exceeded the actual value of the premises at the time when the first lien arose, or in the further alternative priority over the said mortgage to the extent of any unadvanced portions thereof;

(f) for the purposes aforesaid, all proper directions to be given and accounts taken; and

(g) such further and other relief as to this Honourable Court may seem just.

The Plaintiff proposes that this action be tried in the City of Toronto, in the Judicial District of York.

WARNING: If you wish to defend against this claim, you are required to deliver a statement of defence within twenty days. Should you fail to deliver a statement of defence as required, pleadings may be noted closed against you, and you shall be deemed to admit all allegations of fact contained in this claim, and you shall not be entitled to notice of or to participate in the trial or any proceeding in respect of this claim and judgment may be given against you.

DELIVERED at Toronto, this 17th day of November, 1983 by KIRSH & KIRSH, Barristers and Solicitors, 45 Bay Street, Toronto, Ontario, solicitors for the Plaintiff.

Precedent No. 40

CLA 1234/83

IN THE SUPREME COURT OF ONTARIO

IN THE MATTER OF the *Construction Lien Act*, S.O. 1983, c. 6

B E T W E E N:

SUBCONTRACTOR LTD.,

Plaintiff,

- and -

GENERAL CONTRACTOR LTD.,
OWNER LTD. and
MORTGAGEE LTD.,

Defendants

STATEMENT OF DEFENCE OF THE DEFENDANT, GENERAL CONTRACTOR LTD.

1. This Defendant admits the allegations contained in paragraphs 1, 2, 3 and 4 of the Plaintiff's statement of claim, but, save and except as may hereinafter be expressly admitted, denies each and every other allegation contained in the statement of claim as if set out and traversed seriatim.

2. This Defendant admits that, on the 2nd day of April, 1983, it entered into a written agreement under seal with the Plaintiff whereby the Plaintiff agreed to supply and install plumbing materials, in consideration for an agreed price, in connection with the renovation of an industrial building situated on the lands referred to in Schedule A annexed to the Plaintiff's statement of claim. This Defendant pleads that it was an implied term of the said agreement that the Plaintiff would perform its work in a good, proper and workmanlike manner, and that the materials supplied by the Plaintiff would be of good quality and suitable for the purposes for which they were intended. This Defendant alleges that part of the work done by the Plaintiff was done negligently, carelessly and unskilfully, and that some of the materials supplied by the Plaintiff were not of good quality, particulars of which are as follows:

    (a) . . .
    (b) . . .
    (c) . . .

3. This Defendant alleges that the Plaintiff failed to preserve its lien within

the time allowed for doing so under Section 31 of the *Construction Lien Act*, and accordingly the Plaintiff is not entitled to a lien in respect of the premises.

4. This Defendant further alleges that the Plaintiff failed to perfect its lien within the time allowed for doing so under Section 36 of the *Construction Lien Act*, and accordingly the Plaintiff's lien has expired.

5. By virtue of the foregoing, this Defendant states that it is not indebted to the Plaintiff in the sum of $75,000 as alleged, and either that the Plaintiff is not entitled to a lien in respect of the premises or that the Plaintiff's lien has expired.

6. This Defendant therefore submits that this action be dismissed with costs.

DELIVERED at Toronto, this 5th day of December, 1983, by PETERS & RICHARDS, Barristers and Solicitors, 210 Bay Street, Toronto, Ontario, solicitors for the Defendant, General Contractor Ltd.

Precedent No. 41

CLA 1234/83

IN THE SUPREME COURT OF ONTARIO

IN THE MATTER OF the *Construction Lien Act*, S.O. 1983, c. 6

B E T W E E N:

SUBCONTRACTOR LTD.,

Plaintiff,

- and -

GENERAL CONTRACTOR LTD.,
OWNER LTD. and
MORTGAGEE LTD.,

Defendants.

CROSSCLAIM OF THE DEFENDANT, OWNER LTD.

1. At all material times, the Defendant, Owner Ltd., was the registered owner of the lands referred to in Schedule A annexed to the Plaintiff's statement of claim herein (hereinafter referred to as the "Lands").

2. On the 2nd day of April, 1983, the Defendant, Owner Ltd., entered into a written agreement under seal (hereinafter referred to as the "Contract") with the Defendant, General Contractor Ltd., whereby the Defendant, General Contractor Ltd., agreed to supply all services and materials in connection with the renovation of an industrial building situated on the Lands.

3. The Defendant, Owner Ltd., pleads that it was an implied term of the Contract that the Defendant, General Contractor Ltd., would perform the work set out in the Contract in a good, proper and workmanlike manner, and that the materials supplied by the Defendant, General Contractor Ltd., would be of good quality and suitable for the purposes for which they were intended. The Defendant, Owner Ltd., alleges that part of the work done by the Defendant, General Contractor Ltd., was done negligently, carelessly and unskilfully, and that some of the materials supplied by the Defendant, General Contractor Ltd., were not of good quality, particulars of which are as follows:

(a) . . .
(b) . . .
(c) . . .

4. By virtue of the allegations contained in paragraph 3 above, the Defendant, Owner Ltd., was obliged to retain other forces to complete construction and to rectify deficiencies in the work performed by the Defendant, General Contractor Ltd., thereby incurring damages in the sum of $99,000.

5. The Defendant, Owner Ltd., therefore crossclaims as against the Defendant, General Contractor Ltd., for:

> (a) damages in the sum of $99,000, or the right to set off a like sum from any amount which may be found to be due and owing by the Defendant, Owner Ltd., to the Defendant, General Contractor Ltd., pursuant to the Contract;
>
> (b) interest on the said sum of $99,000 pursuant to the provisions of Section 36 of the *Judicature Act*, R.S.O. 1980, c. 223;
>
> (c) its costs of this crossclaim;
>
> (d) such further and other relief as to this Honourable Court may seem just.

WARNING: If you wish to defend against this claim, you are required to deliver a statement of defence within twenty days. Should you fail to deliver a statement of defence as required, pleadings may be noted closed against you, and you shall be deemed to admit all allegations of fact contained in this claim, and you shall not be entitled to notice of or to participate in the trial or any proceeding in respect of this claim and judgment may be given against you.

DELIVERED at Toronto, this 5th day of December, 1983, by STEPHENS & MITCHELL, Barristers and Solicitors, 206 Torson Avenue, Toronto, Ontario, solicitors for the Defendant, Owner Ltd.

Precedent No. 42

CLA 1234/83

IN THE SUPREME COURT OF ONTARIO

IN THE MATTER OF the *Construction Lien Act*, S.O. 1983, c. 6

B E T W E E N:

GENERAL CONTRACTOR LTD.,

Plaintiff by Counterclaim,

- and -

SUBCONTRACTOR LTD.,

Defendant by Counterclaim.

COUNTERCLAIM OF GENERAL CONTRACTOR LTD.

1. The Plaintiff by Counterclaim repeats and adopts the allegations contained in its statement of defence delivered herewith.

2. By reason of the Defendant by Counterclaim's negligence, carelessness and lack of skill, as particularized in paragraph 2 of the Plaintiff by Counterclaim's statement of defence, the Plaintiff by Counterclaim was obliged to retain other forces to rectify deficiencies in the work performed by the Defendant by Counterclaim, thereby incurring damages in the sum of $25,000.

3. The Plaintiff by Counterclaim alleges that the claim for lien of the Defendant by Counterclaim is for an amount which the Defendant by Counterclaim knows or ought to know is grossly in excess of the amount which is owing. By preserving an exaggerated lien as aforesaid, the Defendant by Counterclaim has caused the Plaintiff by Counterclaim to incur damages in the sum of $5,000 in that the Plaintiff by Counterclaim has lost the use of monies which would otherwise have been paid to it by the Defendant, Owner Ltd., but for the preservation of an exaggerated lien.

4. The Plaintiff by Counterclaim therefore claims:

    (a) damages, pursuant to paragraphs 2 and 3 above, in the sum of $30,000;

    (b) interest on the said damages pursuant to the provisions of Section 36 of the *Judicature Act*, R.S.O. 1980, c. 223;

    (c) its costs of this counterclaim; and

    (d) such further and other relief as to this Honourable Court may seem just.

WARNING: If you wish to defend against this claim, you are required to deliver a statement of defence within twenty days. Should you fail to deliver a statement of defence as required, pleadings may be noted closed against you, and you shall be deemed to admit all allegations of fact contained in this claim, and you shall not be entitled to notice of or to participate in the trial or any proceeding in respect of this claim and judgment may be given against you.

DELIVERED at Toronto, this 5th day of December, 1983 by PETERS & RICHARDS, Barristers and Solicitors, 210 Bay Street, Toronto, Ontario, solicitors for the Plaintiff by Counterclaim, General Contractor Ltd.

Precedent No. 43

CLA 1234/83

IN THE SUPREME COURT OF ONTARIO

IN THE MATTER OF the *Construction Lien Act*, S.O. 1983, c. 6

B E T W E E N:

GENERAL CONTRACTOR LTD.,

Plaintiff by Counterclaim,

- and -

SUBCONTRACTOR LTD.,

Defendant by Counterclaim.

STATEMENT OF DEFENCE TO COUNTERCLAIM OF DEFENDANT BY COUNTERCLAIM, SUBCONTRACTOR LTD.

1. The Defendant by Counterclaim denies the allegations contained in the counterclaim and puts the Plaintiff by Counterclaim to the strict proof thereof.

2. The Defendant by Counterclaim denies that the Plaintiff by Counterclaim incurred the damages as alleged, or at all, and further denies that the Plaintiff by Counterclaim retained any other forces to complete or rectify any of the work performed by the Defendant by Counterclaim.

3. The Defendant by Counterclaim denies having preserved an exaggerated lien, and alleges that the lien which was preserved was for the amount owing to the Defendant by Counterclaim.

4. The Defendant by Counterclaim therefore submits that this counterclaim be dismissed with costs.

DELIVERED at Toronto, this 12th day of December, 1983, by KIRSH & KIRSH, Barristers and Solicitors, 45 Bay Street, Toronto, Ontario, solicitors for the Defendant by Counterclaim.

Precedent No. 44

CLA 1234/83

IN THE SUPREME COURT OF ONTARIO

IN THE MATTER OF the *Construction Lien Act*, S.O. 1983, c. 6

B E T W E E N:

SUBCONTRACTOR LTD.,

Plaintiff,

- and -

GENERAL CONTRACTOR LTD.,
OWNER LTD. and
MORTGAGEE LTD.,

Defendants.

NOTICE OF MOTION

TAKE NOTICE that a motion will be made to the Master on behalf of the Defendant, Owner Ltd., at 145 Queen Street West, Toronto, Ontario, on Monday, the 12th day of December, 1983, at the hour of 10:00 o'clock in the forenoon, or so soon thereafter as Counsel can be heard, for leave, pursuant to Section 58 of the *Construction Lien Act*, S.O. 1983, c. 6, to join Partner Ltd. as a third party in the within action, or for such further or other Order as to this Honourable Court may seem just.

AND TAKE NOTICE that in support of such motion will be filed the Affidavit of Andrew Owner, and such further and other material as Counsel may advise.

DATED at Toronto this 3rd day of December, 1983.

STEPHENS & MITCHELL
Barristers and Solicitors
206 Torson Avenue
Toronto, Ontario

Solicitors for the Defendant,
Owner Ltd.

Precedent No. 45

CLA 1234/83

IN THE SUPREME COURT OF ONTARIO

IN THE MATTER OF the *Construction Lien Act*, S.O. 1983, c. 6

B E T W E E N:

SUBCONTRACTOR LTD.,

Plaintiff,

- and -

GENERAL CONTRACTOR LTD.,
OWNER LTD. and
MORTGAGEE LTD.,

Defendants.

AFFIDAVIT

I, ANDREW OWNER, of the City of Toronto, in the Municipality of Metropolitan Toronto, Executive, MAKE OATH AND SAY AS FOLLOWS:

1. I am President of Owner Ltd., and as such have knowledge of the matters hereinafter deposed to.

2. Owner Ltd. is the registered owner of the lands referred to in Schedule A annexed hereto (hereinafter referred to as the "Lands").

3. On the 2nd day of April, 1983, Owner Ltd. entered into a written agreement with General Contractor Ltd. whereby General Contractor Ltd. agreed to supply all services and materials required in connection with the renovation of an industrial building situated on the Lands.

4. Now shown to me and marked Exhibit 1 to this my Affidavit is a true copy of a joint venture agreement between Owner Ltd., of the first part, and Partner Ltd., of the second part, whereby the parties thereto agreed initially to purchase the Lands, taking title only in the name of Owner Ltd.; to renovate the existing industrial building situated on the Lands; and to attempt to sell or lease the Lands and industrial building thereafter. The said joint venture agreement further provided that both parties would undertake the same financial investment and that any profits realized were to be split between them equally.

5. Peter Partner, the President of Partner Ltd., attended at the site daily, actively participated in all decisions which were made relating to the construction work, and had numerous dealings with both General Contractor Ltd. and all of

the sub-trades. On the basis of the foregoing, I verily believe that Partner Ltd. is a statutory owner within the meaning of the *Construction Lien Act*.

6. By virtue of the aforesaid joint venture agreement, I verily believe that Owner Ltd. is entitled to initiate third party proceedings against Partner Ltd. for contribution in respect of the Plaintiff's claim herein.

7. I further verily believe that the taking of third party proceedings against Partner Ltd. will not unduly prejudice the ability of Partner Ltd., or of any lien claimant or Defendant, to prosecute his claim or conduct his defence, and will not unduly delay or complicate the resolution of the lien action.

8. This Affidavit is made in support of a motion for leave to join Partner Ltd. as a third party in this action, and for no improper purpose.

SWORN before me (etc.) . . . .   )
)
)
)   _____
)   ANDREW OWNER
)
)

A Commissioner, etc.

Precedent No. 46

CLA 1234/83

IN THE SUPREME COURT OF ONTARIO

IN THE MATTER OF the *Construction Lien Act*, S.O. 1983, c. 6

MASTER) MONDAY, THE 12TH DAY OF
)
) DECEMBER, 1983.

B E T W E E N:

SUBCONTRACTOR LTD.,

Plaintiff,

- and -

GENERAL CONTRACTOR LTD.,
OWNER LTD. and
MORTGAGEE LTD.,

Defendants.

O R D E R

UPON motion made this day on behalf of the Defendant, Owner Ltd., for leave, pursuant to Section 58 of the *Construction Lien Act*, S.O. 1983, c. 6, to join Partner Ltd. as a third party in the within action, in the presence of Counsel for the Defendant, Owner Ltd., and Counsel for the Plaintiff, upon reading the Affidavit of Andrew Owner, filed, and upon hearing Counsel aforesaid:

1. IT IS ORDERED that the Defendant, Owner Ltd., be and is hereby given leave to join Partner Ltd. as a third party in this action.

2. AND IT IS ORDERED that the Defendant, Owner Ltd., be and is hereby given leave to deliver its third party claim, together with a true copy of this Order and all other pleadings in this action, within twenty days of the date of this Order by serving the same upon the third party in the manner prescribed by the Supreme Court Rules of Practice for service upon a corporation.

3. IT IS FURTHER ORDERED that Partner Ltd. shall have twenty days from the date of service to deliver a statement of defence to the third party claim, and to deliver a statement of defence to the Plaintiff's statement of claim, if so advised.

Precedent No. 47

CLA 1234/83

IN THE SUPREME COURT OF ONTARIO

IN THE MATTER OF the *Construction Lien Act*, S.O. 1983, c. 6

B E T W E E N:

SUBCONTRACTOR LTD.,

Plaintiff,

- and -

GENERAL CONTRACTOR LTD.,
OWNER LTD. and
MORTGAGEE LTD.,

Defendants,

- and -

PARTNER LTD.,

Third Party.

THIRD PARTY CLAIM OF THE DEFENDANT,
OWNER LTD.

1. The third party, Partner Ltd., is a corporation incorporated pursuant to the laws of the Province of Ontario, having its head office in the Municipality of Metropolitan Toronto, in the Province of Ontario.

2. The Plaintiff has commenced this action against the Defendant, Owner Ltd., and others for the relief set forth in the statement of claim which is delivered herewith.

3. The Defendant, Owner Ltd., has defended the within action on the basis of those pleadings and allegations contained in its statement of defence which is delivered herewith.

4. On the 2nd day of April, 1983, the Defendant, Owner Ltd., entered into a written joint venture agreement under seal with the third party, Partner Ltd., whereby the parties thereto agreed to purchase certain lands more particularly described in Schedule A annexed to the Plantiff's statement of claim (hereinafter referred to as the "Lands"), taking title only in the name of Owner Ltd.; to renovate the existing industrial building situated on the Lands; and to attempt to

sell or lease the Lands and industrial building thereafter. The said joint venture agreement further provided that both parties would undertake the same financial investment and that any profits realized were to be split between them equally.

5. At all material times, the Defendant, Owner Ltd., held the Lands and industrial building in trust for itself and Partner Ltd. in equal shares.

6. The Defendant, Owner Ltd., therefore claims as against the third party:

> (a) contribution with respect to any judgment which may be obtained in this action as against the Defendant, Owner Ltd.;
> (b) its costs of these third party proceedings;
> (c) such further and other relief as to this Honourable Court may seem just.

WARNING: If you wish to defend against this claim, you are required to deliver a statement of defence within twenty days. Should you fail to deliver a statement of defence as required, pleadings may be noted closed against you, and you shall be deemed to admit all allegations of fact contained in this claim, and you shall not be entitled to notice of or to participate in the trial or any proceeding in respect of this claim and judgment may be given against you.

DELIVERED at Toronto, this 14th day of December, 1983, by STEPHENS & MITCHELL, Barristers and Solicitors, 206 Torson Avenue, Toronto, Ontario, solicitors for the Defendant, Owner Ltd.

Precedent No. 48

IN THE SUPREME COURT OF ONTARIO IN BANKRUPTCY

THE REGISTRAR IN BANKRUPTCY	)))	WEDNESDAY, THE 16TH DAY OF NOVEMBER, 1983.

IN THE MATTER OF the bankruptcy of
General Contractor Ltd.;

AND IN THE MATTER OF the *Construction Lien Act*, S.O. 1983, c. 6;

AND IN THE MATTER OF an action between:

SUBCONTRACTOR LTD.,

Plaintiff,

- and -

GENERAL CONTRACTOR LTD.,
OWNER LTD. and
MORTGAGEE LTD.,

Defendants.

ORDER

UPON the application of Subcontractor Ltd. for leave to commence and prosecute its claim for lien upon the estate of Owner Ltd. in the lands described in Schedule A annexed hereto in respect of the supply and installation of plumbing materials to General Contractor Ltd., and the claims of other lienholders against the lands hereinbefore referred to, in the presence of Counsel for the Plaintiff Applicant, upon reading the Consent of Timothy Trustee, filed, and upon hearing Counsel aforesaid:

1. IT IS ORDERED that the Plaintiff Applicant be and it is hereby authorized to commence and prosecute an action in the Supreme Court of Ontario under the *Construction Lien Act* and to add the trustee of the estate of General Contractor Ltd., namely Timothy Trustee, as a party Defendant thereto, to enforce its lien against the lands described in Schedule A annexed to this Order.

2. AND IT IS ORDERED that the time for filing a declaration under Section 99(1) of the *Bankruptcy Act* be and the same is hereby extended until after the expiration of thirty days from the completion of the sale of the said lands pursuant to the judgment of the Court adjudicating upon the Plaintiff Applicant's

claim for lien for whatever amount may be found owing thereunder as against the said trustee.

3. IT IS FURTHER ORDERED that the time for filing any claim which the Plaintiff Applicant may have as an unsecured creditor after realization under its lien as required by Section 99(1) of the *Bankruptcy Act* be and the same is hereby extended until it shall have been ascertained what amount the Plaintiff Applicant shall have received under its lien.

4. AND IT IS FURTHER ORDERED that all other persons who may be entitled to enforce construction lien claims against the said lands be and they are hereby authorized to take such proceedings as may be necessary to protect their rights thereunder and that the provisions of paragraphs 2 and 3 of this Order shall apply to such lien holders in the bankruptcy proceedings.

5. AND IT IS FURTHER ORDERED that, if the trustee does not defend the action, he shall not be subject to discovery or production of documents nor shall any costs be awarded against him.

_____

REGISTRAR

Precedent No. 49

IN THE SUPREME COURT OF ONTARIO IN BANKRUPTCY

IN THE MATTER OF the bankruptcy
of General Contractor Ltd.;

IN THE MATTER OF the *Construction Lien Act*, S.O. 1983, c. 6;

AND IN THE MATTER OF an action
between:

SUBCONTRACTOR LTD.,

Plaintiff,

- and -

GENERAL CONTRACTOR LTD.,
OWNER LTD. and
MORTGAGEE LTD.,

Defendants.

CONSENT

I, TIMOTHY TRUSTEE, trustee of the estate of General Contractor Ltd., a bankrupt, hereby consent to an Order being made as follows:

1. Giving leave to Subcontractor Ltd. to commence and prosecute an action in the Supreme Court of Ontario under the Construction Lien Act and to add me, as trustee of the estate of General Contractor Ltd., as a party Defendant thereto to enforce its lien against the lands described in Schedule A annexed hereto.

2. Extending the time for filing a declaration under Section 99(1) of the *Bankruptcy Act* until after the expiration of thirty days from the completion of the sale of the said lands pursuant to a judgment of the court adjudicating upon the Plaintiff Applicant's claim for lien for whatever amount may be found owing thereunder as against me, as trustee.

3. Extending the time for the filing of any claim which the Plaintiff Applicant may have as an unsecured creditor after realization under its lien as required by Section 99(1) of the *Bankruptcy Act* until it shall have ascertained what amount the Plaintiff Applicant shall receive under its lien.

4. Authorizing all other persons who may be entitled to enforce construction lien claims against the said lands to take such proceedings to protect their rights thereunder and that the provisions of paragraphs 2 and 3 of this Consent shall apply to all such lienholders in the bankruptcy proceedings.

DATED at Toronto this 16th day of November, 1983.

Trustee

Precedent No. 50

CLA 1234/83

IN THE SUPREME COURT OF ONTARIO

IN THE MATTER OF the *Construction Lien Act*, S.O. 1983, c. 6

B E T W E E N:

SUBCONTRACTOR LTD.,

Plaintiff,

- and -

GENERAL CONTRACTOR LTD.,
OWNER LTD. and
MORTGAGEE LTD.,

Defendants.

NOTICE OF MOTION

TAKE NOTICE that a motion will be made to the Court on behalf of the Plaintiff at Osgoode Hall, Queen Street West, Toronto, Ontario, on Monday, the 12th day of December, 1983, at 10:30 o'clock in the forenoon, or so soon thereafter as Counsel can be heard, for judgment, pursuant to Section 60(1)(a) of the *Construction Lien Act*, S.O. 1983, c. 6, referring the within action to the Master at Toronto for trial, or for such further or other Order as to this Honourable Court may seem just.

AND TAKE NOTICE that in support of such motion will be read the Affidavit of Stanley Subcontractor, and such further and other material as Counsel may advise.

DATED at Toronto this 3rd day of December, 1983.

KIRSH & KIRSH
Barristers and Solicitors
45 Bay Street
Toronto, Ontario

Solicitors for the Plaintiff.

Precedent No. 51

CLA 1234/83

IN THE SUPREME COURT OF ONTARIO

IN THE MATTER OF the *Construction Lien Act*, S.O. 1983, c. 6

B E T W E E N:

SUBCONTRACTOR LTD.,

Plaintiff,

- and -

GENERAL CONTRACTOR LTD.,
OWNER LTD. and
MORTGAGEE LTD.,

Defendants.

AFFIDAVIT

I, STANLEY SUBCONTRACTOR, of the Municipality of Metropolitan Toronto, in the Province of Ontario, Executive, MAKE OATH AND SAY AS FOLLOWS:

1. I am President of the Plaintiff, Subcontractor Ltd., and as such have knowledge of the matters hereinafter deposed to.

2. Statements of defence on behalf of each of the Defendants have been delivered in the within action. None of the Defendants has delivered a counterclaim or a crossclaim, and the time for their delivery has expired. Furthermore, none of the Defendants has sought or obtained leave to join any person as a third party to the within action.

3. This Affidavit is made in support of a motion for judgment referring the within action to the Master at Toronto for trial, and for no improper purpose.

SWORN before me (etc.) . . . .   )
)
)   _____
)   STANLEY SUBCONTRACTOR
)
)

A Commissioner, etc.

Precedent No. 52

CLA 1234/83

IN THE SUPREME COURT OF ONTARIO

IN THE MATTER OF the *Construction Lien Act*, S.O. 1983, c. 6

THE HONOURABLE	)	MONDAY, THE 12TH DAY OF
MR. JUSTICE	)	
	)	DECEMBER, 1983.

B E T W E E N:

SUBCONTRACTOR LTD.,

Plaintiff,

- and -

GENERAL CONTRACTOR LTD.,
OWNER LTD. and
MORTGAGEE LTD.,

Defendants.

O R D E R

UPON motion made this day on behalf of the Plaintiff for judgment, pursuant to Section 60(1)(a) of the *Construction Lien Act,* S.O. 1983, c. 6, referring the within action to the Master at Toronto for trial, in the presence of Counsel for the Plaintiff and for the Defendants, upon reading the Affidavit of Stanley Subcontractor, filed, and the pleadings and proceedings herein, and upon hearing Counsel aforesaid:

1. THIS COURT ORDERS AND ADJUDGES that this action be and the same is hereby referred to the Master at Toronto for trial.

2. AND THIS COURT ORDERS AND ADJUDGES that the parties found liable forthwith after confirmation of the report of the Master pay to the parties the respective amounts due them.

3. THIS COURT FURTHER ORDERS AND ADJUDGES that the Master determine all questions arising in this action and on the reference and all questions arising under the *Construction Lien Act, 1983* and that the findings of the Master be effective on the confirmation of the report.

4. AND THIS COURT FURTHER ORDERS AND ADJUDGES that
the Master determine the question of costs in this action and of the reference, and
the costs be taxed and paid as the Master shall direct.

JUDGMENT signed the 12th day of December, 1983.

REGISTRAR, S.C.O.

Precedent No. 53

CLA 1234/83

IN THE SUPREME COURT OF ONTARIO

IN THE MATTER OF the *Construction Lien Act*, S.O. 1983, c. 6

B E T W E E N:

SUBCONTRACTOR LTD.,

Plaintiff,

- and -

GENERAL CONTRACTOR LTD.,
OWNER LTD. and
MORTGAGEE LTD.,

Defendants,

- and -

PARTNER LTD.,

Third Party.

NOTICE OF MOTION

TAKE NOTICE that a motion will be made to the Court on behalf of the third party, Partner Ltd., at Osgoode Hall, Queen Street West, Toronto, Ontario, on Tuesday, the 20th day of December, 1983, at the hour of 10:30 o'clock in the forenoon, or so soon thereafter as Counsel can be heard, for an Order, pursuant to Section 60(3) of the *Construction Lien Act,* S.O. 1983, c. 6, setting aside the judgment of the Honourable Mr. Justice   directing a reference of the within action to the Master at Toronto for trial, and for a further Order that the within action be tried together with an action commenced in the Supreme Court of Ontario by the third party, as Plaintiff, against the Defendant herein, Owner Ltd., as Defendant, being Action No. 13579/83, or for such further or other Order as to this Honourable Court may seem just.

AND TAKE NOTICE that in support of such motion will be read the

Affidavit of Peter Partner and such further and other material as Counsel may advise.

DATED at Toronto, this 13th day of December, 1983.

BLACK & JETTA
963 Sky Avenue
Toronto, Ontario

Solicitors for the third party,
Partner Ltd.

Precedent No. 54

CLA 1234/83

IN THE SUPREME COURT OF ONTARIO

IN THE MATTER OF the *Construction Lien Act*, S.O. 1983, c. 6

B E T W E E N:

SUBCONTRACTOR LTD.,

Plaintiff,

- and -

GENERAL CONTRACTOR LTD.,
OWNER LTD. and
MORTGAGEE LTD.,

Defendants,

- and -

PARTNER LTD.,

Third Party.

A F F I D A V I T

I, PETER PARTNER, of the Municipality of Metropolitan Toronto, in the Province of Ontario, Executive, MAKE OATH AND SAY AS FOLLOWS:

1. I am President of the third party, Partner Ltd., and as such have knowledge of the matters hereinafter deposed to.

2. By Order of Master   dated the 12th day of December, 1983, Partner Ltd. was joined as a third party in this action upon the motion of the Defendant, Owner Ltd. Now shown to me and marked Exhibit 1 to this my Affidavit is a true copy of the said Order.

3. By Writ of Summons issued the 8th day of June, 1983, Partner Ltd. commenced an action in the Supreme Court of Ontario (hereinafter referred to as the "Supreme Court Action") against Owner Ltd., General Contractor Ltd. and Mortgagee Ltd. for, inter alia, certain declaratory relief relating to a construction project which is the subject matter of the within action, and to the interpretation of a joint venture agreement, in respect of that construction project, entered into between Partner Ltd. and Owner Ltd. Now shown to me and marked Exhibits 2

and 3 to this my Affidavit are true copies of the Writ of Summons and Statement of Claim in the Supreme Court Action.

4. The issues involved in the Supreme Court Action involve an examination of the dealings of Partner Ltd., Owner Ltd., Mortgagee Ltd., General Contractor Ltd., and the various sub-trades claiming through General Contractor Ltd. I therefore verily believe that the factual issues in the within action and the Supreme Court Action are similar in substance. Furthermore, save as to the Plaintiff in the within action, the parties named in the within action and in the Supreme Court Action are identical. I therefore verily believe that much of the evidence in the actions will be duplicated if they are not tried together. Additionally, unless both actions are tried together, there is the risk that different courts will make different findings of fact.

5. This Affidavit is made in support of a motion to set aside the judgment of the Honourable Mr. Justice   , dated the 12th day of December, 1983, wherein the within action was referred to the Master at Toronto for trial, and for an Order that the within action be tried together with the Supreme Court Action or that the said actions be placed on the trial list to be tried one after the other, and for no improper purpose.

SWORN before me (etc.) . . . .   )
)
)
)   _____
)   PETER PARTNER
)
)

A Commissioner, etc.

Precedent No. 55

CLA 1234/83

IN THE SUPREME COURT OF ONTARIO

IN THE MATTER OF the *Construction Lien Act*, S.O. 1983, c. 6

THE HONOURABLE	)	TUESDAY, THE 20TH DAY OF
MR. JUSTICE	)	
	)	DECEMBER, 1983.

B E T W E E N:

SUBCONTRACTOR LTD.,

Plaintiff,

- and -

GENERAL CONTRACTOR LTD.,
OWNER LTD. and
MORTGAGEE LTD.,

Defendants,

- and -

PARTNER LTD.,

Third Party.

O R D E R

UPON motion made this day on behalf of the third party, Partner Ltd., for an Order, pursuant to Section 60(3) of the *Construction Lien Act*, S.O. 1983, c. 6, setting aside the judgment of the Honourable Mr. Justice , dated the 12th day of December, 1983, and for an Order that the within action be tried together with the action commenced in the Supreme Court of Ontario by the third party, being Action No. 13579/83, in the presence of Counsel for the third party, Counsel for the Plaintiff and Counsel for the Defendants, upon reading the Affidavit of Peter Partner, filed, and the pleadings and proceedings herein and the pleadings and proceedings in Supreme Court Action No. 13579/83, and upon hearing Counsel aforesaid:

1. IT IS ORDERED that the judgment of the Honourable Mr. Justice
                   , dated the 12th day of December, 1983, be and the same is
hereby set aside.

2. AND IT IS ORDERED that the within action be tried together with the
action commenced in the Supreme Court of Ontario by the third party against the
named Defendants herein, being Action No. 13579/83.

3. IT IS FURTHER ORDERED that there be examinations for discovery
and production of documents in the within action in accordance with the Rules
of Practice, and that the same be common with those in the action commenced by
the third party in the Supreme Court of Ontario, Action No. 13579/83.

Precedent No. 56

CLA 1234/83

IN THE SUPREME COURT OF ONTARIO

IN THE MATTER OF the *Construction Lien Act*, S.O. 1983, c. 6

B E T W E E N:

SUBCONTRACTOR LTD.,

Plaintiff,

- and -

GENERAL CONTRACTOR LTD.,
OWNER LTD. and
MORTGAGEE LTD.,

Defendants.

NOTICE OF MOTION

TAKE NOTICE that a motion will be made to the Master on behalf of the Plaintiff at 145 Queen Street West, Toronto, Ontario, on Monday, the 23rd day of January, 1984, at the hour of 10:00 o'clock in the forenoon, or so soon thereafter as Counsel can be heard, for an Order, pursuant to Section 62(1) of the *Construction Lien Act*, S.O. 1983, c. 6, fixing the day, time and place for the trial of the within action and for the holding of a settlement meeting, or for such further or other Order as to this Honourable Court may seem just.

AND TAKE NOTICE that in support of such motion will be read the Affidavit of Stanley Subcontractor, and such further and other material as Counsel may advise.

DATED at Toronto, this 16th day of January, 1984.

KIRSH & KIRSH
Barristers and Solicitors
45 Bay Street
Toronto, Ontario

Solicitors for the Plaintiff.

Precedent No. 57

CLA 1234/83

IN THE SUPREME COURT OF ONTARIO

IN THE MATTER OF the *Construction
Lien Act*, S.O. 1983, c. 6

B E T W E E N:

SUBCONTRACTOR LTD.,

Plaintiff,

- and -

GENERAL CONTRACTOR LTD.,
OWNER LTD. and
MORTGAGEE LTD.,

Defendants.

AFFIDAVIT

I, STANLEY SUBCONTRACTOR, of the Municipality of Metropolitan Toronto, in the Province of Ontario, Executive, MAKE OATH AND SAY AS FOLLOWS:

1. I am President of the Plaintiff, Subcontractor Ltd., and as such have knowledge of the matters hereinafter deposed to.

2. On the 13th day of January, 1984, I caused a search to be made of the Supreme Court file in the within action. The said search disclosed that:

    (a) all of the Defendants in the within action have filed their statements of defence with the court;

    (b) none of the Defendants has filed a crossclaim or a counterclaim with the court, and neither Subcontractor Ltd. nor its solicitors have been served with legal process in this regard; and

    (c) no order has been obtained by any of the Defendants for leave to join a third party herein.

3. Now shown to me and marked Exhibit 1 to this my Affidavit is a true copy of the judgment of the Honourable Mr. Justice   dated the 12th day of December, 1983, wherein the within action was referred to the Master at Toronto for trial.

4. Now shown to me and marked Exhibit 2 to this my Affidavit is a true

copy of the abstract of title with respect to the lands and premises which are the subject of the within lien action. As indicated therein, seven lien claims have been registered. On the basis of the allegations contained in the statement of defence of the Defendant, General Contractor Ltd., I verily believe that there will be a dispute as to whether some or all of the said liens were preserved and perfected within the time allowed for so doing. Furthermore, on the basis of the allegations contained in the statement of defence of the Defendant, Owner Ltd., there is an issue as to the extent of the holdback obligations of that Defendant. In view of the foregoing, I verily believe that it is desirable that a settlement meeting be ordered so that the various issues referred to above may be canvassed by the parties with a view to narrowing or resolving the same.

5. This Affidavit is made in support of a motion for an Order fixing the day, time and place for the trial of the within action and for the holding of a settlement meeting, and for no improper purpose.

SWORN before me (etc.) . . . .　　　　)
　　　　　　　　　　　　　　　　　　)
　　　　　　　　　　　　　　　　　　)　　_____
　　　　　　　　　　　　　　　　　　)　　STANLEY SUBCONTRACTOR
　　　　　　　　　　　　　　　　　　)
　　　　　　　　　　　　　　　　　　)

A Commissioner, etc.

Precedent No. 58

CLA 1234/83

IN THE SUPREME COURT OF ONTARIO

IN THE MATTER OF the *Construction Lien Act*, S.O. 1983, c. 6

MASTER		
	)	MONDAY, THE 23RD DAY OF
	)	
	)	JANUARY, 1984.

B E T W E E N:

SUBCONTRACTOR LTD.,

Plaintiff,

- and -

GENERAL CONTRACTOR LTD.,
OWNER LTD. and
MORTGAGEE LTD.,

Defendants.

O R D E R

UPON ex parte motion made this day on behalf of the Plaintiff for an Order, pursuant to Section 62(1) of the *Construction Lien Act*, S.O. 1983, c. 6, fixing the day, time and place for the trial of the within action, and for the holding of a settlement meeting, in the presence of Counsel for the Plaintiff, upon reading the Affidavit of Stanley Subcontractor, filed, and upon hearing Counsel aforesaid:

1. IT IS ORDERED that the trial of this action shall take place at 145 Queen Street West, in the City of Toronto, in the Municipality of Metropolitan Toronto, on Friday, the 8th day of June, 1984 at 10:00 o'clock in the forenoon.

2. AND IT IS ORDERED that a settlement meeting with respect to this action shall take place in room 222 at 145 Queen Street West, in the City of Toronto, in the Municipality of Metropolitan Toronto, on Friday, the 4th day of May, 1984 at 10:00 o'clock in the forenoon.

Precedent No. 59

CLA 1234/83

IN THE SUPREME COURT OF ONTARIO

IN THE MATTER OF the *Construction Lien Act*, S.O. 1983, c. 6

MASTER	) FRIDAY, THE 8TH DAY OF
	)
	) JUNE, 1984.

B E T W E E N:

SUBCONTRACTOR LTD.,

Plaintiff,

- and -

GENERAL CONTRACTOR LTD.,
OWNER LTD. and
MORTGAGEE LTD.,

Defendants.

O R D E R

UPON motion made this day on behalf of the Plaintiff for an Order, pursuant to Section 61(2) of the *Construction Lien Act*, S.O. 1983, c. 6, for consolidation and carriage, in the presence of Counsel for the Plaintiff, Counsel for the Defendants, and Counsel for the lien claimants, Excavation Ltd., Lumber Ltd. and Masonry Ltd., upon reading the pleadings and proceedings in the within action and the pleadings and proceedings in those actions commenced by the aforesaid lien claimants in Action Nos. CLA 2345/83, CLA 2346/83 and CLA 2347/83 respectively, and upon hearing Counsel aforesaid:

1. IT IS ORDERED that the within action, together with Action Nos. CLA 2345/83, CLA 2346/83 and CLA 2347/83 in the Supreme Court of Ontario be and the same are hereby consolidated into one action.

2. AND IT IS ORDERED that the action consolidated by this Order shall henceforth be carried on bearing the following style of cause:

CLA 1234/83

B E T W E E N:

SUBCONTRACTOR LTD.,

Plaintiff,

- and -

GENERAL CONTRACTOR LTD.,
OWNER LTD. and
MORTGAGEE LTD.,

Defendants.

3. IT IS FURTHER ORDERED that the Plaintiff is awarded carriage of the consolidated action.

4. AND IT IS FURTHER ORDERED that the costs of this motion and the Plaintiff's salvage costs shall be taxed and paid as the Master shall direct.

Precedent No. 60

CLA 1234/83

IN THE SUPREME COURT OF ONTARIO

IN THE MATTER OF the *Construction Lien Act*, S.O. 1983, c. 6

B E T W E E N:

SUBCONTRACTOR LTD.,

Plaintiff,

- and -

GENERAL CONTRACTOR LTD.,
OWNER LTD. and
MORTGAGEE LTD.,

Defendants.

NOTICE OF FILING OF REPORT

TAKE NOTICE that the Report of Master   herein, dated the 8th day of June, 1984, was filed with the Supreme Court office at 145 Queen Street West, Toronto, Ontario, on Monday, the 18th day of June, 1984.

DATED at Toronto, this 19th day of June, 1984.

KIRSH & KIRSH
Barristers and Solicitors
45 Bay Street
Toronto, Ontario

Solicitors for the Plaintiff.

Precedent No. 61

CLA 1234/83

IN THE SUPREME COURT OF ONTARIO

IN THE MATTER OF the *Construction Lien Act*, S.O. 1983, c. 6

B E T W E E N:

SUBCONTRACTOR LTD.,

Plaintiff,

- and -

GENERAL CONTRACTOR LTD.,
OWNER LTD. and
MORTGAGEE LTD.,

Defendants.

NOTICE OF APPEAL

TAKE NOTICE that the Plaintiff appeals to the Divisional Court from the Report of Master   , dated the 8th day of June, 1984, and asks that the findings contained in the said Report may be reversed, and that the Plaintiff be found to be entitled to a lien and to judgment in the sum of $75,000 plus interest, upon the following grounds:

1. That the findings of fact made by the learned Master were inconsistent with the evidence;
2. That . . .;
3. That . . .;
4. Such further and other grounds as Counsel may advise and this Honourable Court may permit.

The Plaintiff proposes that this Appeal be heard at the City of Toronto.
DATED at Toronto, this 15th day of June, 1984.

KIRSH & KIRSH
Barristers and Solicitors
45 Bay Street
Toronto, Ontario

Solicitors for the Plaintiff.

Precedent No. 62

CLA 1234/83

IN THE SUPREME COURT OF ONTARIO

IN THE MATTER OF the *Construction Lien Act*, S.O. 1983, c. 6

B E T W E E N:

SUBCONTRACTOR LTD.,

Plaintiff,

- and -

GENERAL CONTRACTOR LTD.,
OWNER LTD. and
MORTGAGEE LTD.,

Defendants.

NOTICE OF APPEAL

TAKE NOTICE that the Plaintiff appeals to the Divisional Court from the Judgment of the Honourable Mr. Justice   dated the 8th day of June, 1984, and asks that the said Judgment may be reversed, and that the Plaintiff be found to be entitled to a lien and to Judgment in the sum of $75,000 plus interest, upon the following grounds:

1. That the findings of fact made by the learned trial judge were inconsistent with the evidence;
2. That . . .;
3. That . . .;
4. Such further and other grounds as Counsel may advise and this Honourable Court may permit.

The Plaintiff proposes that this Appeal be heard at the City of Toronto. DATED at Toronto, this 15th day of June, 1984.

KIRSH & KIRSH
Barristers and Solicitors
45 Bay Street
Toronto, Ontario

Solicitors for the Plaintiff.

Precedent No. 63

CLA 1234/83

IN THE SUPREME COURT OF ONTARIO

IN THE MATTER OF the *Construction Lien Act*, S.O. 1983, c. 6

MASTER	)	MONDAY, THE 25TH DAY OF
	)	
	)	JUNE, 1983.

B E T W E E N:

SUBCONTRACTOR LTD.,

Plaintiff,

- and -

GENERAL CONTRACTOR LTD.,
OWNER LTD. and
MORTGAGEE LTD.,

Defendants.

VESTING ORDER

UPON motion made this day on behalf of the Plaintiff, pursuant to the Report of Master   dated the 8th day of June, 1984 directing that the lands and premises described in Schedule A annexed hereto be sold in pursuance of and in the manner directed by the said Report, for an Order vesting the said lands and premises in Percy Purchaser, in the presence of Counsel for the Plaintiff, for the Defendants, Owner Ltd. and Mortgagee Ltd., and for Percy Purchaser, no one appearing for the Defendant, General Contractor Ltd., although duly served, upon reading the Affidavit of Stanley Subcontractor and the offer to Purchase the said lands and premises submitted by Percy Purchaser as well as the statement of adjustments submitted by the solicitor for the Plaintiff, and upon hearing Counsel aforesaid:

1. IT IS ORDERED that the estate, right, title and interest of the Defendant, Owner Ltd., in and to the lands and premises described in Schedule A annexed to this Order be and the same are hereby vested in Percy Purchaser.

2. AND IT IS ORDERED that the Master of Titles for the Land Titles Office of the Land Titles Division of Toronto be and he is hereby directed to enter and register Percy Purchaser as owner in fee simple of the said lands and premises.

Precedent No. 64

No. 222 A.D. 1983

IN THE SUPREME COURT OF ONTARIO

Between:

SUBCONTRACTOR LTD.,

Plaintiff

- and -

GENERAL CONTRACTOR LTD.,
DAVID DIRECTOR and
ORVILLE OFFICER,

Defendants

Elizabeth the Second, by the Grace of God, of the United Kingdom, Canada and Her other Realms and Territories Queen, Head of the Commonwealth, Defender of the Faith.

TO: GENERAL CONTRACTOR LTD.
99 Queen Street
Toronto, Ontario

AND TO: DAVID DIRECTOR
6 Trojan Crescent
Toronto, Ontario

AND TO: ORVILLE OFFICER
3 Winston Street
Toronto, Ontario

We Command that, if you wish to defend this action, either you or your lawyer shall file an Appearance in the office of this Court at 145 Queen Street West, Toronto, Ontario within ten days after the day this Writ was served upon you; AND TAKE NOTICE that, where a Statement of Claim is also served with this Writ, or is served upon you at some later date, and you fail to serve upon the plaintiff or its lawyer AND file your Statement of Defence in the same Court office within twenty days after the Statement of Claim has been filed and served upon you, pleadings may be noted closed against you and you may not be permitted to deliver your Statement of Defence;

And Further Take Notice that where pleadings have been noted closed against you, you may be deemed to have admitted the plaintiff's claim and you may not be entitled to notice of any motion for judgment or notice of trial, AND JUDGMENT MAY BE GIVEN AGAINST YOU IN YOUR ABSENCE.

In Witness Whereof this Writ is signed for the Supreme Court of Ontario by WARREN JOHN DUNLOP Local Registrar of the said Court at Toronto this 12th day of December, 1983.

"Warren John Dunlop"
(signature of officer)

N.B.—This Writ is to be served within twelve calendar months from the date thereof, or if renewed, within twelve calendar months from the date of such renewal, including the day of such date and not afterwards.

The Plaintiff's claim is against the Defendants for:

1. A declaration that certain monies appropriated or converted by the Defendants are trust monies and are held in trust by the Defendants for the Plaintiff;
2. Damages for breach of trust;
3. An accounting with respect to all trust monies received, held, appropriated and converted by the Defendants, and judgment in accordance with such accounting;
4. Interest, pursuant to Section 36 of the *Judicature Act*, R.S.O. 1980, c. 223, upon all amounts awarded to the Plaintiff;
5. Costs on a solicitor-client basis.

Precedent No. 65

No. 222/83

IN THE SUPREME COURT OF ONTARIO

B E T W E E N:

SUBCONTRACTOR LTD.,

Plaintiff,

- and -

GENERAL CONTRACTOR LTD.,
DAVID DIRECTOR and
ORVILLE OFFICER,

Defendants.

STATEMENT OF CLAIM

(Writ issued the 12th day of December, 1983)

1. The Plaintiff is a corporation incorporated pursuant to the laws of the Province of Ontario, having its head office in the Municipality of Metropolitan Toronto, in the Province of Ontario.

2. The Defendant, General Contractor Ltd., is a corporation incorporated pursuant to the laws of the Province of Ontario, having its head office in the Municipality of Metropolitan Toronto, in the Province of Ontario.

3. The Defendants, David Director and Orville Officer, each reside in the City of Toronto, in the Municipality of Metropolitan Toronto, and at all material times were the sole directors and officers of General Contractor Ltd. and had effective control of that corporation and its relevant activities.

4. On the 2nd day of April, 1983, the Plaintiff entered into a written agreement under seal with the Defendant, General Contractor Ltd., whereby the Plaintiff agreed to supply and install plumbing materials, in consideration for an agreed price, in connection with the renovation of an industrial building situated on lands referred to in Schedule A annexed hereto.

5. The Plaintiff has completed its work in accordance with the terms of its said agreement with the Defendant, General Contractor Ltd. However, the said Defendant has refused or neglected to pay the amount owing therefor to the Plaintiff, namely the sum of $75,000 plus interest.

6. On or about the 11th day of July, 1983, and the 5th day of September, 1983, the Defendant, General Contractor Ltd., received the sums of $50,000 and $60,000 respectively from the owner of the aforesaid lands, Owner Ltd., on

account of the contract price. The Plaintiff pleads that the said progress payments received by the Defendant, General Contractor Ltd., constitute a trust fund for the benefit of the Plaintiff pursuant to the provisions of Section 8 of the *Construction Lien Act*.

7. The Plaintiff alleges that the said progress payments received by the Defendant, General Contractor Ltd., were deposited by the said Defendant in its bank account and were converted by the said Defendant in the retirement of the said Defendant's indebtedness to its bank, The Bank of Toronto. The Plaintiff pleads that the said Defendant has thereby appropriated and converted the said monies, and that such actions constitute a breach of trust by the Defendant, General Contractor Ltd.

8. The Plaintiff further alleges that the Defendants, David Director and Orville Officer, at all material times had effective control of the Defendant, General Contractor Ltd., and its relevant activities, and assented to and acquiesced in the appropriation and conversion of the said monies, which the Defendants, David Director and Orville Officer, knew or reasonably ought to have known amounted to a breach of trust by the Defendant, General Contractor Ltd.

9. The Plaintiff pleads and relies upon the provisions of Section 13 of the *Construction Lien Act*.

10. The Plaintiff further alleges that it has suffered damages by virtue of the aforesaid actions of the Defendants.

11. The Plaintiff therefore claims:

(a) A declaration that the monies received by the Defendant, General Contractor Ltd., and applied to reduce its bank indebtedness, constituted a trust fund for the benefit of the Plaintiff pursuant to the provisions of the *Construction Lien Act*;

(b) An accounting with respect to the trust monies converted by the Defendants as aforesaid, and judgment in accordance therewith;

(c) Damages for breach of trust;

(d) Interest, pursuant to the provisions of Section 36 of the *Judicature Act*, R.S.O. 1980, c. 223, upon all amounts found due and owing to the Plaintiff;

(e) Costs on a solicitor-client basis;

(f) Such further and other relief as to this Honourable Court may seem just.

DELIVERED at Toronto, this 12th day of December, 1983 by Messrs. Kirsh & Kirsh, Barristers and Solicitors, 45 Bay Street, Toronto, Ontario, solicitors for the Plaintiff.

Precedent No. 66

LABOUR AND MATERIAL PAYMENT BOND
(TRUSTEE FORM)

No. . . . . $. . . . .
Note: This Bond is issued simultaneously with another Bond in favour of the
Obligee conditioned for the full and faithful performance of the Contract.

KNOW ALL MEN BY THESE PRESENTS THAT . . . .
. . . . as Principal
hereinafter called the Principal, and . . . .
a corporation created and existing under the laws of . . . .
and duly authorized to transact the business of Suretyship in . . . .
as Surety, hereinafter called the Surety are, subject to the conditions hereinafter
contained, held and firmly bound unto . . . . as Trustee
hereinafter called the Obligee, for the use and benefit of the Claimants, their and
each of their heirs, executors, administrators, successors and assigns, in the
amount of . . . .
. . . . Dollars ($. . . . .)
of lawful money of Canada for the payment of which sum well and truly to be
made the Principal and the Surety bind themselves, their heirs, executors,
administrators, successors and assigns, jointly and severally, firmly by these
presents.

WHEREAS, the Principal has entered into a written contract with the Obligee,
dated the . . . . day of . . . . 19 . . . , for
. . . .
. . . .
. . . .
which Contract Documents are by reference made a part hereof, and are here-
inafter referred to as the Contract.

NOW, THEREFORE, THE CONDITION OF THIS OBLIGATION is such
that, if the Principal shall make payment to all Claimants for all labour and
material used or reasonably required for use in the performance of the Contract,
then this obligation shall be null and void; otherwise it shall remain in full force
and effect, subject, however, to the following conditions:

1. A Claimant for the purpose of this Bond is defined as one having a direct
   contract with the Principal for labour, material, or both, used or
   reasonably required for use in the performance of the Contract, labour
   and material being construed to include that part of water, gas, power,
   light, heat, oil, gasoline, telephone service or rental equipment directly
   applicable to the Contract provided that a person, firm or corporation
   who rents equipment to the Principal to be used in the performance of the
   Contract under a contract which provides that all or any part of the rent

is to be applied towards the purchase price thereof, shall only be a Claimant to the extent of the prevailing industrial rental value of such equipment for the period during which the equipment was used in the performance of the Contract. The prevailing industrial value of equipment shall be determined, insofar as it is practical to do so, in accordance with and in the manner provided for in the latest revised edition of the publication of the Canadian Construction Association titled "Rental Rates on Contractors Equipment" published prior to the period during which the equipment was used in the performance of the Contract.

2. The Principal and the Surety, hereby jointly and severally agree with the Obligee, as Trustee, that every Claimant who has not been paid as provided for under the terms of his contract with the Principal, before the expiration of a period of ninety (90) days after the date on which the last of such Claimant's work or labour was done or performed or materials were furnished by such Claimant, may as a beneficiary of the trust herein provided for, sue on this Bond, prosecute the suit to final judgment for such sum or sums as may be justly due to such Claimant under the terms of his contract with the Principal and have execution thereon. Provided that the Obligee is not obliged to do or take any act, action or proceeding against the Surety on behalf of the Claimants, or any of them, to enforce the provisions of this Bond. If any act, action or proceeding is taken either in the name of the Obligee or by joining the Obligee as a party to such proceeding, then such act, action or proceeding, shall be taken on the understanding and basis that the Claimants; or any of them, who take such act, action or proceeding shall indemnify and save harmless the Obligee against all costs, charges and expenses or liabilities incurred thereon and any loss or damage resulting to the Obligee by reason thereof. Provided still further that, subject to the foregoing terms and conditions, the Claimants, or any of them may use the name of the Obligee to sue on and enforce the provisions of this Bond.

3. No suit or action shall be commenced hereunder by any Claimant:
   (a) unless such Claimant shall have given written notice within the time limits hereinafter set forth to each of the Principal, the Surety and the Obligee, stating with substantial accuracy the amount claimed. Such notice shall be served by mailing the same by registered mail to the Principal, the Surety and the Obligee, at any place where an office is regularly maintained for the transaction of business by such persons or served in any manner in which legal process may be served in the Province or other part of Canada in which the subject matter of the Contract is located. Such notice shall be given
      (1) in respect of any claim for the amount or any portion thereof, required to be held back from the Claimant by the Principal, under either the terms of the Claimant's contract with the Principal, or under the Mechanics' Liens Legislation applicable to the Claimant's contract with the Principal, whichever is the greater, within one hundred and twenty (120) days after such Claimant should have been paid in full under the Claimant's contract with the Principal;

(2) in respect of any claim other than for the holdback, or portion thereof, referred to above, within one hundred and twenty (120) days after the date upon which such Claimant did, or performed, the last of the work or labour or furnished the last of the materials for which such claim is made under the Claimant's contract with the Principal;

(b) after the expiration of one (1) year following the date on which the Principal ceased work on the Contract, including work performed under the guarantees provided in the Contract;

(c) other than in a Court of competent jurisdiction in the Province or District of Canada in which the subject matter of the Contract, or any part thereof, is situated and not elsewhere, and the parties hereto agree to submit to the jurisdiction of such Court.

4. The Surety agrees not to take advantage of Article 1959 of the Civil Code of the Province of Quebec in the event that, by an act or an omission of a Claimant, the Surety can no longer be subrogated in the rights, hypothecs and privileges of Said Claimant.

5. Any material change in the contract between the Principal and the Obligee shall not prejudice the rights or interest of any Claimant under this Bond, who is not instrumental in bringing about or has not caused such change.

6. The amount of this Bond shall be reduced by, and to the extent of any payment or payments made in good faith, and in accordance with the provisions hereof, inclusive of the payment by the Surety of Mechanics' Liens which may be filed of record against the subject matter of the Contract, whether or not claim for the amount of such lien be presented under and against this Bond.

7. The Surety shall not be liable for a greater sum than the specified penalty of this Bond.

IN WITNESS WHEREOF, the Principal and the Surety have Signed and Sealed this Bond this . . . . day of . . . . 19 . . . .

SIGNED AND SEALED
In the presence of   (
                          (
                          (
                          (. . . . (Seal)
                          (Principal
                          (
                          (
                          (. . . . (Seal)
                                               Surety

Precedent No. 67

CONSTRUCTION LIEN HOLDBACK DEFICIENCY BOND

BOND NO.   AMOUNT: NOT TO EXCEED $
EFFECTIVE DATE:

WHEREAS:

The surety of this Bond is The Mortgage Insurance Company of Canada, a company incorporated under the laws of Canada and duly authorized to transact the business of suretyship in the Province of Ontario (the "Surety");

Unless otherwise defined herein all terms used in this Bond have the meanings ascribed to them in the Construction Lien Act, 1983, as the same may be amended from time to time (the "Act");

The principal of this Bond is   as   (the "Principal"), the Owner of lands and premises described as   (the "Property") who has entered into the written or verbal agreement with respect to certain Improvements to the Property (the "Contract"), details of which have been provided to the Surety prior to the execution of this Bond by the Surety;

The obligee of this Bond is   (the "Obligee"), the holder of the mortgage (the "Mortgage") details of which have been provided to the Surety by the Obligee prior to the execution of this Bond by the Surety; and

The Act provides that under certain circumstances liens arising from Improvements shall have priority over certain mortgages to the extent of the deficiency in the Holdbacks required to be retained by Owners under Part IV of the Act.

NOW, THEREFORE, subject to the conditions hereof, including those on the reverse side of this Bond, the Principal and the Surety bind themselves, their heirs, administrators, executors, successors and assigns, jointly and severally, by this Bond to the Obligee in an amount equal to the lesser of:

(A) the sum of   Dollars ($) of lawful money of Canada (inclusive of all legal costs and expenses); and

(B) the total amount of all outstanding liens against the Property as settled by the Obligee with the approval of the Surety or as finally determined by the Court to have priority in accordance with the Act over the Mortgage as a result of a deficiency in the Holdbacks required to be retained by the Principal, together with all reasonable legal fees incurred by the Obligee in the defence or resolution of claims made by Lien Claimants asserting priority over the Mortgage as a result of a deficiency in the Holdbacks,

provided that the liability of the Surety hereunder shall be reduced by and to the extent of:

(C) any monies and the value of other security held or controlled by the Obligee specifically for the purpose of protecting the priority of the

Mortgage from any lien claims resulting out of any deficiency in the Holdbacks;

(D) in the event the Property is sold by the Obligee following foreclosure, under power of sale, or otherwise, the amount by which the net sale proceeds exceeds the amount then owing to the Obligee under the Mortgage; and

(E) any payments made to the Obligee by the Surety in good faith and in accordance with the provisions hereof.

IN WITNESS WHEREOF the Principal and Surety have duly executed this Bond this day of   , 19 .

SIGNED, SEALED AND DELIVERED)
    in the presence of:)

)	
)	
)	
)	

________________________) ______________________ (seal)
)   (Principal)

) THE MORTGAGE INSURANCE COMPANY
) OF CANADA

) By: ___________________
                                                                          Attorney in Fact

CONDITIONS OF THIS BOND

This Bond is subject to the following conditions:

1. <u>Information</u> — The Obligee shall make available to the Surety upon request copies of the reports of the Payment Certifier, if any, under the Contract and any other information available to the Obligee relating to the Principal, the Contract, the Mortgage, the Property and any potential liability of the Surety under this Bond.

2. <u>Required Notices</u> — This Bond is an agreement of the utmost good faith between the parties hereto and, consequently, the Obligee shall deliver notice in writing and copies of all related documentation to the Surety at its address shown on the face hereof immediately (and in any event within five days) after:

(a) the Obligee has become aware of the registration of a claim for lien against title to the Property;

(b) the Obligee has received a claim for lien;

(c) the Obligee has received notice that a person intends to make a claim for lien; or

(d) the Obligee has become aware of any information that constitutes a material change in the circumstances of the Principal, the Contract, the Mortgage or the Property or any potential liability of the Surety under this Bond.

3. Settlements — The Obligee, at the direction or with the consent of the Surety, shall use all reasonable efforts to enter into settlements with Lien Claimants of their claims for priority over any Mortgage arising as a result of an alleged deficiency in the Holdbacks, such settlements to be on such terms as may be approved by the Surety. Upon payment by the Surety to the Obligee of any settlement sum together with all reasonable legal fees incurred by the Obligee in the defence or resolution of the claims made by Lien Claimants, the liability of the Surety hereunder shall be reduced by the amount so paid.

4. Sale Proceeds — In the event the Property is sold by the Obligee following foreclosure, under power of sale, or otherwise and the Obligee realizes net sale proceeds in excess of the amount then owing to the Obligee under the Mortgage, the Obligee shall retain sufficient of such excess funds to satisfy any potential but yet unascertained deficiency in the Holdbacks.

5. Filing of Claims — If the Principal shall fail to pay any lien claims having priority over the Mortgage by reason of a deficiency in any Holdbacks, the Obligee shall file with the Surety a claim for payment under this Bond within 30 days (or such longer period as the Surety may approve) after the Obligee has made payment to the Lien Claimants pursuant to any settlement referred to in paragraph 3 of this Bond, or if not so settled, when there has been a final determination by the Court of priority of the liens and a finding by the Court that there is a deficiency in the Holdbacks.

6. Payment of Claims — The Surety shall make payment to the Obligee in the amount of the Surety's liability hereunder within 30 days after receipt by the Surety of a duly completed valid claim of the Obligee on such forms as are satisfactory to the Surety accompanied by such other documentation with respect to the claim as is reasonably requested by the Surety.

7. Subrogation — Upon satisfaction of the liabilities of the Surety hereunder, the Surety shall be subrogated to the rights of the Obligee under the Mortgage but subordinated to the position of the Obligee and, in return for payment of the Obligee's claim hereunder, the Surety shall be entitled to demand and receive an express assignemnt of a subordinated interest in the Mortgage, any security therefor and any proceedings arising thereunder in an amount equal to the payment made by the Surety hereunder.

8. Limitation Period — The Surety shall be released from its obligations to the Obligee unless the Obligee has instituted legal proceedings against the Surety with respect to its claim hereunder within one year after the Obligee was required, in accordance with paragraph 5, to file such claim with the Surety.

9. Sale by Principal — The Surety shall be liable to the Obligee in accordance with the terms of this Bond for any failure of the Principal to retain any required Holdbacks arising during the time the Principal owns the Property and, unless otherwise agreed to by the Surety, immediately upon the Principal ceasing to own the Property (other than by virtue of a conveyance of the Property

or a part thereof to an individual who intends to use the property or the part conveyed to him as his personal residence) the Surety shall cease to be liable for any subsequent failure by any successor Owner of such conveyed property to retain the Holdbacks required by the Act.

10. Release of Surety — The Surety shall be released from its liability to the Obligee hereunder if the Obligee, without the prior consent of the Surety, makes any material change in the terms of the Mortgage or the security therefor or any documentation related thereto or the method of making progress advances under the Mortgage from the terms, security, documentation and methods disclosed by the Obligee to the Surety prior to the execution of this Bond by the Surety, it being hereby declared that the Surety has relied upon such information in issuing this Bond.

11. Term of Bond — The liability of the Surety under this Bond shall terminate at such time as the Contract has been completed and the Principal is under no further obligation to retain the Holdbacks referred to in the Act.

12. Assignment by Obligee — The Obligee shall be entitled to assign the benefits of this Bond in conjunction with an absolute assignment of the Mortgage provided that the Obligee has obtained the prior written consent of the Surety.

13. Successors and Assigns — This Bond shall enure to the benefit of and be binding upon the respective successors and permitted assigns of the Obligee, the Principal and the Surety.

14. Interpretation — Words importing the singular number include the plural and vice versa and words importing the neuter gender include the feminine and masculine gender. The division of this Bond into paragraphs and the insertion of headings are for convenience of reference only and shall not affect the construction or interpretation of this Bond. This Bond shall be interpreted in accordance with the laws of the Province of Ontario and shall for all purposes be deemed to be an Ontario contract. This Bond shall only be effective upon the due execution thereof by both the Principal and the Surety and the subsequent delivery thereof to the Obligee.

Precedent No. 68

CONSTRUCTION LIEN HOLDBACK DEFICIENCY BLANKET BOND

BOND NO.   AMOUNT: ENDORSEMENTS NOT TO EXCEED
                          IN THE AGGREGATE — $

WHEREAS:

The surety of this Bond is The Mortgage Insurance Company of Canada, a company incorporated under the laws of Canada and duly authorized to transact the business of suretyship in the Province of Ontario (the "Surety");

Unless otherwise defined herein all terms used in this Bond have the meanings ascribed to them in the Construction Lien Act, 1983, as the same may be amended from time to time (the "Act");

The principal of this Bond is   (the "Principal"), the Owner from time to time of lands and premises to be made subject to the terms of this Bond (collectively the "Properties" and individually a "Property") pursuant to endorsements made to this Bond in the manner specified below who has entered into or will enter into certain written or verbal agreements with respect to certain Improvements to the Properties (the "Contracts"), details of which will be provided to the Surety prior to the execution by the Surety of each endorsement adding each Property to this Bond;

The obligee of this Bond is   (the "Obligee"), the holder of certain mortgages (collectively the "Mortgages" and individually a "Mortgage") details of which will be provided to the Surety by the Obligee prior to the execution by the Surety of each endorsement adding each Property to this Bond; and

The Act provides that under certain circumstances liens arising from Improvements shall have priority over certain mortgages to the extent of the deficiency in the Holdbacks required to be retained by Owners under Part IV of the Act.

NOW, THEREFORE, subject to the conditions hereof, including those on the reverse side of this Bond, the Principal and the Surety bind themselves, their heirs, administrators, executors, successors and assigns, jointly and severally, by this Bond and any endorsements issued hereunder to the Obligee with respect to each Property referred to in such endorsement in an amount equal to the lesser of:

   (A) the amount of the liability of the Surety with respect to such Property specified in such endorsement (inclusive of all legal costs and expenses); and

   (B) the total amount of all outstanding liens against such Property as settled by the Obligee with the approval of the Surety or as finally determined by the Court to have priority in accordance with the Act over the Mortgage registered against title to such Property as a result of deficiencies in the Holdbacks required to be retained by the Principal, together with all reasonable legal fees incurred by the Obligee in the defence or resolution of claims made by Lien Claimants asserting priority over the Mortgage registered against title to such Property as a result of a deficiency in the Holdbacks, provided that the liability of the Surety hereunder shall be reduced by and to the extent of:

(C) any monies and the value of other security held or controlled by the Obligee specifically for the purpose of protecting the priority of the Mortgage registered against title to such Property from any lien claims resulting out of any deficiencies in the Holdbacks;

(D) in the event the Property is sold by the Obligee following foreclosure, under power of sale, or otherwise, the amount by which the net sale proceeds with respect to any such sale exceed the amount then owing to the Obligee under the Mortgage registered against title to such sold Property; and

(E) any payments made to the Obligee by the Surety in good faith and in accordance with the provisions hereof.

This Bond may be extended to each Property to be made subject to the terms of this Bond by the issuance by the Surety of endorsements to this Bond provided, however, that any such endorsement shall only be effective upon the due execution of such endorsement by both the Principal and the Surety and the subsequent delivery of such endorsement to the Obligee. This Bond and any endorsements hereto shall only be amended by the due execution and delivery of a subsequent endorsement.

IN WITNESS WHEREOF the Principal and Surety have duly executed this Bond this day of   , 19   .

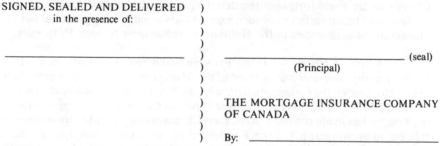

SIGNED, SEALED AND DELIVERED)
in the presence of:)
)
)
————————————————————   ) ——————————————————— (seal)
)   (Principal)
)
)
) THE MORTGAGE INSURANCE COMPANY
) OF CANADA
)
) By: ———————————————————
                                           Attorney in Fact

CONDITIONS OF THIS BOND

This Bond is subject to the following conditions:

1. <u>Information</u> — The Obligee shall make available to the Surety upon request copies of the reports of the Payment Certifier, if any, under any of the Contracts and any other information available to the Obligee relating to the Principal, the Contracts, the Mortgages, the Properties and any potential liability of the Surety under this Bond.

2. <u>Required Notices</u> — This Bond is an agreement of the utmost good faith between the parties hereto and, consequently, the Obligee shall deliver notice in writing and copies of all related documentation to the Surety at its address shown on the face hereof immediately (and in any event within five days) after:

(a) the Obligee has become aware of the registration of a claim for lien against title to any of the Properties;

(b) the Obligee has received a claim for lien with respect to any of the Properties;

(c) the Obligee has received notice that a person intends to make a claim for lien with respect to any of the Properties; or

(d) the Obligee has become aware of any information that constitutes a material change in the circumstances of the Principal, or any one or more of the Contracts, the Mortgages or the Properties or any potential liability of the Surety under this Bond.

3. Settlements — The Obligee, at the direction or with the consent of the Surety, shall use all reasonable efforts to enter into settlements with Lien Claimants of their claims for priority over any of the Mortgages arising as a result of an alleged deficiency in the Holdbacks, such settlements to be on such terms as may be approved by the Surety. Upon payment by the Surety to the Obligee of any settlement sum together with all reasonable legal fees incurred by the Obligee in the defence or resolution of the claims made by Lien Claimants, the liability of the Surety hereunder shall be reduced by the amount so paid.

4. Sale Proceeds — In the event any one or more of the Properties is sold by the Obligee following foreclosure, under power of sale, or otherwise and the Obligee realizes net sale proceeds in excess of the amount then owing to the Obligee under the Mortgages registered against title to such Properties, the Obligee shall retain sufficient of such excess funds to satisfy any potential but yet unascertained deficiencies in the Holdbacks with respect to such Properties.

5. Filing of Claims — If the Principal shall fail to pay any lien claims having priority over any one or more of the Mortgages by reason of a deficiency in any Holdbacks, the Obligee shall file with the Surety a claim for payment under this Bond within 30 days (or such longer period as the Surety may approve) after the Obligee has made payment to the Lien Claimants pursuant to any settlement referred to in paragraph 3 of this Bond, or if not so settled, when there has been a final determination by the Court of priority of such liens and a finding by the Court that there is a deficiency in the Holdbacks.

6. Payment of Claims — The Surety shall make payment to the Obligee in the amount of the Surety's liability hereunder within 30 days after receipt by the Surety of a duly completed valid claim of the Obligee on such forms as are satisfactory to the Surety accompanied by such other documentation with respect to the claim as is reasonably requested by the Surety.

7. Subrogation — Upon satisfaction at any time or times of the liabilities of the Surety hereunder in respect of any one of the Mortgages, the Surety shall be subrogated to the rights of the Obligee under such Mortgage but subordinated to the position of the Obligee and, in return for payment of the Obligee's claim hereunder, the Surety shall be entitled to demand and receive an express assignment of a subordinated interest in the Mortgage, any security therefor and any

proceedings arising thereunder in an amount equal to any payment made by the Surety hereunder in respect to such Mortgage.

8. <u>Limitation Period</u> — The Surety shall be released from its obligations to the Obligee with respect to any one claim hereunder unless the Obligee has instituted legal proceedings against the Surety with respect to such claim within one year after the Obligee was required, in accordance with paragraph 5, to file the claim with the Surety.

9. <u>Sale by Principal</u> — The Surety shall be liable to the Obligee in accordance with the terms of this Bond for any failure of the Principal to retain any required Holdbacks arising during the time the Principal owns any Property and, unless otherwise agreed to by the Surety, immediately upon the Principal ceasing to own any such Property (other than by virtue of a conveyance of the Property or a part thereof to an individual who intends to use the Property or the part conveyed to him as his personal residence) the Surety shall cease to be liable for any subsequent failure by any successor Owner of such conveyed property to retain the Holdbacks required by the Act.

10. <u>Release of Surety</u> — The Surety shall be released from its liability to the Obligee hereunder with respect to any Property if the Obligee, without the prior consent of the Surety, makes any material change in the terms of the Mortgage registered against title to such Property or the security therefor or any documentation related thereto or the method of making progress advances under the Mortgage from the terms, security, documentation and methods disclosed by the Obligee to the Surety prior to the execution of this Bond or any endorsements thereto by the Surety, it being hereby declared that the Surety has relied upon such information in issuing this Bond and such endorsements hereto.

11. <u>Term of Bond</u> — The liability of the Surety under this Bond with respect to each Property shall terminate at such time as the Contract with respect to such Property has been completed and the Principal is under no further obligation to retain the Holdbacks referred to in the Act with respect to such Contract.

12. <u>Assignment by Obligee</u> — The Obligee shall be entitled to assign the benefits of this Bond and any endorsements with respect to any Property as it applies to any Mortgage registered against title to such Property in conjunction with an absolute assignment of the Mortgage provided that the Obligee has obtained the prior written consent of the Surety.

13. <u>Successors and Assigns</u> — This Bond and all endorsements hereto shall enure to the benefit of and be binding upon the respective successors and permitted assigns of the Obligee, the Principal and the Surety.

14. <u>Interpretation</u> — Words importing the singular number include the plural and vice versa and words importing the neuter gender include the feminine and masculine gender. The division of this Bond and all endorsements herto into paragraphs and the insertion of headings are for convenience of reference only

and shall not affect the construction or interpretation of this Bond or any endorsements herto. This Bond and all endorsements hereto shall be interpreted in accordance with the laws of the Province of Ontario and shall for all purposes be deemed to be Ontario contracts. This Bond and all endorsements hereto shall only be effective upon the due execution thereof by both the Principal and the Surety and the subsequent delivery thereof to the Obligee.

CONSTRUCTION LIEN HOLDBACK DEFICIENCY BLANKET BOND ENDORSEMENT

Endorsement No: .... Amount Not To Exceed $..............

Attached to and forming part of Construction Lien Holdback Deficiency Blanket Bond No. ...., dated ...., (the "Bond") and executed by The Mortgage Insurance Company of Canada, as Surety, and ...., as Principal, in favour of .... , as Obligee.

In consideration of receipt of the premium paid by the Principal to the Surety, the Principal and the Surety hereby declare and agree:

1.   Property — The Bond shall extend to the following property:

....
....
....
....

(Municipal Address and Legal Description — If additional space required, add by way of a Schedule)

2.   Limitation of Liability — The amount of the liability of the Surety with respect to the above Property shall, for the purposes of Paragraph (A) on the face of the Bond, not exceed the sum of .... Dollars ($..................) of lawful money of Canada.

3.   Interpretation — The Bond and all prior endorsements, if any, as amended by this endorsement, shall be read together. Save as otherwise defined herein, all terms defined in the Bond and used herein shall have the meaning ascribed to them in the Bond. The conditions of the Bond, save as herein modified, shall continue to full force and effect.

IN WITNESS WHEREOF the Principal and Surety have duly executed this endorsement this .... day of ...., 19...

```
SIGNED, SEALED AND DELIVERED )
     in the presence of:       ) By: ...........................(seal)
                               )     (Principal)
                               )
                               ) THE MORTGAGE INSURANCE COMPANY
                               ) OF CANADA
                               )
_____) By: _____
                                      (Attorney in Fact)
```

Precedent No. 69

MINISTRY OF TRANSPORTATION AND COMMUNICATIONS CREDITORS PAYMENT ACT

NOTICE OF CLAIM

Contract No. ....

.... of ....
(Name of Creditor)   (Address of Creditor)

.... hereby gives notice under The Ministry of Transportation and Communications Creditors Payment Act, of a claim against ....

....
(name and address of contractor)

....
in respect of labour, materials or services used or reasonably required for use in the performance of a contract with The Ministry of Transportation and Communications, Ontario, for the construction, alteration, repair or maintenance of the following work:

1.   (here give a short description of the work) ....
        ....
        ....
        ....

2.   The nature of the claim is as follows: (here set out particulars of the labour, material or services supplied) ....
        ....
        ....
        ....
        ....

3.   The last day on which labour, material or services were provided was the .... day of .... 19 ....

4.   The amount of the claim is $ ....

Dated at .... this .... day of .... 19 ....

                                    ....
                                    (Signature of Creditor)

NOTE: This form is to be sent by registered mail to The Ministry of Transportation and Communications, Ontario, within **120** days from the time that the last work, etc. was done.

        Please forward to —
                Qualification Accountant,
                Financial Branch,
                Ministry of Transportation and Communications, Ontario,
                1201 Wilson Avenue,
                Downsview, Ontario, M3M 1J8

Appendix B

Construction Lien Act, 1983

AN ACT TO REVISE THE MECHANICS' LIEN ACT

HER MAJESTY, by and with the advice and consent of the Legislative Assembly of the Province of Ontario, enacts as follows:

1.—(1) In this Act, Interpretation

1. "action" means an action under Part VIII;

2. "construction trade newspaper" means a newspaper having circulation generally throughout Ontario, that is published no less frequently than on all days except Saturdays and holidays, and in which calls for tender on construction contracts are customarily published, and that is primarily devoted to the publication of matters of concern to the construction industry;

3. "contract" means the contract between the owner and the contractor, and includes any amendment to that contract;

4. "contractor" means a person contracting with or employed directly by the owner or his agent to supply services or materials to an improvement;

5. "court" means the Supreme Court of Ontario;

6. "Crown" includes a Crown agency to which the *Crown Agency Act* applies; R.S.O. 1980, c. 106

7. "holdback" means the 10 per cent of the value of the services or materials supplied under a contract or subcontract required to be withheld from payment by Part IV;

8. "improvement" means,

    i. any alteration, addition or repair to, or

    ii. any construction, erection or installation on,

any land, and includes the demolition or removal of any building, structure or works or part thereof, and "improved" has a corresponding meaning;

9. "interest in the premises" means an estate or interest of any nature, and includes a statutory right given or reserved to the Crown to enter any lands or premises belonging to any person or public authority for the purpose of doing any work, construction, repair or maintenance in, upon, through, over or under any lands or premises;

10. "land" includes any building, structure or works affixed to the land, or an appurtenance to any of them, but does not include the improvement;

11. "lien claimant" means a person having a preserved or perfected lien;

12. "materials" means every kind of movable property,

    i. that becomes, or is intended to become, part of the improvement, or that is used directly in the making of the improvement, or that is used to facilitate directly the making of the improvement,

    ii. that is equipment rented without an operator for use in the making of the improvement;

13. "mortgage" includes a charge and "mortgagee" includes a chargee;

14. "municipality" means a municipality as defined in the *Municipal Affairs Act* or a metropolitan, regional or district municipality, or a local board thereof;

R.S.O. 1980,
c. 303

15. "owner" means any person, including the Crown, having an interest in a premises at whose request and,

    i. upon whose credit, or

    ii. on whose behalf, or

    iii. with whose privity or consent, or

    iv. for whose direct benefit,

    an improvement is made to the premises;

16. "payer" means the owner, contractor or subcontractor who is liable to pay for the materials or services supplied to an improvement under a contract or subcontract;

17. "payment certifier" means an architect, engineer or any other person upon whose certificate payments are made under a contract or subcontract;

18. "person having a lien" includes both a lien claimant and a person with an unpreserved lien;

19. "premises" includes,

    i. the improvement,

    ii. all materials supplied to the improvement, and

    iii. the land occupied by the improvement, or enjoyed therewith, or the land upon or in respect of which the improvement was done or made;

20. "price" means the contract or subcontract price,

    i. agreed upon between the parties, or

    ii. where no specific price has been agreed upon between them, the actual value of the services or materials that have been supplied to the improvement under the contract or subcontract;

21. "services or materials" includes both services and materials;

22. "subcontract" means any agreement between the contractor and a subcontractor, or between two or more subcontractors, relating to the supply of services or materials to the improvement and includes any amendment to that agreement;

23. "subcontractor" means a person not contracting with or employed directly by the owner or his agent but who supplies services or materials to the improvement under an agreement with the contractor or under him with another subcontractor;

24. "suffers damages as a result" means suffers damages that could be reasonably foreseen to result;

25. "supply of services" means any work done or service performed upon or in respect of an improvement, and includes,

i. the rental of equipment with an operator, and

ii. where the making of the planned improvement is not commenced, the supply of a design, plan, drawing or specification that in itself enhances the value of the owner's interest in the land,

and a corresponding expression has a corresponding meaning;

26. "wages" means the money earned by a worker for work done by time or as piece work, and includes all monetary supplementary benefits, whether provided for by statute, contract or collective bargaining agreement;

27. "worker" means a person employed for wages in any kind of labour;

28. "workers' trust fund" means any trust fund maintained in whole or in part on behalf of any worker on an improvement and into which any monetary supplementary benefit is payable as wages for work done by the worker in respect of the improvement;

29. "written notice of a lien" includes a claim for lien and any written notice given by a lien claimant that,

i. identifies his payer and identifies the premises, and

ii. states the amount that he has not been paid and is owed to him by his payer.

When materials supplied

(2) For the purposes of this Act, materials are supplied to an improvement when they are,

(a) placed on the land on which the improvement is being made;

(b) placed upon land designated by the owner or his agent that is in the immediate vicinity of the premises, but placing materials on the land so designated does not, of itself, make that land subject to a lien; or

(c) in any event, incorporated into or used in making or facilitating directly the making of the improvement.

Idem

(3) A contractor or subcontractor to whom materials are supplied and who designates land under clause (2) (b) is deemed to be the

owner's agent for that purpose, unless the person supplying the materials has actual notice to the contrary.

2.—(1) For the purposes of this Act, a contract is substantially performed,

    (a) when the improvement to be made under that contract or a substantial part thereof is ready for use or is being used for the purposes intended; and

    (b) when the improvement to be made under that contract is capable of completion or, where there is a known defect, correction, at a cost of not more than,

        (i) 3 per cent of the first $500,000 of the contract price,

        (ii) 2 per cent of the next $500,000 of the contract price, and

        (iii) 1 per cent of the balance of the contract price.

(2) For the purposes of this Act, where the improvement or a substantial part thereof is ready for use or is being used for the purposes intended and the remainder of the improvement cannot be completed expeditiously for reasons beyond the control of the contractor or, where the owner and the contractor agree not to complete the improvement expeditiously, the price of the services or materials remaining to be supplied and required to complete the improvement shall be deducted from the contract price in determining substantial performance.

(3) For the purposes of this Act, a contract shall be deemed to be completed and services or materials shall be deemed to be last supplied to the improvement when the price of completion, correction of a known defect or last supply is not more than the lesser of,

    (a) 1 per cent of the contract price; and

    (b) $1,000.

PART I

GENERAL

3.—(1) Subject to section 16 (where lien does not attach to the premises), this Act binds the Crown but does not apply in respect of a

R.S.O. 1980, c. 290

contract as defined in the *Ministry of Transportation and Communications Creditors Payment Act*, and to which that Act applies.

Non-application of R.S.O. 1980, c. 393, s. 7

(2) Section 7 of the *Proceedings Against the Crown Act* does not apply in respect of an action against the Crown under this Act.

Architect does not have lien R.S.O. 1980, c. 26

(3) Despite subsection 14(1), an architect or the holder of a certificate of practice under the *Architects Act* does not have a lien.

No waiver of rights

4. An agreement by any person who supplies services or materials to an improvement that this Act does not apply to him or that the remedies provided by it are not available for his benefit is void.

Contracts to conform

5. Every contract or subcontract related to an improvement is deemed to be amended in so far as is necessary to be in conformity with this Act.

Minor irregularities

6. No certificate, declaration or claim for lien is invalidated by reason only of a failure to comply strictly with subsection 32 (2) or (5), subsection 33 (1) or subsection 34 (5), unless in the opinion of the court a person has been prejudiced thereby, and then only to the extent of the prejudice suffered.

PART II

TRUST PROVISIONS

Owner's trust, amounts received for financing a trust

7.—(1) All amounts received by an owner, other than the Crown or a municipality, that are to be used in the financing of the improvement, including any amount that is to be used in the payment of the purchase price of the land and the payment or prior encumbrances, constitute, subject to the payment of the purchase price of the land and prior encumbrances, a trust fund for the benefit of the contractor.

Amounts certified as payable

(2) Where amounts become payable under a contract to a contractor by the owner on a certificate of a payment certifier, an amount that is equal to an amount so certified that is in the owner's hands or received by him at any time thereafter constitutes a trust fund for the benefit of the contractor.

Where substantial performance certified

(3) Where the substantial performance of a contract has been certified, or has been declared by the court, an amount that is equal to the unpaid price of the substantially performed portion of the contract that is in the owner's hands or is received by him at any time thereafter constitutes a trust fund for the benefit of the contractor.

(4) The owner is the trustee of the trust fund created by subsection (1), (2) or (3), and he shall not appropriate or convert any part of a fund to his own use or to any use inconsistent with the trust until the contractor is paid all amounts related to the improvement owed to him by the owner.

8.—(1) All amounts,

    (a) owing to a contractor or subcontractor, whether or not due or payable; or

    (b) received by a contractor or subcontractor,

on account of the contract or subcontract price of an improvement constitute a trust fund for the benefit of the subcontractors and other persons who have supplied services or materials to the improvement who are owed amounts by the contractor or subcontractor.

(2) The contractor or subcontractor is the trustee of the trust fund created by subsection (1) and he shall not appropriate or convert any part of the fund to his own use or to any use inconsistent with the trust until all subcontractors and other persons who supply services or materials to the improvement are paid all amounts related to the improvement owed to them by him.

9.—(1) Where the owner's interest in a premises is sold by the owner, an amount equal to,

    (a) the value of the consideration received by the owner as a result of the sale,

less,

    (b) the reasonable expenses arising from the sale and the amount, if any, paid by the vendor to discharge any existing mortgage indebtedness on the premises,

constitutes a trust fund for the benefit of the contractor.

(2) The former owner is the trustee of the trust created by sub-section (1), and he shall not appropriate or convert any part of the trust property to his own use or to any use inconsistent with the trust until the contractor is paid all amounts owed to him related to the improvement.

10. Subject to Part IV (holdbacks), every payment by a trustee to a person he is liable to pay for services or materials supplied to the improvement discharges the trust of the trustee making the payment and his obligations and liability as trustee to all beneficiaries of the trust to the extent of the payment made by him.

Where trust funds may be reduced

11.—(1) Subject to Part IV, a trustee who pays in whole or in part for the supply of services or materials to an improvement out of money that is not subject to a trust under this Part may retain from trust funds an amount equal to that paid by him without being in breach of the trust.

Application of trust funds to discharge loan

(2) Subject to Part IV, where a trustee pays in whole or in part for the supply of services or materials to an improvement out of money that is loaned to him, trust funds may be applied to discharge the loan to the extent that the lender's money was so used by the trustee, and the application of trust money does not constitute a breach of the trust.

Set-off by trustee

12. Subject to Part IV, a trustee may, without being in breach of trust, retain from trust funds an amount that, as between himself and the person he is liable to pay under a contract or subcontract related to the improvement, is equal to the balance in the trustee's favour of all outstanding debts, claims or damages, whether or not related to the improvement.

Liability for breach of trust by corporation

13.—(1) In addition to the persons who are otherwise liable in an action for breach of trust under this Part,

(a) every director or officer of a corporation; and

(b) any person, including an employee or agent of the corporation, who has effective control of a corporation or its relevant activities,

who assents to, or acquiesces in, conduct that he knows or reasonably ought to know amounts to breach of trust by the corporation is liable for the breach of trust.

Effective control of corporation

(2) The question of whether a person has effective control of a corporation or its relevant activities is one of fact and in determining this the court may disregard the form of any transaction and the separate corporate existence of any participant.

Joint and several liability

(3) Where more than one person is found liable or has admitted liability for a particular breach of trust under this Part, those persons are jointly and severally liable.

Contribution

(4) A person who is found liable, or who has admitted liability, for a particular breach of a trust under this Part is entitled to recover contribution from any other person also liable for the breach in such amount as will result in equal contribution by all parties liable for the

breach unless the court considers such apportionment would not be fair and, in that case, the court may direct such contribution or indemnity as the court considers appropriate in the circumstances.

PART III

THE LIEN

14.—(1) A person who supplies services or materials to an improvement for an owner, contractor or subcontractor, has a lien upon the interest of the owner in the premises improved for the price of those services or materials.

Creation of lien

(2) No person is entitled to a lien for any interest on the amount owed to him in respect of the services or materials that have been supplied by him, but nothing in this subsection affects any right that he may otherwise have to recover that interest.

No lien for interest

15. A person's lien arises and takes effect when he first supplies his services or materials to the improvement.

When lien arises

16.—(1) A lien does not attach to the interest of the Crown in a premises.

Interest of Crown

(2) Where an improvement is made to a premises in which the Crown has an interest, but the Crown is not an owner within the meaning of this Act, the lien may attach to the interest of any other person in that premises.

Interest of person other than Crown

(3) Where the Crown is the owner of a premises within the meaning of this Act, or where the premises is,

Where lien does not attach to premises

    (a) a public street or highway owned by a municipality; or

    (b) a railway right-of-way,

the lien does not attach to the premises but constitutes a charge as provided in section 21, and the provisions of this Act shall have effect without requiring the registration of a claim for lien against the premises.

17.—(1) The lien of a person is limited to the amount owing to him in relation to the improvement and, subject to Part IV (holdbacks), it is further limited to the least amount owed in relation to the improvement by a payer to the contractor or to any subcontractor whose contract or subcontract was in whole or in part performed by the supply of services or materials giving rise to the lien.

Limitation on value of lien

Idem

(2) Subject to Part IV, the total value of the liens of all members of a class, as defined in section 81, is limited to the least amount owed in relation to the improvement by a payer to the contractor or to any subcontractor whose contract or subcontract was in whole or in part performed by the supply of services or materials made by the members of the class.

Set-off

(3) Subject to Part IV, in determining the amount of a lien under subsection (1) or (2), there may be taken into account the amount that is, as between a payer and the person he is liable to pay, equal to the balance in the payer's favour of all outstanding debts, claims or damages, whether or not related to the improvement.

Public highway, liability of municipality re

(4) Despite subsection (1), where land is dedicated to a municipality as a public street or highway and an improvement is made to the land at the written request of, or under an agreement with, the municipality, but not at its expense, the municipality shall nevertheless, on default of payment by the proper payer, be liable to the value of the holdbacks under Part IV that would have been required were the improvement made at the expense of the municipality, and the procedure for making a claim under this subsection shall be the same as for enforcing a claim for lien against a municipality in respect of a public street or highway.

Joint or common interests

18. Where the interest of the owner in the premises is held jointly or in common with another person who knew or ought reasonably to have known of the making of the improvement, the joint or common interest in the premises of that person is also subject to the lien unless the contractor receives actual notice, before the supply of services or materials to the improvement is commenced, that the person having the joint or common interest assumes no responsibility for the improvement to be made.

Where owner's interest leasehold

19.—(1) Where the interest of the owner to which the lien attaches is leasehold, the interest of the landlord shall also be subject to the lien to the same extent as the interest of the owner if the contractor gives the landlord written notice of the improvement to be made, unless the landlord, within fifteen days of receiving the notice from the contractor, gives the contractor written notice that the landlord assumes no responsibility for the improvement to be made.

Forfeiture or termination of lease, effect of

(2) No forfeiture of a lease to, or termination of a lease by, a landlord, except for non-payment of rent, deprives any person having a lien against the leasehold of the benfit of his lien.

Notice to lien claimants

(3) Where a landlord intends to enforce forfeiture or terminate a lease of the premises because of non-payment of rent, and there is a claim for lien registered against the premises in the proper land

registry office, the landlord shall give notice in writing of his intention to enforce forfeiture or terminate the lease and of the amount of the unpaid rent to each person who has registered a claim for lien against the premises.

(4) A person receiving notice under subsection (3) may, within ten days thereafter, pay to the landlord the amount of the unpaid rent, and the amount so paid may be added by that person to his claim for lien.

Payment of unpaid rent

20. Where an owner enters into a single contract for improvements on more than one premises owned by him, any person supplying services or materials under that contract, or under a subcontract under that contract, may choose to have his lien follow the form of the contract and be a general lien against each of those premises for the price of all services and materials he supplied to all the premises.

General lien

21. The lien of a person is a charge upon the holdbacks required to be retained by Part IV, and subject to subsection 17 (3), any additional amount owed in relation to the improvement by a payer to the contractor or to any subcontractor whose contract or subcontract was in whole or in part performed by the supply of services or materials giving rise to the lien.

Lien a charge

PART IV

HOLDBACKS

22.—(1) Each payer upon a contract or subcontract under which a lien may arise shall retain a holdback equal to 10 per cent of the price of the services or materials as they arc actually supplied under the contract or subcontract until all liens that may be claimed against the holdback have expired as provided in Part V, or have been satisfied, discharged or provided for under section 44 (payment into court).

Basic holdback

(2) Where the contract has been certified or declared to be substantially performed but services or materials remain to be supplied to complete the contract, the payer upon the contract, or a subcontract, under which a lien may arise shall retain, from the date certified or declared to be the date of substantial performance of the contract, a separate holdback equal to 10 per cent of the price of the remaining services or materials as they are actually supplied under the contract or subcontract, until all liens that may be claimed against the holdback have expired as provided in Part V, or have been satisfied, discharged or provided for under section 44.

Separate holdback for finishing work

When
obligation to
retain applies

(3) The obligation to retain the holdbacks under subsections (1) and (2) applies irrespective of whether the contract or subcontract provides for partial payments or payment on completion.

Personal
liability of
owner

23.—(1) An owner is personally liable to those lien claimants who have valid liens against his interest in the premises to the extent of the holdbacks that he is required to retain under this Part.

How
determined

(2) The personal liability of an owner under subsection (1) may only be determined in an action under this Act.

Payments
that may be
made

24.—(1) A payer may, without jeopardy, make payments on a contract or subcontract up to 90 per cent of the price of the services and materials that have been supplied under that contract or subcontract unless, prior to making payment, the payer has received written notice of a lien.

Idem

(2) Where a payer has received written notice of a lien and has retained, in addition to the holdbacks required by this Part, an amount sufficient to satisfy the lien, the payer may, without jeopardy, make payment on a contract or subcontract up to 90 per cent of the price of the services and materials that have been supplied under that contract or subcontract, less the amount retained.

Payment
where
subcontract
certified
complete

25. Where a subcontract has been certified complete under section 33, each payer upon the contract and any subcontract may, without jeopardy, make payment reducing the holdbacks required by this Part to the extent of the amount of holdback he has retained in respect of the completed subcontract, where all liens in respect of the completed subcontract have expired as provided in Part V, or have been satisfied, discharged or provided for under section 44 (payment into court).

Payment of
basic holdback

26. Each payer upon the contract or a subcontract may, without jeopardy, make payment of the holdback he is required to retain by subsection 22 (1) (basic holdback), so as to discharge all claims in respect of that holdback, where all liens that may be claimed against that holdback have expired as provided in Part V, or have been satisfied, discharged or provided for under section 44.

Payment of
holdback for
finishing work

27. Each payer upon the contract or a subcontract may, without jeopardy, make payment of the holdback he is required to retain by subsection 22 (2) (holdback for finishing work), so as to discharge all claims in respect of that holdback, where all liens that may be claimed against that holdback have expired as provided in Part V, or have been satisfied, discharged or provided for under section 44.

Direct
payment
to person
having lien

28. Where an owner, contractor or subcontractor makes a payment without obligation to do so to any person having a lien for or on account of any amount owing to that person for services or materials supplied to the improvement and gives written notice of the payment or his intention to pay to the proper payer of that person, the payment shall be deemed to be a payment by the owner, contractor or subcontractor to the proper payer of that person, but no such payment reduces the amount of the holdback required to be retained under this Part or reduces the amount that must be retained in response to a written notice of lien given by a person other than the person to whom payment is made.

29. Payments made in accordance with this Part operate as a discharge of the lien to the extent of the amount paid.

Discharge, extent of

30. Where the contractor or a subcontractor defaults in the performance of his contract or subcontract, a holdback shall not be applied by any payer toward obtaining services or materials in substitution for those that were to have been supplied by the person in default, nor in payment or satisfaction of any claim against the person in default, until all liens that may be claimed against that holdback have expired as provided in Part V, or have been satisfied, discharged or provided for under section 44 (payment into court).

How holdback not to be applied

PART V

EXPIRY, PRESERVATION AND PERFECTION OF LIENS

31.—(1) Unless preserved under section 34, the liens arising from the supply of services or materials to an improvement expire as provided in this section.

Expiry of liens

(2) Subject to subsection (4), the lien of a contractor,

Contractor's liens

(a) for services or materials supplied to an improvement on or before the date certified or declared to be the date of the substantial performance of the contract, expires at the conclusion of the forty-five day period next following the occurrence of the earlier of,

(i) the date on which a copy of the certificate or declaration of the substantial performance of the contract is published, as provided in section 32, and

(ii) the date the contract is completed or abandoned; and

(b) for services or materials supplied to the improvement where there is no certification or declaration of the substantial performance of the contract, or for services or materials supplied to the improvement after the date certified or declared to be the date of substantial performance, expires at the conclusion of the forty-five day period next following the occurrence of the earlier of,

(i) the date the contract is completed, and

(ii) the date the contract is abandoned.

Liens of
other persons

(3) Subject to subsection (4), the lien of any other person,

    (a) for services or materials supplied to an improvement on or before the date certified or declared to be the date of the substantial performance of the contract, expires at the conclusion of the forty-five day period next following the occurrence of the earliest of,

        (i) the date on which a copy of the certificate or declaration of the substantial performance of the contract is published, as provided in section 32, and

        (ii) the date on which he last supplies services or materials to the improvement, and

        (iii) the date a subcontract is certified to be completed under section 33, where the services or materials were supplied under or in respect of that subcontract; and

    (b) for services or materials supplied to the improvement where there is no certification or declaration of the substantial performance of the contract, or for services or materials supplied to the improvement after the date certified or declared to be the date of the substantial performance of the contract, expires at the conclusion of the forty-five day period next following the occurrence of the earlier of,

        (i) the date on which he last supplied services or materials to the improvement, and

        (ii) the date a subcontract is certified to be completed under section 33, where the services or materials were supplied under or in respect of that subcontract.

Separate liens
when ongoing
supply

(4) Where a person has supplied services or materials to an improvement on or before the date certified or declared to be the date of the substantial performance of the contract and has also supplied, or is to supply, services or materials after that date, his lien in respect of the services or materials supplied on or before the date of substantial performance expires without affecting any lien that he may have for the supply of services or materials after that date.

(5) Where a person who has supplied services or materials under a contract or subcontract makes a declaration in the prescribed form declaring, Declaration of last supply

(a) the date on which he last supplied services or materials under that contract or subcontract; and

(b) that he will not supply any further services or materials under that contract or subcontract,

then the facts so stated shall be deemed to be true against the person making the declaration.

32.—(1) The following rules govern the certification and declaration of the substantial performance of a contract: Rules governing certification or declaration of substantial performance

1. On the application of the contractor, the payment certifier, or if there is no payment certifier, the owner and the contractor jointly shall determine whether a contract has been substantially performed in accordance with section 2, and where he or they so determine, shall certify the substantial performance of the contract by signing a certificate in the prescribed form.

2. The payment certifier or the owner and the contractor jointly, as the case may be, shall set out in the certificate the date on which the contract was substantially performed.

3. The date set out in the certificate as the date on which the contract was substantially performed is deemed for the purpose of this Act to be the date on which that event occurred.

4. Where the payment certifier certifies the substantial performance of a contract he shall within seven days of the day the certificate is signed give a copy of the certificate to the owner and to the contractor.

5. The contractor shall publish a copy of the certificate once in a construction trade newspaper.

6. Where the contractor does not publish a copy of the certificate within seven days of receiving a copy of the certificate signed by the payment certifier or, where there is no payment certifier, signed by the owner, any person may publish a copy of the certificate.

7. Where there is a failure or refusal to certify substantial performance of the contract within a reasonable time, any

person may apply to the court, and the court, upon being satisfied that the contract is substantially performed, and upon such terms as to costs or otherwise as it considers fit, may declare that the contract has been substantially performed, and the declaration has the same force and effect as a certificate of substantial performance of the contract.

8. Unless the court otherwise orders, the day the declaration is made shall be deemed to be the date the contract was substantially performed.

9. The person who applied to the court shall publish a copy of the declaration of substantial performance once in a construction trade newspaper.

10. For the purposes of this Part, a certificate or declaration of the substantial performance of a contract has no effect until a copy of the certificate or declaration is published.

Contents of
certificate

(2) Every certificate or declaration made or given under this section shall include,

(a) the name and address for service of the owner and of the contractor;

(b) the name and address of the payment certifier, where there is one;

(c) a short description of the improvement;

(d) the date on which the contract was substantially performed;

(e) where the lien attaches to the premises, a concise description containing a reference to lot and plan or instrument registration number sufficient to identify the premises; and

(f) the street address, if any, of the premises.

Liability for
refusal to
certify

(3) Any person who is required by this section to make a determination of the substantial performance of a contract, and who after receiving an application fails or refuses within a reasonable time to certify the substantial performance of the contract, even though there is no reasonable doubt that the contract has, in fact, been substantially performed, is liable to anyone who suffers damages as a result.

(4) A payment certifier who fails to comply with paragraph 4 of subsection 32 (1) is liable to anyone who suffers damages as a result.

(5) A construction trade newspaper shall publish upon commercially reasonable terms copies of certificates or declarations of substantial performance in the prescribed form and manner.

33.—(1) Upon the request of the contractor, the payment certifier on the contract, or the owner and the contractor jointly, may determine whether a subcontract has been completed, and where he or they so determine, he or they may certify the completion of the subcontract in the prescribed form.

(2) Where a subcontract is certified to be completed, the subcontract shall be deemed to have been completed on the date of certification.

(3) If services or materials are supplied to the improvement under or in respect of a subcontract after the date the subcontract is certified to be completed, those services or materials shall be deemed to have been last supplied on the date of certification.

(4) Within seven days of the date the subcontract is certified to be completed, the payment certifier or the owner and the contractor, as the case may be, shall give a copy of the certificate,

(a) to the subcontractor whose subcontract has been certified as complete; and

(b) to the owner and the contractor, where certification is by the payment certifier.

34.—(1) A lien may be preserved during the supplying of services or materials or at any time before it expires,

(a) where the lien attaches to the premises, by the registration in the proper land registry office of a claim for lien on the title of the premises in accordance with this Part; and

(b) where the lien does not attach to the premises, by giving to the owner a copy of the claim for lien together with the affidavit of verification required by subsection (6).

(2) Where a claim for lien is in respect of a public street or highway owned by a municipality, the copy of the claim for lien and affidavit shall be given to the clerk of the municipality.

Premises
owned by
Crown

(3) Where the owner of the premises is the Crown, the copy of the claim for lien and affidavit shall be given to the office prescribed by regulation, or where no office has been prescribed, to the ministry or Crown agency for whom the improvement is made.

Railway
right-of-way

(4) Where the premises is a railway right-of-way, the copy of the claim for lien and affidavit shall be given to the manager or any person apparently in charge of any office of the railway in Ontario.

Contents of
claim for lien

(5) Every claim for lien shall set out,

(a) the name and address for service of the person claiming the lien and the name and address of the owner of the premises and of the person for whom the services or materials were supplied and the time within which those services or materials were supplied;

(b) a short description of the services or materials that were supplied;

(c) the contract price or subcontract price;

(d) the amount claimed in respect of services or materials that have been supplied; and

(e) a description of the premises,

R.S.O. 1980,
cc. 230, 445

(i) where the lien attaches to the premises, sufficient for registration under the *Land Titles Act* or the *Registry Act*, as the case may be, or

(ii) where the lien does not attach to the premises, being the address or other identification of the location of the premises.

Affidavit of
verification

(6) A claim for lien shall be verified by an affidavit of the person claiming the lien, including a trustee of the workers' trust fund where subsection 83 (2) applies, or of an agent or assignee of the claimant who has informed himself of the facts set out in the claim, and the affidavit of the agent or assignee shall state that he believes those facts to be true.

Preservation
of general
lien

(7) Subject to subsection 44 (4) (apportionment), a general lien shall be preserved against each of the premises that the person having the lien desires the lien to continue to apply against, and the claim against each premises may be for the price of the services or materials that have been supplied to all the premises.

(8) Any number of persons having liens upon the same premises may unite in a claim for lien, but where more than one lien is included in one claim, each person's lien shall be verified by affidavit as required by subsection (6). Who may join in claim

35. In addition to any other ground on which he may be liable, any person who preserves a claim for lien or who gives written notice of a lien, Liability for exaggerated claim, etc.

    (a) for an amount which he knows or ought to know is grossly in excess of the amount which he is owed; or

    (b) where he knows or ought to know that he does not have a lien,

is liable to any person who suffers damages as a result.

36.—(1) A lien may not be perfected unless it is preserved. What liens may be perfected

(2) A lien that has been preserved expires unless it is perfected prior to the end of the forty-five day period next following the last day, under section 31, on which the lien could have been preserved. Expiry of preserved lien

(3) A lien claimant perfects his preserved lien, How lien perfected

    (a) where the lien attaches to the premises, when he commences an action to enforce his lien and, except where an order to vacate the registration of his lien is made, he registers a certificate of action in the prescribed form on the title of the premises; or

    (b) where the lien does not attach to the premises, when he commences an action to enforce his lien.

(4) A preserved lien becomes perfected by sheltering under a lien perfected by another lien claimant in respect of the same improvement in accordance with the following rules: Rules re sheltering

    1. The preserved lien of a lien claimant is perfected by sheltering under the perfected lien of another lien claimant in respect of the same improvement where,

        i. the lien of that other lien claimant was a subsisting perfected lien at the time when the lien of the lien claimant was preserved, or

        ii. the lien of that other lien claimant is perfected in accordance with clause (3) (a) or (b) between the time when the lien of the lien claimant was preserved and the time that the lien of the lien claimant would have expired under subsection (2).

2. The validity of the perfection of a sheltered lien does not depend upon the validity, proper preservation or perfection of the lien under which it is sheltered.

3. A sheltered claim for lien is perfected only as to the defendants and the nature of the relief claimed in the statement of claim under which it is sheltered.

4. Upon notice given by a defendant named in a statement of claim, any lien claimant whose lien is sheltered under that statement of claim shall provide the defendant with further particulars of his claim or of any fact alleged in his claim for lien.

General lien

(5) Subject to subsection 44 (4) (apportionment), a preserved general lien that attaches to the premises shall be perfected against each premises to which the person having the lien desires the lien to continue to apply.

Expiry of perfected lien

37.—(1) A perfected lien expires where,

(a) no day is fixed under section 62 for the trial of an action in which that lien may be realized; or

(b) an action in which that lien may be realized is not set down for trial,

within two years of the date of the commencement of the action which perfected that lien.

Application under s. 46

(2) Where a lien has expired under subsection (1), an application may be made under section 46.

Saving other rights

38. The expiration of a lien under this Act shall not affect any other legal or equitable right or remedy otherwise available to the person whose lien has expired.

PART VI

RIGHT TO INFORMATION

Right to information;

39.—(1) Any person having a lien or who is the beneficiary of a trust under Part II or who is a mortgagee may, at any time, by written request, require information to be provided within a reasonable time, not to exceed twenty-one days, as follows:

1. By the owner or contractor, with, from owner or contractor

   i. the names of the parties to the contract,

   ii. the contract price,

   iii. the state of accounts between the owner and the contractor, and

   iv. a copy of any labour and material payment bond in respect of the contract posted by the contractor with the owner.

2. By the contractor or a subcontractor, with, from contractor or subcontractor

   i. the names of the parties to a subcontract,

   ii. the state of accounts between the contractor and a subcontractor or between a subcontractor and another subcontractor,

   iii. a statement of whether there is a provision in a subcontract providing for certification of the subcontract,

   iv. a statement of whether a subcontract has been certified as complete, and

   v. a copy of any labour and material payment bond posted by a subcontractor with the contractor or by a subcontractor with another subcontractor.

(2) Any person having a lien or any beneficiary of a trust under Part II may, at any time, by written request, require a mortgagee or unpaid vendor to provide him within a reasonable time, not to exceed twenty-one days, with, from mortgagee or unpaid vendor

   (a) sufficient details concerning any mortgage on the premises to enable the person who requests the information to determine whether the mortgage was taken by the mortgagee for the purposes of financing the making of the improvement;

   (b) a statement showing the amount advanced under the mortgage, the dates of those advances, and any arrears in payment including any arrears in the payment of interest; or

   (c) a statement showing the amount secured under the agreement of purchase and sale and any arrears in payment including any arrears in the payment of interest.

by trustee or workers' trust fund

(3) The trustee of a workers' trust fund may at any time by written request require any contractor or subcontractor to permit him, within a reasonable time after making the request, not to exceed twenty-one days, to inspect the payroll records of all workers who are beneficiaries of the fund, and who have supplied labour to the making of the improvement, and who are employed by the contractor or the subcontractor.

respecting publication of certificate of substantial performance

(4) A contractor shall, upon written request whenever made to him by any person, within a reasonable time furnish in writing to the person the date of publication and the name of the construction trade newspaper in which a copy of a certificate of substantial performance has been published under subsection 32 (1).

Liability for failure to provide information

(5) Where a person, who is required under subsection (1), (2), (3) or (4) to provide information or access to information, does not provide the information or access to information as required or knowingly or negligently mis-states that information, he is liable to the person who made the request for any damages sustained by reason thereof.

Order by court to comply with request

(6) Upon motion, the court may at any time, whether or not an action has been commenced, order a person to comply with a request that has been made to him under this section and when making the order, the court may make any order as to costs as it considers appropriate in the circumstances, including an order for the payment of costs on a solicitor-and-client basis.

Cross-examination on claim for lien

40.—(1) Any person who has verified a claim for lien that has been preserved is liable to be cross-examined without an order on the claim for lien at any time, irrespective of whether an action has been commenced.

Who may participate

(2) There shall be only one examination under subsection (1), but the contractor, the payer of the lien claimant, and every person named in the claim for lien who has an interest in the premises are entitled to participate therein.

Notice

(3) Any person intending to examine a person under subsection (1) shall give at least seven days notice of the examination specifying the time and place for the examination to,

(a) the person to be examined or his solicitor;

(b) every other person named in the claim for lien as having an interest in the premises;

(c) the contractor; and

(d) the payer of the lien claimant.

(4) The Supreme Court Rules of Practice pertaining to examinations apply, with necessary modifications, to cross-examinations under this section.

Application of rules of practice

PART VII

DISCHARGE OF PRESERVED OR PERFECTED LIENS

Discharge of lien claim by release

41.—(1) A preserved or perfected lien may be discharged,

(a) where the lien attaches to the premises, by the registration of a release in the prescribed form on the title to the premises and the release shall, except where the lien claimant is a corporation, be supported by an affidavit of execution; or

(b) where the lien does not attach to the premises, by giving a release in the prescribed form to the owner, in the manner set out in section 34 for the giving of copies of the claim for lien.

(2) A written notice of a lien may be withdrawn by giving a withdrawal in writing to the person to whom the written notice of a lien was given, and a payer given the withdrawal shall, in respect of the operation of subsection 24 (2), be in the same position as if the written notice of a lien had never been given.

Withdrawal of notice of lien

42. A preserved or perfected general lien may be discharged against any one or more of the premises that are subject to it, without affecting its application to any other premises to which it applies, by the registration of a release in the prescribed form on the title to the premises released.

Discharge of general lien

43. A preserved or perfected lien may be postponed in favour of the interest of another person in the premises by the registration on the title to the premises of a notice of postponement in the prescribed form, and in that case, subsection 80 (8) applies (priorities in event of postponement).

Postponement of lien claim

44.—(1) Upon the motion of any person, without notice to any other person, the court shall make an order vacating,

Vacating lien by payment into court; without notice

(a) where the lien attaches to the premises, the registration of a claim for lien and any certificate of action in respect of that lien; or

    (b) where the lien does not attach to the premises, the claim for lien,

where the person bringing the motion pays into court, or posts security in an amount equal to, the total of,

    (c) the full amount claimed as owing in the claim for lien; and

    (d) the lesser of $50,000 or 25 per cent of the amount described in clause (c), as security for costs.

on payment in of reasonable amount

(2) Upon the motion of any person, the court may make an order vacating the registration of a claim for lien, and any certificate of action in respect of that lien, upon the payment into court or the posting of security of an amount that the court determines to be reasonable in the circumstances to satisfy the lien.

Where lien does not attach to premises

(3) Where the lien does not attach to the premises, the court may make an order, upon the motion of any person, vacating a claim for lien given to the owner, upon the payment into court or the posting of security of an amount that the court determines to be reasonable in the circumstances to satisfy the lien.

When general lien

(4) Where a motion is made to vacate the registration of a general lien against one or more of the premises subject to that lien, the court may apportion the general lien between the premises in respect of which the application is made and all other premises that are subject to the lien.

Reduction of amount paid into court

(5) Where an amount has been paid into court or security has been posted with the court under this section, the court, upon notice to such persons as it may require, may order where it is appropriate to do so,

    (a) the reduction of the amount paid into court, and the payment of any part of the amount paid into court to the person entitled; or

    (b) the reduction of the amount of security posted with the court, and the delivery up of the security posted with the court for cancellation or substitution, as the case may be.

Lien a charge upon amount paid into court

(6) Where an order is made under clause (1) (a) or subsection (2), the lien ceases to attach to the premises and ceases to attach to the holdbacks and other amounts subject to a charge under section 21, and becomes instead a charge upon the amount paid into court or security posted, and the owner or payer shall, in respect of the

operation of sections 21, 23 and 24, be in the same position as if the lien had not been preserved or written notice of the lien had not been given.

(7) Where an order is made under clause (1) (b) or subsection (3), the lien ceases to attach to the holdbacks and other amounts subject to a charge under section 21 and becomes instead a charge upon the amount paid into court or security posted and the owner or payer shall, in respect of the operation of sections 21, 23 and 24, be in the same position as if the lien had not been preserved or written notice of the lien had not been given. — Idem

(8) Where more than one motion is made under subsection (1), (2) or (3) for the payment into court or posting of security to obtain an order vacating the registration of one or more preserved or perfected liens arising from the same improvement, the court may consolidate the motions and require that the amount paid into court or security posted be adequate to satisfy all the liens that are the subject of each of the motions, or make any other order that it considers appropriate. — Consolidation of motions

(9) Where an order is made under subsection (1), (2) or (3), the following rules apply: — Rules

1. The lien claimant whose lien was the subject of the order may proceed with an action to enforce his claim against the amount paid into court or security posted in accordance with the procedures set out in Part VIII, but no certificate of action shall be registered against the premises.

2. The amount paid into court or security posted is subject to the claims of all persons having a lien to the same extent as if the amount paid into court or security posted was realized by the sale of the premises in an action to enforce the lien and shall be distributed among all lien claimants in accordance with the priorities provided for in section 82.

3. Where an amount is realized in a lien action by the sale of the premises or otherwise, it shall be pooled into a common fund with the amount paid into court or security posted under this section, and shall be distributed among all lien claimants in accordance with the priorities provided for in section 82.

45.—(1) Where a lien that attaches to the premises is not preserved or is not perfected within the time allowed for doing so under section 31 or 36, the court upon, — Declaration by court that preserved lien has expired

(a) the motion of any person without notice to any other person;

(b) proof that the lien has not been preserved or perfected within the time allowed; and

(c) production of,

R.S.O. 1980,
c. 230

(i) a certificate of search under the *Land Titles Act*, or

R.S.O. 1980,
c. 445

(ii) a registrar's abstract under the *Registry Act*,

together with a certified copy of the claim for lien,

shall declare that the lien has expired and order that the registration of the claim for lien be vacated.

Idem

(2) Where the court is satisfied that a lien that does not attach to the premises has not been preserved or perfected within the time allowed for doing so under section 31 or 36, the court upon the motion of any person without notice to any other person shall declare that the lien has expired.

Order
returning
amount paid
into court or
cancelling
security

(3) Where a declaration is made under subsection (1) or (2), the court shall order that,

(a) any amount that has been paid into court under section 44 in respect of that lien be returned to the person who paid the amount into court; and

(b) any security that has been posted under section 44 in respect of that lien be cancelled.

Order
dismissing
action, etc.

46.—(1) Where a perfected lien that attaches to the premises has expired under section 37, the court, upon the motion of any person, shall declare that the lien has expired and shall make an order dismissing the action to enforce that lien and vacating the registration of a claim for lien and the certificate of action in respect of that action.

Idem

(2) Where a perfected lien that does not attach to the premises has expired under section 37, the court, upon the motion of any person, shall declare that the lien has expired and shall make an order dismissing the action to realize upon that lien.

Costs

(3) A motion under subsection (1) or (2) may be brought without notice, but no order as to costs in the action may be made upon the motion unless notice of that motion was given to the person against whom the order for costs is sought.

(4) Where an action, is dismissed under subsection (1) or (2), the court shall order that, Order returning money paid into court or cancelling security

(a) any amount that has been paid into court under section 44 in respect of that action be returned to the person who paid the amount into court; and

(b) any security that has been posted under section 44 in respect of that action be cancelled.

47.—(1) Upon motion, the court may, General power to discharge lien

(a) order the discharge of a lien;

(b) order that the registration of,

(i) a claim for lien, or

(ii) a certificate of action,

or both, be vacated;

(c) declare, where written notice of a lien has been given, that the lien has expired, or that the written notice of the lien shall no longer bind the person to whom it was given; or

(d) dismiss an action,

upon any proper ground and subject to any terms and conditions that the court considers appropriate in the circumstances.

(2) Where a certificate of action is vacated under subsection (1), and there remain liens which may be enforced in the action to which that certificate relates, the court shall give any directions that are necessary in the circumstances in respect of the continuation of that action. Direction by court

48. A discharge of a lien under this Part is irrevocable and the discharged lien cannot be revived, but no discharge affects the right of the person whose lien was discharged to claim a lien in respect of services or materials supplied by him subsequent to the preservation of the discharged lien. Discharge irrevocable

49. Where the lien attaches to the premises, an order declaring that a lien has expired, or discharging a lien, or vacating the registration of a claim for lien or a certificate of action, may be registered by regis- Registration

tering on the title to the premises a certified copy of the order that includes a description of the premises sufficient for registration under the *Registry Act* or the *Land Titles Act*, as the case may be, and a reference to the registration number of every preserved or perfected claim for lien and certificate of action thereby affected.

R.S.O. 1980, cc. 445, 230

PART VIII

JURISDICTION AND PROCEDURE

Lien claim enforceable in action

50.—(1) A lien claim is enforceable in an action in the Supreme Court in accordance with the procedure set out in this Part.

Trust claim and lien claim not to be joined

(2) A trust claim shall not be joined with a lien claim but may be brought in any court of competent jurisdiction.

Joinder in action

(3) Any number of lien claimants whose liens are in respect of the same owner and the same premises may join in the same action.

Where premises situate in Judicial District of York

51.—(1) Where the premises or a part thereof are situate in the Judicial District of York, an action shall be tried by a judge of the court.

Where premises situate outside Judicial District of York

(2) Where the premises are situate outside the Judicial District of York, an action shall be tried,

(a) by a local judge of the court having jurisdiction in the county or district in which the premises or a part thereof are situate;

(b) on consent of the persons to whom a notice of trial must be given and on the order of the local judge otherwise having jurisdiction over the action, by a local judge of the court in a county or district other than the one in which the premises or a part thereof are situate, but not in the Judicial District of York; or

(c) where upon motion the local judge so orders, by a judge of the court at the regular sittings of the court for the trial of actions in the county or district in which the premises or a part thereof are situate.

Where premises situate in more than one county

(3) Where the premises or a part thereof are situate in more than one county or district, an action may be tried by any judge or local judge who has jurisdiction under subsection (1) or (2) in any of the counties or districts in which the premises are situate.

52.—(1) Except as provided in subsection (2),

(a) a master, where the premises or a part thereof are situate in the Judicial District of York;

(b) a local master appointed for, or a master assigned to, the county or district in which the premises or a part thereof are situate, where the premises are situate outside the Judicial District of York;

(c) a local judge, where the local judge has ordered that the action be tried by a judge of the court under clause 51 (2) (c),

has jurisdiction to hear and dispose of any motion under this Act, including a motion brought prior to the commencement of an action, and all motions relating to the conduct of an action or reference under this Act.

(2) A master or appointed local master shall not hear or dispose of,

What matters
not to be dealt
with by master

(a) a motion for the trial of the action by a judge under clause 51 (2) (c);

(b) a motion for the reference of an action to a master or appointed local master for trial;

(c) an originating application; or

(d) a motion in respect of an appeal.

(3) In addition to his jurisdiction under subsection (1), a master or appointed local master to whom a reference has been directed has all the jurisdiction, powers and authority of the court to try and completely dispose of the action and all matters and questions arising in connection with the action, including the giving of leave to amend any pleading and the giving of directions to a receiver or trustee appointed by the court.

53. The court, whether the action is being tried by a judge or local judge, or by a master or an appointed local master on a reference,

(a) shall try the action, including any set-off, crossclaim, counterclaim, and, subject to section 58, third party claim, and all questions that arise therein or that are necessary to be tried in order to dispose completely of the action and to adjust the rights and liabilities of the persons appearing before it or upon whom notice of trial has been served; and

(b) shall take all accounts, make all inquiries, give all directions and do all things necessary to dispose finally of the action and all matters, questions and accounts arising therein or at the trial and to adjust the rights and liabilities of, and give all necessary relief to, all parties to the action.

Where exclusive jurisdiction not acquired

54. A judge, local judge, master or an appointed local master does not acquire exclusive jurisdiction over the trial of an action or reference by reason only of his appointing the time and place for the trial of the action or reference, or for the holding of a settlement meeting.

How action commenced

55.—(1) An action shall be commenced by filing a statement of claim in the office of the registrar or local registrar of the court in the county or district in which the premises or a part thereof are situate.

Service of statement of claim

(2) The statement of claim shall be served within ninety days after it is filed, but the court may, upon a motion made before or after the expiration of that period of time, extend the time for service.

Crossclaim or counterclaim

(3) A crossclaim or counterclaim by any person shall accompany his statement of defence, but on motion the court may grant leave to deliver a crossclaim or counterclaim after this time where it is appropriate to do so, and where leave is granted, the court may,

(a) make any order as to costs that it considers appropriate; and

(b) give directions as to the conduct of the action.

Time for delivery of pleadings

56.—(1) The time for delivering a statement of defence to a lien claim, crossclaim, counterclaim or third party claim shall be twenty days.

Noting pleadings closed

(2) Where a person against whom a claim is made in a statement of claim, counterclaim, crossclaim or third party claim defaults in the delivery of a statement of defence in respect of that claim, pleadings may be noted closed against him in respect of that claim.

Effect of default in defence

(3) Where pleadings have been noted closed against a defendant or third party under subsection (2), he shall not be permitted to contest the claim of the person who named him as a defendant or third party, or to file a statement of defence, except with leave of the court, to be given only where the court is satisfied that there is evidence to support a defence, and where leave is granted, the court,

(a) may make any order as to costs that it considers appropriate; and

(b) may give directions as to the conduct of the action.

(4) Except where leave has been granted under subsection (3), a defendant or third party against whom pleadings have been noted closed under subsection (2) shall be deemed to admit all allegations of fact made in the statement of claim, counterclaim, crossclaim or third party claim, as the case may be, and shall not be entitled to notice of or to participate in the trial of the action or any proceeding in respect of the action and judgment may be given against him. *Allegations of fact deemed admitted*

(5) Every statement of claim, crossclaim, counterclaim or third party claim shall include the following warning: *Warning to be included*

> "WARNING: If you wish to defend against this claim, you are required to deliver a statement of defence within twenty days. Should you fail to deliver a statement of defence as required, pleadings may be noted closed against you, and you shall be deemed to admit all allegations of fact contained in this claim, and you shall not be entitled to notice of or to participate in the trial or any proceeding in respect of this claim and judgment may be given against you."

57.—(1) A plaintiff in an action may join with his lien claim a claim for breach of his contract or subcontract. *Joinder of claims*

(2) A defendant in an action may, *Counter-claims and crossclaims*

(a) counterclaim against the person who named him as a defendant in respect of any claim that he may be entitled to make against that person, whether or not that claim is related to the making of the improvement;

(b) crossclaim against a co-defendant in respect of any claim that he may be entitled to make against that person related to the making of the improvement.

58. The following rules govern third party proceedings: *Rules re third party proceedings*

1. Subject to paragraph 2, a person against whom a claim is made in a statement of claim, crossclaim, counterclaim or third party claim may join a person who is not a party to the action as a third party for the purpose of claiming contribution or indemnity from the third party in respect of that claim.

2. A person may only be joined as a third party with leave of the court upon a motion made with notice to the owner and all persons having subsisting preserved or perfected liens at

the time of the motion, but such leave shall not be given unless the court is satisfied that the trial of the third party claim will not,

    i. unduly prejudice the ability of the third party or of any lien claimant or defendant to prosecute his claim or conduct his defence, or

      ii. unduly delay or complicate the resolution of the lien action.

3. The court may give such directions as it considers appropriate in the circumstances in respect of the conduct of third party proceedings.

Parties

59.—(1) The person serving the notice of trial and all persons served with notice of trial are parties to the action.

Adding parties

(2) Subject to section 56, the court may at any time add or join any person as a party to the action.

Reference to master, etc.

60.—(1) On motion made after the delivery of all statements of defence, or the statements of defence to all crossclaims, counterclaims, or third party claims, if any, or the time for their delivery has expired,

    (a) a judge may refer to a master; or

    (b) a local judge may refer to a master assigned to, or a local master appointed for, the county or district in which the trial is to take place,

R.S.O. 1980, c. 223

the whole action for trial under section 71 of the *Judicature Act.*

Idem

(2) At the trial,

    (a) a judge may direct a reference to a master; or

    (b) a local judge may direct a reference to a master assigned to, or a local master appointed for, the county or district in which the trial is to take place,

R.S.O. 1980, c. 223

under section 70 or 71 of the *Judicature Act.*

Application to set aside order of reference

(3) Where under subsection (1), the action has been referred to the master or local master for trial, any person who subsequently becomes a party to the action may, within seven days after becoming a party to the action, make a motion to a judge or the local judge of

the court who directed the reference to set aside the judgment directing the reference.

(4) Where no motion is made under subsection (3), or where the motion is refused, the person who subsequently became a party to the action is bound by the judgment directing the reference as if he had been a party to the action at the time the reference was directed.

Effect on subsequent party to action

61.—(1) The court may at any time make an order awarding carriage of the action to any person who has a perfected lien.

Carriage of action

(2) Where more than one action is brought to enforce liens in respect of the same improvement, the court may,

Consolidation of actions

(a) consolidate all the actions into one action; and

(b) award carriage of the action to any person who has a perfected lien.

62.—(1) Any party may make a motion to the court without notice to any other person at any time after,

Application to fix date for trial or settlement, meeting

(a) the delivery of the statements of defence, or the statements of defence to all crossclaims, counterclaims or third party claims, if any, where the plaintiff's claim is disputed; or

(b) the expiry of the time for the delivery of these statements of defence in all other cases,

to have a day, time and place fixed for the trial of the action, or for the holding of a settlement meeting under section 63, or both.

(2) Where the court orders the holding of a settlement meeting, then at least ten days before the date appointed for the holding of the meeting, the party who obtained the appointment shall serve a notice of settlement meeting upon any person who was, on the twelfth day before the date appointed,

Notice of settlement meeting

(a) subject to section 56 (default in filing defence), the owner and every other person named as a defendant in every statement of claim in respect of the action;

(b) where the lien attaches to the premises, a person with a registered interest in the premises;

(c) where the lien attaches to the premises, an execution creditor of the owner;

(d) any other person having a preserved or perfected lien against the premises; and

(e) a person joined as a third party under section 58.

Request to identify other persons having lien

(3) Where the lien does not attach to the premises, the party who obtained the appointment for the holding of the settlement meeting shall request the owner to inform him of the identity of every person described in clause (2) (d).

Service of notice of trial

(4) Subject to section 56, where the court fixes a date for trial, the party who obtained the appointment shall serve a notice of trial, at least ten days before the date appointed for trial, upon any person who is or would be entitled to a notice of a settlement meeting under subsection (2).

Conduct of settlement meeting

63.—(1) Where a settlement meeting is ordered by the court, it shall be conducted in accordance with this section.

Idem

(2) The settlement meeting shall be conducted by,

(a) a person selected by a majority of the persons present at the meeting; or

(b) where no person is selected, by the person who took out the appointment.

and shall be for the purpose of resolving or narrowing any issues to be tried in the action.

Idem

(3) The results of the settlement meeting shall be embodied in a statement of settlement which shall summarize those issues of fact and law which have been settled by the parties.

Statement of settlement

(4) The statement of settlement shall be filed with the court and shall be attached to and form part of the record, and the settlement shall be binding upon all persons served with notice of the settlement meeting, and upon all defendants against whom pleadings have been noted closed under section 56, but subject to subsection 56 (3), the court may vary or set aside the statement of settlement upon such order as to costs or otherwise as it considers appropriate.

Power of court

(5) Upon the filing of the statement of settlement with the court, the court may,

(a) if there was no dispute at the meeting to a claim for lien, declare the lien valid and give such further judgment as it considers appropriate;

(b) enter a judgment or make a report upon consent on those issues which have been settled by the parties;

(c) make any order that is necessary in order to give effect to any judgment or report of the court under clause (a) or (b); and

(d) make any order that is necessary for, or will expedite the conduct of, the trial.

(6) Rule 244 of the Supreme Court Rules of Practice does not apply to an action under this Act.

Non-application of rule 244

64.—(1) The results of the trial shall be embodied,

Judgment or report

(a) in a judgment in the prescribed form, where the trial is conducted by a judge or local judge of the court; or

(b) in a report in the prescribed form, where the trial is conducted by a master or an appointed local master of the court on a reference.

(2) The prescribed form of judgment or report may be varied by the court in order to meet the circumstances of the case so as to afford to any party to the proceedings any right or remedy in the judgment or report to which he is entitled.

Varying form

(3) The report of a master or an appointed local master shall be deemed to be confirmed at the expiration of the fifteen-day period next following the date that the notice of filing was given, unless notice of appeal is served within that time.

When report deemed confirmed

(4) The judgment or report may direct any party found liable to make a payment, to make such payment forthwith, and execution may be issued,

Issue of execution

(a) immediately, in the case of a judgment; or

(b) after confirmation, in the case of a report.

(5) The court may order that the interest in the premises be sold and may direct the sale to take place at any time after the judgment or confirmation of the report, allowing a reasonable time for advertising the sale.

Order for sale

(6) The court may allow any person with a perfected lien,

Persons who may be let in

(a) who was not served with a notice of trial; or

R.S.O. 1980,
c. 25

(b) whose action was stayed by reason of an order under the *Arbitrations Act,*

to be let in to prove his claim at any time before the amount realized in the action for the satisfaction of the lien has been distributed, and where his claim is allowed, the judgment or report shall be amended to include his claim.

Personal judgment

65. Subject to paragraph 3 of subsection 36 (4) (sheltering), the court may award any lien claimant a personal judgment, whether he proves his lien or not, upon any ground relating to his claim that is disclosed by the evidence against any party to the action for any amount that may be due to him and that he might have recovered in a proceeding against that party.

Right to share in proceeds

66. Where an interest in the premises is sold under court order, or by a trustee appointed under Part IX, a person with a perfected lien is entitled to share in the proceeds of sale in respect of the amount owing to him, although that amount or part thereof was not payable at the time of the commencement of the action or at the time of the distribution of the proceeds.

Orders for completion of sale

67.—(1) The court may make all orders necessary for the completion of a sale and for vesting an interest in the premises in the purchaser.

Payment into court of proceeds

(2) Where an interest in the premises is sold under court order, or by a trustee appointed under Part IX, the proceeds of the sale shall be paid into court to the credit of the action.

Fees and disbursements

(3) The court may add to the claim of the party having carriage of the action his fees and actual disbursements in connection with the sale.

To whom proceeds paid

(4) The court shall direct to whom the proceeds shall be paid in accordance with the priorities established by this Act.

Where proceeds insufficient to satisfy judgment

(5) Where the proceeds of the sale are not sufficient to satisfy the judgment and costs, the court shall certify the amount of the deficiency and give personal judgment in the appropriate amount to each person whose judgment is not satisfied out of the proceeds against each person who has been found liable to him.

Application to court for directions

68. Where a person has in his possession an amount that may be subject to a trust under Part II, he may apply to the court for direction and the court may give any direction or make any order that the court considers appropriate in the circumstances.

69.—(1) The procedure in an action shall be as far as possible of a summary character, having regard to the amount and nature of the liens in question.

(2) Interlocutory proceedings, other than those provided for in this Act, shall not be taken without the consent of the court obtained upon proof that the proceedings are necessary or would expedite the resolution of the issues in dispute.

(3) Except where inconsistent with this Act, and subject to subsection (2), the *Judicature Act* and the Supreme Court Rules of Practice apply to pleadings and proceedings under this Act.

(4) The court may obtain the assistance of any merchant, accountant, actuary, building contractor, architect, engineer or other person in such a way as it considers fit, to enable it to determine better any matter of fact in question, and may fix the remuneration of such person and direct the payment thereof by any of the parties.

(5) A lien claimant whose claim is for an amount within the monetary jurisdiction of a small claims court may by represented by an agent who is not a barrister and solicitor.

(6) Where in this Act the court is empowered to do anything upon motion, the motion may be made in the manner provided for in the Supreme Court Rules of Practice for the making of interlocutory motions, regardless of whether any action has been commenced at the time the motion is made.

PART IX

EXTRAORDINARY REMEDIES

70.—(1) Any person having a lien, or any other person having an interest in the premises, may apply to the court for the appointment of a trustee and the court may appoint a trustee upon such terms as to the giving of security or otherwise as the court considers appropriate.

(2) Subject to the supervision and direction of the court, a trustee appointed under subsection (1) may,

(a) act as a receiver and manager and, subject to the *Planning Act* and the approval of the court, mortgage, sell or lease the premises or any part thereof;

(b) complete or partially complete the improvement;

(c) take appropriate steps for the preservation of the premises; and

(d) subject to the approval of the court, take such other steps as are appropriate in the circumstances.

Liens a charge on amounts recovered

(3) Subject to subsection 80 (7), all liens shall be a charge upon any amount recovered by the trustee after payment of the reasonable business expenses and management costs incurred by the trustee in the exercise of any power under subsection (2).

Sale subject to encumbrances

(4) Any interest in the premises that is to be sold may be offered for sale subject to any mortgage, charge, interest or other encumbrance that the court directs.

Orders for completion of sale, etc.

(5) The court may make all orders necessary for the completion of any mortgage, lease or sale by a trustee under this section.

Labour and material payment bonds

71.—(1) Where a labour and material payment bond is in effect in respect of an improvement, any person whose payment is guaranteed by that bond has a right of action to recover the amount of his claim, in accordance with the terms and conditions of the bond, against the surety on the bond, where the principal on the bond defaults in making the payment guaranteed by the bond.

Saving

(2) Nothing in this section makes the surety liable for an amount in excess of the amount that he undertakes to pay under the bond and the surety's liability under the bond shall be reduced by and to the extent of any payment made in good faith by the surety either before or after judgment is obtained against the surety.

Subrogation

(3) The surety, upon satisfaction of its obligation to any person whose payment is guaranteed by the bond, shall be subrogated to all the rights of that person.

PART X

APPEALS

Stated case

72.—(1) Where in the course of an action a question of law arises, the court may state the question in the form of a stated case for the opinion of the Divisional Court, and the stated case shall thereupon be set down to be heard before the Divisional Court and notice of hearing shall be served by the party setting down the matter upon all parties concerned.

Facts to be set out

(2) The stated case shall set forth those facts material to the determination of the question raised.

73.—(1) Subject to subsection (3), an appeal lies from a judgment or a report under this Act to the Divisional Court.

(2) A party wishing to appeal a judgment or report shall file and serve his notice of appeal,

    (a) prior to the confirmation of the report where the appeal is in respect of a report; or

    (b) within fifteen days of the date of judgment in all other cases,

but the time for filing or serving the notice of appeal may be extended by the written consent of all parties, or by a single judge of the Divisional Court where an appropriate case is made out for doing so.

(3) No appeal lies from,

    (a) a judgment or a report under this Act, where the amount claimed is $1,000 or less; or

    (b) an interlocutory order made by the court.

PART XI

PRIORITIES

74. A person who has supplied services or materials in respect of an improvement may enforce his lien despite the noncompletion or abandonment of the contract or a subcontract by any other person.

75. The rights of a person having a lien may be assigned by an instrument in writing and, if not assigned, upon his death pass to his personal representative.

76.—(1) Subject to section 84, where one or more premises that are subject to an unpreserved general lien are sold, the general lien continues for the full amount of the lien against those premises that are subject to the lien, that were not sold.

(2) Where a person having a preserved or perfected general lien releases the lien against one or more of the premises subject to the lien, the lien continues for the full amount of the lien against those premises that were not released.

77.—(1) The taking of any security for, or the acceptance of any promissory note or bill of exchange for, or the taking of any acknowledgment of, or the giving of time for the payment of, or the taking of proceedings for the recovery of, or the obtaining of a personal judgment for, the claim, does not in itself merge, waive, pay, satisfy, prejudice or destroy a lien.

Where note
or bill
negotiated

(2) Where any promissory note or bill of exchange has been negotiated, the person having the lien may still enforce the lien if he is the holder of the promissory note or bill of exchange at the time when he proves his claim.

Time not
extended

(3) Nothing in this section extends the time for, or dispenses with the requirement for, the preservation or perfection of a lien.

Lien claimant
deemed
purchaser
R.S.O. 1980,
cc. 445, 230

78. Where a claim for lien is preserved by registration, the lien claimant shall be deemed to be a purchaser to the extent of his lien within the provisions of the *Registry Act* and *Land Titles Act*, but except as otherwise provided in this Act, those Acts do not apply to any lien arising under this Act.

Priority of
liens over
executions,
etc.

79. The liens arising from an improvement have priority over all judgments, executions, assignments, attachments, garnishments and receiving orders except those executed or recovered upon before the time when the first lien arose in respect of the improvement.

Priority over
mortgages, etc.

80.—(1) Except as provided in this section, the liens arising from an improvement have priority over all conveyances, mortgages or other agreements affecting the owner's interest in the premises.

Building
mortgage

(2) Where a mortgagee takes a mortgage with the intention to secure the financing of an improvement, the liens arising from the improvement have priority over that mortgage, and any mortgage taken out to repay that mortgage, to the extent of any deficiency in the holdbacks required to be retained by the owner under Part IV, irrespective of when that mortgage, or the mortgage taken out to repay it, is registered.

Prior
mortgages,
prior advances

(3) Subject to subsection (2), and without limiting the effect of subsection (4), all conveyances, mortgages or other agreements affecting the owner's interest in the premises that were registered prior to the time when the first lien arose in respect of an improvement have priority over the liens arising from the improvement to the extent of the lessor of,

    (a) the actual value of the premises at the time when the first lien arose; and

    (b) the total of all amounts that prior to that time were,

        (i) advanced in the case of a mortgage, and

(ii) advanced or secured in the case of a conveyance or other agreement.

(4) Subject to subsection (2), a conveyance, mortgage or other agreement affecting the owner's interest in the premises that was registered prior to the time when the first lien arose in respect of an improvement, has priority, in addition to the priority to which it is entitled under subsection (3), over the liens arising from the improvement, to the extent of any advance made in respect of that conveyance, mortgage or other agreement after the time when the first lien arose, unless,

    (a) at the time when the advance was made, there was a preserved or perfected lien against the premises; or

    (b) prior to the time when the advance was made, the person making the advance had received written notice of a lien.

Prior mortgages, subsequent advances

(5) Where any mortgage is registered after the time when the first lien arose in respect of an improvement, the liens arising from the improvement have priority over the mortgage to the extent of any deficiency in the holdbacks required to be retained by the owner under Part IV.

Special priority against subsequent advances

(6) Subject to subsections (2) and (5), a conveyance, mortgage or other agreement affecting the owner's interest in the premises that is registered after the time when the first lien arose in respect to the improvement, has priority over the liens arising from the improvement to the extent of any advance made in respect of that conveyance, mortgage or other agreement, unless,

    (a) at the time when the advance was made, there was a preserved or perfected lien against the premises; or

    (b) prior to the time when the advance was made, the person making the advance had received written notice of a lien.

General priority against subsequent mortgages

(7) Despite anything in this Act, where an amount is advanced to a trustee appointed under Part IX as a result of the exercise of any powers conferred upon him under that Part,

Advances to trustee under Part IX

    (a) the interest in the premises acquired by the person making the advance takes priority, to the extent of the advance, over every lien existing at the date of the trustee's appointment; and

    (b) the amount received is not subject to any lien existing at the date of the trustee's appointment.

Where
postponement

(8) Despite subsections (4) and (6), where a preserved or perfected lien is postponed in favour of the interest of some other person in the premises, that person shall enjoy priority in accordance with the postponement over,

   (a) the postponed lien; and

   (b) where an advance is made, any unpreserved lien in respect of which no written notice has been received by the person in whose favour the postponement is made at the time of the advance,

but nothing in this subsection affects the priority of the liens under subsections (2) and (5).

Saving

(9) Subsections (2) and (5) do not apply in respect of a mortgage that was registered prior to the day on which this Act comes into force.

Registration
of financial
guarantee
bond

(10) A financial guarantee bond in a form prescribed may be registered on the title to the premises, and where the bond is registered a purchaser who takes title from the mortgagee takes title to the premises free of the priority of the liens created by subsections (2) and (5), the security of the bond takes the place of the priority created by those subsections and persons who have proved liens have a right of action against the surety on the bond.

Persons who
comprise class

81. All persons having a lien who have supplied services or materials to the same payer comprise a class, and a person who has supplied services or materials to more than one payer is a member of every class to the extent to which his lien relates to that class.

Priority
between and
within class

82.—(1) Except where it is otherwise provided by this Act,

   (a) no person having a lien is entitled to any priority over another member of the same class;

   (b) all amounts available to satisfy the liens in respect of an improvement shall be distributed rateably among the members of each class according to their respective rights; and

   (c) the lien of every member of a class has priority over the lien of the payer of that class.

Where
conveyance or
mortgage void

(2) Any conveyance or mortgage in respect of the premises to any person entitled to a lien on the premises, in payment of or as security for that claim, whether given before or after that lien arises, is void against all other persons entitled to a lien on the premises.

83.—(1) The lien of a worker has priority over the lien of any other person belonging to the same class to the extent of the amount of forty regular-time working days' wages.

(2) Where monetary supplementary benefits are payable to a workers' trust fund instead of to a worker, the trustee of the workers' trust fund is subrogated to the rights of the worker under this Act with respect to those benefits.

(3) Every device to defeat the priority given to workers by this section is void.

84. Where a general lien is realized against a premises in an action in which other liens are also realized against the premises,

(a) the general lien shall rank with the other liens according to the rules of priority set out in section 82 only to the extent of,

(i) the total value of the general lien,

divided by,

(ii) the total number of premises to which the person having the general lien supplied services or materials under his contract or subcontract; and

(b) in respect of the balance of the general lien, it shall rank next in priority to all other liens against the premises, whether or not of the same class.

85. Where a premises that is subject to a lien is destroyed in whole or in part, any amount received by the owner or a mortgagee by reason of any insurance on the premises shall take the place of the premises so destroyed and shall be distributed in accordance with the priorities set out in this Part.

86. Where an interest in the premises is sold or leased under an order of the court or by a trustee appointed under Part IX, the proceeds received as a result of that disposition, together with any amount paid into court under subsection 67 (2), shall be distributed in accordance with the priorities set out in this Part.

87.—(1) Where a payer becomes insolvent, the trust fund of which that payer is trustee shall be distributed so that priority over all others is given to a beneficiary of that trust who has proved a lien and a beneficiary of a trust created by section 8 that is derived from that trust, who has proved a lien.

Idem

(2) Priority in the distribution of trust funds among those who have proved liens shall be in accordance with the respective priorities of their liens as set out in this Part.

Idem

(3) The remaining trust funds shall be distributed among the beneficiaries of that trust and the beneficiaries of trusts created by section 8 that are derived from that trust, whose liens have not been proved, in accordance with the respective priorities to which those liens would have been entitled as set out in this Part, had those liens been proved.

PART XII

MISCELLANEOUS RULES

Costs

88.—(1) Subject to subsection (2), any order as to the costs in an action, application, motion or settlement meeting is in the discretion of the court, and an order as to costs may be made against,

    (a) any party to the action or motion; or

    (b) the solicitor or agent of any party to the action, application or motion, where the solicitor or agent has,

        (i) knowingly participated in the preservation or perfection of a lien, or represented a party at the trial of an action, where it is clear that the claim for lien is without foundation or is for a grossly excessive amount, or that the lien has expired, or

        (ii) by his conduct prejudiced or delayed the conduct of the action,

and the order may be made on a solicitor-and-client basis, including where the motion is heard by, or the action has been referred under section 60 to, a master or an appointed local master.

Where least expensive course not taken

(2) Where the least expensive course is not taken by a party, the costs allowed to him shall not exceed what would have been incurred had the least expensive course been taken.

Scale of costs

(3) Except where otherwise ordered by the court hearing an appeal, the costs of an appeal shall be on the scale of costs allowed in county court appeals where the amount involved is within the proper competence of the county court and where it exceeds that amount shall be on the Supreme Court scale.

89.—(1) Subject to subsection (3) and, except where otherwise ordered by the court, all documents and notices required to be given or that may be given under this Act, may be served in any manner permitted under the Rules of the Supreme Court or, in the alternative, may be sent by certified or registered mail addressed to the intended recipient at his last known mailing address, How documents may be given

(a) according to the records of the person sending the document; or

(b) as stated on the most recently registered instrument identifying him as a person having an interest in the premises.

(2) In the absence of evidence to the contrary, a document or notice sent to a person by certified or registered mail shall be deemed to have been received by him on the fifth day following the date on which it was mailed, exclusive of Saturdays and holidays. When document deemed received

(3) Except where otherwise ordered by the court, the following shall not be sent by certified or registered mail but shall be served in the manner provided in the Rules of the Supreme Court for service of a writ of summons: Service of particular documents, etc.

1. Statement of claim.

2. Notice of trial or settlement meeting.

3. Notice of appeal.

(4) Where a document or notice is sent by registered mail, the date appearing on the postal registration receipt shall be deemed conclusively to be the date of mailing. Date of mailing

90. The Lieutenant Governor in Council may make regulations, Regulations

(a) prescribing forms and providing for their use;

(b) prescribing the appropriate offices of the Crown to which claims for lien must be sent;

(c) prescribing the form and manner of publication of copies of certificates and declarations of substantial performance under section 32.

91. Sections 1 to 51 and sections 53 of the *Mechanics' Lien Act*, being chapter 261 of the Revised Statutes of Ontario, 1980, are repealed. Repeal

362

Appendix B: Construction Lien Act, 1983

Commence-
ment and
application

92.—(1) This Act comes into force on the 2nd day of April, 1983, and applies to all contracts entered into on or after that date and to the subcontracts arising under those contracts and to all services or materials supplied thereunder.

Transitional
R.S.O. 1980,
c. 261

(2) Despite section 91, the *Mechanics' Lien Act* continues to apply to all contracts entered into before the 2nd day of April, 1983, and to the subcontracts arising under those contracts and to all services or materials supplied thereunder.

Idem

(3) Despite section 91, where a contract entered into before the 2nd day of April, 1983 is amended in good faith on or after that date, the *Mechanics' Lien Act* applies to that amendment and to all subcontracts arising under it and to all services or materials supplied thereunder.

Short title

93. The short title of this Act is the *Construction Lien Act, 1983*.

Appendix C

Regulation Made Under The Construction Lien Act, 1983

O. Reg. 159/83.
General.
Made—March 16th, 1983.
Filed—March 18th, 1983.

---

1. The office of the Crown to which a copy of a claim for lien must be given under subsection 34 (3) of the Act is as follows:

1. Where the contract is with a Ministry of the Crown, the office of the Director of Legal Services of that Ministry.

2. Where the contract is with the Ontario Housing Corporation, the office of the Director of Legal Services of the Ministry of Municipal Affairs and Housing.

3. Where the contract is with a college of applied arts and technology, the office of the president of the college.

4. Where the contract is with any other office of the Crown, the chief executive officer of that office. O. Reg. 159/83, s. 1.

2.—(1) A notice to a contractor under section 18 of the Act may be in Form 1.

(2) A notice to a landlord under subsection 19 (1) of the Act may be in Form 2.

(3) A notice to a contractor under subsection 19 (1) of the Act may be in Form 3.

(4) A notice to a lien claimant under subsection 19 (3) of the Act may be in Form 4.

(5) A declaration of last supply under subsection 31 (5) of the Act shall be in Form 5.

(6) A certificate of the substantial performance of a contract under section 32 of the Act shall be in Form 6.

(7) A certificate of completion of a subcontract under subsection 33 (1) of the Act shall be in Form 7.

(8) A claim for lien under section 34 of the Act shall be in Form 8.

(9) An affidavit of verification of a claim for lien under section 34 of the Act may be in Form 9.

(10) A certificate of action under section 36 of the Act shall be in Form 10.

(11) A notice requiring a lien claimant whose lien is sheltered under the statement of claim of some other person to provide further particulars of his claim or of any fact alleged in his claim under paragraph 4 of subsection 36 (4) of the Act may be in Form 11.

(12) A notice under clause 40 (3) (*b*), (*c*) or (*d*) of the Act may be in Form 12.

(13) A notice under clause 40 (3) (*a*) of the Act may be in Form 13.

(14) A release of lien under section 41 of the Act shall be in Form 14.

(15) A notice of postponement under section 43 of the Act shall be in Form 15.

(16) A judgment under section 60 of the Act directing a reference of the whole action to a master or appointed local master for trial shall be in Form 16.

(17) A notice of trial under section 62 of the Act may be in Form 17.

(18) A notice of settlement meeting under section 62 of the Act may be in Form 18.

(19) A judgment under section 64 of the Act shall be,

(*a*) in Form 19, where the lien attaches to the premises; or

(*b*) in Form 20, where the lien does not attach to the premises.

(20) A report under section 64 of the Act shall be,

(*a*) in Form 21, where the lien attaches to the premises; or

(*b*) in Form 22, where the lien does not attach to the premises.

(21) A financial guarantee bond under subsection 80 (10) of the Act shall be in Form 23.

(22) Where an affidavit provided for in this Regulation is sworn or affirmed by an illiterate person, the jurat to the affidavit shall be in the form prescribed in the Supreme Court Rules of Practice. O. Reg. 159/83, s. 2.

3.—(1) Copies of certificates of the substantial performance of a contract shall be published in a construction trade newspaper in the following form and manner:

1. In each issue, all certificates shall appear on a single page or consecutive pages, and shall be arranged alphabetically.

    i. by the county, district or regional municipality in which the premises is situate, except where the premises is situate in The Municipality of Metropolitan Toronto, or

    ii. by the city or borough of The Municipality of Metropolitan Toronto in which the premises is situate, where the premises is situate, in The Municipality of Metropolitan Toronto.

2. The contents of each certificate of the substantial performance of a contract published in a construction trade newspaper shall be the same as in the original of the certificate, except that the signature of the payment certifier or other persons certifying substantial performance shall be deleted.

(2) Declarations of the substantial performance of a contract shall be published in the same form and manner as certificates of the substantial performance of a contract. O. Reg. 159/83, s. 3.

Form 1

Construction Lien Act, 1983

NOTICE TO CONTRACTOR
UNDER SECTION 18 OF THE ACT

TO: . . . . , contractor.

FROM: . . . . , a joint owner or owner

in common with . . . .

of the following premises:

. . . .
(give address of premises)

The joint owner or owner in common assumes no responsibility for the improvements to the premises, to be made by you under a contract between you and ....

(name of owner)

Date: ....

(joint owner or owner in common or agent)

O. Reg. 159/83, Form 1.

Form 2

Construction Lien Act, 1983

NOTICE TO LANDLORD
UNDER SUBSECTION 19 (1) OF THE ACT

TO: ....

the landlord of

....

(address of premises)

FROM: .... , a contractor, who has entered into

a contract with your tenant, ... to supply services or
materials to make the following improvement to the above named premises:

(describe improvement to be made)

This contract was entered into on ....

(date)

(Use A, B or C as appropriate)

A. A copy of the contract is enclosed.

B. The contract is oral and the following are the details of the contract.

C. You may inspect a copy of this contract at ....

(place)

.... between the hours of .... and

every ....

(days of the week)

Date: ....
                                        (contractor or agent)

                        ....
                        (address for service of contractor)

WARNING: Subsection 19 (1) of the *Construction Lien Act, 1983* provides as follows:

19.—(1) Where the interest of the owner to which the lien attaches is leasehold, the interest of the landlord shall also be subject to the lien to the same extent as the interest of the owner if the contractor gives the landlord written notice of the improvement to be made, unless the landlord, within fifteen days of receiving the notice from the contractor, gives the contractor written notice that the landlord assumes no responsibility for the improvement to be made. O. Reg. 159/83, Form 2.

Form 3

Construction Lien Act, 1983

NOTICE TO CONTRACTOR
UNDER SUBSECTION 19 (1) OF THE ACT

TO: .... , contractor.

FROM: .... ,

the landlord of:

(give address of premises)

The landlord of the premises assumes no responsibility for the improvement to be made by you under a contract dated .... between you and

.... , a tenant.
                        (name of tenant)

Date: ....
                                        (landlord or agent)

O. Reg. 159/83, Form 3.

Form 4

Construction Lien Act, 1983

NOTICE TO LIEN CLAIMANT
UNDER SUBSECTION 19 (3) OF THE ACT

TO: ...., lien claimant.

FROM: .... the landlord of

the following premises: ....

(give address of premises)

The landlord intends to (*use A or B, whichever is applicable*)

   A. enforce forfeiture against the lease of the premises;

   B. terminate the lease of the premises

for non-payment of rent.

In order to protect your lien rights against the interest of the tenant, the amount of the unpaid rent as stated below must be paid to the landlord within ten days of your receiving this notice. If you pay this amount, you may add it to your claim for lien.

Amount of unpaid rent: $...............

Payment of this amount may be made on ....

(days)

between the hours of .... and ...., at ....

....

(address for payment)

Date: ....

(landlord or agent)

O. Reg. 159/83, Form 4.

Form 5

Construction Lien Act, 1983

DECLARATION OF LAST SUPPLY
UNDER SUBSECTION 31 (5) OF THE ACT

. . . .

(name of supplier)

a supplier of services or materials to an improvement being made to:

. . . .

(address of premises)

declares that:

1. The following services or materials were supplied:

    (description of services or materials)

2. These services or materials were supplied under a contract *(or subcontract)*

    with . . . . dated the . . . .

    (name of payer)

    day of . . . . , 19 . . . .

3. The last supply of services or materials made by the supplier to the improvement under the contract *(or subcontract)*, was made on . . . .

    (date of last supply)

4. No further services or materials will be supplied under the contract *(or subcontract)*.

Declared before me at the . . . . of

. . . . in the . . . . of

. . . .

on the . . . . day of . . . . . . , ...

19 . . . .   *(supplier)*

. . . .

A Commissioner, etc.

O. Reg. 159/83, Form 5.

Form 6

Construction Lien Act, 1983

CERTIFICATE OF SUBSTANTIAL PERFORMANCE OF THE CONTRACT UNDER SECTION 32 OF THE ACT

. . . .
(County/District or Regional Municipality/City or Borough of Municipality of Metropolitan Toronto in which premises are situate)

. . . .
(Street address and city, town, etc., or, if there is no street address, the location of the premises)

This is to certify that the contract for the following improvement:

. . . .
(short description of the improvement)

to the above premises was substantially performed on . . . .
                                                       (date substantially performed)

Date certificate signed: . . . .
                                                               *(payment certifier
                                                               where there is one)*

                                                               . . . .

                                                               . . . .
                                                               *(owner and contractor,
                                                               where there is no
                                                               payment certifier)*

Name of owner: . . . .

Address of service: . . . .

Name of contractor: . . . .

Address for service: . . . .

Name of payment certifier: . . . .
                                                       (where applicable)

Address: . . . .

(Use A or B whichever is appropriate)

A. Identification of premises for preservation of liens:

. . . .

(where liens attach to premises, reference to lot and plan or instrument registration number)

B. Office to which claim for lien and affidavit must be given to preserve lien:

. . . .

(where liens do not attach to premises)

O. Reg. 159/83, Form 6.

Form 7

Construction Lien Act, 1983

CERTIFICATE OF COMPLETION OF SUBCONTRACT UNDER SUBSECTION 33 (1) OF THE ACT

This is to certify the completion of a subcontract for the supply of services or

materials between . . . .

. . . .

(name of subcontractor)

and . . . . dated the . . . . day of . . . . , 19. . . .

The subcontract provided for the supply of the following services or materials

. . . .

to the following improvement:

. . . .

(short description of the improvement)

of premises at . . . .

(street address, or if there is none, the location of the premises)

Date of certification: . . . .

(payment certifier, where there is one)

. . . .

. . . .

(owner and contractor)

Name of owner: ....

Address for service: ....

Name of contractor: ....

Address for service: ....

Name of payment certifier *(where applicable):* ....

Address: ....

(Use A or B whichever is appropriate)

   A. Identification of premises for preservation of liens:

....

       (where liens attach to premises, lot and plan number or instrument registration number)

   B. Office to which claim for lien and affidavit must be given to preserve lien:

....

       (where liens do not attach to premises)

O. Reg. 159/83, Form 7.

Form 8

Construction Lien Act, 1983

CLAIM FOR LIEN UNDER SECTION 34 OF THE ACT

Name of lien claimant: ....

Address for service: ....

Name of owner: ....

Address: ....

Name of person to whom lien claimant supplied services or materials: ......

....

Address: ....

Time within which services or materials were supplied:

from .... to ....
   (date supply commenced)   *(date of most recent supply)*

Short description of services or materials that have been supplied:

....

Contract price or subcontract price: $............

Amount claimed as owing in respect of services or materials
that have been supplied: $............

(Use A where the lien attaches to the premises; use B where the lien does not attach to the premises).

A. The lien claimant *(if claimant is personal representative or assignee this must be stated)* claims a lien against the interest of every person identified above as an owner of the premises described in Schedule A to this claim for lien.

B. The lien claimant *(if claimant is personal representative or assignee this must be stated)* claims a charge against the holdbacks required to be retained under the Act and any additional amount owed by a payer to the contractor or to any subcontractor whose contract or subcontract was in whole or in part performed by the services or materials that have been supplied by the lien claimant in relation to the premises at:

....
   (address or other identification of the location of the premises)

Date: ...., ...
                                   (signature of claimant or agent)

SCHEDULE A

To the claim for lien of ....

Description of premises:

(Where the lien attaches to the premises, provide a description of the premises sufficient for registration under the Land Titles Act or the Registry Act, as the case may be).

O. Reg. 159/83, Form 8.

Form 9

Construction Lien Act, 1983

AFFIDAVIT OF VERIFICATION OF LIEN CLAIM UNDER SECTION 34
OF THE ACT

I, ..., make oath and say *(or affirm)* as follows: *(use A, B or C as applicable)*

A.1. I am the lien claimant named in the attached claim for lien;

  2. The facts stated in the claim for lien are true.

B.1. I am the agent *(or assignee)* of the lien claimant named in the attached claim for lien;

  2. I have informed myself of the facts stated in the claim for lien, and I believe those facts to be true.

C.1. I am a trustee of the workers' trust fund which is named as the lien claimant in the attached claim for lien;

  2. I have informed myself of the facts stated in the claim for lien, and I believe those facts to be true.

Sworn *(or affirmed)* before me at the

. . . . of . . . .

in the . . . . of . . . .

this . . . . . . day of . . . . , 19. . .

. . . .
    A Commissioner, etc.

. . . .
      (deponent)

O. Reg. 159/83, Form 9.

Form 10

Construction Lien Act, 1983

CERTIFICATE OF ACTION
UNDER SECTION 36 OF THE ACT

Court File No.

. . . .

SUPREME COURT OF ONTARIO

BETWEEN

Plaintiff(s)

(court seal) and

Defendant(s)

CERTIFICATE OF ACTION

I certify that an action has been commenced in the Supreme Court of Ontario under the *Construction Lien Act, 1983* between the above parties in respect of the premises described in Schedule A to this certificate, and relating to the claim(s) for lien bearing the following registration numbers:

. . . .

Date: . . . .
                                          (registrar or local registrar)

SCHEDULE A

Description of Premises:

(The description of the premises must be the same as in the statement of claim, and must be sufficient for registration under the Land Titles Act or Registry Act, as the case may be).

O. Reg. 159/83, Form 10.

Form 11

Construction Lien Act, 1983

NOTICE REQUIRING PARTICULARS OF SHELTERED CLAIM FOR LIEN UNDER PARAGRAPH 4 OF SUBSECTION 36 (4) OF THE ACT

Court File No.

. . . .

SUPREME COURT OF ONTARIO

BETWEEN

Plaintiff(s)

(court seal)   and

Defendant(s)

TO: . . . ., lien claimant

FROM: . . . ., a defendant

in the above named action.

This action has been commenced to realize a claim for lien in respect of an improvement to the following premises:

. . . .
(address)

and you may be entitled to realize your lien in this action.

You are required to furnish the above-named defendant with particulars of your claim and, specifically, the following facts alleged in your claim for lien:

. . . .
(set out facts)

Date: . . . .
                                                       (defendant, counsel or agent)

Address for service:

. . . .

O. Reg. 159/83, Form 11.

Form 12

Construction Lien Act, 1983

NOTICE OF CROSS-EXAMINATION OF PERSON VERIFYING CLAIM FOR LIEN UNDER SECTION 40 OF THE ACT

TO: ....

(a person named in the claim for lien as having an interest in the premises, the contractor, or the payer of the lien claimant or the solicitor of any of the foregoing).

This is notice that ...., a person

who has verified a claim for lien by ....
                                            (name of lien claimant)

in respect of an improvement to the following premises: ....

....

(street address of premises)

will be cross-examined regarding that claim on ...., ..., at
                                                    (day)   *(date)*

............., at the office of ....
(time)

....

(name, address and telephone number of examiner)

You are entitled to be present at the cross-examination either personally or by counsel and to participate in the cross-examination. Only one cross-examination may be held in respect of this claim for lien.

Date: ....

                                     (name, address and telephone
                                     number of person or solicitor
                                     requiring cross-examination)

                                     O. Reg. 159/83, Form 12.

Form 13

Construction Lien Act, 1983

NOTICE OF CROSS-EXAMINATION
UNDER SECTION 40 OF THE ACT

TO: .... , a person

who has verified a claim for lien by ....
(name of lien claimant)

dated .... with respect to the following premises:

....
(street address of premises)

YOU ARE REQUIRED TO ATTEND TO BE CROSS-EXAMINED ON OATH respecting the claim for lien on ...., ..., at
(day)   (date)

.............., at the office of ....
(time)   (name, address and telephone number of examiner)

.... and to bring with you all documents relating to the claim.

If you fail, without due cause, to attend your lien may be discharged or you may be liable for any legal costs arising from your non-attendance.

Date: ....
(Name, address and telephone
number of person or solicitor
requiring the cross-examination)

O. Reg. 159/83, Form 13.

Form 14

Construction Lien Act, 1983

RELEASE OF LIEN
UNDER SECTION 41 OF THE ACT

Name of lien claimant: ....

Address: ....

1. The lien claimant releases the lien claimed in the claim for lien dated ......,

   in respect of an improvement to the premises owned by .... and described in Schedule A to this release.

2. *(complete where lien attaches to the premises)*
   The registration number of the claim for lien is ....

Date: ....

....
          (witness)   *(lien claimant)*

NOTE:
        Where the lien claimant is not a corporation, the release must be verified by an affidavit of a subscribing witness.

SCHEDULE A

(Where the lien attaches to the premises, provide a description of the premises sufficient for registration under the Land Titles Act, or the Registry Act, as the case may be).

(Where the lien does not attach to the premises, provide the street address, or, where there is none, the location of the premises).

O. Reg. 159/83, Form 14.

Form 15

Construction Lien Act, 1983

NOTICE OF POSTPONEMENT OF LIEN
UNDER SECTION 43 OF THE ACT

Name of lien claimant ....

Address ....

The lien claimant postpones the lien claimed in the claim for lien dated ....,

19...., registered as Instrument No.......... to Instrument No...........,

in respect of the lands described in Schedule A upon the following terms and

conditions: ....

....

....

Date: ....

....
      (witness)   *(signature of lien claimant)*

NOTE:
      Where the lien claimant is not a corporation, the postponement must be
      verified by the affidavit of a subscribing witness.

SCHEDULE A

(Where the lien attaches to the premises, provide a description of the premises sufficient for registration under the Land Titles Act, or the Registry Act, as the case may be).

(Where the lien does not attach to the premises, provide the street address, or, where there is none, the location of the premises).

O. Reg. 159/83, Form 15.

Form 16

Construction Lien Act, 1983

JUDGMENT DIRECTING A
REFERENCE FOR TRIAL
UNDER SECTION 60 OF THE ACT

Court File No.

. . . .

SUPREME COURT OF ONTARIO

(name of judge)   *(day and date)*

BETWEEN

. . . .
Plaintiff(s)

(court seal)   and

. . . .
Defendant(s)

JUDGMENT

On motion of the plaintiff made under the provisions of subsection 60 (1) of the *Construction Lien Act, 1983* in the presence of counsel for the plaintiff(s) and the defendant(s), and on reading the pleadings in this action and on hearing what was alleged by counsel for the parties, *(or the parties by their counsel consenting to judgment, or as the case may be).*

1. THIS COURT ORDERS AND ADJUDGES that this action be referred to the master *(or appointed local master)* at Toronto *(or other place)* for trial.

2. AND THIS COURT ORDERS AND ADJUDGES that the parties found liable forthwith after confirmation of the report of the master *(or appointed local master)* pay to the parties the respective amounts due them.

3. AND THIS COURT ORDERS AND ADJUDGES that the master *(or appointed local master)* determine all questions arising in this action and on the reference and all questions arising under the *Construction Lien Act, 1983* and that the findings of the master *(or appointed local master)* be effective on the confirmation of the report.

4. AND THIS COURT ORDERS AND ADJUDGES that the master *(or appointed local master)* determine the question of costs in this action and of the reference, and the costs be taxed and paid as the master *(or appointed local master)* shall direct.

Date: ....   Signed by: ....
                                        (judge or local judge)
                                      (registrar or local registrar)

O. Reg. 159/83, Form 16.

Form 17

Construction Lien Act, 1983

NOTICE OF TRIAL
UNDER SECTION 62 OF THE ACT

Court File No.

....

SUPREME COURT OF ONTARIO

BETWEEN

....
                                            Plaintiff(s)
                and

....
                                            Defendant(s)

NOTICE

(Use A or B, whichever is applicable)

A. The Supreme Court of Ontario has directed that this action shall be tried on

.........., ..., at ...., at ....
   (day)   *(date)*   *(time)*   *(place)*

B. This action has been set down for trial by the Supreme Court of Ontario, at the non-jury sittings commencing on ....,
                                            (day)   *(date)*

at ...., at ....
       (time)   *(place)*

If you do not appear at the trial, proceedings may be taken in your absence and you may be deprived of all benefit of the action and your rights may be disposed of in your absence.

All parties are required to be prepared to proceed with the trial, and to bring with them on the trial day all evidence and witnesses necessary to prove their respective claims or defences. If any person fails to comply with these directions, the costs of the day may be given against that party should it be necessary to adjourn the trial of this action.

This is an action to enforce a construction lien arising from an improvement of the following premises:

. . . .

(concise description sufficient to identify premises)

This notice is served by . . . .

Date: . . . .

To: . . . .

O. Reg. 159/83, Form 17.

Form 18

Construction Lien Act, 1983

NOTICE OF SETTLEMENT MEETING
UNDER SECTION 62 OF THE ACT

Court File No.

. . . .

SUPREME COURT OF ONTARIO

BETWEEN

. . . .

Plaintiff(s)

and

. . . .

Defendant(s)

NOTICE

The Supreme Court of Ontario has directed that the settlement meeting in respect

of the above action shall be held on . . . . , ... ,
(day)   *(date)*

at . . . . , at . . . .
(time)   *(place)*

(Use A or B, whichever is applicable)

A. The Supreme Court of Ontario has also directed that this action shall be tried
    on . . . . , ... , at . . . . , at . . . .
(day)   *(date)*   *(time)*   *(place)*

B. In addition, this action has been set down for trial by the Supreme Court of
    Ontario, at the non-jury sittings commencing

    on . . . . , ... ,
(day)   *(date)*

    at . . . . , at . . . .
(time)   *(place)*

Any settlement reached at a settlement meeting is binding upon every person
served with notice of the settlement meeting, regardless of whether the person
attends the settlement meeting, and orders may be made by the court affecting
your rights.

(Use where applicable)

If you do not appear at the trial, proceedings may be taken in your absence
and you may be deprived of all benefit of the action and your rights may be
disposed of in your absence.

All parties are required to be prepared to proceed with the trial, and to bring
with them on the trial day all evidence and witnesses necessary to prove their
respective claims or defences. If any person fails to comply with these
directions, the costs of the day may be given against that party should it be
necessary to adjourn the trial of this action.

This is an action to enforce a construction lien arising from an improvement
of the following premises:

. . . .
(concise description sufficient to identify premises)

This notice is served by ....

Date: ....

To: ....

O. Reg. 159/83, form 18.

Form 19

Construction Lien Act, 1983

JUDGMENT AT TRIAL UNDER SECTION 64 OF THE ACT WHERE LIEN ATTACHES TO PREMISES

Court File No.

....

SUPREME COURT OF ONTARIO

(name of judge)   *(day and date)*

BETWEEN

....

Plaintiff(s)

(court seal)   and

....

Defendant(s)

JUDGMENT

THIS ACTION was heard on ...., at ...., in

(date)   *(place)*

the presence of all parties *(or the solicitors for identified parties,* ....

appearing in person, no one appearing for ....,

or as the case may be).

ON READING THE PLEADINGS AND HEARING THE EVIDENCE and the submissions of the solicitors for the parties *(or* ....

appearing in person, or as the case may be).

(use the appropriate paragraphs)

1. THIS COURT DECLARES AND ADJUDGES that the persons named in Column 1 of Schedule A to this judgment are respectively entitled to a lien under the *Construction Lien Act, 1983,* upon

the interest of the owner, ... ,
(name of owner)

in the premises described in Schedule B of this judgment for the amounts set opposite their respective names in Column 5 of Schedule A, and the primary debtors of those persons respectively are as set out in Column 6 of Schedule A.

2. AND THIS COURT DECLARES AND ADJUDGES that the persons mentioned in Column 1 of Schedule C to this judgment are entitled to some charge or encumbrance other than a lien under this Act on the interest of the owner in the premises for the amounts set opposite their respective names in Column 4 of Schedule C.

3. AND THIS COURT ORDERS AND ADJUDGES that the personal liability of the owner .... to the persons named in Column 1 of Schedule E in respect of the holdbacks the owner was required to retain is

$..........., and writs of execution may be issued forthwith for the amounts set out opposite their respective names in Column 2 of Schedule E.

4. AND THIS COURT ORDERS AND ADJUDGES that upon the defendant

.... paying into court to the credit of this action the
(the owner)

amount of $............ on or before the .... day of .... ,

19...., the liens mentioned in Schedule A are discharged and the registration of those liens and the certificates of action in relation to those liens are vacated and the money paid into court is to be paid in payment of the persons entitled to a lien.

5. AND THIS COURT ORDERS AND ADJUDGES that if the defendant

.... makes default in payment of the money into Court
(owner)
that the owner's interest in the premises be sold under the supervision of the master *(or appointed local master)* of this court and that the purchase money be paid into court to the credit of this action.

6. AND THIS COURT ORDERS AND ADJUDGES that the purchase money be applied in or towards payment of the claims mentioned in Schedule(s) A *(and C)* as the master *(or appointed local master)* directs, with subsequent interest and subsequent costs to be computed and taxed by the master *(or appointed local master)*.

7. AND THIS COURT ORDERS AND ADJUDGES that if the purchase money paid into court is insufficient to pay in full the proven claims of the persons mentioned in Column 1 of Schedule A, the primary debtor of each of those persons, as set out in Column 6 of Schedule A, shall pay the amount remaining due to those persons forthwith after the amount has been ascertained by the master *(or appointed local master)*.

8. AND THIS COURT ORDERS AND ADJUDGES that the persons named in Column 1 of Schedule F have not proved any lien under the *Construction Liens Act, 1983,* and orders and adjudges that the claims for lien registered by them and the certificates of action related to those claims as set out in Column 2 of Schedule F are vacated against the premises described in Schedule B.

9. AND THIS COURT ORDERS AND ADJUDGES that the persons whose names are set out in Column 1 of Schedule D to this judgment, although they have not proved their claims for lien, are entitled to personal judgment for the amounts set opposite their respective names in Column 4 of Schedule D against their respective debtors as set out in Column 5 opposite their names and the respective debtors shall forthwith pay to their respective judgment creditors the amount found due.

10. AND THIS COURT ORDERS AND ADJUDGES, that since the owner's interest in the premises has been sold by . . . . , a mortgagee, and it has been determined by this court that the liens were entitled to priority over the mortgage under subsection 80 (2) [*or subsection 80 (5) as the case may be*] of the Act, therefore the mortgagee shall pay to the persons named in Schedule E the amount set out opposite each of their

respective names on or before the . . . . day of . . . . , 19. . .

. . . .

(signature of judge or local judge)

Schedule A

Column 1	Column 2	Column 3	Column 4	Column 5	Column 6
Names of persons entitled to construction lien	Registration numbers of claims for lien and certificates of action	Amount of debt and interest (if any)	Costs	Total	Names of primary debtors

. . . .

(signature of judge or local judge)

Schedule B

The premises in respect of which this action is brought is as follows:

....

(Set out a description sufficient for registration purposes)

....
*(signature of judge
or local judge)*

Schedule C

COLUMN 1	COLUMN 2	COLUMN 3	COLUMN 4
Names of persons entitled to encumbrances other than construction liens	Amount of debt and interest (if any)	Costs	Total

....
*(signature of judge
or local judge)*

Schedule D

COLUMN 1	COLUMN 2	COLUMN 3	COLUMN 4	COLUMN 5
Judgment creditors not entitled to liens	Amount of debt and interest (if any)	Costs	Total	Names of Debtors

....
*(signature of judge or
local judge)*

Schedule E

COLUMN 1	COLUMN 2
Name of persons entitled to share in holdback	Amount to be paid

....
(signature of judge or
local judge)

Schedule F

COLUMN 1	COLUMN 2
Names of Persons not entitled to lien	Registration numbers of claims for lien and certificates of action

....
(signature of judge or
local judge)

O. Reg. 159/83, Form 19.

Form 20

Construction Lien Act, 1983

JUDGMENT AT TRIAL UNDER SECTION 64 OF THE ACT
WHERE LIEN DOES NOT ATTACH TO PREMISES

Court File No.

....

SUPREME COURT OF ONTARIO

(name of judge)   *(day and date)*

BETWEEN

. . . .   Plaintiff(s)

and

. . . .   Defendant(s)

JUDGMENT

THIS ACTION was heard on . . . . , at . . . . , in the
                                         (date)   *(place)*

presence of the solicitors for all parties *(or the solicitors for identified parties,*

. . . . *appearing in person, no one appearing for* . . . . ,
or as the case may be).

ON READING THE PLEADINGS AND HEARING THE EVIDENCE and
the submissions of the solicitors for the parties *(or as the case may be),*

(use the appropriate paragraphs)

1. THIS COURT DECLARES AND ADJUDGES that the amount for which

   the defendant-owner . . . . is liable under
                                                    (owner)
   section 21 [*or subsection 17 (4)*] of the *Construction Lien Act, 1983* is $ . . . . . .

2. AND THIS COURT DECLARES AND ADJUDGES that the persons
   named in Column 1 of Schedule A to this judgment are respectively entitled to
   a lien under the *Construction Lien Act, 1983* which lien is a charge under
   section 21 upon the amount for which the defendant-owner is liable; for the
   amounts set opposite their respective names in Column 4 and the primary
   debtors of those persons are set out in Column 5 of Schedule A.

3. AND THIS COURT ORDERS AND ADJUDGES that upon the

   defendant-owner . . . . paying into court to the
                                                    (owner)
   credit of this action the amount of $ . . . . for which the owner is

   liable on or before the . . . . , ...
                                       (day)   *(date)*
   that the liens mentioned in Schedule A are discharged, that the money paid
   into court is to be paid in payment of the persons entitled to a lien.

4. AND THIS COURT ORDERS AND ADJUDGES that if the money paid into court is insufficient to pay in full the proven claims of the persons mentioned in Column 1 of Schedule A, the primary debtor of each of those persons as set out in Column 5 of Schedule A shall pay the amount remaining due to those persons forthwith after this amount has been ascertained by the master *(or appointed local master)*.

5. AND THIS COURT DECLARES AND ADJUDGES that the following persons have not proved any lien under the *Construction Lien Act, 1983:*

. . . .
(names of persons)

and are not entitled to a personal judgment against any of the parties to this action.

6. AND THIS COURT ADJUDGES that the persons whose names are set out in Column 1 of Schedule B to this judgment, although they have not proven their claims for lien are entitled to personal judgment for the amounts set opposite their respective name in Column 4 of Schedule B against their respective debtors as set out in Column 5 opposite their names and the respective debtors shall forthwith pay to their respective judgment creditors the amount found due.

. . . .
(signature of judge or
local judge)

Schedule A

COLUMN 1	COLUMN 2	COLUMN 3	COLUMN 4	COLUMN 5
Names of persons entitled to construction lien	Amount of debt and interest (if any)	Costs	Total	Names of primary debtors

. . . .
(signature of judge or
local judge)

Schedule B

COLUMN 1	COLUMN 2	COLUMN 3	COLUMN 4	COLUMN 5
Judgment creditors not entitled to liens	Amount of debt and interest (if any)	Costs	Total	Names of Debtors

. . . .
(signature of judge or local judge)

O. Reg. 159/83, Form 20.

Form 21

Construction Lien Act, 1983

REPORT UNDER SECTION 64 OF THE ACT WHERE LIEN ATTACHES TO PREMISES

Court File No.

. . . .

SUPREME COURT OF ONTARIO

(name of master)   *(day and date)*
(or appointed local master)

BETWEEN

. . . .   Plaintiff(s)

(court seal)   and

. . . .   Defendant(s)

REPORT

In accordance with a judgment of reference dated . . . . ,

trial of this action was heard on . . . . , at . . . . ,
　　　　　　　　　　　　　(date)　　　　　　　　　*(place)*

in the presence of all parties *(or the solicitors for identified parties,* . . . .

appearing in person, no one appearing for . . . . ,
or as the case may be).

ON READING THE PLEADINGS AND HEARING THE EVIDENCE and
the submissions of the solicitors for the parties *(or as the case may be).*

(use the appropriate paragraphs)

1. I FIND AND DECLARE THAT the persons named in Column 1 of
   Schedule A to this report are respectively entitled to a lien under the

   Construction Lien Act, 1983, upon the interest of the owner, ... ,
   　　　　　　　　　　　　　　　　　　　　　　　　　　　　(name of owner)

   in the premises described in Schedule B of this report for the amounts set
   opposite their respective names in Column 5 of Schedule A, and the primary
   debtors of those persons respectively are as set out in Column 6 of Schedule
   A.

2. I FIND AND DECLARE THAT the persons mentioned in Column 1 of
   Schedule C to this report are entitled to some charge or encumbrance other
   than a lien under this Act on the interest of the owner in the premises for the
   amounts set opposite their respective names in Column 4 of Schedule C.

3. AND I FIND, DECLARE AND DIRECT that the personal liability of the

   owner . . . . to the persons named in Column 1 of
   Schedule E in respect of the holdbacks the owner was required to retain is

   $. . . . . and writs of execution may be issued forthwith after
   confirmation of this order for the amounts set opposite their respective
   names in Column 2 of Schedule E.

4. AND I DIRECT that upon the defendant . . . .
   　　　　　　　　　　　　　　　　　　　　　　　(the owner)

   paying into court to the credit of this action the amount of $ . . . .

   on or before the . . . . day of . . . . , 19. . . . ,
   the liens mentioned in Schedule A are discharged and the registration of
   those liens and the certificates of action in relation to those liens are vacated
   and the money paid into court is to be paid in payment of the persons entitled
   to a lien.

5. AND I DIRECT that if the defendant ....

(owner)

makes default in payment of the money into Court that the owner's interest in the premises be sold under the supervision of the master *(or appointed local master)* of this court and that the purchase money be paid into court to the credit of this action.

6. AND I DIRECT that the purchase money be applied in or towards payment of the claims mentioned in Schedule(s) A *(and C)* as the master *(or appointed local master)* directs, with subsequent interest and subsequent costs to be computed and taxed by the master *(or appointed local master).*

7. AND I DIRECT that if the purchase money paid into court is insufficient to pay in full the proven claims of the persons mentioned in Column 1 of Schedule A, the primary debtor of each of those persons, as set out in Column 6 of Schedule A, shall pay the amount remaining due to those persons forthwith after the amount has been ascertained by the master *(or appointed local master).*

8. AND I FIND AND DECLARE THAT the persons named in Column 1 of Schedule F have not proved any lien under the *Construction Lien Act, 1983,* and I direct that the claims for lien registered by them and the certificates of action related to those claims as set out in Column 2 of Schedule F be vacated against the premises described in Schedule B.

9. AND I FIND AND DECLARE THAT the persons whose names are set out in Column 1 of Schedule D to this report, although they have not proven their claims for lien, are entitled to personal judgment for the amounts set opposite their respective names in Column 4 of Schedule D against their respective debtors as set out in Column 5 opposite their names and the respective debtors shall forthwith after confirmation of this report pay to their respective judgment creditors the amount found due.

10. AND I DIRECT that since the owner's interest in the premises has been sold

by ...., a mortgagee, and it has been determined by this court that the lien claimants were entitled to priority over the mortgagee under subsection 80 (2) [*or subsection 80 (5) as the case may be*] of the Act, therefore the mortgagee shall pay to the persons named in Schedule E the amount set out opposite each of their respective names on or before the .... day of ...., 19....

....

(master or appointed local master)

Schedule A

COLUMN 1	COLUMN 2	COLUMN 3	COLUMN 4	COLUMN 5	COLUMN 6
Names of persons entitled to construction lien	Registration numbers of claims for lien and certificates of action	Amount of debt and interest (if any)	Costs	Total	Names of primary debtors

. . . .

(signature of master or appointed local master)

Schedule B

The premises in respect of which this action is brought is as follows:

. . . .

(Set out a description sufficient for registration purposes)

. . . .

(signature of master or appointed local master)

Schedule C

COLUMN 1	COLUMN 2	COLUMN 3	COLUMN 4
Names of persons entitled to encumbrances other than construction liens	Amount of debt and interest (if any)	Costs	Total

. . . .

(signature of master or appointed local master)

Schedule D

COLUMN 1	COLUMN 2	COLUMN 3	COLUMN 4	COLUMN 5
Judgment creditors not entitled to liens	Amount of debt and interest (if any)	Costs	Total	Names of Debtors

. . . .
(signature of master or appointed local master)

Schedule E

COLUMN 1	COLUMN 2
Name of persons entitled to share in holdback	Amount to be paid

. . . .
(signature of master or appointed local master)

Schedule F

COLUMN 1	COLUMN 2
Names of persons not entitled to lien	Registration numbers of claims for lien and certificates of action

. . . .
(signature of master or appointed local master)

O. Reg. 159/83, Form 21.

Form 22

Construction Lien Act, 1983

REPORT UNDER SECTION 64 OF THE ACT
WHERE LIEN DOES NOT ATTACH TO PREMISES

Court File No.

. . . .

SUPREME COURT OF ONTARIO

(master or appointed   *(day and date)*
   local master)

BETWEEN

. . . .   Plaintiff(s)

and

. . . .   Defendant(s)

REPORT

In accordance with a judgment of reference dated . . . . ,

trial of this action was heard on . . . . , at . . . . ,
                                                    (date)   *(place)*
in the presence of the solicitors for all parties *(or the solicitors for identified*

parties, ... *appearing in person, no one appearing for*

. . . . , *or as the case may be).*

ON READING THE PLEADINGS AND HEARING THE EVIDENCE and
the submissions of the solicitors for the parties *(or as the case may be).*

(use the appropriate paragraphs)

1. I FIND AND DECLARE that the amount for which the defendant-owner

. . . . is liable under section 21 [*or subsection 17 (4)*] of the
      (owner)

Construction Lien Act, 1983 is $. . . . .

2. I FIND AND DECLARE that the persons named in Column 1 of Schedule A to this report are respectively entitled to a lien under the *Construction Lien Act, 1983* which lien is a charge under section 21 of the Act upon the amount for which the defendant-owner is liable; for the amounts set opposite their respective names in Column 4 and the primary debtors of those persons are set out in Column 5 of Schedule A.

3. AND I DIRECT that upon the defendant-owner ....

(owner)

paying into court to the credit of this action the amount of $ ....

for which the owner is liable on or before the ....,

(day)   *(date)*

the liens mentioned in Schedule A are discharged, and that the money paid into court is to be paid in payment of the persons entitled to a lien.

4. AND I DIRECT that if the money paid into court is insufficient to pay in full the proven claims of the persons mentioned in Column 1 of Schedule A, the primary debtor of each of those persons as set out in Column 5 of Schedule A shall pay the amount remaining due to those persons forthwith after this amount has been ascertained by the master *(or appointed local master).*

5. AND I FIND AND DECLARE that the following persons have not proved any lien under the *Construction Lien Act, 1983:*

....

(names of persons)

and are not entitled to a personal judgment against any of the parties to this action.

6. AND I FIND AND DECLARE that the persons whose names are set out in Column 1 of Schedule B to this report, although they have not proved their claims for lien are entitled to personal judgment for the amounts set opposite their respective names in Column 5 after confirmation of this report and the respective debtors shall forthwith after confirmation of this report pay to their respective judgment creditors the amount found due.

....

(master or appointed
local master)

Schedule A

COLUMN 1	COLUMN 2	COLUMN 3	COLUMN 4	COLUMN 5
Names of persons entitled to construction lien	Amount of debt and interest (if any)	Costs	Total	Names of primary debtors

....

(signature of master or appointed local master)

Schedule B

COLUMN 1	COLUMN 2	COLUMN 3	COLUMN 4	COLUMN 5
Judgment creditors not entitled to liens	Amount of debt and interest (if any)	Costs	Total	Names of Debtors

....

(signature of master or appointed local master)

O. Reg. 159/83, Form 22.

Form 23

Construction Lien Act, 1983

FINANCIAL GUARANTEE BOND UNDER SUBSECTION 80 (10) OF THE ACT

The surety of this bond is ...., a guarantee

company to which the *Guarantee Companies Securities Act* applies.

The principal of this bond is ....,

a mortgagee of the interest of the owner ....

in the premises described in Schedule A to this bond.

The obligees of this bond are all persons having liens whose liens are entitled to priority over the interest of the principal under subsection 80 (2) or (5) of the Act.

WHEREAS it is the intention of the principal to sell the interest of the owner under a power of sale.

THEREFORE, subject to the conditions contained in this bond, the surety and the principal bind themselves, their heirs, executors, administrators, successors and assigns, jointly and severally to the obligees as follows:

1. The principal shall, on or before the date set out in the judgment or report for payment, pay to each obligee who has proved a lien the amount determined by the court to be owing to that obligee under subsection 80 (2) or (5) of the Act by the principal as mortgagee, unless in the meantime an appeal has been taken from the judgment or report in which case payment is not required until the final disposition of all appeals.

2. The surety, in default of payment by the principal shall pay to each obligee the amount owing to him by the principal, but the surety is not

liable to pay more than a total maximum amount of $ ....
(*an amount equal to 20 per cent of the amount stated to be the contract price in the affidavit attached as Schedule B to this bond*).

This bond is subject to the following conditions:

1. An obligee shall not make a claim against the surety unless the principal is in default of his obligations under this bond.

2. An obligee shall give the surety thirty days' written notice of his claim prior to commencing an action against the surety.

3. The surety is released from its obligation to an obligee unless the obligee has given written notice of his claim to the surety within one year after the default by the principal.

4. The total amount of this bond is reduced by and to the extent of any payment made under the bond.

5. The surety is entitled to an assignment of the rights of an obligee against the principal to the extent of the payment made by the surety.

Signed and sealed by the principal and the surety on the .... day of

.........................., 19.... and registration of this bond on the title to the premises constitutes delivery of this bond to each obligee.

SIGNED AND SEALED
in the presence of: .... *(seal)*

(principal)

.... *(seal)*

(surety)

NOTE:

Where the principal is not a corporation, the principal's signature must be verified by an affidavit of a subscribing witness.

Schedule A

FINANCIAL GUARANTEE BOND

(provide a description of the premises sufficient for registration under the Land Titles Act or the Registry Act, as the case may be)

Schedule B

FINANCIAL GUARANTEE BOND

AFFIDAVIT OF GOOD FAITH BY MORTGAGEE

I, ..., make oath and say *(or affirm)* as follows:

1. I am a mortgagee of the interest of ....
   (name of owner)
   described in Schedule A to the attached bond.

2. Under the terms of the mortgage, or under the *Mortgages Act,* I am entitled to exercise a power of sale with respect to that interest.

3. It is my intention to exercise that power of sale, even though there are claims for lien registered against the interest of the owner under the *Construction Lien Act, 1983* that may have priority to the mortgage under the Act.

4. I have inquired of the contractor and the owner with respect to the contract price of the contract to which that improvement relates, and to the best of

my information and belief the amount of the contract price *(including the price of all services and materials supplied under all amendments to that contract)* is ....

5. The attached bond has been obtained by me in good faith, without any intention of depriving any lien claimant of his rights under the *Construction Lien Act, 1983.*

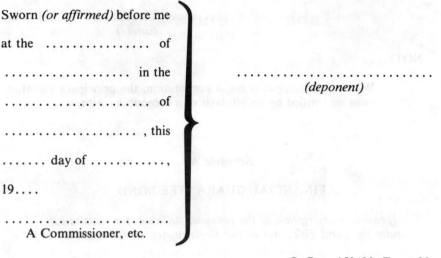

Sworn *(or affirmed)* before me

at the .... of

.... in the

.... of

.... , this

.... day of .... ,

19....

....
    A Commissioner, etc.

....
          (deponent)

O. Reg. 159/83, Form 23.

Appendix D

Table of Concordance:

Mechanics' Lien Act to Construction Lien Act, 1983

MECHANICS' LIEN ACT PROVISION	ATTORNEY GENERAL'S COMMITTEE DRAFT PROVISION	MECHANICS' LIEN ACT PROVISION	ATTORNEY GENERAL'S COMMITTEE DRAFT PROVISION
1(1)(a)	deleted		1(1)20
1(1)(b)	1(1)4		1(2)
1(1)(c)	1(1)6		14(1)
1(1)(c)	1(1)9		17(1)
1(1)(d)	1(1)12	6(2)	16
1(1)(e)	1(1)12	6(3)	1(2)
1(1)(f)	1(1)15	6(4)	1(3)
1(1)(g)	deleted	6(5)	1(1)12
1(1)(h)	1(1)22		1(1)24
1(1)(i)	1(1)25	7	18
1(1)(j)	1(1)26	8(1)	19(1)
1(2)	1(1)24	8(2)	19(2), (3), (4)
1(3)	2(1)	8(3)	80(3), (4)
1(4)	2(2)	8(4)	15
2	3		80(3), (4)
3(1)	8(1)	8(5)	deleted
3(2)	11	8(6)	80(3), (4), (6)
3(3)	7(2)	9	85
3(4)	7(1)	10	17(1)
3(5)	11	11	17(1)
3(6)	11	12(1)	1(1)20
3(7)	13		22(1)
4	deleted	12(2)	1(1)17
5	4		25
6(1)	1(1)8	12(3)	deleted
	1(1)19		but see s. 31(5)

12(4)	32(1)7	29(4)	55(6)
12(5)	21	29(5)	45
12(6)	24	29(6)	44(5)
12(7)	24	29(7)	48
	29		49
12(8)	26	30(1), (2), (3)	77
12(9)	5	30(3), (4)	deleted
12(10)	30	31	deleted
13	28	32(1)	39(1), (4)
14	74	32(2)	39(2), (5)
15(1)	80(4), (6)	32(3)	39(6)
15(2)	82(1)	33(1)	50(1)
15(3)	82(2)	33(2)	55(1)
16(1)	83(1)	33(3)	55(2)
16(2)	74	33(4)	56(1)
16(3)	deleted	39(5)	59
16(4)	83(3)	39(6)	deleted
17(1)	34(1), (4)	34	50(3)
17(2)	34(5)	35(1)	51(2)
17(3)	deleted	35(2)	51(1)
	but see s. 16(3)		60(1)
18	34(7)	35(3)	60(3), (4)
19(1)	6(1)	35(4)	52
19(2)	6(2)	36	52
20	deleted	37	20
21	78		76
22	31	38(1)	deleted
	34(1)	38(2), (3), (4),	70
21(1)	deleted	(5), (6)	80(7)
23(2)	34(1)(b)	39	deleted
23(3)	34(2)	40	61
23(4)	34(3)	41	61
23(5)	deleted	42(1)	62(1)
23(6)	deleted	42(2)	62(2)
23(7)	34(4)	42(3)	deleted
24(1)	34(1)	42(4)(a), (b)	53
24(2)	36(3)(a)	42(4)(c)	64(1), (4)
24(3)	37	42(5)	64(2)
	46	42(6)	64(5)
24(4)	deleted	42(7)	64(6)
25	34	42(8)	69(5)
26	36	42(9)	54
27	36	42(10)	deleted
28	75	43	67
29(1)	41		68
29(2)(a)	44		86
29(2)(b)	47	44	65
29(2)(c)	47	45	66
29(3)	44(6), (7)	46	72

47(1)	73(1), (3)	49(4)	88(2)
47(2)	73(2)	49(5)	deleted
47(3)	64(3)	50	69
47(4)	88(3)	51	89
48(1)	deleted	52	remains in force
49(1)	88(1)		unaffected
49(2)	deleted	53	90
49(3)	deleted		

Table of Concordance:

Construction Lien Act, 1983 to Mechanics' Lien Act

ATTORNEY GENERAL'S COMMITTEE DRAFT PROVISION	MECHANICS' LIEN ACT PROVISION	ATTORNEY GENERAL'S COMMITTEE DRAFT PROVISION	MECHANICS' LIEN ACT PROVISION
1(1)1	-	1(1)23	-
1(1)2	-	1(1)24	1(2)
1(1)3	-		6(5)
1(1)4	1(1)(b)	1(1)25	1(1)(i)
1(1)5	-	1(1)26	1(1)(j)
1(1)6	1(1)(c)	1(1)27	-
1(1)7	-	1(1)28	-
1(1)8	6(1) part	1(2)	6(1), (3) and
1(1)9	1(1)(d)		(4) part
1(1)10	-	1(3)	6(1), (3) and
1(1)11	-		(4) part
1(1)12	1(1)(e)	2(1)	1(3)
1(1)13	-	2(2)	1(4)
1(1)14	-	3	2
1(1)15	1(1)(f)	4	5
1(1)16	-	5	12(9)
1(1)17	12(2) part	6	19
1(1)18	-	7(1)	3(4)
1(1)19	6(1) part	7(2)	3(3)
1(1)20	6(1) part	7(3)	-
	12(1) part	7(4)	-
1(1)21	-	8(1)	3(1)
1(1)22	-	8(2)	-

9	-	39(3)	-
10	-	39(4)	-
11	3(2), (5) and (6)	39(5)	32(1) and (2)
12	-	39(6)	28(3)
13	-	40	-
14(1)	6(1) part	41	29(1)
14(2)	-	42	-
15	6(4)	43	-
16	6(2)	44(1)	29(2)
17(1)	6(1)	44(2)	-
	10	44(3)	-
	11	44(4)	-
17(2)	-	44(5)	29(6)
17(3)	-	44(6)(7)	29(3) and (4)
17(4)	-	44(8)	-
18	7	44(9)	-
19	8	45	29(5)
20	37	46	24(3)
21	12(5)	47	41(4)
22(1)	12(1)	48	-
22(2)	-	49	29(7)
22(3)	-	50	33(1)
23	-		34
24	12(7)	51	35(1) and (2)
25	12(3)	52	-
26	12(8)	53	42(4)(a) and (b)
27	-	54	42(9)
28	13	55(1)	33(2)
29	-	55(2)	33(3)
30	12(10)	55(3)	-
31	22	56	-
32	-	57	-
33	12(2) part	58	-
34(1)	17(1)	59	33(5)
	24(1)	60	35(2) and (3)
	25(1)	61	40
34(2)	23(3)		41
34(3)	23(4)	62	42(1), (2) and (3)
34(4)	17(1)	63	-
34(5)	17(2)	64	42(4)(c), 42(5),
34(16)	-		(6), (7), 47(3)
34(5)	18(1)	65	44
35	-	66	45
36	26	67	43
	27	68	-
37	24(3)	69	50
38	-	69(5)	42(5)
39(1)	32(1)	70	38
39(2)	32(2)	71	-

72	46(1)	80(9)	-
73	47	81	-
74	14	82	15
	16(2)	83	16
75	28	84	-
76	37	85	9
77	30(1), (2), (3)	86	38(4)
78	21		43
79	15(1)	87	-
80(1)	-	88	49
80(2)	-		47(4)
80(3)	8(3), (4) part	89	51
80(4)	8(3), (4) part	90	53
80(5)	-	91	-
80(6)	15(1)	92	-
80(7)	15(3) and (2)	93	-
80(8)	-		

Appendix E

Mechanics' Lien Act
R.S.O. 1980, c. 261

1.—(1) In this Act,

(*a*) "completion of the contract" means substantial performance, not necessarily total performance, of the contract;

(*b*) "contractor" means a person contracting with or employed directly by the owner or his agent for the doing of work or the placing or furnishing of materials for any of the purposes mentioned in this Act;

(*c*) "Crown" includes Crown agencies to which the *Crown Agency Act* applies;

(*d*) "estate or interest in land" includes a statutory right given or reserved to the Crown to enter any lands or premises of any person or public authority for the purpose of doing any work, construction, repair or maintenance in, upon, through, over or under any such lands or premises;

(*e*) "materials" includes every kind of movable property;

(*f*) "owner" includes any person and corporation, including the Crown, a municipal corporation and a railway company, having any estate or interest in the land upon which or in respect of which work is done or materials are placed or furnished, at whose request, and

    (i) upon whose credit, or

    (ii) on whose behalf, or

    (iii) with whose privity or consent, or

    (iv) for whose direct benefit,

work is done or materials are placed or furnished and all persons claiming under him or it whose rights are acquired after the work in respect of which the lien is claimed is commenced or the materials placed or furnished have been commenced to be placed or furnished;

(g) "public work" means the property of the Crown and includes land in which the Crown has an estate or interest, and also includes all works and properties acquired, constructed, extended, enlarged, repaired, equipped or improved at the expense of the Crown, or for the acquisition, construction, repairing, equipping, extending, enlarging or improving of which any public money is appropriated by the Legislature, but not any work for which money is appropriated as a subsidy only;

(h) "subcontractor" means a person not contracting with or employed directly by the owner or his agent for any of the purposes mentioned in this Act, but contracting with or employed by a contractor or, under him, by another subcontractor;

(i) "wages" means the money earned by a workman for work done by time or as piece work, and includes all monetary supplementary benefits, whether by statute, contract or collective bargaining agreement;

(j) "workman" means a person employed for wages in any kind of labour, whether employed under a contract of service or not. R.S.O. 1970, c. 267, s. 1(1); 1975, c. 43, s. 1, *revised.*

Work includes service   (2) In this Act, the expression "the doing of work" includes the performance of a service, and corresponding expressions have corresponding meanings.

Substantial performance   (3) For the purposes of this Act, a contract shall be deemed to be substantially performed,

(a) when the work or a substantial part thereof is ready for use or is being used for the purpose intended; and

(b) when the work to be done under the contract is capable of completion or correction at a cost of not more than,

(i) 3 per cent of the first $250,000 of the contract price,

(ii) 2 per cent of the next $250,000 of the contract price, and

(iii) 1 per cent of the balance of the contract price.

(4) For the purpose of this Act, where the work or a substantial part thereof is ready for use or is being used.for the purpose intended and where the work cannot be completed expeditiously for reasons beyond the control of the contractor, the value of the work to be completed shall be deducted from the contract price in determining substantial performance. R.S.O. 1970, c. 267, s. 1 (2-4). *Idem*

2.—(1) Subject to subsection 6 (2), this Act binds the Crown but does not apply in respect of work under a contract as defined in the *Ministry of Transportation and Communications Creditors Payment Act* and to which that Act applies. *Application of Act* *R.S.O. 1980, c. 290*

(2) Section 7 of the *Proceedings Against the Crown Act* does not apply in respect of proceedings against the Crown under this Act. 1975, c. 43, s. 2. *Application of R.S.O. 1980, c. 393*

GENERAL

3.—(1) All sums received by a builder, contractor or subcontractor on account of the contract price constitute a trust fund in his hands for the benefit of the owner, builder, contractor, subcontractor, Workmen's Compensation Board, workmen, and persons who have supplied materials on account of the contract or who have rented equipment to be used on the contract site, and the builder, contractor or subcontractor, as the case may be, is the trustee of all such sums so received by him and he shall not appropriate or convert any part thereof to his own use or to any use not authorized by the trust until all workmen and all persons who have supplied materials on the contract or who have rented equipment to be used on the contract site and all subcontractors are paid for work done or materials supplied on the contract and the Workmen's Compensation Board is paid any assessment with respect thereto. *Trust funds in hands of contractors*

(2) Notwithstanding subsection (1), where a builder, contractor or subcontractor has paid in whole or in part for any materials supplied on account of the contract or for any rented equipment or has paid any workman who has performed any work or any subcontractor who has placed or furnished any materials in respect of the contract, the retention by such builder, contractor or subcontractor of a sum equal to the sum so paid by him shall be deemed not to be an appropriation or conversion thereof to his own use or to any use not authorized by the trust. *Exception*

(3) Where a sum becomes payable under a contract to a contractor by an owner on the certificate of a person authorized under the contract to make such a certificate, an amount equal to the sum so *Trust funds in hands of owners*

certified that is in the owner's hands or received by him at any time thereafter shall, until paid to the contractor, constitute a trust fund in the owner's hands for the benefit of the contractor, subcontractor, Workmen's Compensation Board, workmen, and persons who have supplied materials on account of the contract or who have rented equipment to be used on the contract site, and the owner shall not appropriate or convert any part thereof to his own use or to any use not authorized by the trust until all workmen and all persons who have supplied materials on the contract or who have rented equipment to be used on the contract site and all contractors and subcontractors are paid for work done or materials supplied on the contract and the Workmen's Compensation Board is paid any assessment with respect thereto. R.S.O. 1970, c. 267, s. 2 (1-3).

Advances on mortgage, etc., a trust fund R.S.O. 1980, c. 303

(4) All sums received by an owner, other than the Crown, a municipality as defined in the *Municipal Affairs Act* or a metropolitan or regional municipality or a local board thereof, which are to be used in the financing, including the purchase price of the land and the payment of prior encumbrances, of a building, structure or work, constitute, subject to the payment of the purchase price of the land and prior encumbrances, a trust fund in the hands of the owner for the benefit of the persons mentioned in subsection (1), and, until the claims of all such persons have been paid, the owner shall not appropriate or convert any part thereof to his own use or to any use not authorized by the trust. R.S.O. 1970, c. 267, s. 2 (4); 1972, c. 1, s. 104 (5); 1975, c. 43, s. 3.

Exception

(5) Notwithstanding subsection (4), where an owner has himself paid in whole or in part for any work done, for any materials placed or furnished or for any rented equipment, the retention by him from any moneys received from the lender under subsection (4) of a sum equal to the sum so paid by him shall be deemed not to be an appropriation or conversion thereof to his own use or to any use not authorized by the trust.

Protection for money lenders

(6) Notwithstanding anything in this section, where money is lent to a person upon whom a trust is imposed by this section and is used by him to pay in whole or in part for any work done, for any materials placed or furnished or for any rented equipment, trust moneys may be applied to discharge the loan to the extent that the lender's money was so used by the trustee, and any sum so applied shall be deemed not to be an appropriation or conversion to the trustee's own use or to any use not authorized by the trust.

Offence and penalty

(7) Every person upon whom a trust is imposed by this section who knowingly appropriates or converts any part of any trust moneys referred to in subsection (1), (3) or (4) to his own use or to any use not authorized by the trust is guilty of an offence and on con-

viction is liable to a fine of not more than $5,000 or to imprisonment for a term of not more than two years, or to both, and every director or officer of a corporation who knowingly assents to or acquiesces in any such offence by the corporation is guilty of such offence, in addition to the corporation, and on conviction is liable to a fine of not more than $5,000 or to imprisonment for a term of not more than two years, or to both. R.S.O. 1970, c. 267, s. 2 (5-7).

4. No action to assert any claim to trust moneys referred to in section 3 shall be commenced against a lender of money to a person upon whom a trust is imposed by that section except,

Limit of time for asserting claims to trust moneys

> (*a*) in the case of a claim by a contractor or subcontractor in cases not provided for in clauses (*b*), (*c*) and (*d*), within nine months after the completion or abandonment of the contract or subcontract;
>
> (*b*) in the case of a claim for materials, within nine months after the placing or furnishing of the last material;
>
> (*c*) in the case of a claim for services, within nine months after the completion of the service; or
>
> (*d*) in the case of a claim for wages, within nine months after the last work was done for which the claim is made. R.S.O. 1970, c. 267, s. 3.

5.—(1) Every agreement, oral or written, express or implied, on the part of any workman that this Act does not apply to him or that the remedies provided by it are not available for his benefit is void.

Agreements waiving application of Act are void

(2) Subsection (1) does not apply.

Exception

> (*a*) to a manager, officer or foreman; or
>
> (*b*) to any person whose wages are more than $50 a day.

(3) No agreement deprives any person otherwise entitled to a lien under this Act, who is not a party to the agreement, of the benefit of the lien, but it attaches, notwithstanding such agreement. R.S.O. 1970, c. 267, s. 4.

Effect upon third party of agreement waiving lien

CREATION OF LIENS

6.—(1) Unless he signs an express agreement to the contrary and in that case subject to section 5, any person who does any work upon or in respect of, or places or furnishes any materials to be used in, the making, constructing, erecting, fitting, altering, improving or

General right to a lien

repairing of any land, building, structure or works or the appurtenances to any of them for any owner, contractor or subcontractor by virtue thereof has a lien for the price of the work or materials upon the estate or interest of the owner in the land, building, structure or works and appurtenances and the land occupied thereby or enjoyed therewith, or upon or in respect of which the work is done, or upon which the materials are placed or furnished to be used, limited, however, in amount to the sum justly due to the person entitled to the lien and to the sum justly owing, except as herein provided, by the owner, and the placing or furnishing of the materials to be used upon the land or such other place in the immediate vicinity of the land designated by the owner or his agent is good and sufficient delivery for the purpose of this Act, but delivery on the designated land does not make such land subject to a lien. R.S.O. 1970, c. 267, s. 5 (1).

Where lien against Crown or municipality

(2) Where the land or premises upon or in respect of which any work is done or materials are placed or furnished is,

    (*a*) a public street or highway owned by a municipality; or

    (*b*) a public work,

the lien given by subsection (1) does not in any event attach to such land or premises but shall instead constitute a charge on amounts directed to be retained by section 12, and the provisions of this Act shall be construed, with necessary modifications, to have effect without requiring the registration or enforcement of a lien or a claim for lien against such land or premises. 1975, c. 43, s. 4.

Lien attaches where materials incorporated into building

(3) The lien given by subsection (1) attaches as therein set out where the materials delivered to be used are incorporated into the land, building, structure or works, notwithstanding that the materials may not have been delivered in strict accordance with subsection (1).

Interpretation

(4) In subsection (1), "agent" includes the contractor or subcontractor for whom the materials are placed or furnished, unless the person placing or furnishing the materials has had actual notice from the owner to the contrary.

Lien for rented equipment

(5) A person who rents equipment to an owner, contractor or subcontractor for use on a contract site shall be deemed for the purposes of this Act to have performed a service for which he has a lien for the price of the rental of the equipment used on the contract site, limited, however, in amount to the sum justly owed and due to the person entitled to the lien from the owner, builder, contractor or subcontractor in respect of the rental of the equipment. R.S.O. 1970, c. 267, s. 5 (3-5).

7. Where work is done or materials are placed or furnished to be used upon or in respect of the land of a married woman, or in which she has an interest, with the privity or consent of her husband, he shall be presumed conclusively to be acting as her agent as well as for himself for the purposes of this Act unless before doing the work or placing or furnishing the materials the person doing the work or placing or furnishing the materials has had actual notice to the contrary. R.S.O. 1970, c. 267, s. 6, *revised*.

When husband's interest liable for work done or materials furnished on land of spouse

8.—(1) Where the estate or interest upon which the lien attaches is leasehold, the fee simple is also subject to the lien if the person doing the work or placing or furnishing the materials gives notice in writing, by personal service, to the owner in fee simple or his agent of the work to be done or materials to be placed or furnished unless the owner in fee simple or his agent within fifteen days thereafter gives notice in writing, by personal service, to such person that he will not be responsible therefor.

Where estate charged is leasehold

(2) No forfeiture or attempted forfeiture of the lease on the part of the landlord, or cancellation or attempted cancellation of the lease except for non-payment of rent, deprives any person otherwise entitled to a lien of the benefit of the lien, but the person entitled to the lien may pay any rent accruing after he becomes so entitled, and the amount so paid may be added to his claim.

Forfeiture or cancellation of lease, effect of on lienholder

(3) Where the land and premises upon or in respect of which any work is done or materials are placed or furnished are encumbered by a mortgage or other charge that was registered in the proper land registry office before any lien under this Act arose, the mortgage or other charge has priority over all liens under this Act to the extent of the actual value of the land and premises at the time the first lien arose, such value to be ascertained by the judge or officer having jurisdiction to try an action under this Act.

Prior mortgages

(4) The time at which the first lien arose shall be deemed to be the time at which the first work was done or the first materials placed or furnished, irrespective of whether a claim for lien in respect thereof is registered or enforced and whether or not such lien is before the court.

When first lien arose

(5) Any mortgage existing as a valid security, notwithstanding that it is a prior mortgage within the meaning of subsection (3), may also secure future advances, subject to subsection 15(1).

Future advances

(6) A registered agreement for the sale and purchase of land and any moneys *bona fide* secured or payable thereunder has the same priority over a lien as is provided for a mortgage and mortgage moneys in subsection (3) and (5), and for the purposes of this Act the seller shall be deemed to be a mortgagee, and any moneys *bona fide*

Registered agreement for sale and purchase of land has same priority as mortgage secured and payable under such agreement shall be deemed to be mortgage moneys *bona fide* secured or advanced. R.S.O. 1970, c. 267, s. 7.

Application of insurance

9. Where any of the property upon which a lien attaches is wholly or partly destroyed by fire, any money received by reason of any insurance thereon by an owner or prior mortgagee or chargee shall take the place of the property so destroyed and is, after satisfying any prior mortgage or charge in the manner and to the extent set out in subsection 8 (3), subject to the claims of all persons for liens to the same extent as if the money had been realized by a sale of the property in an action to enforce the lien. R.S.O. 1970, c. 267, s. 8.

Limit of amount of owner's liability

10. Save as herein otherwise provided, the lien does not attach so as to make the owner liable for a greater sum than the sum payable by the owner to the contractor. R.S.O. 1970, c. 267, s. 9.

Limit of lien when claimed by other than contractor

11. Save as herein otherwise provided, where the lien is claimed by any person other than the contractor, the amount that may be claimed in respect thereof is limited to the amount owing to the contractor or subcontractor or other person for whom the work has been done or the materials were placed or furnished. R.S.O. 1970, c. 267, s. 10.

Holdback

12.—(1) In all cases, the person primarily liable upon a contract under or by virtue of which a lien may arise shall, as the work is done or the materials are furnished under the contract, retain for a period of thirty-seven days after the completion or abandonment of the work done or to be done under the contract 15 per cent of the value of the work and materials actually done, placed or furnished, as mentioned in section 6, irrespective of whether the contract or subcontract provides for partial payments or payment on completion of the work, and the value shall be calculated upon evidence given in that regard on the basis of the contract price or, if there is no specific contract price, on the basis of the actual value of the work or materials.

Reduction in amount retained

(2) Where a contract is under the supervision of an architect, engineer or other person upon whose certificate payments are to be made and thirty-seven days have elapsed after a certificate issued by that architect, engineer or other person to the effect that the subcontract has been completed to his satisfaction has been given to the person primarily liable upon that contract and to the person who became a subcontractor by a subcontract made directly under that contract, the amount to be retained by the person primarily liable upon that contract shall be reduced by 15 per cent of the subcontract price or, if there is no specific subcontract price, by 15 per cent of the actual value of the work done or materials placed or furnished under

that subcontract, but this subsection does not operate if and so long as any lien derived under that subcontract is preserved by anything done under this Act. R.S.O. 1970, c. 267, s. 11 (1, 2).

(3) Where a certificate issued by an architect, engineer or other person to the effect that a subcontract by which a subcontractor became a subcontractor has been completed to the satisfaction of that architect, engineer or other person has been given to that subcontractor, then, for the purposes of subsections 22 (1), (2) and (3), section 26 and section 27, that subcontract and any materials placed or furnished or to be placed or furnished thereunder and any work done or to be done thereunder shall, so far as concerns any lien thereunder of that subcontractor, be deemed to have been completed or placed or furnished not later than the time at which the certificate was so given. R.S.O. 1970, c. 267, s. 11 (3); 1975, c. 43, s. 5 (1). *Idem*

(4) Where an architect, engineer or other person neglects or refuses to issue and deliver a certificate upon which payments are to be made under a contract or subcontract, the judge or officer having jurisdiction to try an action under this Act, upon application and upon being satisfied that the certificate should have been issued and delivered may, upon such terms and conditions as to costs and otherwise as he deems just, make an order that the work or materials to which the certificate would have related has been done or placed or furnished, as the case may be, and any such order has the same force and effect as if the certificate had been issued and delivered by the architect, engineer or other person. R.S.O. 1970, c. 267, s. 11 (4). *Court order in lieu of certificate*

(5) The lien is a charge upon the amount directed to be retained by this section in favour of lien claimants whose liens are derived under persons to whom the moneys so required to be retained are respectively payable. *Charge on holdback*

(6) Where the lien does not attach to the land by virtue of subsection 6 (2), and a person claiming a lien gives to the owner, or a contractor or subcontractor notice in writing of the lien, the owner, contractor or subcontractor so notified shall retain out of amounts payable to the contractor or subcontractor under whom the lien is derived an amount equal to the amount claimed in the notice. 1975, c. 43, s. 5 (2). *Charge on further amounts payable in case of Crown or municipality*

(7) All payments up to 85 per cent as fixed by subsection (1) and payments permitted as a result of the operation of subsections (2) and (3) made in good faith by an owner to a contractor, or by a contractor to a subcontractor, or by one subcontractor to another subcontractor, before notice in writing of the lien given by the person claiming the lien to the owner, contractor or subcontractor, as the case may be, operate as a discharge *pro tanto* of the lien. R.S.O. 1970, c. 267, s. 11 (6). *Payments made in good faith without notice of lien*

Payment of
percentage and
discharge
of liens

(8) Payment of the percentage required to be retained under this section may be validly made so as to discharge all claims in respect of such percentage after the expiration of the period of thirty-seven days mentioned in subsection (1) unless in the meantime the appropriate steps have been taken to preserve the lien as provided by sections 24 and 26, or 25 and 27, as the case may be, in which case the owner may pay the percentage into court in the proceedings, and such payment constitutes valid payment in discharge of the owner to the amount thereof. R.S.O. 1970, c. 267, s. 11 (7); 1975, c. 43, s. 5 (3).

Amendment
of contracts

(9) Every contract shall be deemed to be amended in so far as is necessary to be in conformity with this section.

Where
percentage
not to be
applied

(10) Where the contractor or subcontractor makes default in completing his contract, the percentage required to be retained shall not, as against any lien claimant who by virtue of subsection (5) has a charge thereupon, be applied by the owner, contractor or subcontractor to the completion of the contract or for any other purpose nor to the payment of damages for the non-completion of the contract by the contractor or subcontractor nor in payment or satisfaction of any claim against the contractor or subcontractor. R.S.O. 1970, c. 267, s. 11 (8, 9).

Payments
made directly
by owner
to persons
entitled to lien

13. If an owner, contractor or subcontractor makes a payment to any person entitled to a lien under section 6 for or on account of any debt, justly due to him for work done or for materials placed or furnished to be used as therein mentioned, for which he is not primarily liable, and within three days afterwards gives written notice of the payment to the person primarily liable, or his agent, the payment shall be deemed to be a payment on his contract generally to the contractor or subcontractor primarily liable but not so as to affect the percentage to be retained by the owner as provided by section 12. R.S.O. 1970, c. 267, s. 12; 1975, c. 43, s. 6.

Rights of
subcontractor

14. Every subcontractor is entitled to enforce his lien notwithstanding the non-completion or abandonment of the contract by any contractor or subcontractor under whom he claims. R.S.O. 1970, c. 267, s. 13.

Priority
of lien

15.—(1) The lien has priority over all judgments, executions, assignments, attachments, garnishments and receiving orders recovered, issued or made after the lien arises, and over all payments or advances made on account of any conveyance or mortgage after notice in writing of the lien has been given to the person making such payments or after registration of a claim for the lien as hereinafter provided, and, in the absence of such notice in writing or the registration of a claim for lien, all such payments or advances have priority over any such lien.

(2) Except where it is otherwise provided by this Act, no person entitled to a lien on any property or money is entitled to any priority or preference over another person of the same class entitled to a lien on such property or money, and each class of lienholders ranks *pari passu* for their several amounts, and the proceeds of any sale shall be distributed among them *pro rata* according to their several classes and rights.

Priority among lienholders

(3) Any conveyance, mortgage or charge of or on land given to any person entitled to a lien thereon under this Act in payment of or as security for any such claim, whether given before or after such lien claim has arisen, shall, as against other parties entitled to liens under this Act, on any such land be deemed to be fraudulent and void. R.S.O. 1970, c. 267, s. 14.

Mortgage given to person entitled to lien void as against lienholders

PRIORITY OF WAGES

16.—(1) Every workman whose lien is for wages has priority to the extent of thirty days wages over all other liens derived through the same contractor or subcontractor to the extent of and on the 15 per cent directed to be retained by section 12 to which the contractor or subcontractor through whom the lien is derived is entitled, and all such workmen rank thereon *pari passu.*

Priority of liens for wages

(2) Every workman is entitled to enforce a lien in respect of any contract or subcontract that has not been completed and, notwithstanding anything to the contrary in this Act, may serve a notice of motion on the proper persons, returnable in four days after service thereof before the judge or officer having jurisdiction to try an action under this Act, that the applicant will on the return of the motion ask for judgment on his claim for lien, registered particulars of which shall accompany the notice of motion duly verified by affidavit.

Enforcing lien in such cases

(3) If the contract has not been completed when the lien is claimed by a workman, the percentage shall be calculated on the value of the work done or materials placed or furnished by the contractor or subcontractor by whom the workman is employed, having regard to the contract price, if any.

Calculating percentage when contract not fulfilled

(4) Every device by an owner, contractor or subcontractor to defeat the priority given to a workman for his wages and every payment made for the purpose of defeating or impairing a lien are void. R.S.O. 1970, c. 267, s. 15.

Devices to defeat priority of workmen

REGISTRATION

17.—(1) A claim for a lien may be registered in the proper land registry office and shall set out,

Registration of claim for lien

(*a*) the name and an address for service of the person claiming the lien and of the owner or of the person whom the person claiming the lien, or his agent, believes to be the owner of the land, and of the person for whom the work was or is to be done, or the materials were or are to be placed or furnished, and the time within which the same was or was to be done or placed or furnished;

(*b*) a short description of the work done or to be done, or the materials placed or furnished or to be placed or furnished;

(*c*) the sum claimed as due or to become due;

R.S.O. 1980,
cc. 230, 445

(*d*) a description of the land as required by the *Land Titles Act* or the *Registry Act* and the regulations thereunder, as the case may be; and

(*e*) the date of expiry of the period of credit if credit has been given.

Verification
of claim

(2) The claim shall be verified in duplicate by the affidavit of the person claiming the lien, or of his agent or assignee who has a personal knowledge of the matters required to be verified, and the affidavit of the agent or assignee shall state that he has such knowledge.

Lien against
railway

(3) When it is desired to register a claim for lien against a railway, it is sufficient description of the land of the railway company to describe it as the land of the railway company, and every such claim shall be registered in the general register in the land registry office for the land registry division within which the lien is claimed to have arisen. R.S.O. 1970, c. 267, s. 16.

What may
be included
in claim

18.—(1) A claim for lien may include claims against any number of properties, and any number of persons claiming liens upon the same property may unite therein, but, where more than one lien is included in one claim, each claim for lien shall be verified by affidavit as provided in section 17.

Apportionment
of claims

(2) The judge or officer trying the action has jurisdiction equitably to apportion against the respective properties the amounts included in any claim or claims under subsection (1). R.S.O. 1970, c. 267, s. 17.

Informality

19.—(1) Substantial compliance with sections 17, 18, 23 and 33 is sufficient and no claim for lien is invalidated by reason of failure to comply with any of the requirements of such sections unless, in the opinion of the judge or officer trying the action, the owner, contractor or subcontractor, mortgagee or other person is prejudiced thereby, and then only to the extent to which he is thereby prejudiced. R.S.O. 1970, c. 267, s. 18 (1); 1975, c. 43, s. 7.

(2) Nothing in this section dispenses with the requirement of registration of the claim for lien. R.S.O. 1970, c. 267, s. 18(2).

Registration necessary

20. A duplicate of the claim for lien, bearing the registrar's certificate of registration, shall be filed on or before the trial of the action, where the action is to be tried in the Judicial District of York, in the office of the master of the Supreme Court, or, where the action is to be tried elsewhere, in the office of the clerk of the county or district court of the county or district in which the action is to be tried. R.S.O. 1970, c. 267, s. 19.

Duplicate to be filed

21. Where a claim is so registered, the person entitled to a lien shall be deemed to be a purchaser *pro tanto* and a purchaser within the provisions of the *Registry Act* and the *Land Titles Act*, but, except as herein otherwise provided, those Acts do not apply to any lien arising under this Act. R.S.O. 1970, c. 267, s. 20.

Status of lien claimant R.S.O. 1980, cc. 445, 230

22.—(1) A claim for lien by a contractor or subcontractor in cases not otherwise provided for may be registered before or during the performance of the contract or of the subcontract or within thirty-seven days after the completion or abandonment of the contract or of the subcontract, as the case may be.

Limit of time for registration

(2) A claim for lien for materials may be registered before or during the placing or furnishing thereof, or within thirty-seven days after the placing or furnishing of the last material so placed or furnished.

Materials

(3) A claim for lien for services may be registered at any time during the performance of the service or within thirty-seven days after the completion of the service.

Services

(4) A claim for lien for wages may be registered at any time during the doing of the work for which the wages are claimed or within thirty-seven days after the last work was done for which the lien is claimed. R.S.O. 1970, c. 267, s. 21 (1-4).

Wages

23.—(1) Without limiting the generality of subsection 6 (2), where the lien does not attach to the land by virtue of subsection 6 (2), sections 17, 18, 20 and 21 do not apply.

Crown and municipal contracts

(2) Where the lien does not attach to the land by virtue of subsection 6 (2), any person who is claiming a lien shall give notice thereof in writing to the owner in the manner hereafter provided.

Notice of claim to hold back

Service on
municipality

(3) Where the claim is in respect of a public street or highway owned by a municipality, the notice required to be given to the owner by subsection (2) shall be given to the clerk of the municipality.

Service on
Crown

(4) Where the claim is in respect of a public work, the notice required by subsection (2) to be given to the owner shall be given to the Ministry or Crown agency for whom the work is done or the materials are placed or furnished, or to such office as is prescribed by the regulations.

Time for
service

(5) The notice required by subsection (2) shall be given within the time allowed for registration under section 22.

Method of
service

(6) The notice required by subsection (2) may be served personally, or it may be sent by registered mail, in which case the date of mailing shall be deemed to be the date on which the notice was given.

Contents of
notice

(7) The notice required shall set out,

> (*a*) the name and address of the person making the claim and of the person for whom the work was done or the materials were placed or furnished, and the time within which the same was done or placed or furnished;
>
> (*b*) a short description of the work done or the materials placed or furnished;
>
> (*c*) the sum claimed as due;
>
> (*d*) the address or a description of the location of the land;
>
> (*e*) the date of expiry of the period of credit if credit has been given.

Verification

(8) The matters set out in the notice shall be verified by the affidavit of the person claiming the lien, or his agent or assignee who has a personal knowledge of the matters, and the affidavit of the agent or assignee shall state that he has such knowledge. 1975, c. 43, s. 9.

EXPIRY AND DISCHARGE

Expiry of
liens

24.—(1) Every lien for which a claim is not registered ceases to exist on the expiration of the time limited in section 22 for the registration thereof.

Registration
of certificate
of action

(2) Upon an action under this Act being commenced, a certificate thereof shall be registered in the land registry office in which the claim for lien is registered.

(3) Where a certificate of action has been registered for two years or more in the land registry office and no appointment has been taken out for the trial of the action, the judge or, in the Judicial District of York, the master, may, upon the application *ex parte* of any interested person, make an order vacating the certificate of action and discharging all liens depending thereon. R.S.O. 1970, c. 267, s. 22.

Vacating orders

(4) This section does not apply to liens which, by virtue of subsection 6 (2), do not attach to the land. 1975, c. 43, s. 10.

Not applicable to Crown and municipal contracts

25. Where the lien does not attach to the land by virtue of subsection 6 (2), every lien for which notice has not been given as required by section 23 ceases to exist at the expiration of the time limited in section 23 for giving notice of claim thereof. 1975, c. 43, s. 11.

Time for claiming liens against Crown and municipalities

26. Every lien for which a claim is registered ceases to exist on the expiration of ninety days after the work has been completed or the materials have been placed or furnished, or after the expiry of the period of credit, where such period is mentioned in the registered claim for lien, unless in the meantime an action is commenced to realize the claim or in which a subsisting claim may be realized, and a certificate is registered as provided by section 24. R.S.O. 1970, c. 267, s. 23 (1).

When lien to cease if registered and not proceeded upon

27. Every lien which by virtue of subsection 6 (2) does not attach to the land ceases to exist on the expiration of ninety days after,

Expiration of liens against Crown and municipalities

    (*a*) the work has been completed or abandoned;

    (*b*) the materials have been placed or furnished; or

    (*c*) the expiry of the period of credit, where such period is mentioned in the notice referred to in section 23,

unless in the meantime an action under this Act is commenced to realize the claim or in which a subsisting claim may be realized. 1975, c. 43, s. 13.

28. The rights of a lien claimant may be assigned by an instrument in writing and, if not assigned, upon his death pass to his personal representative. R.S.O. 1970, c. 267, s. 24.

Assignment or death of lien claimant

29.—(1) A claim for lien may be discharged by the registration of a receipt acknowledging payment,

Discharge of lien

    (*a*) where made by a lien claimant that is not a corporation, signed by the lien claimant or his agent duly authorized in writing and verified by affidavit; or

(b) where made by a lien claimant that is a corporation sealed with its corporate seal.

Security or
payment
into court
and vacating
lien and
certificate
of action

(2) Upon application, the judge or, in the Judicial District of York, the master, may, at any time,

(a) allow security for or payment into court of the amount of the claim of the lien claimant and the amount of the claims of any other subsisting lien claimants together with such costs as he may fix, and thereupon order that the registration of the claim for lien or liens and the registration of the certificate of action, if any, be vacated;

(b) upon any other proper ground, order that the registration of the claim for lien or liens and the registration of the certificate of action, if any, be vacated; or

(c) upon proper grounds, dismiss the action.

Effect of order
under subs.
(2) (a) or (b)

(3) Notwithstanding sections 24 and 26, where an order to vacate the registration of a lien is made under clause (2) (a) or (b), the lien does not cease to exist for the reason that no certificate of action is registered.

Money paid
into court

(4) Any money so paid into court, or any bond or other security for securing the like amount and satisfactory to the judge or officer, takes the place of the property discharged and is subject to the claims of every person who has at the time of the application a subsisting claim for lien or given notice of the claim under subsection 12 (7) or section 15 to the same extent as if the money, bond or other security was realized by a sale of the property in an action to enforce the lien, but such amount as the judge or officer finds to be owing to the person whose lien has been so vacated is a first charge upon the money, bond or other security.

Where notice
of application
to vacate not
requisite

R.S.O. 1980,
cc. 230, 445

(5) Where the certificate required by section 24 or 26 has not been registered within the prescribed time and an application is made to vacate the registration of a claim for lien after the time for registration of the certificate, the order vacating the lien may be made *ex parte* upon production of a certificate of search under the *Land Titles Act* or of a registrar's abstract under the *Registry Act*, as the case may be, together with a certified copy of the registered claim for lien.

Payment of
money out
of court

(6) Where money has been paid into court or a bond deposited in court pursuant to an order under subsection (2), the judge or, in the

Judicial District of York, the master, may, upon such notice to the parties as he may require, order the money to be paid out to the persons entitled thereto or the delivery up of the bond for cancellation, as the case may be.

(7) An order discharging a claim for lien or vacating a certificate of action shall be registered by registering the order or a certificate thereof, under the seal of the court, that includes a description of the land as required by the *Land Titles Act* or the *Registry Act* and the regulations thereunder, as the case may be, and a reference to the registration number of every registered claim for lien and certificate of action affected thereby. R.S.O. 1970, c. 267, s. 25.

Registration number

EFFECT OF TAKING SECURITY OR EXTENDING TIME

30.—(1) The taking of any security for, or the acceptance of any promissory note or bill of exchange for, or the taking of any acknowledgment of the claim, or the giving of time for the payment thereof, or the taking of any proceedings for the recovery, or the recovery of a personal judgment for the claim, does not merge, waive, pay, satisfy, prejudice or destroy the lien unless the lien claimant agrees in writing that it has that effect.

Effect generally

(2) Where any such promissory note or bill of exchange has been negotiated, the lien claimant does not thereby lose his right to claim for lien if, at the time of bringing his action to enforce it or where an action is brought by another lien claimant, he is, at the time of proving his claim in the action, the holder of such promissory note or bill of exchange.

Where period of credit not expired

(3) Nothing in subsection (2) extends the time limited by this Act for bringing an action to enforce a claim for lien.

Time for bringing action not extended

(4) A person who has extended the time for payment of a claim for which he has a claim for lien in order to obtain the benefit of this section shall commence an action to enforce the claim within the time prescribed by this Act and shall register a certificate as required by sections 24 and 26, but no further proceedings shall be taken in the action until the expiration of such extension of time. R.S.O. 1970, c. 267, s. 26.

Time for bringing action by person who gave time for payment

31. Where the period of credit in respect of a claim has not expired or there has been an extension of time for payment of the claim, the lien claimant may nevertheless, if an action is commenced by any other person to enforce a claim for lien against the same property, prove and obtain payment of his claim in the action as if the period of credit or the extended time had expired. R.S.O. 1970, c. 267, s. 27.

Proving claim in action by another person

LIEN CLAIMANTS RIGHTS TO INFORMATION

Production of contract or agreement

32.—(1) Any lien claimant may in writing at any time demand of the owner or his agent the production, for inspection, of the contract or agreement with the contractor for or in respect of which the work was or is to be done or the materials were or are to be placed or furnished, if the contract or agreement is in writing or, if not in writing, the terms of the contract or agreement and the state of the accounts between the owner and the contractor, and, if the owner or his agent does not, at the time of the demand or within a reasonable time thereafter, produce the contract or agreement if in writing or, if not in writing, does not inform the person making the demand of the terms of the contract or agreement and the amount due and unpaid upon the contract or agreement or if he knowingly falsely states the terms of the contract or agreement or the amount due or unpaid thereon and if the person claiming the lien sustains loss by reason of the refusal or neglect or false statement, the owner is liable to him for the amount of the loss in an action therefor or in any action for the enforcement of a lien under this Act, and subsection 42 (4) applies.

Statement of mortgagee or unpaid vendor

(2) Any lien claimant may in writing at any time demand of a mortgagee or unpaid vendor or his agent the terms of any mortgage on the land or of any agreement for the purchase of the land in respect of which the work was or is to be done or the materials were or are to be placed or furnished and a statement showing the amount advanced on the mortgage or the amount owing on the agreement, as the case may be, and, if the mortgagee or vendor or his agent fails to inform the lien claimant at the time of the demand or within a reasonable time thereafter of the terms of the mortgage or agreement and the amount advanced or owing thereon or if he knowingly falsely states the terms of the mortgage or agreement and the amount owing thereon and the lien claimant sustains loss by the refusal or neglect or mis-statement, the mortgagee or vendor is liable to him for the amount of the loss in an action therefor or in any action for the enforcement of a lien under this Act, and subsection 42 (4) applies.

Production of contract or agreement

(3) The judge or, in the Judicial District of York, the master, may, on a summary application at any time before or after an action is commenced for the enforcement of the claim for lien, make an order requiring the owner or his agent or the mortgagee or his agent or the unpaid vendor or his agent or the contractor or his agent or the subcontractor or his agent, as the case may be, to produce and permit any lien claimant to inspect any such contract or agreement or mortgage or agreement for sale or the accounts or any other relevant document upon such terms as to costs as the judge or master considers just. R.S.O. 1970, c. 267, s. 28.

ACTIONS

33.—(1) A claim for lien is enforceable in an action in the Supreme Court.

How claim enforceable

(2) An action under this section shall be commenced by filing a statement of claim in the office of the local registrar of the Supreme Court in the county or district in which the land or part thereof is situate.

Statement of claim, filing of

(3) The statement of claim shall be served within thirty days after it is filed, but the judge having jurisdiction to try the action or, in the Judicial District of York, the master, may extend the time for service.

Idem, service

(4) The time for delivering the statement of defence in the action shall be the same as for entering an appearance in an action in the Supreme Court.

Statement of defence

(5) It is not necessary to make any lien claimants parties defendant to the action, but all lien claimants served with the notice of trial shall for all purposes be deemed to be parties to the action.

Parties

(6) After the commencement of the action, any lien claimant or other person interested may apply to the judge having jurisdiction to try the action or, in the Judicial District of York, a judge of the Supreme Court, to speed the trial of the action. R.S.O. 1970, c. 267, s. 29.

Motion to speed trial

34. Any number of lien claimants claiming liens on the same land may join in an action, and an action brought by a lien claimant shall be deemed to be brought on behalf of himself and all other lien claimants. R.S.O. 1970, c. 267, s. 30.

Lien claimants joining in action

35.—(1) Except in the Judicial District of York, the action shall be tried by the local judge of the Supreme Court in the county or district in which the action was commenced, but, upon the application of any party or other interested person made according to the practice of the Supreme Court and upon notice, the court may direct that the action be tried by a judge of the Supreme Court at the regular sittings of the court for the trial of actions in the county or district in which the action was commenced.

Tribunal and place of trial

(2) In the Judicial District of York, the action shall be tried by a judge of the Supreme Court, but,

Idem, York

    (*a*) on motion after defence or defence to counterclaim, if any, has been delivered or the time for such delivery has expired,

R.S.O. 1980,
c. 223
a judge of the Supreme Court may refer the whole action to the master for trial pursuant to section 71 of the *Judicature Act*; or

(*b*) at the trial, a judge of the Supreme Court may direct a reference to the master pursuant to section 70 or 71 of the *Judicature Act*.

Application to set aside judgment directing a reference

(3) Where on motion the whole action is referred to the master for trial, any person brought into the proceedings subsequent thereto and served with a notice of trial may apply to a judge of the Supreme Court to set aside the judgment directing the reference within seven days after service of notice of trial and, if such person fails to make such application, he is bound by such judgment as if he were originally a party thereto.

Amendment of pleadings on reference

(4) Where the action is referred to the master for trial, he may grant leave to amend any pleading. R.S.O. 1970, c. 267, s. 31.

Powers of local judges S.C.O., etc.

36. The local judges of the Supreme Court and the master to whom a reference for trial has been directed, in addition to their ordinary powers, have all the jurisdiction, powers and authority of the Supreme Court to try and completely dispose of the action and questions arising therein and all questions of set-off and counterclaim arising under the building contract or out of the work done or materials furnished to the property in question. R.S.O. 1970, c. 267, s. 32.

Where contract covers several buildings

37. Where an owner enters into an entire contract for the supply of materials to be used in several buildings, the person supplying the materials may ask to have his lien follow the form of the contract and that it be for an entire sum upon all the buildings, but, in case the owner has sold one or more of the buildings, the judge or officer trying the action has jurisdiction equitably to apportion against the respective buildings the amount included in the claim for lien under the entire contract. R.S.O. 1970, c. 267, s. 33.

Power to appoint a receiver of rents and profits

38.—(1) At any time after the delivery of the statement of claim, the judge having jurisdiction to try the action or, in the Judicial District of York, a judge of the Supreme Court, may, on the application of any lien claimant, mortgagee or other person interested, appoint a receiver of the rents and profits of the property against which the claim for lien is registered upon such terms and upon the giving of such security or without security as the judge considers just.

Power to direct sale and appoint trustee

(2) Any lien claimant, mortgagee or other person interested may make an application to the judge having jurisdiction to try the action or, in the Judicial District of York, a judge of the Supreme Court, at any time before or after judgment, who may hear *viva voce* or

affidavit evidence or both and appoint, upon such terms and upon the giving of such security or without security as the judge considers just, a trustee or trustees with power to manage, mortgage, lease and sell, or manage, mortgage, lease or sell, the property against which the claim for lien is registered, and the exercise of such powers shall be under the supervision and direction of the court, and with power, when so directed by the court, to complete or partially complete the property, and, in the event that mortgage moneys are advanced to the trustee or trustees as the result of any of the powers conferred upon him or them under this subsection, such moneys take priority over every claim of lien existing as of the date of the appointment.

(3) Any property directed to be sold under subsection (2) may be offered for sale subject to any mortgage or other charge or encumbrance if the judge so directs.

Property offered for sale

(4) The proceeds of any sale made by a trustee or trustees under subsection (2) shall be paid into court and are subject to the claims of all lien claimants, mortgagees or other persons interested in the property so sold as their respective rights are determined, and, in so far as applicable, section 43 applies.

Proceeds to be paid into court

(5) The judge shall make all necessary orders for the completion of any mortgage, lease or sale authorized to be made under subsection (2).

Orders for completion of sale

(6) Any vesting order made of property sold by a trustee or trustees appointed under subsection (2) vests the title of the property free from all claims for liens, encumbrances and interests of any kind, except in cases where sale is made subject to any mortgage, charge, encumbrance or interest as hereinbefore provided. R.S.O. 1970, c. 267, s. 34, *revised.*

Vesting of title

39. At any time after delivery of the statement of claim and before judgment, or after judgment and pending the hearing and determination of any appeal, any lien claimant, mortgagee or other interested person may make an application to the judge having jurisdiction to try the action or who tried the action, as the case may be, or, in the Judicial District of York, a judge of the Supreme Court, who may hear *viva voce* or affidavit evidence or both and make an order for the preservation of any property pending the determination of the action and any appeal. R.S.O. 1970, c. 267, s. 35.

Order for preservation of property

40. Where more actions than one are brought to realize liens in respect of the same land, the judge or officer having jurisdiction to try the action may, on the application of any party to any one of the actions or on the application of any other person interested, consolidate all such actions into one action and award the conduct of the consolidated action to any plaintiff as the judge or officer considers just. R.S.O. 1970, c. 267, s. 36.

Consolidation of actions

Transferring
carriage of
proceedings

41. Any lien claimant entitled to the benefit of an action may at any time apply to the judge or officer having jurisdiction to try the action for the carriage of the proceedings, and the judge or officer may make an order awarding such lien claimant the carriage of the proceedings. R.S.O. 1970, c. 267, s. 37.

Appointing
day for trial

42.—(1) After the delivery of the statement of defence where the plaintiff's claim is disputed, or after the time for delivery of defence in all other cases, either party may apply *ex parte* to a judge or officer having jurisdiction to try the action to fix a day for the trial thereof, and the judge or officer shall appoint the time and place of trial, and the order, signed by the judge or officer, shall form part of the record of the proceedings.

Notice of trial
and service

(2) The party obtaining an appointment for the trial shall, at least ten clear days before the day appointed, serve notice of trial upon the solicitors for the defendants who appear by solicitors and upon the defendants who appear in person, and upon all the lienholders who have registered their claims as required by this Act or of whose claims he has notice, and upon all other persons having any charge, encumbrance or claim on the land subsequent in priority to the lien, who are not parties, and such service shall be personal unless otherwise directed by the judge or officer who may direct in what manner the notice of trial is to be served.

Idem

(3) Where any person interested in the land has been served with a statement of claim and makes default in delivering a statement of defence, he shall nevertheless be served with notice of trial and is entitled to defend on such terms as to costs and otherwise as the judge or officer having jurisdiction to try the action considers just.

Trial

(4) The judge, or where a reference for trial is directed, the master,

    (*a*) shall try the action, including any set-off and counterclaim, and all questions that arise therein or that are necessary to be tried in order to completely dispose of the action and to adjust the rights and liabilities of the persons appearing before him or upon whom notice of trial has been served;

    (*b*) shall take all accounts, make all inquiries, give all directions and do all other things necessary to finally dispose of the action and of all matters, questions and accounts arising therein or at the trial, and to adjust the rights and liabilities of and give all necessary relief to all parties to the action and all persons who have been served with the notice of trial; and

    (*c*) shall embody the results of the trial,

> (i) in the case of a judge, in a judgment, and
>
> (ii) in the case of a master, in a report,
>
> > which judgment or report may direct payment forthwith by the person or persons primarily liable to pay the amount of the claims and costs as ascertained by the judgment or report, and execution may be issued therefor forthwith in the case of a judgment and after confirmation thereof, in the case of a report.

(5) The form of the judgment or report may be varied by the judge or officer in order to meet the circumstances of the case so as to afford to any party to the proceedings any right or remedy in the judgment or report to which he may be entitled.

Power to vary form of judgment

(6) The judge or officer may order that the estate or interest charged with the lien be sold, and may direct the sale to take place at any time after judgment or confirmation of the report, allowing, however, a reasonable time for advertising the sale.

Sale

(7) A lien claimant who did not prove his claim at the trial, on application to the judge or officer before whom the action or reference was tried, may be let in to prove his claim, on such terms as to costs and otherwise as are deemed just, at any time before the amount realized in the action for the satisfaction of liens has been distributed, and, where his claim is allowed, the judgment or report shall be amended so as to include his claim.

Letting in lien claimants

(8) Any lien claimant for an amount not exceeding $200 may be represented by an agent who is not a barrister and solicitor.

Right of lien claimants to representation

(9) An action or reference under this Act may be tried by any judge or officer having jurisdiction to try the action or reference notwithstanding that the time and place for the trial or reference thereof were appointed and fixed by another judge or officer.

Action may be tried by any judge

(10) Any party to an action under this Act or any other interested person may at any time and from time to time apply to the judge having jurisdiction to try the action or, in the Judicial District of York, the master, for directions as to pleadings, discovery, production or any other matter relating to the action or reference, including the cross-examination of a lien claimant or his agent or assignee on his affidavit verifying the claim. R.S.O. 1970, c. 267, s. 38.

Applications for directions

43.—(1) Where a sale is had, the moneys arising therefrom shall be paid into court to the credit of the action, and the judge or officer before whom the action was tried shall direct to whom the moneys in

Report where sale is had

court shall be paid and may add to the claim of the person conducting the action his fees and actual disbursements incurred in connection with the sale, and, where sufficient to satisfy the judgment and costs is not realized from the sale, he shall certify the amount of the deficiency and the names of the persons who are entitled to recover the same, showing the amount that each is entitled to recover and the persons adjudged to pay the same, giving credit for payments made, if any, under subsection 42 (4), and the persons so entitled may enforce payment of the amounts so found to be due by execution or otherwise.

Completion of sale

(2) The judge or officer before whom the action was tried may make all necessary orders for the completion of the sale and for vesting the property in the purchaser. R.S.O. 1970, c. 267, s. 39.

Where lien not established

44. Where a lien claimant fails to establish a lien, he may nevertheless recover a personal judgment against any party to the action for such sum as may appear to be due to him and which he might recover in an action against such party. R.S.O. 1970, c. 267, s. 40.

Right of lienholders whose claims are not payable to share in proceeds

45. Where property subject to a lien is sold in an action to enforce a lien, every lienholder is entitled to share in the proceeds of the sale in respect of the amount then owing to him, although the same or part thereof was not payable at the time of the commencement of the action or is not then presently payable. R.S.O. 1970, c. 267, s. 41.

STATED CASE

Stated case

46.—(1) If in the course of proceedings to enforce a lien a question of law arises, the judge or officer trying the case may, at the request of any party, state the question in the form of a stated case for the opinion of the Divisional Court, and the stated case shall thereupon be set down to be heard before the Divisional Court and notice of hearing shall be served by the party setting down upon all parties concerned.

Transmission of papers

(2) The stated case shall set forth the facts material for the determination of the question raised, and all papers necessary for the hearing of the stated case by the Divisional Court shall be transmitted to the registrar of the Supreme Court. R.S.O. 1970, c. 267, s. 42.

APPEAL

Appeal

47.—(1) Except where the amount of a judgment or report made on a reference for trial in respect of a claim or counterclaim is $200 or less, an appeal lies from any judgment or report under this Act to the Divisional Court.

(2) Where a question is referred to the master for inquiry and report under subsection 35 (2), an appeal lies in the manner prescribed by the rules of court.

Appeal from reference

(3) Where an action is referred to the master for trial under subsection 35 (2), the report shall be filed and shall be deemed to be confirmed at the expiration of fifteen days from the date of service of notice of filing the same, unless notice of appeal is served within that time.

Confirmation of master's report

(4) The costs of an appeal shall not be governed by subsections 49 (2) and (3) but, subject to any order of the Divisional Court, shall be upon the scale of costs allowed in county court appeals where the amount involved is within the proper competence of the county court, and, where it exceeds that amount, upon the Supreme Court scale. R.S.O. 1970, c. 267, s. 43, *revised.*

Costs of appeal

FEES AND COSTS

48. The fee payable by every plaintiff, every plaintiff by counterclaim and every lien claimant, including every person recovering a personal judgment, in any action to realize a lien under this Act is,

Fee

(*a*) $5 on a claim or counterclaim not exceeding $500;

(*b*) $10 on a claim or counterclaim exceeding $500 but not exceeding $1,000;

(*c*) $10 on a claim or counterclaim exceeding $1,000, plus $1 for every $1,000 or fraction thereof in excess of $1,000,

but no fee is payable on a claim for wages only, and in no case shall the fee on a claim exceed $75 or on a counterclaim exceed $25. R.S.O. 1970, c. 267, s. 44.

49. (1) Subject to subsections (2), (3), (4) and (5), any order as to costs in an action under this Act is in the discretion of the judge or officer who tries the action.

Costs not otherwise provided for

(2) The costs of the action, exclusive of actual disbursements, awarded to the plaintiffs and successful lienholders, shall not exceed in the aggregate 25 per cent of the total amount found to have been actually due on the liens at the time of the registration thereof, and shall be apportioned and borne in such proportion as the judge or officer who tries the action may direct, but in making the apportionment he shall have regard to the actual services rendered by or on behalf of the parties respectively, provided that, where a counterclaim is set up by a defendant, the amount and apportionment of the

Limit of costs to plaintiffs

costs in respect thereof are in the discretion of the judge or officer who tries the action.

Limit of
costs against
plaintiffs

(3) Where costs are awarded against the plaintiff or other persons claiming liens, they shall not exceed, except in the case of a counter-claim, 25 per cent of the claim of the plaintiff and the other claimants, besides actual disbursements, and shall be apportioned and borne as the judge or officer who tries the action may direct.

Costs
where least
expensive
course not
taken

(4) Where the least expensive course is not taken by a plaintiff, the costs allowed to him shall in no case exceed what would have been incurred if the least expensive course had been taken.

Costs of
drawing and
registering
and vacating
registration
of lien

(5) Where a lien is discharged or vacated under section 29 or where judgment is given in favour of or against a claim for a lien, in addition to the costs of the action, the judge or officer who tries the action may allow a reasonable amount for the costs of drawing and registering the claim for lien or of vacating the registration thereof, but this does not apply where the claimant fails to establish a valid lien. R.S.O. 1970, c. 267, s. 45.

RULES OF PRACTICE

Rules of
practice

50.—(1) The object of this Act being to enforce liens at the least expense, the procedure shall be as far as possible of a summary character, having regard to the amount and nature of the liens in question.

Interlocutory
proceedings

(2) Except where otherwise provided by this Act, no interlocutory proceedings shall be permitted without the consent of the judge having jurisdiction to try the action or, in the Judicial District of York, the master, and then only upon proper proof that such pro-ceedings are necessary.

Assistance
of experts

(3) The judge or officer having jurisdiction to try the action may obtain the assistance of any merchant, accountant, actuary, building contractor, achitect, engineer or person in such way as he deems fit, the better to enable him to determine any matter of fact in question, and may fix the remuneration of any such person and direct payment thereof by any of the parties.

Rules of
practice

(4) Unless otherwise provided in this Act, the Rules of Practice and Procedure of the Supreme Court apply to proceedings under this Act. R.S.O. 1970, c. 267, s. 46.

SERVICE OF DOCUMENTS

Service of
documents

51. Except where otherwise directed by the judge having jurisdic-tion to try the action or, in the Judicial District of York, the master, all documents relating to an action under this Act, other than statements of claim and notices of trial, are sufficiently served upon the intended recipient if sent by registered mail addressed to the intended recipient at his address for service. R.S.O. 1970, c. 267, s. 47.

LIENS ON CHATTELS

52.—(1) Every person who has bestowed money, skill or materials upon any chattel or thing in the alteration or improvement of its properties or for the purpose of imparting an additional value to it, so as thereby to be entitled to a lien upon the chattel or thing for the amount or value of the money or skill and material bestowed, has, while the lien exists but not afterwards, in case the amount to which he is entitled remains unpaid for three months after it ought to have been paid, the right, in addition to any other remedy to which he may be entitled, to sell by auction the chattel or thing on giving one week's notice by advertisement in a newspaper having general circulation in the municipality in which the work was done, setting forth the name of the person indebted, the amount of the debt, a description of the chattel or thing to be sold, the time and place of sale, and the name of the auctioneer, and leaving a like notice in writing at the last known place of residence, if any, of the owner, if he is a resident of the municipality. Right of chattel lienholder to sell chattel

(2) Such person shall apply the proceeds of the sale in payment of the amount due to him and the costs of advertising and sale and shall upon application pay over any surplus to the person entitled thereto. R.S.O. 1970, c. 267, s. 48. Application of proceeds of sale

REGULATIONS

53. The Lieutenant Governor in Council may make regulations, Regulations

(*a*) prescribing forms and providing for their use;

(*b*) providing for and requiring the posting of notices on building sites;

(*c*) prescribing the appropriate offices of the Crown to which notice of a claim for lien must be sent. 1975, c. 43, s. 14.

Appendix F

Ministry of Transportation and Communications Creditors Payment Act
R.S.O. 1980, c. 290

1. In this Act,

Interpretation

 (a) "claimant" means a creditor who has sent a notice under subsection 2 (1);

 (b) "contract" means a written agreement between the Minister and a person for the performance of work and under which the Minister is obligated to pay for the total cost thereof;

 (c) "contractor" means a person who enters into a contract with the Minister;

 (d) "creditor" means a person who supplies labour, materials or services used or reasonably required for use in the performance of work as set out in a contract;

 (e) "Minister" means the Minister of Transportation and Communications;

 (f) "Ministry" means the Ministry of Transportation and Communications;

 (g) "person" means an individual, partnership or corporation but does not include a municipal corporation;

 (h) "surety" means a person who guarantees to the Minister the payment of creditors under a bond with the Minister;

 (i) "work" means a construction, reconstruction, improvement, alteration, expansion, addition to, repair or maintenance of property. 1975, c. 44, s. 1.

2.—(1) Where a contractor does not pay a creditor in accordance with his obligation to do so under the contract, the creditor may, not later than 120 days after the last day on which the labour, materials or services were provided, send to the appropriate office of the Ministry

Service of
notice of
non-payment

by registered mail a notice setting out the nature and amount of his claim.

Payment of claim

(2) The Minister may, after notice in writing to the contractor and surety, if any, pay the claimant the amount settled upon and deduct the amount so paid from any moneys due or that may become due to the contractor on any account or from the moneys or securities, if any, deposited by the contractor with the Ministry, and, if there are insufficient moneys due or to become due to the contractor to permit of such deduction, the surety, if any, shall pay to the Ministry upon demand an amount sufficient to make up the deficiency.

Amount paid final

(3) In paying a claim under subsection (2), the Minister may act upon any evidence that he considers sufficient and may compromise any disputed liability, and such payment is not open to dispute or question by the contractor or the surety, if any, but is final and binding upon them. 1975, c. 44, s. 2.

Minister may demand list of creditors

3. The Minister may, in writing, require a contractor to send to him by registered mail, within fifteen days from the date of the mailing of the demand, a list of the names of and the amounts owing to his creditors. 1975, c. 44, s. 3.

Contractors to display s. 2(1)

4. Every contractor shall display and keep displayed in a conspicuous place where the work is being performed a copy of subsection 2 (1). 1975, c. 44, s. 4.

Offences

5. A contractor who does not file a list when required to do so under section 3 or who does not display and keep displayed a copy of subsection 2 (1) as required by section 4 is guilty of an offence and on conviction is liable to a fine of not less than $10 and not more than $100 for every day during which the default continues. 1975, c. 44, s. 5.

Regulations

6.—(1) The Lieutenant Governor in Council may make regulations,

(*a*) extending or reducing the periods of time referred to in sections 2 and 3;

(*b*) providing for and requiring notices in addition to the notice mentioned in section 2;

(*c*) respecting any matter necessary or advisable to carry out effectively the intent and purpose of this Act.

Application

(2) Any regulation made under subsection (1) or any provision thereof may be made applicable in respect of any class or classes of contractor. 1975, c. 44, s. 6.

Index